The Effects of
Urban Growth

Richard P. Appelbaum
Jennifer Bigelow
Henry P. Kramer
Harvey L. Molotch
Paul M. Relis

The Praeger Special Studies program—
utilizing the most modern and efficient book
production techniques and a selective
worldwide distribution network—makes
available to the academic, government, and
business communities significant, timely
research in U.S. and international economic, social, and political development.

The Effects of Urban Growth

A Population Impact Analysis

PRAEGER SPECIAL STUDIES IN U.S. ECONOMIC, SOCIAL, AND POLITICAL ISSUES

Praeger Publishers   New York   Washington   London

Library of Congress Cataloging in Publication Data
Main entry under title:

The Effects of urban growth.

(Praeger special studies in U.S. economic, social, and
political issues)
    Includes index.
    1. Cities and towns—Growth. 2. Population.
3. Urbanization—California—Santa Barbara. 4. Santa Barbara,
California—Population. I. Appelbaum, Richard P
HT371.E34   301.36'3   75-23952
ISBN 0-275-55980-7

PRAEGER PUBLISHERS
111 Fourth Avenue, New York, N.Y. 10003, U.S.A.

Published in the United States of America in 1976
by Praeger Publishers, Inc.

Printed in the United States of America

This book represents a community effort, and there have been many people whose support has been crucial to our work. In the earliest phases of our thinking about the study, we were encouraged or informed by a number of people, including Julio Bortolazzo, Patrice Drolet, Pamela Emerson, Carole Faxon, Paul Ginberg, John Karubian, Claudia Madsen, Richard Temple, and William Wittausch. Frances Kramer helped us set up our office and get into business.

We are grateful to Cliff Pauley and to these others on the Santa Barbara County Planning staff: George Kammer, Carl Kramer, Richard Honn. Sandy Korbelik, and Norman Schultz. Our studies on property assessment would not have been possible without the enthusiastic cooperation of William Cook, County Assessor, and Walter Alves, Chief Appraiser, who provided basic data and assembled historical information at our request. We are similarly grateful to Karl Grahn, Business Manager, and Henry Mealy, Office of Accounting, of the Santa Barbara City School District.

Our study of water costs was strengthened by the guidance provided by David Kleinecke and John Hamilton. Ray Spencer greatly assisted us in our study of wastewater. Our study of the city's habitats was supported through the advice and suggestions of Waldo Abbott, Jackie Broughton, Janet Hamber, Poppett Hill, Virginia Puddicombe, Cliff Smith, Sidney Tarbox, and Cecilia Terry. Our legal analyses were aided through consultation with Michael Heyman and Sho Soto of the Law School, University of California, Berkeley; and, through the research assistance of Robert Bush and Susan Dewey.

In our study of city esthetics, we benefited from consultation with David Gebhard, Wales Holbrook, Leo Pedersen, and Herbert Andree. In our research on circulation and air pollution, and in a number of other phases of our work, we relied upon the assistance of the Santa Barbara County Transportation Study. Our study of disaster impacts was supported through consultation with Phil G. Olsen of the Earth Sciences Department, Santa Barbara City College; and Cynthia Sage of Hinningson, Durham, and Richardson.

In carrying out our economic analyses, we were able to draw upon the knowledge of a wide array of people: Stanley Lowry of the Chamber of Commerce; William Gawzner (in regard to general tourism); James Gildea of the West Beach Motel Owners Association; the UCSB Economics Department; Miriam Ciochon of the Research Department, Federal Reserve Bank, San Francisco; Rueben Irvin,

Chairman of the Board, Santa Barbara National Bank; Ellen Lococo, the Downtown Organization; Anthony Nakazawa, UCSB Urban Economics Program; Donald Rook, La Cumbre Plaza Management; Shirley Stephensen, Security Pacific Bank, Los Angeles.

Others who provided us with information of various sorts included David Gold, Robert Smith, and Bruce Straits, Sociology Department, UCSB; Brian J. L. Berry, University of Chicago; and Otis Dudley Duncan, University of Arizona. The South Central Coastal Regional Commission staff, particularly Pamela Emerson and David Loomis, also provided assistance. Other help was furnished by Russell Barcroft, Circulation Manager, Santa Barbara News Press; Judith Horn and her conscientious colleagues at the Government Publications section of the UCSB library; Eric Lyons of Lyons Realty; and Lee Rook, UCSB Associate Campus Community Planner. Linda Molotch provided helpful editing assistance.

Anthony Shih and the staff of the UCSB Sociology Department Computer Facility served us well beyond the call of duty. Conscientious research assistance was provided by Bonnie Cornwall and Sheikh-Mohammad Sartajuddin.

Our work efficiency has been enhanced by the courteous and understanding support of the managers of the Balboa Building where we were housed, Curtis and Mary Kay Schmeisser. Pattern Analysis Corporation provided us with additional work space and computer facilities. Damon Combs of Sun Sierra Systems was instrumental in providing us with the courtesy use of a copying machine. The final phase of our work was greatly enhanced through the support of the Sunflower Foundation.

Those who shared in the production work, the time-consuming and tedious labors of typing, layout, proofreading, and collating, deserve our special thanks. They are Jamie Barr, Glyn Davies, Claire Glennon, Jeffrey King, Jeremy Kramer, Sasha Newborn, Gertrude Platt, Diane Salisbury, June Tierney, and Meridith Pometti.

We are grateful to the staffs of the city departments, who provided us with their time and their enthusiasm. Their helpful advice and information are reflected in most of the chapters that follow.

Our final acknowledgment is to the staff of the Santa Barbara City Planning Department: Anne Bagnall, Mary Louise Days, Thomas Giordano, William Haskell, James Perry, and Bruce Thompson. Each was involved in this study in an important way, and we are grateful that each was always there when we were in need.

GENERAL SUPPORT STAFF

Gerald DeWitt
Amelia Fitts
Eric Mankin

ADDITIONAL TASK GROUPS

Air Quality

For General Research Corporation
Jose R. Martinez
Richard A. Nordsieck

With the Assistance of Task Force
Staff
Richard Laula
and
Douglas Bauer
Chandra Muller
David Slesnick

Cross-City Analysis
Ross Follet

With the assistance of
Cynthia Eisenhut
John Forbes

Economic Analysis

Private Sector
Linda Lillow
Stephen Logan

Public Sector
Carmen Lodise
With the Assistance of
Christopher Attwood
Robert Leiter
Granville Pool
With Consultation from
Robert Crouch
Edward Kirshner
Douglas Morgan
William Wittausch

Habitats

Lee Waian

With the Assistance of
Jennifer Fairfax
Gerrie Human
Helen Wolfe
and
Thomas Bush
Thomas Dudley
Susan Hogan
Steve Junack
Russell Mark
Lee Phifer
Terry Rochester
Lynda Thompson

Legal Research

Philip Marking

With the Assistance of
Lee Rosenberg

Report Preparation

Composition
Kathleen Sullivan

Editing
William Glennon
John Seeley

Graphics
Jules Worthington

Photography
David Whittaker

CONTENTS

                                                Page

ACKNOWLEDGMENTS   v

SANTA BARBARA PLANNING TASK FORCE   vii

LIST OF TABLES   xiv

LIST OF FIGURES   xviii

INTRODUCTION   xix

Chapter

1   PRINCIPLES AND METHODS   1

     Orientation   1.
       General Purpose   1
       Organization of This Volume   2
     Explaining Population Change   4
       The Hazards of Prediction   6
       Sources of Growth   8
       Case Illustration: The Impact of UCSB on
         Area Growth   9
     General Methods   12
       Population Impact Points   12
       The Assumption of All Other Things Being Equal   15
     General Data Base   17
     Notes   18

2   CROSS-CITY ANALYSIS   19
     Methods: Cross-Sectional and Longitudinal Analysis   20
     The Findings   23
       Economic Indicators   23
       Public Safety   27
       Health   29
       Municipal Expenditures   32
       Residential Segregation   35
     Summary   35
     Notes   36

Chapter		Page
3	SOCIAL IMPACTS OF GROWTH	41
	Opinion as a Cost-Benefit Factor	41
	Survey Methods	42
	Findings	42
	Summary	43
	Land Use and Housing Type	44
	Parks	45
	Circulation	47
	Effects on Road-Network Capacities	47
	Parking	58
	Area Impacts	60
	Summary of Findings	61
	Social Consequences	62
	Life-Style and Social Tensions	62
	Space Disorganization	62
	Access to Local Institutions	63
	Local Bureaucracies	64
	Segregation by Race and Income	65
	Range of Retail and Service Facilities	67
	Freedom and Spontaneity	69
	Horses and Dogs	69
	Notes	71
4	ENVIRONMENTAL EFFECTS OF GROWTH	72
	Air Quality	72
	Approaches to Emissions Analysis	73
	Results of Emissions Analysis	80
	Present and Future Air Quality	83
	Summary and Conclusions	86
	Noise	87
	Urban Habitats	89
	Identifying, Classifying, and Ranking Open Space	90
	Stream Environment	92
	Specific Neighborhood Investigations	96
	Disasters	100
	Disaster Impacts Due to Earthquakes	101
	Tsunami Hazards	104
	Disaster Potential from Fire	105
	Disaster Potential from Floods	105
	Summary	106
	Esthetics	106
	Notes	109

Chapter		Page
5	ECONOMIC EFFECTS OF GROWTH: THE PRIVATE SECTOR	113
	Growth and the Individual	114
	Per Capita Income	115
	Wealth	117
	Local Retailing	119
	Monopoly Versus Competitive Business	119
	Skilled, Well-Financed Business Versus Marginal Business	119
	"Unique" Versus Undifferentiated Establishments	120
	Local Ownership Versus Chain Stores, and CBD Versus Outlying Shopping Centers	120
	Conclusion	123
	Unemployment	123
	Employment in Construction: A Special Case	128
	Cost of Living: Housing and Other Expenses	131
	Half-Density Ordinance Effects	134
	Summary	140
	Notes	141
6	ECONOMIC EFFECTS OF GROWTH: THE PUBLIC SECTOR	142
	The General Fund: Expenditures and Revenues	144
	General Fund Expenditures at Future PIPs	145
	Police	145
	Fire	146
	City Library	147
	Parks and Recreation	151
	Public Works: Streets and Highways	161
	Overview: Total General Fund Expenditures	161
	General Fund Revenues at Future PIPs	165
	Property-Tax Revenues	165
	Revenues from All Other Sources	171
	Net Effects of Growth on the General Fund	173
	Specially Funded Services	176
	Education	179
	Population Growth and School Requirements: The Recent Experience	179
	Estimating the Costs of Education: Methods and Assumptions	181

Water   194
　　Present Supply   194
　　Basis for Determining Water Requirements
　　　and Costs Resulting from Growth   195
　　Interpretation of Net Costs per Resident for
　　　Five PIPs   202
　　Conclusion   203
Wastewater   205
　　Projecting Expenditures and Revenues   206
　　Net Effects of Growth: Expenditures/Revenue
　　　Synthesis   214
　　Summary and Conclusion   214
Summary of Public Sector Analysis   218
The Effects of Growth on Property Taxes   218
The Effects of Growth on Revenue Requirements
　for Water and Wastewater   220
Overall Conclusions   221
Notes   223

7   ALTERNATIVE ECONOMIC SCENARIOS   228

Salient Costs and Benefits   228
　　Relevant Costs and Benefits   228
　　Choice of Economic Scenarios   230
　　Summary: Direct and Indirect Salient Revenue
　　　Benefits   235
Special Studies: Two Proposed Projects   238
　　New Resort Hotel   238
　　New Downtown Regional Shopping Center   239
Relative Costs of Economic Sectors   240
　　Retailing   242
　　Research and Development   243
　　Technical Manufacturing   243
　　Light Manufacturing   244
　　Tourism   244
A Note on Property and Pensions Income   246
Summary   246
Notes   248

8   SUMMARY OF FINDINGS: POPULATION EFFECTS
     AT EACH PIP   249

The Social Effects   250
The Environmental Effects   252

Chapter   Page

           The Economic Effects   253
           Choices   257

    9   POLICY IMPLICATIONS   258

           Housing Intervention   258
              Rent Control   259
              Price Control   260
              Tax Methods   260
           Labor-Force Intervention   261
              Zoning Methods to Decrease Labor-Force Growth 262
              Retaining Modest Interregional Transportation
                 Facilities   263
              Restraining City Promotion   263
              Nonexpansion of Public Institutions   264
           Evaluating Specific Projects   264
           Need for Coordination   266

   10   MANAGING GROWTH: LEGAL ISSUES AND TOOLS   268

           Temporary Zoning: Continuation of Interim
              Ordinance   270
              Extension of Half-Density Ordinance   270
              New Water-Service Moratorium and Rationing   271
              Other Interim Devices   272
              Comment and Conclusions   272
           Preparation of a Growth-Management Plan   273
              Reason for the Plan   274
              Conclusions   274
           Regional Considerations   274
              Significance of Regional Issue   275
              Regional Planning Methods   276
           Contrast of Growth Issues in the City of Santa
              Barbara with Issues and Plans of Selected
              Other California Communities   277
           Recommended Procedures to Follow in
              Establishing a Santa Barbara Growth-
              Management Plan   277
              Regional Status   277
              Population-Growth Impacts   278
              Disasters   278
              Projected Population   279

Chapter   Page

    "Phasing" and "Sequencing" of Growth-
      Allowing Facilities   279
    Low-Income Housing   280
  Ordinances and Other Tools to Carry Out the
    Growth-Management Plan   280
    Rezoning of Residential Property to Lower
      Density   281
    Amendment of Multiple-Dwelling Density
      Ordinances   282
    Mixed Residential Zoning as a Possible Solution   283
    Increased Minimum Lot Size: Open-Space Zoning
      and Substandard-Lot Problem   284
    Development-Right Acquisition   284
    Property-Tax Issues   285
    Migration Opportunity Limitations   286
    Subdivision and Subdivision-type Exactions   288
    Historical and Esthetic Zoning   288
    Point or Scoring System for Proposed New
      Development   289
  Low- and Moderate-Income Housing   290
    Two Problems   290
    Low-Income Housing Options   291
  Notes   297

EPILOGUE   302

APPENDIX   304

BIBLIOGRAPHY   319

ABOUT THE AUTHORS   331

LIST OF TABLES

Table   Page

1.1   Annual Population, by PIP, for the City of Santa
Barbara to the Year 2000   16

1.2   PIP Totals, City and Total South Coast, Year 2000   17

3.1   Number and Percentage of City Residents with
Various Population Preferences   43

3.2   Screenline Capacities and Demands   50

3.3   Bus Requirements   57

3.4   Space Demand for Downtown Parking at Various PIPs   59

4.1   Pollutant Emission Factors for California Motor
Vehicles   76

4.2   Estimated Ratios of Emissions from Future Aircraft,
Year 2000, to Current Aircraft Emissions, Year 1972   77

4.3   Projected Land-Use Areas   77

4.4   Stationary-Source Emissions in the South Coast Air
Basin of Santa Barbara County, 1972   79

4.5   Aggregated Pollutant Emissions by Source Type,
for Year 2000 and Selected Intermediate Years   82

4.6   Current and Predicted Ozone Concentrations   85

4.7   Historical Comparison of Habitat Resources   91

4.8   Comparative Habitat Resources of Four High-
Income Neighborhoods and Four Low-Income
Neighborhoods   93

4.9   Stream "Stabilization" Modifications   94

5.1   Comparison of Median Family Income, Santa Barbara
and United States, 1950, 1960, and 1970   116

Table   Page

5.2   La Cumbre Plaza and Downtown Core: Independents
        Versus Chain Stores   122

5.3   Growth and Unemployment Rates of 25 Most Quickly
        Growing SMSAs, 1950-60   125

5.4   Growth and Unemployment Rates of 25 Most Quickly
        Growing SMSAs, 1960-70   126

5.5   Growth and Unemployment Rates of All California
        SMSAs, 1960-66   127

5.6   Building Permit Activity: City and State, 1968-74   135

6.1   Library Construction Schedule, 1975-2000, Half-
        Density PIPs   149

6.2   City Library Bond Costs, 1974-2000   150

6.3   Impact of Population on Park Acreage Requirements   157

6.4   Costs of Land and Development for Parks at Each PIP   158

6.5   Parks and Recreation Bond Costs, 1974-2000   160

6.6   Public-Works (Streets and Highways) Bond Costs,
        1974-2000   162

6.7   Costs of Municipal Services per Resident, City of
        Santa Barbara, 1968/69 Through 1972/73, and
        Five-Year Average   163

6.8   Total Costs, Operating Plus Capital, for Each
        PIP, 1974-2000   164

6.9   Comparative Values of Overzoned R-3/R-4 Areas
        and Proximate R-1 Areas: Tax Loss Due to
        Downzoning   168

6.10   Per Capita Revenues from Principal Sources to the
        General Fund, Excluding Property Taxes,
        1963-73   172

Table   Page

6.11   Total Revenues for Each PIP, 1974–2000   174

6.12   Net Revenues (Revenues Less Costs) for Each PIP,
       1974–2000   177

6.13   Change in Property Tax on a $30,000 Home, for
       Different PIPs, Selected Years   178

6.14   Selected Characteristics of Schools, Santa Barbara
       School Districts   182

6.15   Program for Expansion of School Capacity: Current
       and Total Costs   186

6.16   Elementary Schools, Total Average Daily
       Attendance, 1974–2000   187

6.17   High School District, Average Daily Attendance,
       1974–2000   188

6.18   Capital Costs: Elementary Schools, Projected
       Capital Outlays, 1974–2000   190

6.19   Elementary Schools, Revenue Less Costs for Each
       PIP, 1974–2000   191

6.20   Change in Property Tax on a $30,000 Home, for
       Combined Santa Barbara School Districts at
       Different PIPs   193

6.21   Supplemental Sources of Water and Incremental Costs   197

6.22   Water: Demand and Costs, Half-Density Probable,
       1974–2000   200

6.23   Water: Revenues Less Costs, 1974–2000   201

6.24   Water: Per Capita Net Revenues Less Costs,
       Selected Years   202

6.25   Year and Population at Which Supplemental Water
       Will Be Needed, at Various PIPs   204

Table		Page
6.26	Wastewater: Population and Year of Capacity, Limits of New 11 Million gpd Treatment Plant	207
6.27	Wastewater: Estimated Annual Operating Expenditures, 1974/75 and 1977/78	208
6.28	Schedule of Wastewater Treatment Plant Expansion Under Each PIP, 1974-2000	210
6.29	Wastewater: Estimated Number of Users, by Class, in Year 2000, for Each PIP	212
6.30	Wastewater: Current Revenue, by User Class	212
6.31	Wastewater: Percent Changes in Revenue, Population, and per Capita Revenue for Each PIP, 1974-2000	213
6.32	Half-Density Probable Wastewater Analysis: Expenditures, Revenues, and per Capita Deficit, 1974-2000	215
6.33	Change in Property Tax Rates for Combined School Districts and City of Santa Barbara, 1995	219
6.34	Projected Revenue Increases Required, Water and Wastewater, 1995	220
6.35	Present Value of Revenue Requirements (Revenues Less Costs) for All Services, 1974-2000	222
7.1	City Revenues per Employee, by Economic Sector	236
7.2	Total Revenue for General Fund, If Entire Labor Force Were of a Given Sector, by Each Sector	238
7.3	Impacts of Various Economic Sectors on the City	247
8.1	The Public Sector: Net Effects of Growth, by PIP	255
8.2	PIP Ratings for Each Growth Variable	256

LIST OF FIGURES

Figure		Page
1.1	Growth of City, Remaining South Coast, South Coast, and UCSB	5
1.2	Population, City of Santa Barbara, and Comparison of City Population with South Coast and Santa Barbara County, 1840-1980 Projection	7
1.3	Contribution of UCSB, National Increase, and All Other Causes to Population Growth of South Coast Area, 1960-73	10
3.1	Screenline Map, City of Santa Barbara	49
4.1	Two-by-Two Kilometer Grid Overlay for Geographical Distribution of Pollutant Emissions	75
4.2	Geographical Distribution of the Difference in NO_x Emissions Between the High and Low PIPs in the Year 2000	81
4.3	Future Trends in Total Emissions of NO_x and Reactive HC	83
4.4	Future Trends in Total Emissions of CO	84
4.5	Disaster Map, City of Santa Barbara	102
5.1	Total Valuation: Residential Building Permits, City and State, 1968-74	136
5.2	Number of Units: Building Permits, City and State, 1968-74	138
5.3	Valuation per Unit: Residential Building Permits, City and State, 1968-74	139
6.1	Comparative Demand for Supplemental Water	196
6.2	Wastewater Revenue Requirements for Each PIP, 1977-2000	216

The authors of this work made up the Santa Barbara Planning Task Force, a group of local citizens who were asked by the Santa Barbara City Council to provide an analytic base to help determine an optimum level of population for the City of Santa Barbara. In response to a proposed work program prepared by the Task Force, $47,000 in city funds were allocated, and a work and production period of approximately seven months was provided to accomplish the task.

The five members of the Task Force, a group of people who had never before worked together, enlisted the aid of scores of citizens--some professional and some amateur--in a series of projects that involved dozens of simultaneous studies. It would have been appropriate, in many instances, to have collected the results of one study before embarking upon another, but our time limits did not permit such a reasonable approach. Similarly, it would have been desirable to issue a series of preliminary reports, with ample time for community and self-criticism; again, the time pressure of our deadline did not allow for such a course of action.

We have sought to reveal the basis of our reasoning and to include the calculations upon which our conclusions rest. Demystifying the planning process has been one of our key goals throughout.

As originally prepared and presented to its city sponsors, this study consisted of three volumes; this book represents an abridged and somewhat modified version of Volume 1 of the original study, which is an analysis of the effects of growth on the city as a whole. In Volume 2 of the original series, the Neighborhood Fact Book, the general growth effect findings were applied to each of the city's 26 neighborhoods and six business and cultural center areas. The third volume contained technical appendixes, some of which have been incorporated directly, wherever necessary, into this book. Along with the three volumes of study reports, other materials produced by the Task Force included a 13-page popular summary, distributed as a special section of the metropolitan newspaper, and a slide show presentation of research findings, presented at various neighborhood association meetings and community forums.

The original three-volume series is referred to in the notes sections of the present text by the designations "Volume 1," "Volume 2," or "Volume 3." We make reference to these volumes where we have omitted from the present book materials specifically relevant only to Santa Barbara or involving analyses unduly repetitive. We have endeavored always to include sufficient material from the original volumes to show "how it is done" and hence to facilitate replication. We have been forced, for practical reasons, to omit some of the more detailed maps and figures.

In publishing the study results for a larger national audience, we act on the assumption that the issue of local growth is becoming a pressing concern of cities across the country and that our attempt to discern the effects of growth in one place could have much relevance to the future of many other places as well. We believe that in its comprehensiveness and in the logic of its analysis this Santa Barbara study represents a potential model for those wishing to assess the effects of growth in other areas. The results of such analyses may or may not lead to similar findings; the effects of additional people are obviously not going to be the same everywhere. Specific local conditions, such as the existing stock of unused capacities in roadways, water supply, sewage treatment, and so forth will help to determine where, and under what circumstances, additional people will benefit or detract from the quality of life of different citizens. Our study merely points to the fact that it is possible to know such effects, to know them in advance, and to use public policy so that beneficial consequences are maximized.

1

PRINCIPLES AND
METHODS

ORIENTATION

General Purpose

There is increasing appreciation among urban Americans of
the fact that, however warranted it might be on some grounds, continuous metropolitan growth carries with it certain obvious cost to
the quality of life. Because of Santa Barbara's strategic ocean-front
location in the midst of a rapidly developing industrial and agricultural region almost contiguous to the expanding Los Angeles megalop-
olis, its future as a small-scale community of high environmental
quality may be in jeopardy. Over the long term, Santa Barbara's
future growth is not limited by its zoning, its general plan, its water
supply, or its land acreage. General plans and zoning laws can be
changed; additional water supplies can be purchased; a finite supply
of land can be developed and redeveloped to intensities that are almost infinite.

This population impact study is intended as an aid to citizens,
elected officials, and city staffs to enable them to assess the probable consequences of future growth. Our goal is to determine those
aspects of population growth that improve the quality of life, those
aspects that have no effect whatsoever, and those that adversely affect it. Wherever possible, these consequences are expressed quan-
titatively so as to highlight the net effects, positive or negative, of
increasing the city's population. Where relevant, the distribution of
these effects upon particular neighborhoods of the city is highlighted

---

Gerald DeWitt is coauthor of this chapter.

so that future changes may be accommodated in the most rational manner possible.

From the outset, it has <u>not</u> been our task to determine the optimum size of the city's population, and so we make no judgment of the optimum size of Santa Barbara. But the facts and concepts are here for other citizens to do so. In order to reach such a determination, they will be faced with the most fundamental questions that can be asked: What sort of lives are most worth leading, and what sort of prices are worth paying to have such lives? Our job has been to lay out the prices: There is no optimum level of growth or population size, apart from the values and interests of different people. Because of these differences, there will continue to be disagreements about the optimum population size of Santa Barbara even after this study has been read and digested. Thus, the debate will not stop with this report; we only hope to enable it to continue at a higher level of informed intelligence. The land-use-control policies that are eventually chosen by the city, whether through a revised General Plan or some other means, will be a result of the political process-- the only mechanism we know for settling disagreements among people who have varying interests and values. May that process continue, in such a manner that the majority is both informed and in a position to prevail.

Organization of This Volume

In this chapter we provide an orientation to our basic conceptual apparatus--how we approach a population study. We make clear one basic assumption: Population cannot be predicted.

In the second part of this chapter we provide a general explanation of the methods used in the study, in particular our decision to develop Population Impact Points (PIPs) to use as hypothetical scenarios for future levels of populations. We use these PIPs as the population bench marks for changes in the city's economy, social life, and land-use pattern.

Chapter 2 describes the results of a statistical examination of the effects of size and growth rates on the economic and social well-being of the 115 American cities we have used for comparative purposes. With these effects on cities in general as a background, the following two chapters examine the likely effects of growth on the social and environmental characteristics of Santa Barbara. Chapter 3 analyzes the likely effects of growth on the social well-being of Santa Barbarans: the traffic congestion that will surround them, their relationships with one another and with their government, their access to parks and recreation facilities, and the general use of the land and the style by which they live a routine day. Perhaps most important, we examine the current opinions of Santa Barbara's residents on the subject of growth and thus are able to compare the opinions they hold and the levels of growth expected for the city under the city's current land-use growth-control restrictions.

Chapter 4 analyzes the effects of growth on the natural environment of the city: the quality of air, the level of noise, the status of its habitats, animal species and creeks, its esthetic resources, and the ability of the city to withstand the consequences of natural disaster.

The next series of chapters investigates the relationship between Santa Barbara's population growth and its citizens' economic well-being. Chapter 5, devoted to an analysis of the private economic sector, examines expected effects of population growth on per capita income, unemployment rates, and the cost of living. We also discuss some issues relevant to the effects of growth upon local wealth, particularly upon the financial health of locally owned businesses.

Chapter 6 describes our findings on the effects of growth on the public sector of the economy. Due to its length and complexity, this chapter has been divided into three parts. Part I analyzes General Fund expenditures and revenues likely to develop at various growth points. Part II analyzes the effects of various growth alternatives on expenditures and revenues for non-General Fund services, particularly education, water, and sewers. Drawing upon the findings of the previous two parts, Part III summarizes the general public sector effects of growth.

In Chapter 7 the study takes a slight analytical detour to examine the ways that changes in the economic base of the city may come to alter the general costs and benefits of growth as revealed in the previous chapters. That is, while other chapters have discussed the effects of growth on various quality-of-life indicators, Chapter 7 asks how these effects might be mitigated or exacerbated, should the economic base of the city change. Each of the major economic sectors-- hotel-motels, research and development, retailing, technical manufacturing, and light industry--is separately analyzed and then compared with the others.

Finally, our last series of chapters summarizes our findings and describes options for the future. Chapter 8 is a summary of findings, organized around an attempt to lay out scenarios of the quality of life of Santa Barbarans at each of the future PIPs. Chapter 9 sets forth certain policy implications of our study, particularly the ways that different methods used to control growth will be likely to yield very different consequences. Chapter 10 discusses the legal constraints under which the city must operate in determining future land-use patterns and the tools that are available to the city to provide policy makers with maximum ability to reach their goals.

We now turn to the discussion of first principles.

EXPLAINING POPULATION CHANGE

Cities historically have followed very different courses of growth. Some expand rapidly and then slow down; some never expand much at all; some never seem to stop expanding. There is neither a single pattern that fits all cities nor a "classic" pattern that can be used to explain growth in one place based on the growth experience of another. There are ample precedents for almost any possible Santa Barbara future: It may remain absolutely stable, as Beaumont, Texas, or Buffalo, New York, did between 1960 and 1970; it may become the equal of boom cities like Anaheim, California, that more than doubled with a 10 percent average yearly growth rate experienced over the same decade. The range of possibilities is enormous: Santa Barbara contains within its 17 square miles more acreage than Jersey City, New Jersey, (population 261,000) and has not much less than Manhattan, also once a rather small and charming ocean-front town.

Of course these examples are far-fetched, but so are all scenarios of rapid growth that are imagined before they occur. They are unimaginable, even when scaled down to more moderate levels, because urban residents have a habit of thinking that the history of growth in their area somehow sets "natural" limits on guiding projections for its future growth patterns.

Any attempt to determine a "natural" growth rate for an area on the basis of past experience is as likely to fail as it is to succeed, as the growth history of Santa Barbara demonstrates. Figure 1.1 summarizes the pattern of growth over the past 35 years. During the 1940s, both the city and the surrounding South Coast areas grew at moderate rates.[1] The city sustained these moderate rates throughout the 1950s and early 1960s, at which time its rate of increase declined sharply. The remaining South Coast, however, began to grow rapidly in the 1950s, averaging almost 10 percent annually in that decade and from 13 to 14 percent during the next (see Figure 1.1). This marked increase occurred primarily in the Goleta Valley, and much of it was due to the University of California, which moved to Goleta and became a General Campus of the University in 1958. Student enrollment quadrupled between 1960 and 1970, and University planners as recently as 1968 envisioned continuous enrollment increases to 25,000 by 1985. But student enrollments peaked around 1969-70 and then declined; with this decline, the growth of the South Coast has slowed. During the past few years, the total South Coast population has increased at the average annual rate of only 2 percent, and the city itself has increased only 1 percent for the past eight years.

FIGURE 1.1

Growth of City, Remaining South Coast, South Coast, and UCSB

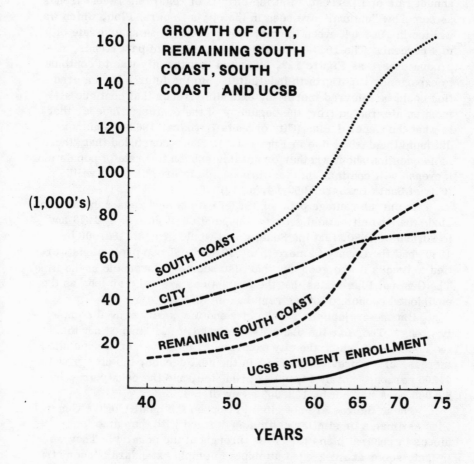

GROWTH OF CITY, REMAINING SOUTH COAST, SOUTH COAST AND UCSB

The Hazards of Prediction

It is tempting to simplify our planning problem dramatically by merely projecting the rates of growth experienced by the city over the past eight years. After all, a clear pattern is evident: a steady annual rate of 1 percent. But the pitfalls of regarding recent trends as somehow "natural" are seen in the city's General Plan, which was written in 1963-64, when the city was growing at an annual rate of 3 to 4 percent. The 1964 General Plan projection of past trends, reproduced here as Figure 1.2, indicated that the city was to continue to experience rapid growth indefinitely into the future; such a prediction could be inferred merely by extending trends that continue almost uninterrupted from the beginning of the century. Indeed, that is what the General Plan (City of Santa Barbara 1963-64) authors did (note the dashed line in Figure 1.2). They concluded that "there is no question about whether or not this substantial rate of population increase will continue into the foreseeable future. . . . It will" (City of Santa Barbara 1963-64, p. 18).

From the vantage point of 1963-64 it seemed reasonable to conclude that the city would grow to a population of 80,000 by 1973 and to 90,000 by 1980, that the South Coast would grow to 180,000 by 1980, and the County to more than 350,000. These projections were tied to trends in the economy that also seemed reasonable at the time. The General Plan states that the projections are valid so long as the envisioned economic forces remained in effect.

But the projections for the city and the county proved completely wrong. The year the plan was published, 1964, turned out to be the last year in which the city experienced the substantial population increase of the previous years. In the next decade, the city grew by 7,500 persons, not by 14,400 as predicted, and the county grew by 52,000 persons, not by 103,000 as predicted.

These figures are not cited to impugn the quality of the General Plan estimates or similar estimates derived with the same techniques in general plans for cities throughout the country. They were, in fact, sober and reasoned attempts to employ standard econometric models as the basis for intelligent population forecasting. Rather, we argue that there is no solid basis for inducing natural tendencies of population growth from past trends and the existing economic and population structure. What seemed "natural" in the light of the data in 1964 was clearly not "natural" only a few years later. Similarly, an attempt to induce a "natural" rate from the current 1 percent rate of the past eight years would be equally fallacious, even if tied to forecasts of the regional economy: National economic downturns (or upturns), a decision of a major industry to locate a branch in the South Coast region, or the decision of local residents regarding water importation are all unpredictable sources of influence on the future of this area.

FIGURE 1.2

Population, City of Santa Barbara, and Comparison of City Population
with South Coast and Santa Barbara County, 1840-1980 Projection

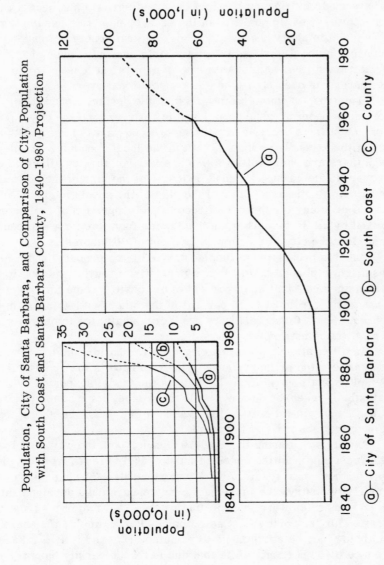

ⓐ— City of Santa Barbara   ⓑ— South coast   ⓒ— County

Source: City of Santa Barbara, General Plan, 1963-64.

Sources of Growth

To see how this is so, it may be of some value to discuss in somewhat more detail the immediate causes of local population growth. Given the undeniable beauty of the Santa Barbara area, some observers have made the assumption that the area's growth has been a response to the esthetic qualities of the area. Under this assumption, people move to a city because they seek natural beauty and superior community amenities. Santa Barbara, this reasoning goes, has superior amenities, and thus its rate of growth, at least prior to recent years, has been above the state and national average.

One group of immigrants for whom the "esthetic attraction" theory does seem to make good sense is retirees. Of the city's population, 18 percent consists of persons over 65 years of age. Although some of these people do indeed work in the local economy, and although there are some retirees who are younger than 65, the size of this over-65 age group is a good indicator of the size of the retired population. Another indicator of the size of the population not tied to the local economy for their livelihood is the proportion of the income received by all Santa Barbarans that comes from property and pensions. For the city this is now 31 percent of all income.

But this proportion of income derived from property and pensions has not increased with recent population growth. Indeed, it has remained constant at 13 percent of net basic income for the city but has shrunk from 21 to 18 percent in the other South Coast communities. South Coast residents are increasingly tied to nearby employment opportunities.

An alternative explanation of growth is that for this area, as for any other, the primary cause of in-migration is the opportunity for employment that is present. This is the model supported by the great bulk of research on why people move (see, for example, Rossi 1965). The argument here is that people follow jobs, and those areas that have the jobs will get the people.

And in fact, during the 1960-70 decade, both the city and other South Coast communities received most of their growth from people who went there as a result of work opportunities. The expansion of the tourist industry, the University, and research and development (R & D) companies were the impetus for the great majority of new migration for the South Coast as a whole. For example, the share of net basic income attributable to manufacturing and to R & D has increased by 56 percent, while that due to the University has increased by 167 percent. Of course, some people may have chosen to accept offers or establish businesses in Santa Barbara rather than elsewhere precisely because of the area's amenities. But they would not have moved there were there not the possibility of making a living

in the area. Santa Barbara's amenities thus act primarily to determine the type of persons who are there--for example, those who appreciate Santa Barbara's qualities and who may even be willing to
make certain income sacrifices to experience them. Except for the
significant minority who live on pensions, royalties, and dividends,
Santa Barbara's income base is made up of people whose residence
in the area is tied to the local economy.

Another way of summarizing this finding is that growth in the
city and in the South Coast generally is primarily a result of people
following job opportunities or establishing businesses there. People
currently move there primarily because of their work, not to retire,
write, or play. The degree to which opportunities are provided for
this work is the degree to which those who might want to live in Santa
Barbara will have the opportunity to do so.

Case Illustration: The Impact of UCSB on Area Growth

The single most important new source of South Coast jobs
since 1960 has been the University of California at Santa Barbara
(UCSB). A close look at its impact illustrates the significance of
economic development as a factor in the area's population growth
experience.

It is possible to make a crude estimate of the impact of the
University on the growth of the entire South Coast area, including
the city. The UCSB Office of Architects and Engineering currently
estimates that approximately 1.017 additional persons--primarily,
University employees and their families, and, to a lesser degree,
persons supported by service-activity employment generated by the
presence of the University--are "induced" to live in this area by each
student enrolled in the University (these multiplier estimates are approximate and are used here only to obtain a general idea of the University's impact).

Thus, each additional student generates 2.017 South Coast residents, including himself/herself. Using County Planning Department
estimates of yearly population in the South Coast area, as well as estimates of natural increase (excess of births over deaths) derived from
the 1970 census and the County Health Department, it is possible to
make rough estimates of the proportion of population growth caused by
the University and by natural increase, respectively. These estimates are presented graphically in Figure 1.3, and should be taken
as an illustration of general trends, rather than as precise estimates
for specific years. On the one hand, they probably underestimate the
growth-inducing influence of the University, particularly in the growth
period of the early and middle 1960s when extensive construction work

FIGURE 1.3

Contribution of UCSB, Natural Increase, and All Other Causes to
Population Growth of South Coast Area, 1960-73

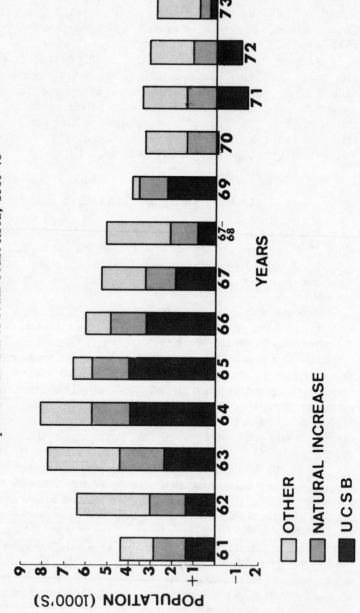

on the physical plant was in progress. They also fail to take into account industries that were attracted to the Santa Barbara area because of the presence of the University campus; for example, a recent survey by the UCSB Office of Architects and Engineers of Goleta firms found that 32 percent gave "proximity to UCSB" as a reason for locating in the Santa Barbara area; 80 percent make use of University facilities and personnel.

Figure 1.3 graphically presents the results of this analysis. We may conclude that the period of rapid growth of the South Coast closely paralleled the period of rapid growth of the University; indeed, in the initial rapid-growth years (1963-66) the University probably accounted for at least half of the population increase in the South Coast area, with natural increase accounting for another quarter. The impact of the University expansion on the city itself is more difficult to ascertain. Although city population growth began to slow down during the height of University expansion, it is possible that this slowdown would have been even greater in the absence of the stimulus of the University.

The purpose of this analysis has been to demonstrate the impact that a single political decision can have upon the future growth of an area and the folly of attempting to predict future growth on the basis of "natural" past trends. When the Regents made the new Goleta campus a "General Campus" of the University of California in 1958, growth patterns in the South Coast area were altered in ways that would not have been predictable from any knowledge available a decade earlier. The rate of population increase in the Goleta Valley for a time doubled and then redoubled over earlier levels, while that of the city declined. Now it appears that the growth "impulse" generated by the rapid expansion of the UCSB campus is at an end as campus enrollments stabilize. This effect, combined with the also unforeseen rapid decline in the birth rate, has meant that since 1970 annual South Coast growth rates have been around 2 percent and declining. As mentioned previously, city rates of growth have been even lower. It should be emphasized that there is no "natural" rate of growth for the Santa Barbara area. For Santa Barbara, as for any other locality, growth is the consequence of decisions: decisions by University Regents, aerospace firms, corporate executives, water districts, national and state politicians, planners, and the public. If growth is left to occur "naturally," it will reflect the preferences of those sufficiently influential to determine the location of major economic entities--entities that bring jobs and people. Growth is a consequence of decisions. The key issue involves determining who will decide.

GENERAL METHODS

Population Impact Points

Because this study does not predict growth but rather measures its impacts, we created a series of population bench marks to use as analytic points of departure for our studies. We ask what will happen to Santa Barbara at one level of population or another and have chosen our population levels to reflect the populations that would result, given various alternative city land-use policies that have been enacted over the years. There are three such city land-use policies that we have used to create our PIPs.

Maximum Future Populations

The City's Zoning Ordinance. This categorizes land use as residential, commercial, or manufacturing. Within each category there are numerous subcategories that vary the intensity of allowable land use and establish other constraints. Existing residential zones permit a range of development that runs from the sparseness of one housing unit per net acre (A-1) to the density of 43 or more units per acre (R-3). The ordinance is cumulative, or "pyramid"--that is, lower-density developments can occur within higher-density zones. Because of the pyramid principle, high-density (R-3 or R-4) residential construction is also legal in commercial zones.

Our task was to determine the level of population implied by current zoning. We computed allowable densities on a parcel-by-parcel basis for the entire city, and hence the maximum population permissible under current zoning. We term this the Zoning Maximum PIP; it is estimated at 170,039 persons, or two and one-third times the present estimated population of 73,132.[2] To reach Zoning Maximum by the year 2000 the population of Santa Barbara would have to grow at an average annual rate of 5.1 percent, substantially above the current rate, but well under rates experienced recently in other California cities, such as San Jose.

The City's General Plan. This is not a law; there are no provisions for its enforcement. Since its adoption a decade ago, the city has not reconciled the Zoning Ordinance with the policies expressed in the General Plan. Nonetheless, proposed developments in recent years have been judged in part according to their conformity with the Plan, thus justifying its use in the present study as an authentic alternative scenario for the city.

The General Plan has numerous designations for different kinds of land use, including parks and parkways, various residential densities (from one dwelling unit to 30 per gross acre), and a number of "mixed" zones, suggesting a combination of residential and commercial development. Its land-use categories correspond closely to those in the Zoning Ordinance; the discrepancy between the two policies has mostly to do with the intensity of development in areas designated for a given sort of use. The conceptual bases of the categories, stressing homogeneity of proximate uses, is the same for both documents. The General Plan is hence an alternative land-use policy in terms of the level of population that would result if its recommendations were given the force of law through changes in the Zoning Ordinance. Our estimate of the maximum number of persons that could live in the city under a General Plan that led to such zone changes is 139,720, or almost twice the present population. This represents an average growth rate of 3.5 percent to the year 2000.

The City's Half-Density Ordinance. This was adopted by the City Council in April 1973 as an interim measure to limit development until appropriate studies could be undertaken preparatory to still another revision of the General Plan. The half-density ordinance halved all densities in multiple zones. The half-density ordinance, or some modification of it, is potentially a permanent city land-use and population policy. We calculated as 117,486 the maximum number of people who would live in the city under a permanent version of the present half-density ordinance, or a little more than one and one-half times the present population. To reach half-density maximum population by the year 2000 the city would have to grow at an average annual rate of 2.3 percent, or about twice the rate of the past eight years.

Probable Future Populations

There are a number of reasons to believe that the figures affixed to the maximum PIPs overstate the population levels that could be expected to develop even under strong growth pressure in the region. Many areas of the city are currently fully developed at lower densities than those permitted under zoning or suggested by the General Plan. Major demolition of recently constructed single-family homes and duplexes is unlikely, even if the areas in question are zoned for apartments. Furthermore, there are areas in the city with extremely rugged terrain that are not likely to be developed. Similar considerations exist with respect to ocean-front property and areas adjacent to creek beds. Development at full legal density is not likely to be permitted. Finally, there are areas likely to experience zoning changes in the near future--changes designated as part of the city's open-space element, or where zoning reductions have already been recommended to the Council by the Planning Commission.[3]

Because of such considerations, we have estimated probable populations for each PIP previously discussed. Together with staff from the City Planning Department, the Task Force reviewed each parcel map (usually two city blocks) in the city's land-use inventory field sheets, estimating probable future populations under each policy (Zoning, General Plan, Half-Density Ordinance). The results are three additional PIPs:

1. Half-Density Probable. This is calculated to be a population of 93,555 persons or about 1.25 times the present population. To reach this level by the year 2000 the city would have to grow at an average rate of about 1.1 percent--a rate slightly higher than the rate of growth experienced over the past half-decade. This PIP most closely approximates the most recent growth trajectory of the city population.
2. General Plan Probable. This is a population of 103,444 persons, or 1.4 times the current population, representing an average annual growth rate of 1.6 percent.
3. Zoning Probable. This is a population of 119,460, or 1.6 times the current population, representing an average annual growth rate of 2.4 percent.

When we call these figures "probable," we mean just that: They are likely results of existing laws and policies under current conditions. By current conditions we include the prevailing philosophy among city staff and elected officials concerning the preservation of areas such as open space, major hillsides, and creek beds. Their views could quickly change, and should they become more permissive, the actual figures would be considerably closer to, or even exceed, the maximum figures.

Since the logic of our approach is to present the impacts of growth on a range of policy alternatives, we decided to include as a lower bound to that range a seventh PIP:

4. No-growth. This is a population numerically identical to the present population of 73,132. Even the most stringent no-growth policies cannot prevent increase through excess of births over deaths until at least 1990; only a net out-migration would result in a stable or declining population.

The no-growth PIP, like the other PIPs, was chosen not because we expect it actually to occur in the year 2000, but rather to provide an analytic basis for comparison with the other growth scenarios.

The logic of our study is to make comparison among various PIPs, thus enabling us to estimate the magnitude of growth effects under a variety of different growth scenarios. We have deduced the rates of growth that would accompany each PIP's level of population by horizoning each Impact Point to the year 2000 and then assuming an equal yearly population increase to reach that point.[4] The projections of yearly population growth for each PIP are presented in Table 1.1. This table provides the basis for much of the analysis in this study.

South Coast Population

For many of our purposes it was necessary to know the population levels for the remaining South Coast area that would correspond to various growth levels in the city. Each PIP thus includes a population scenario not only for the city, but one for the remaining South Coast as well. The ratio of populations of the entire South Coast (including the city) compared to the city alone is currently 2.2:1. Based on County General Plan estimates of South Coast population at full development, we assume that by the year 2000, at each PIP, the ratio of total South Coast population to city population will grow to 2.7:1 as the city continues to decrease in population relative to the rest of the region. For the No-Growth PIP we assume no-growth in the remaining areas of the South Coast as well; thus, the ratio between the two populations remains constant at 2.2:1. In Table 1.2 PIP totals for the city and South Coast at the year 2000 are listed.

The Assumption of All Other Things Being Equal

The usefulness of the PIPs is that they permit us to test various notions of what will happen to the city as a result of changes in population level per se. That is, there are many changes in the offing for Santa Barbara, but our key focus is not upon the effects of such variables. During the coming generation that is the time horizon of this study, important changes in technology may occur and result, for example, in the abandonment of the automobile as a means of transportation. Or the basis of school funding may be altered to create full federal or state support. The economic base of the city may change: R & D may grow and tourism decline, or vice versa.

Our basic method, in light of all such possibilities, was generally to assume that none of them would occur. This study tries to determine the effects of growth, all other things being equal. Thus, we do not automatically assume that per capita income or per capita property value will automatically rise with an increase in population,

TABLE 1.1

Annual Population, by PIP, for the City of Santa Barbara to the Year 2000

Year	No Growth	Half-Density		General Plan		Zoning	
		Maximum	Probable	Maximum	Probable	Maximum	Probable
1974	73,132	73,132	73,132	73,132	73,132	73,132	73,132
1975	73,132	74,837	73,917	75,693	74,297	76,859	74,913
1976	73,132	76,543	74,703	78,254	75,463	80,586	76,695
1977	73,132	78,249	75,488	80,815	76,629	84,313	78,477
1978	73,132	79,955	76,274	83,376	77,795	88,040	80,259
1979	73,132	81,661	77,059	85,937	78,961	91,767	82,041
1980	73,132	83,367	77,845	88,498	80,127	95,495	83,823
1981	73,132	85,073	78,630	91,059	81,292	99,222	85,605
1982	73,132	86,779	79,416	93,620	82,458	102,949	87,387
1983	73,132	88,485	80,201	96,182	83,624	106,676	89,168
1984	73,132	90,191	80,987	98,743	84,790	110,403	90,950
1985	73,132	91,897	81,772	101,304	85,956	114,131	92,732
1986	73,132	93,603	82,558	103,865	87,122	117,858	94,514
1987	73,132	95,309	83,343	106,426	88,287	121,585	96,296
1988	73,132	97,015	84,129	108,987	89,453	125,312	98,078
1989	73,132	98,721	84,914	111,548	90,619	129,039	99,860
1990	73,132	100,427	85,700	114,109	91,785	132,767	101,642
1991	73,132	102,133	86,485	116,670	92,951	136,494	103,424
1992	73,132	103,839	87,271	119,232	94,117	140,221	105,205
1993	73,132	105,545	88,056	121,793	95,283	143,948	106,987
1994	73,132	107,251	88,842	124,354	96,448	147,675	108,769
1995	73,132	108,957	89,627	126,915	97,614	151,403	110,551
1996	73,132	110,663	90,413	129,476	98,780	155,130	112,333
1997	73,132	112,369	91,198	132,037	99,946	158,857	114,115
1998	73,132	114,075	91,984	134,598	101,112	162,584	114,115
1999	73,132	115,781	92,769	137,159	102,278	166,311	117,679
2000	73,132	117,486	93,555	139,720	103,443	170,038	119,460

Source: Santa Barbara Planning Task Force.

although the total amount clearly does. Nor do we assume (or attempt to predict) a shift in the economic base of the area--toward a more tourist-oriented economy, or retirement-oriented, or any other possible outcome. We assume that the current economic mix remains unchanged as the city grows, just as we assume constant per capita income or per capita property value. We relax this assumption only when it would violate clear logic or clear, existing evidence. For example, current fertility is at levels where births approximately equal deaths each year; thus, we can expect a gradual "aging" of the population with relatively fewer children entering our schools in the future. Similarly, it appears reasonable to expect that under a now-growth policy, in which no additional housing units were allowed, currently undeveloped land in the city would lose much of its value. Such an assumption is investigated and incorporated into our research in Chapter 6.

TABLE 1.2

PIP Totals, City and Total South Coast, Year 2000

PIP	City		Total South Coast	
	Maximum	Probable	Maximum	Probable
No-growth	73,132		162,469	
Half-density	117,486	93,555	317,214	252,598
General Plan	139,720	103,443	377,246	279,298
Zoning	170,038	119,460	459,105	322,544

Our assumption of generally stable conditions does not argue that we expect the economic mix of the city to remain constant for the next 25 years, but only acknowledges that no one can predict the direction that future changes might take.[5] To build such changes into our analysis would obscure the fact that such changes result from action taken today, and it would imply that they were somehow inevitable. Because we are mindful that changes in the economic base can have effects on the consequences of growth, we do attempt, where relevant, to indicate how such changes would affect the direction of the magnitude of our findings.

GENERAL DATA BASE

We have attempted to mobilize a wide range of sources and to draw upon the numerous studies that have been completed for the

city and other jurisdictions as well as studies of urban finance and
social life that are part of the general literature of urban economics
and urban sociology. Our work has relied upon the following sorts
of materials, each of which is described in the relevant chapters
that follow as well as Volume 3 of the original report:

1. Historical information on the public sector in Santa Barbara,
including our own econometric analyses of revenues and expenditures,
by major service category, over the past 13 years;

2. Materials and consultations provided us by the heads of
city departments and divisions within departments, enabling us to
interpret the historical information of Santa Barbara's revenue and
expenditures to make estimations of major capital costs that will
attend growth;

3. Extensive data and technical assistance provided us by
agencies outside the city government;

4. A comparative study of 115 relevant U.S. cities to provide
us with comparative data on nationwide growth effects;

5. Information on the private sector in Santa Barbara, gathered by interviews with executives at major business institutions;

6. Numerous studies concerning growth effects in other cities.

NOTES

1. The "South Coast" denotes an area generally coincident
with the census-defined Santa Barbara urban area, covering the
coastal plain and foothills from Gaviota in the north and including
the city of Carpinteria in the south.

2. The procedures used for estimating the PIPs and the assumptions employed are presented in Volume 3, Appendix 2.1. By
development to "maximum population permissible" we assume that
all land is developed to its maximum legal capacity, including land
that currently is developed at less than full capacity. Thus, substantial redevelopment would occur under the "maximum" PIPs.

3. Detailed discussion of methods used to calculate probable
populations is contained in Volume 3, Appendix 2.1.

4. The projections are thus straight-line increases. We could
have employed a model based on geometric increases (constant annual
rate rather than amount), but such a model more nearly approximates
natural population increase (through births and deaths) than increase
due primarily to in-migration, the primary source of Santa Barbara's
past growth.

5. It is also the case, as we learned from our cross-city analysis, that variations in the economic base of a city provide little pre-
dictive power on our list of dependent variables.

It is possible that there are patterns in which cities that grow
at similar rates or that have populations of similar sizes also experience common problems and benefits. If we can discover these
common patterns, we will have an indication of how Santa Barbara
is likely to change with future growth. There are other considerations, of course, that influence the way a city will fare as it grows,
particularly a city that is distinctive in a number of ways, such as
Santa Barbara. But many cities are idiosyncratic in one way or
another, and if strong patterns nevertheless emerge as a common
response to growth, it becomes increasingly likely that those patterns have important implications for Santa Barbara as well.

Much has been written about the ways the quality of city life is
affected by urban growth, but there has been little systematic empirical examination of the ways in which concrete indicators of that
quality are associated with differences and changes in the size of
urban places. This chapter represents one of the first comprehensive
studies of the relationships between urban size and growth rate, on
the one hand, and several empirical indicators of well-being, on the
other, including economic conditions, public safety, health, public
expenditures, and residential segregation. While a number of studies
have looked at individual indicators (for comprehensive reviews, see
Appelbaum 1975; Richardson 1973; Baum 1971), few have attempted
to look simultaneously at multiple indicators across the same group
of cities, employing comparable methodologies.

The present study differs from the conventional approach in
that it restricts its analysis of the effects of size and growth to those

---

Ross Follett is coauthor of this chapter.

middle-sized cities that are relatively self-contained.[1] The 115
cities analyzed include all urbanized areas in the continental United
States that (a) contain only one central city of from 50,000 to 400,000
inhabitants and (b) are at least 20 miles from the closest neighboring
urbanized area. These criteria effectively exclude suburbs and cities
that are parts of large metropolitan agglomerations. This serves to
standardize the cities studied: It makes little conceptual sense, for
example, to compare the costs of government services in a relatively isolated, functionally self-contained city with those of a city
that serves as a "dormitory" for a metropolitan town. It should be
emphasized that the 115 places used are not simply a sample. They
constitute all such places that meet our criteria.[2]

It should be noted that while we restricted our analysis to
medium-sized cities, such cities are perhaps more "typical" of the
places in which most urban Americans live than are larger metropolitan areas. According to the 1970 Census of Population (U.S.
Department of Commerce 1973a, sect. 2, pp. 1-44), 26.8 percent
of Americans live in places of 50,000 to 500,000 people; only 15.6
percent live in larger places, while the remainder (more than half
the population) live in smaller towns, unincorporated places, and
rural areas. The largest city in our analysis (Toledo, Ohio) ranked
thirty-fourth among all U.S. cities in size in 1970; that is, there are
only 33 cities excluded from consideration purely because they have
too many people.

METHODS: CROSS-SECTIONAL AND
LONGITUDINAL ANALYSIS

The major analyses that were done related the variables of
size, growth rate, and population increase over time (the independent or "causal" variables) to a set of dependent (or "effect")
variables. Two basic methods were used: a cross-sectional and a
longitudinal analysis. First, we compared the 115 urban areas at
one point in time using U.S. government data for 1970 (the cross-
sectional analysis); then 55 of these urban areas (all those that experienced positive growth over the past decade) were examined using
comparative data for 1960 and 1970 to see the effects of differences
in the rate of growth on changes in the dependent variables over time
(the longitudinal analysis). We thus looked at U.S. cities at one
point in time to see whether their size or recent rate of growth could
explain any differences currently found among them; then we further
examined a subgroup of these cities to determine whether their population change between 1960 and 1970 explained any other changes that
occurred within them over that decade.

The major independent variables are size of city, and size and growth rate of urbanized area(the city plus surrounding suburbs). [3] City growth rate was not used as an independent variable because it proved to be misleading. Almost all growth experienced by the cities was due to annexation and did not entail the relevant dynamics of growth. [4] Independent variables used in the longitudinal analysis are 1960-70 city population change, and 1960-70 urbanized area population change (U.S. Department of Commerce 1963b, 1973a).

The dependent variables selected for use in this analysis included indicators of economic well-being, public safety, health, public expenditures, and segregation. Data on six economic indicators were collected for both cities and urbanized areas: unemployment rate, median family income, percentage of families below poverty, income concentration, median house value, and median gross rent. Data for the remaining variables were available for cities only. These include three measures of public safety (per capita rates of murders and homicides, robberies and burglaries, and automobile thefts), five measures of public health (per capita rates of bronchitis, emphysema, and asthma, motor-vehicle deaths, infant deaths, cirrhosis deaths, and suicides), and six indexes of public-sector expenditures (per capita number of police officers, firepersons, and common function personnel, and per capita expenditures on each of the three categories). Finally, data on residential segregation were available for some 30 cities. Additionally, seven variables are employed as control variables: these include urbanized area growth rate, percentage Black or "of Spanish heritage," urbanized area population size, region (South or non-South), median age, median family income, and proportion of the urbanized area population that is city population ("consolidation"). Those control variables are those that are thought to mask or condition relationships between the independent and dependent variables. [5] All dependent and control variables are expressed either in per capita terms, as rates (percentages), or as median figures. The interest is thus not in examining the effects of size and growth on (for example) the magnitude of police costs or infant mortality, but rather on the effects relative to the population size (for example, police costs per person).

For variables that indicate the state of the economic environment, data were collected for both urbanized areas and cities. The effects of urbanized-area size on urbanized-area economic conditions are reported, as are the effects of city size on city economic variables. These two analyses draw upon different but overlapping data bases; when they nevertheless lead to similar results, as they usually do, they serve to confirm the fact that a strong pattern exists. Relationships are also reported between urbanized-area growth rate and urbanized-area economic variables.

Relationships between both city population and urbanized-area population and these dependent variables are reported. The purpose of the urbanized-area population analysis in this case is to examine the total-context effects of urban size, especially on safety and health. The city population analysis is especially appropriate in examining municipal expenditures.

When we examine the effects of growth over time (the longitudinal analysis), relationships are reported between urbanized-area population change (and, where appropriate, city population change) between 1960 and 1970, and changes in the dependent variables over the same period of time. When dependent variables are in dollar terms, the figures for 1960 and 1970 are deflated to constant dollars. [6]

The purpose of the present analysis is to indicate persistent effects of urban-area size and growth on the quality of life. Thus, we are not interested in specifying causal models of the relationships among numerous variables, of which some refer to size and growth, while others refer to the quality of life. Rather, we are seeking to answer the question: Does size (or growth) make a difference for this particular measure of the quality of life, even when other factors are taken into account? We are therefore reporting empirical regularities that currently obtain in the areas under examination, rather than attempting to develop a theoretical understanding of the underlying processes. In other words, the purpose of the present analysis is to discover variables clearly affected by urban population level or growth rate; we have accordingly conservatively adopted strategies that minimize the possibility that variables will be so deemed. If each of two or more control variables reduces a correlation, the one that reduces the relationship most is employed in any additional control procedures.

The principal statistical techniques employed in this analysis are multiple and partial correlation analysis. Since the correlations are linear techniques, that is, they depend on the straight-line relationships, every possible relationship between urban size or growth rate and each of the dependent variables was checked for curvilinearity through comparisons of correlations in the 1970 data. [7] This procedure, revealing no curves, crudely legitimized the linearity assumption.

The main statistical analysis proceeded as follows. For the cross-sectional analysis, zero-order correlation coefficients were first computed for each of the potential relationships between the independent and dependent variables. Whether or not a statistical relationship was found, every correlation was then computed controlling for each of the control variables as well as for the other independent variable acting as a control variable (singly and in combinations of two) that could statistically affect the zero-order correlation. [8]

Finally, the parallel longitudinal analyses were completed for each of the dependent variables for which longitudinal data were available. The longitudinal analysis was carried out in terms of zero-order correlations and serves to confirm or disconfirm the results of the cross-sectional study.

A further refinement in the analysis is that all potential relationships were reexamined with Southern U.S. cities or urbanized areas removed, and for cities comparable in income to Santa Barbara.[9]

The data sources used in this analysis are very numerous and disparate. There are possibly inconsistent methods of recordkeeping and data compilation across cities. The effect of such inconsistencies is to introduce "noises" into the pattern field, thus inhibiting the discovery of actual relationships with growth. The point is that our findings are conservative statements; we report a relationship at present only when the data produce clear statistical significance at ≤ 0.05.

That so many of our findings are nevertheless consistent with one another is all the more remarkable, given both the diversity in data sources and the diversity of analytic methods we used. Relationships between the same variables were looked at both statically and over time, for the entire group of urban areas and for non-Southern areas only, and for areas more directly comparable in income to Santa Barbara. To a remarkable degree, the findings remain unchanged regardless of method used or area subgroup utilized. It is clear that there are many forces at work, besides the ones we have examined here, in creating changes in cities, but it does appear that the variables of size and growth do play a role.

THE FINDINGS[10]

Economic Indicators

Unemployment

There is conflicting evidence on the relationship between official unemployment rate and urban-area size, although the majority of studies find no relationship between the two (Samuelson 1942; Levy and Arnold 1972, p. 95; Sierra Club of San Diego 1973, pp. 21-30; Molotch 1976). Hadden and Borgatta (1965, p. 108) found no relationship between unemployment and size among places smaller than 150,000 population; larger places did report somewhat higher unemployment rates, but this finding may have been due to the different ecologica! structure of older, larger cities (the working population migrates to the suburbs, leaving the poor and unemployed in the central c.ty). Duncan and Reiss (1956, p. 95) found higher unemployment ra.es in urban places larger than 1 million, although no relationshi.) between size and unemployment obtained in smaller places; Flair (1968), however, found no relationship among the 20 largest cities (all with more than 1 million).

In our analysis, unemployment rates appear to be unrelated to population size; for urbanized areas the zero-order correlation between unemployment rate and population size is nonsignificant at $r = 0.00$; for cities it is nonsignificant at $r = 0.02$. More quickly growing urbanized areas, however, tend to have slightly higher unemployment rates (the zero-order correlation is 0.16; p - 0.064; n = 93), a tendency that can be seen even more clearly when Southern urbanized areas are excluded ($r = 0.26$; $p = 0.03$; n = 52), or when urbanized areas in Santa Barbara's income range are considered separately ($r = 0.37$; $p = 0.021$; n = 31). None of the partial correlations significantly altered the zero-order relationships.

Our longitudinal analysis reveals that as population increases over time, there is no significant tendency for unemployment rates to increase or decrease ($r = 0.00$). The longitudinal analysis thus shows no relationship between population increase and change in unemployment rate for urbanized areas.

The finding that growth does not affect, or may even increase, the unemployment rate, supports the notion that new jobs attract new population, whereas new population does not necessarily attract or create (enough) new jobs.[11]

Median Family Income

Numerous studies have found that mean or median income is higher in larger places (Oliver 1946; Johnson 1952; Schnore and Varley 1955; Duncan and Reiss 1956; Hanna 1959; Schnore 1963; Ogburn and Duncan 1964; ACIR 1968). Furthermore, this relationship remains even after cities are standardized on such variables as race, sex, age, and educational composition (Fuchs 1967); region (ibid.); and cost of living (Hoch 1972b), although this latter control in particular attenuates the relationship somewhat (since larger places also have higher costs of living; see ACIR 1968, p. 51; Hoch 1972a, pp. 310-11, 1972b, p. 240).

The present analysis casts some doubt on these previous findings. Looking first at urbanized areas, larger areas indeed have somewhat higher median family incomes than do smaller ones (the zero-order correlation is 0.21; $p = 0.015$; n = 109), a relationship that is unaffected when urban-area growth rate is controlled (the partial correlation is 0.22; p = 0.016; n = 93). On the other hand, if one considers only urbanized areas outside the South, the zero-order relationship between size and income is no longer significant (r = 0.16); the same is true of urbanized areas in Santa Barbara's income bracket (r = 0.06). It appears, then, that at least for medium-sized areas the relationship between urbanized area size and income is due primarily to the fact that the smaller urbanized areas are found in the South, a region of low average income relative to the rest of the country.

Looking next at cities, the zero-order relationship between size and income is not significant (r = 0.13); only controlling on the percentage of the population that is Black or "of Spanish heritage" (among all our controls) reveals a significant relationship (partial r = 0.25; p = 0.012; n = 84)--perhaps because of the concentration of these relatively poor groups in the central city areas of larger cities.[12]

On the other hand, faster-growing urbanized areas tend to have somewhat higher median incomes than slower-growing ones (zero order r = 0.31; p ≤ 0.001; n > 93), a relationship that remains even when urbanized area size and region are simultaneously controlled (r = 0.29; p = 0.003; n = 93). When one looks at only non-Southern urbanized areas, the zero-order relationship between growth and median income remains significant (r = 0.28; p = 0.034; n = 52), as it does for that subset of urbanized areas in Santa Barbara's income range (r = 0.37; p = 0.021; n = 31).

Over time, as urbanized-area population increases, urbanized-area median family income tends to increase as well (zero-order r = 0.25; p = 0.034; n = 53). This longitudinal finding is consistent with the cross-sectional findings above.

The relationship between growth and higher income may very well stem from people moving to areas where higher incomes are available (in terms of employment opportunities), or may in fact be due to some causal effect of size and growth.[13]

Poverty[14]

Both Alonso (1973, p. 198) and Richardson (1973, pp. 52-54) have argued that the proportion of families living in poverty declines as city size increases--although, because of their increasing absolute numbers and concentration, the poor may become more visible. Among the cities and urbanized areas in our study, however, there is no zero-order relationship between the number of families below the poverty line and size (r = -0.05 and -0.06 for cities and urbanized areas, respectively). This is also the case when one looks only at cities and urbanized areas outside the South and at urbanized areas

in Santa Barbara's income bracket. When one looks at cities in
Santa Barbara's income bracket, however, a mild zero-order relationship emerges (partial $r = 0.29$; $p = 0.040$; $n = 38$).

More quickly growing urbanized areas do show some tendency
to have a lower proportion of poor families than do more slowly
growing ones, under certain conditions. When all single and possible combinations of two-way controls are exerted, controlling
simultaneously for median age and region alone brings out this mild
relationship (partial $r = 0.27$; $p = 0.005$; $n = 93$). Due to a lack of
comparable data for 1960, there is no longitudinal analysis.

As noted above with income, the effect demonstrated here may
be one of poverty on growth, rather than the reverse.

Income Concentration[15]

Alonso (1973, p. 198) has argued that income distribution does
not vary systematically with city size. Betz (1972) has also found
this to be the case, when differences among cities in industrial
diversification, income level, and racial composition are taken into
account. In our analysis there is similarly no relationship between
income concentration and either city or urbanized area size (zero-
order $r = 0.07$ and -0.03, respectively); this is also true for areas
outside the South or in Santa Barbara's income range. There is
somewhat greater concentration of income in more quickly growing
urbanized areas than more slowly growing ones, although this relationship emerges only when differences in median family income
(among all possible control variables) are controlled (partial $r = 0.30$;
$p = 0.002$; $n = 93$); the meaning of this relationship is ambiguous.
There is no longitudinal analysis, due to lack of comparable 1960
data.

Median House Value[16]

Few studies have attempted to measure the relationship between city or urbanized-area size and the cost of housing (house
value or rental). One study that did so was Shefer's study of living
cost differentials by urban size; he found (1970, p. 420) no significant relationship between a family's expenditure on housing and size,
even when controlling on region and budget level.[17] In the present
analysis, no relationship was found between size and median house
value (zero-order $r = -0.03$ for cities and 0.09 for urbanized areas).
This lack of relationship also characterized places outside the South
and urbanized areas in Santa Barbara's income bracket. Among
cities in Santa Barbara's income bracket, however, a relationship
is seen (partial $r = -0.32$; $p = 0.027$; $n = 37$).

More quickly growing urbanized areas quite clearly have higher median house values than do more slowly growing areas (zero-order $r = 0.62$; $p \leq 0.001$; $n = 93$), a relationship that is as strong for areas outside the South ($r = 0.62$; $p \leq 0.001$; $n > 31$).

The same relationship holds over time: The larger the population increase in urbanized areas, the greater the increase in urbanized-area median house value (zero-order $r = 0.31$; $p = 0.012$; $n = 53$).

Gross Rent[18]

The results of the rent analysis support the general patterns derived from the house-value analysis. Population size appears to make no differences to the value of median gross rent in cities; in urbanized areas, zero-order correlations reveal a positive relationship ($r = 0.25$; $p = 0.004$; $n = 109$), but this relationship ceases to be significant when median income differences among the areas are statistically controlled (partial $r = 0.14$). More quickly growing urbanized areas clearly show higher median gross rents than do more slowly growing ones (zero-order $r = 0.64$; $p \leq 0.001$; $n = 93$), even when income differences are statistically controlled (partial $r = 0.67$; $p \leq 0.001$; $n = 93$). This is also true when the analysis is restricted to areas outside the South ($r = 0.70$; $p \leq 0.001$; $n = 52$) or in Santa Barbara's income range ($r = 0.61$; $p \leq 0.001$; $n = 37$).

As urbanized area population increases over time, there is an increase in urbanized area gross rent as well (zero-order $r = 0.47$; $p \leq 0.001$; $n = 53$). The longitudinal analysis thus tends to confirm the cross-sectional analysis.

As with our income effects, these higher housing costs under more rapid growth may be caused by the nature of the migrants (more well-to-do) rather than being a direct effect of growth--for example, pressure on the existing housing supply.

Public Safety[19]

Many studies have noted a correlation between city size and per capita crime rates (for example, Duncan 1951, p. 764; Hoch 1972a, pp. 271-72, 1972b, p. 323; Alonso 1973, p. 197). There is some evidence that larger cities have higher per capita rates for selected categories of crimes even when differentials in age, income, racial composition, crowding, and other related variables are controlled (Hoch 1972a, pp. 271-72, 1972b, p. 323), particularly for such crimes as rape, robbery, and automobile theft. Expenditures on police tend to increase accordingly with city size; Duncan (1951,

p. 764) has suggested that "the large city experiences not only a greater relative amount of crime, but also pays proportionately more heavily for it."

Murders and Nonnegligent Homicides[20]

In the present analysis larger cities were found to have a higher homicide rate per capita (zero-order $r = 0.16$; $p = 0.043$; $n = 115$), a relationship that is a little stronger for urbanized areas (zero-order $r = 0.27$; $p = 0.002$; $n = 109$). These relationships hold when related variables are controlled, including particularly when differences in racial or "Spanish heritage" composition are taken into account ($r = 0.22$; $p = 0.015$; $n = 102$).

When one analyzes the subset of cities more directly comparable to Santa Barbara, the correlations between size and per capita homicide rates increase. Outside the South, the zero-order correlation is 0.34 ($p = 0.003$; $n = 65$) for cities and 0.48 ($p \leq 0.001$; $n = 62$) for urbanized areas. For places comparable to Santa Barbara in income the zero-order correlations are 0.54 for cities ($p \leq 0.001$; $n = 38$), and 0.40 for urbanized areas ($p = 0.006$; $n = 37$).

Growth rate in urbanized areas generally does not appear to be associated with the per capita rate of homicides within the cities, although outside the South the more quickly growing urbanized areas tend to have somewhat higher rates (zero-order $r = 0.36$; $p = 0.005$; $n = 52$).

With population increases in urbanized areas over time, there is an increase in city homicides per capita (zero-order $r = 0.29$; $p = 0.016$; $n = 53$). The longitudinal findings thus bear out the cross-sectional analysis.

Robberies and Burglaries[21]

Larger cities and urbanized areas have more robberies and burglaries per capita (zero-order $r = 0.34$; $p \leq 0.001$; $n = 115$; and $r = 0.53$; $p \leq 0.001$; $n = 109$; respectively). The relationship for urbanized areas is unaffected by any controls, and is strengthened by controls on racial composition and "Spanish heritage" (partial $r = 0.49$; $p \leq 0.001$; $n = 102$) or "consolidation" ($r = 0.43$; $p \leq 0.001$; $n = 109$).[22] Furthermore, the relationship holds for cities and urbanized areas outside the South (zero-order $r = 0.39$; $p \leq 0.001$; $n = 65$; and $r = 0.58$; $p \leq 0.001$; $n = 62$); respectively), and for those in Santa Barbara's income range ($r - 0.49$; $p \leq 0.001$; $n = 38$; and $r = 0.57$; $p \leq 0.001$; $n = 37$; respectively). Urbanized-area growth rate, while associated with the number of robberies and burglaries per capita (zero-order $r = 0.30$; $p = 0.002$; $n = 93$), ceases to be significant in its effect when urbanized-area size and "consolidation" are controlled (partial r = 0.11).

Over time, population increases in urbanized areas are associated with increasing rates of robberies and burglaries (zero order r = 0.41; p ≤ 0.001; n = 53).

Automobile Thefts

As with homicides and robberies and burglaries, there are more automobile thefts per capita in larger cities and urbanized areas (zero-order r = 0.46; p ≤ 0.001; n = 115; and r = 0.50; p ≤ 0.001; n = 109; respectively). The relationships for urbanized areas remain strong when all possible controls are exerted, including those for racial composition and "Spanish heritage" (r = 0.48; p ≤ 0.001; n = 102). This remains true when one analyzes separately the subset of cities and urbanized areas outside the South (zero-order r = 0.36; p = 0.002; n = 65; and r = 0.44; p ≤ 0.001; n = 62; respectively), and it is stronger among those in Santa Barbara's income range (r = 0.58; p ≤ 0.001; n = 38; and r = 0.44; p ≤ 0.001; n = 37; respectively). Again, however, growth rate does not appear to affect the number of city auto thefts per capita (r > 0.16). There is a tendency for increases in the rate of auto thefts to be associated with increases in the urbanized area growth rate (zero-order r = 0.26; p = 0.03; n = 52).

Rates of murder, robbery and burglary, and auto theft all increase with increases in population size, but not with increases in the growth rate (with the exception of homicides in the subset of cities outside the South).

Health[23]

It has long been hypothesized that residents of large, dense cities experience a greater degree of stress, manifested in higher indexes of suicide, nervous disorders, and so forth (see, for example, Jacobs 1961), although many studies have called into question the purported relationship between size, density, health, and social problems (Duncan 1951, pp. 762-63; Hoch 1972a, pp. 272-73, 1972b, p. 320; Alonso 1973, p. 197).

To the extent that such respiratory ailments as bronchitis, emphysema, and asthma result from air pollution, one might expect a correlation with size, if indeed air quality tends to be worse in large places relative to smaller ones. In fact, such health indexes might serve as a partial index of air quality. Motor-vehicle deaths presumably should increase in larger places, per capita, as vehicular

traffic becomes increasingly necessary to traverse large distances:
Traffic congestion and travel time increase with city size (Duncan
1951, pp. 761-62; Morgan et al. 1966, p. 80; Hoch 1972a, p. 243).
Infant deaths should be lower in large cities to the extent that there
is a greater availability of medical services--although not all segments of the population have equal access to such facilities. Cirrhosis might serve as an indicator of stress, insofar as the disease
is often associated with alcoholism, and alcoholism, in turn, presumably reflects in part the stressful conditions of daily life. Finally, suicides are presumably an indicator of social disorganization; several studies have found that the rates of suicide and mental
disorder are higher in denser areas of cities (Schmitt 1966) or in
more quickly growing places (Wechsler 1961).

Bronchitis, Emphysema, and
Asthma Deaths

Neither population size nor growth rate seems to have any
bearing on bronchitis, emphysema, and asthma deaths per capita
(zero-order r = 0.04 for cities and 0.10 for urbanized areas). There
is no longitudinal analysis for this variable due to lack of comparable
1960 data.

Motor-Vehicle Deaths

There appears to be no relationship between population size or
growth rate and motor-vehicle deaths per capita (zero-order r =
-0.15 and -0.05 for cities and urbanized areas, respectively). As
urbanized-area population increases over time, there is a tendency
for city motor-vehicle deaths per capita to decrease (zero-order
r = -0.30; p = 0.016; n = 53).

Infant Deaths[24]

There is some tendency for larger urbanized areas to have
higher per capita rates of infant death in their central cities (zero-
order r = 0.25; p = 0.005; n = 109), but this is not the case for cities
themselves. This relationship remains unchanged for urbanized
areas when all possible controls are exerted. Infant deaths are
higher both in cities (r = 0.21; p = 0.05; n = 65) and in urbanized
areas outside the South (r = 0.29; p = 0.012; n = 62) and in urbanized
areas in Santa Barbara's income bracket (r = 0.34; p = 0.020; n = 37).
Urbanized-area growth rate appears to have no bearing on the
number of city infant deaths per capita. Consistent with these findings is the longitudinal finding that as urbanized-area population

changes, there is no tendency for the number of infant deaths per capita to change (r = 0.04).

Cirrhosis Deaths

Larger urbanized areas have higher per capita rates of cirrhosis deaths in their central cities (zero-order r = 0.27; p = 0.002; n = 109), a relationship that persists when median family income is controlled (partial r = 0.24; p = 0.006; n = 109), and median age and "consolidation" are simultaneously controlled (partial r = 0.16; p = 0.045; n = 109). Thus, structural changes due to these variables, which are often held to be associated with alcoholism, do not appear to explain the relationship between urbanized-area size and the dependent variable. Apparently, however, region is in part a source of the relationship between urbanized-area size and cirrhosis deaths, because the relationship is reduced when only those areas outside the South are analyzed (r is nonsignificant at 0.17). The same is true of places in Santa Barbara's income bracket (-0.01). Among cities themselves, a relationship emerges only when the effect of median age among all controls is controlled (partial r = 0.18; p = 0.028; n = 115).

More quickly growing urbanized areas tend to have slightly higher rates of cirrhosis deaths in their central cities than do more slowly growing ones (zero-order r = 0.18; p = 0.04; n = 93), a relationship that becomes somewhat stronger when the effects of age differences and "consolidation" are simultaneously taken into account (r = 0.23; p = 0.013; n = 93). The same relationship seems to hold over time as well (from our longitudinal analysis) for population increase in urbanized areas (r = 0.30; p = 0.015; n = 53).

Suicides

There seems to be no tendency for larger cities or urbanized areas to have higher numbers of suicides per capita, regardless of the controls that are exerted. However, suicide rates appear to be somewhat higher in more quickly growing urbanized areas (zero-order r = 0.26; p = 0.006; n = 93). This relationship increases in strength when age differences are controlled (partial r = 0.35; p ≤ 0.001; n = 93) and remains about the same when age and "consolidation" are simultaneously controlled (r = 0.28; p = 0.003; n = 93). Suicide rates are higher in more quickly growing urbanized areas (zero-order r = 0.26; p = 0.006; n = 93), a relationship that becomes stronger when the effects of median age are controlled (partial r = 0.35; p ≤ 0.001; n = 93), and when areas outside the South or in Santa Barbara's income bracket are considered separately (zero-order

$r = 0.41$; $p \leq 0.001$; $n = 52$; and $r = 0.43$; $p = 0.008$; $n = 31$; respectively). The longitudinal analysis is somewhat inconsistent with these findings, in that it shows no statistically significant tendency for cities to increase in their suicide rates as population increases in the urbanized areas (zero-order $r = 0.14$).

Municipal Expenditures[25]

Although numerous studies have been undertaken over the past 50 years relating city size to the costs of government (see Appelbaum 1975, for a review), no firm conclusions can be drawn. Initial studies generally found a U-shaped curve, whereby per capita costs decreased initially as economies of scale were realized, "flattened out" over some "optimal" range, and then began to increase again. The trough was placed anywhere from 50,000 to several hundred thousand people (see, for example, Ogburn 1937; Phillips 1942; Lomax 1943; Schmandt and Stephens 1963; Shapiro 1963). Duncan, however, questioned the meaning of such findings, noting that expenditure differentials could very well reflect differences in "unit costs, amount, and quality of services" (1951, p. 766) rather than the effects of size per se. Other writers have argued that the higher expenditure levels in larger cities reflect the generally higher income levels and property values in those places (Scott and Feder 1957; Brazer 1959; Schmandt and Stephens 1963). Yet another confounding factor has to do with what we have termed "consolidation"--the fact that cities often grow faster in their suburban rings than in their urban core, with the consequence that in-commuters (for purposes of work, commerce, or recreation) use city services while residing outside the city limits. One consequence of this pattern is that the costs of services to city residents (who pay in large part through property taxes) increases with city size, to the extent that cities fail to annex surrounding areas and thus consolidate their tax base. A number of studies have in fact found that the cost of municipal services is strongly (if not primarily) related to the proportion of the total urban-area population residing outside the city limits (for example, Hawley 1951; Brazer 1959; Shapiro 1963; Kasarda 1972).

One difficulty with most of the studies undertaken previously in this area is that they fail to take into account the degree of functional dependence of the city in question. Cities that are part of large metropolitan areas may share municipal costs through special district arrangements or with county government; they may also incur costs peculiar to their function as a center of commerce, industry, or residence. Our analysis addresses such difficulties through restricting itself to a set of cities matched on size and relative geographical isolation or independence. One difficulty that we do not address, however, is the difference in quality of services between places of different size.

Fire Personnel and Fire Personnel Expenditures

City size seems to have no significant relationship to the number of sworn fire personnel per capita (0.06), nor to fire personnel per capita (0.06), nor to fire personnel expenditures per capita ($r = 0.14$). This finding holds over time as well, with no apparent relationship between population increase and change in sworn fire personnel per capita ($r = -0.01$) or change in total fire-personnel expenditures per capita ($r = -0.14$) in cities.

Police Officers

While the population size of cities is not significantly related to the number of police officers per capita (-0.04), the size of the urban area is moderately related (zero-order $r = 0.35$; $p \leq 0.001$; $n = 97$). This remains true for urban areas outside the South (zero-order $r = 0.31$; $p = 0.009$; $n = 57$) and for those in Santa Barbara's income bracket ($r = 0.42$; $p = 0.006$; $n = 35$). The relationship between urban-area size and the number of police officers is reduced, however, when differences in percentage black/"Spanish surname" and "consolidation" are simultaneously controlled (partial $r = 0.06$). However, there is some tendency for more quickly growing urbanized areas to have more city police officers per capita than more slowly growing ones (zero-order $r = 0.37$; $p \leq 0.001$; $n = 93$); this remains true—although of reduced magnitude—even when differences in median age and "consolidation" are statistically controlled (zero-order $r = 0.23$; $p = 0.013$; $n = 93$). Furthermore, the relationship is somewhat stronger when considered for that subset of cities outside the South (zero order $r = 0.45$; $p \leq 0.001$; $n = 48$) and those in Santa Barbara's income condition ($r = 0.51$; $p = 0.002$; $n = 30$). The longitudinal findings are consistent: Increases in urbanized-area population are associated with increases in the number of police officers per capita (zero-order $r = 0.33$; $p = 0.01$; $n = 49$). With respect to the number of police personnel per capita, then, our data offer support for the hypothesis that to some extent in quickly growing urbanized areas the residents of the central city are paying for police service incurred by those residing outside the city limits.

Police Personnel Expenditures

Larger cities and urbanized areas have higher police-personnel expenditures per capita than do smaller ones (zero-order $r = 0.23$; $p = 0.01$; $n = 102$; and $r = 0.51$; $p \leq 0.001$; $n = 97$; respectively). This relationship holds true for urbanized areas even when urbanized-area growth rate and "consolidation" are jointly controlled (partial $r = 0.30$; $p = 0.003$; $n = 83$); it also holds true for both cities and urbanized areas outside the South (zero-order $r = 0.30$; $p = 0.011$; $n = 58$; and $r = 0.56$; $p \leq 0.001$; $n = 55$; respectively) and for urbanized areas in Santa Barbara's income bracket ($r = 0.53$; $p \leq 0.001$; $n = 34$).

Furthermore, more rapidly growing urbanized areas have higher city police-personnel expenditures per capita than do more slowly growing ones (zero-order $r = 0.42$; $p \leq 0.001$; $n = 83$), a relationship that holds (although reduced in magnitude) when differences in urban-area population size and "consolidation" are jointly controlled (partial $r = 0.22$; $p = 0.023$; $n = 83$). Police personnel expenditures per capita and urban-area growth remain strongly associated when considered for that subset of cities outside the South (zero-order $r = 0.46$; $p \leq 0.001$; $n = 46$) and in those of Santa Barbara's income bracket ($r = 0.47$; $p = 0.005$; $n = 29$). Consistent with the foregoing, our longitudinal analysis reveals that there is a strong association between change in police personnel expenditures per capita and urbanized-area population increase (zero-order $r - 0.52$; $p \leq 0.001$; $n = 41$).

The overall patterns, when seen in combination with the effects of growth and size on police officers per capita (see "Police Officers," above), suggest that, contrary to those of fire services, the per capita costs of police services increase both with size and with growth rate, and this relationship is stronger for urbanized areas than for the cities on whose payrolls the police serve.

"Common Functions" Personnel
and "Common Functions"-
Personnel Payroll[26]

Because of special district arrangements, overlying metropolitan jurisdictions, special contracting arrangements, and unusual one-time capital expenditures, it is difficult to make intercity comparisons of personnel or general expenditures. Therefore, we focus on functions common to most cities. The common functions include highways, police protection, fire protection, wastewater, and other sanitation, parks and recreation, and water supply.

City size seems to have no bearing on the number of "common functions" personnel per capita, nor on the size of the payroll for such personnel (zero-order r = -0.07 and 0.15, respectively). There is similarly no relationship between urbanized-area population increase and change in the city payroll for this class of personnel.

Residential Segregation[27]

There is a tendency for larger cities to have more residential segregation by race than do smaller cities, although this relationship only emerges when differences in income level are statistically controlled (partial r = 0.34; p = 0.038; n - 30). There is insufficient comparable data for 1960 for a longitudinal analysis.

SUMMARY

Economic Well-Being. Areas that are larger and more quickly growing have slightly higher median family incomes than those that are smaller or that grow at slower rates, but in general size and growth appear to make little difference in this variable. Furthermore, inasmuch as the cost of living tends to be higher in larger places (Hoch 1972a, b), the relationship between size and real income is further attenuated. To the extent that income differentials persist, we do not know whether it is due to the effect of growth or to the possibility that more quickly growing places attract higher-income people.[28] Housing values and rental levels are higher in the more rapidly growing places. This could be due to the fact that larger numbers of people pressing against a more static housing supply cause prices to rise, thus lowering real spending power. Alternatively, it may be due to the fact the people in more quickly growing places have more money and thus demand higher-priced facilities.

Unemployment rates neither rise nor fall with changes in population size, but there is some evidence that unemployment rises with higher rates of area growth.[29]

Public Safety. On a variety of serious types of crimes larger places have higher per capita crime rates.

Health. Larger urbanized areas have slightly higher rates of infant mortality in their central cities than do smaller urbanized areas. Infant mortality is likely to be related to health-care delivery systems that, these data suggest, may be poorer within the cities of the larger urbanized areas.

Death from cirrhosis of the liver, our proxy for alcoholism, increases slightly with size and with growth rate. It may be that rapid growth and large size induce stress. It may be, too, that such places are occupied by the types of people who incidentally tend toward alcoholism. Or, possibly, it may be that such places attract alcoholics from smaller and less rapidly growing places. The results, however, are the same: Larger and more rapidly growing places have somewhat more alcoholics in the population on a per capita basis.

Our suicide data only partially support the stress hypothesis: Only on one variable, growth rate of urbanized areas, are there weak but significant positive relationships with the rate of suicide.

Municipal Expenditures. Consistent with our findings on crime rates, we learn that higher levels of population and growth tend to be associated with higher per capita police costs. None of the other forms of public expenditures seems to vary in any clear way with changes in size or growth rate.

Residential Segregation. Larger cities appear to have slightly more residential segregation by race than do smaller ones, although data are available only for a very small subset of the cities studied.

We would summarize our findings in this way: Economic effects of population size and growth are mixed and ambiguous; public safety effects are generally negative; health effects, where they exist at all, are weak and negative; public expenditure effects seem not to exist except in the case of police, where they are negative.

NOTES

1. The 115 places included in the analysis are Abilene, Texas; Albany, Georgia; Albuquerque, New Mexico; Altoona, Pennsylvania; Amarillo, Texas; Ann Arbor, Michigan; Asheville, North Carolina; Augusta, Georgia; Austin, Texas; Bakersfield, California; Baton Rouge, Louisiana; Billings, Montana; Binghamton, New York; Birmingham, Alabama; Boise City, Idaho; Boulder, Colorado; Cedar Rapids, Iowa; Charleston, South Carolina; Charleston, West Virginia; Charlotte, North Carolina; Chattanooga, Tennessee; Colorado Springs, Colorado; Columbia, Missouri; Columbia, South Carolina; Columbus, Georgia; Corpus Christi, Texas; Decatur, Illinois; Des Moines, Iowa; Dubuque, Iowa; Erie, Pennsylvania; Eugene, Oregon; Evansville, Indiana; Fayettesville, North Carolina; Flint, Michigan; Fort Smith, Arkansas; Fort Wayne, Indiana; Fresno, California; Gadsden, Alabama; Gainesville, Florida; Great Falls, Montana; Green Bay, Wisconsin; Greenville, South Carolina; Harrisburg,

Pennsylvania; Huntsville, Alabama; Jackson, Mississippi; Kalamazoo, Michigan; Knoxville, Tennessee; La Crosse, Wisconsin; LaFayette, Louisiana; Lake Charles, Louisiana; Lancaster, Pennsylvania; Lansing, Michigan; Las Vegas, Nevada; Lawton, Oklahoma; Lexington, Kentucky; Lima, Ohio; Lincoln, Nebraska; Louisville, Kentucky; Lubbock, Texas; Lynchburg, Virginia; Macon, Georgia; Madison, Wisconsin; Mansfield, Ohio; Mobile, Alabama; Modesto, California; Monroe, Louisiana; Montgomery, Alabama; Ogden, Utah; Orlando, Florida; Owensboro, Kentucky; Pensacola, Florida; Peoria, Illinois; Pine Bluff, Arkansas; Pittsfield, Massachusetts; Portland, Maine; Pueblo, Colorado; Reading, Pennsylvania; Reno, Nevada; Richmond, Virginia; Roanoke, Virginia; Rochester, Minnesota; Rockford, Illinois; Sacramento, California; Saint Joseph, Missouri; Salt Lake City, Utah; San Angelo, Texas; Santa Barbara, California; Santa Rosa, California; Savannah, Georgia; Shreveport, Louisiana; Sioux City, Iowa; Sioux Falls, South Dakota; South Bend, Indiana; Spokane, Washington; Springfield, Illinois; Springfield, Missouri; Springfield, Ohio; Stockton, California; Syracuse, New York; Tacoma, Washington; Tallahassee, Florida; Terre Haute, Indiana; Toledo, Ohio; Topeka, Kansas; Tucson, Arizona; Tulsa, Oklahoma; Tuscaloosa, Alabama; Tyler, Texas; Waco, Texas; Waterloo, Iowa; West Palm Beach, Florida; Wichita, Kansas; Wichita Falls, Texas; York, Pennsylvania.

2. For a discussion of the use of statistical tests of significance when a universe rather than a sample is being studied, see Gold (1969).

3. A "city" is defined as "A political subdivision of a State within a defined area over which a municipal corporation has been established to provide local government functions and facilities" (U.S. Department of Commerce 1973a, b). An "urbanized area" is defined as "A central city, or cities, and surrounding closely settled territory" (U.S. 1973).

4. The independent variables actually employed in the zero-order and partial correlations reported are logarithmic (base = ten) transformations of city and urbanized area size, so the size difference between cities of 50,000 and 100,000 is not treated as equivalent to the size difference between cities of 300,000 and 350,000, but both differences are treated as rates of change. For a discussion of this technique see Frank (1966). Since a comparison of each zero-order correlation based on transformed data with the parallel correlation based on untransformed data revealed little difference when the transformation was used, and to facilitate reading the transformations are not referred to in the text.

5. The control variables include those representing every underlying dimension that differentiates cities according to a comprehensive factor analysis of 1960 data by Hadden and Borgatta (1965), which examined 65 variables for 644 U.S. cities. In addition

to the control variables that emerged from the work of Hadden and
Borgatta's, we used several controls related to economic structure,
For a discussion of these techniques, see Blalock (1972), chapters
17-19. For a more detailed analysis of these cities that relies on
analysis of variance and multiple classification analysis (MCA), see
Appelbaum and Follet (1975).

6. A detailed inventory of sources of data keyed to each
variable is contained in Volume 3, pp. 11-20. Most information
comes from several sources. Basic demographic data are from the
U.S. Census of Population, including the volumes on "General Social
and Economic Characteristics of the Population" (vol. 1), "City
Governmental Finances," and the County and City Data Book. Vital
statistics are provided through HEW, Vital Statistics of the United
States, vol. 2. Crime data are obtained through the FBI's Uniform
Crime Reports. Additional information is found in the Municipal
Year Book.

7. The cases (cities or urbanized areas) were divided into
two categories on the basis of the midpoint of the range of the independent variable in question. Evidence of a simple curve would have
been either opposite signs for significant correlations in the two
categories or a significant and stronger correlation in each of the
two categories than for the full set of cases.

8. A third variable can have a "partial" effect only if it is
statistically related to both the independent and dependent variables.
These principles were employed in a thorough search (in the correlation matrix) of the control variables and other independent variables to determine the partial correlations that were to be computed.
For a discussion of these principles see Rosenberg (1968). The
criterion (mild) for a "relationship" between the third variable and
the independent or dependent variable was statistically significant
at $p \leq 0.05$. See Gold (1969) for a discussion of the use of statistical
tests of significance for populations, as well as samples.

9. In this study, Southern states include Texas, Oklahoma,
Arkansas, Louisiana, Kentucky, Tennessee, Mississippi, Alabama,
West Virginia, Virginia, North Carolina, South Carolina, Georgia,
and Florida. "Region" refers to a dichotomous variable, South and
non-South. Santa Barbara's income bracket includes those cities
with a median income between $8,474 and $4,533 and those urbanized
areas with a median income greater than $9,738.

10. In this section both p and n (the number of cases on which
the correlation is based) are reported only when correlations are
significant ($p \leq 0.05$). A detailed listing of all correlation coefficients
and their significance is contained in Volumes 1 and 3.

11. For a discussion of this point see Molotch (1975).

12. We use the term "of Spanish heritage" to encompass the various census usages. According to the 1970 Census of Population, vol. 1, "in 42 states, (the population of 'Spanish' heritage) is identified as 'Persons of Spanish language or Spanish surname'; and in the three Middle Atlantic states, as 'Persons of Puerto Rican birth or parentage.'" The percentage of black of "Spanish heritage" is summed into a single variable.

13. See Volume 1, pp. 6.3-6.6 for additional interpretation.

14. The poverty cut-off point is determined "by such factors as family size, sex of the family head, and number of children under 18 years old. . . . At the core of this definition of poverty is a nutritionally adequate food plan" (Department of Commerce 1973A, app. 32).

15. This measure is derived from the Lorenz curve; it varies from zero to one. As it approaches zero, income is increasingly equally distributed; that is 5 percent of the families will possess 5 percent of the total income; 10 percent of the families, 10 percent of the income; etc.

16. U.S. Department of Commerce (1972) defines "value" as "the respondent's estimate of how much the property (house and lot) would sell for if it were for sale. . . . The statistics on value are . . . only for one-family houses on less than 10 acres without a commercial establishment or medical office on the property" (App. 11).

17. Shefer (1970) looked at four regions and three budget levels (low, moderate, and high). He found a statistically significant correlation between urban-area size and expenditures on housing only among one of the 12 possible categories so determined--the low-budget-level families in the South (tau = 0.45). Shefer did not look specifically at housing value or rentals, however, so his arguments are only indirectly related to the present analysis.

18. Gross rent "is the contract rent plus the estimated average cost of utilities . . . and fuels. Thus, gross rent is intended to eliminate the differentials which result from varying practices with respect to the inclusion of utilities and fuel as part of the rental payment" (U.S. Department of Commerce, Bureau of the Census, 1972, app. 11). The inclusion of utility and fuel costs, of course, means that gross rents will be higher in those regions of the country where severe winters incur substantial heating requirements.

19. The crime statistics are "number of offenses known to the police" by place of occurrence and per year. They are available for cities only.

20. Murders and nonnegligent homicides were summed together for the present analysis.

21. Robberies and burglaries were summed together for the present analysis.

22. "Consolidation" refers to the ratio between city population and urbanized area population; it is an important variable because of the potential tendency of younger, more affluent, or more stable working populations to flee to the suburbs (outside the city limits) in older cities, leaving behind the elderly, the marginally employed, and the unemployed.

23. Vital statistics are by place of residence and per year. They are available for cities only (not for urbanized areas).

24. "Infant death" means "born alive but died within one year."

25. Expenditure figures are for cities only.

26. "Personnel" here refers to full-time equivalent employees. These, in turn, consist of the "number of full-time employees" plus "total expenditures for part-time personnel divided by average expenditure for a full-time employee."

27. The index of residential segregation "represents the minimum percentage of either population (white or nonwhite) that would have to change residence to bring about a zero degree of segregation (i.e., the situation of each city block having the same white to nonwhite ratio as the entire city)" (Sorensen et al. 1974; see this source for computation details). Findings on this variable must be taken as tentative, because of the severely reduced number of cities for which the index of racial segregation was available (30).

28. See Volume 1, pp. 6.2-6.6 for additional discussion of this point.

29. A detailed interpretation of this point is contained in Volume 1, pp. 6.12-6.20.

3

SOCIAL IMPACTS
OF GROWTH

In this chapter we examine the social consequences of growth upon the people of the city. How will the ways people live together change as the city moves from one PIP to another? We begin with our survey results that reveal the kind of growth that people in the city currently desire. We then examine how the population levels implied by current city policy will affect the way residents will be using the city's land, have access to parks and recreational facilities, and experience traffic, and how the tone of daily life will change.

OPINION AS A COST-BENEFIT FACTOR

The opinions of a city's residents, according to the assumptions of a democratic society, are supposed to be the determinant of public policies. To the extent that a given population policy, such as that contained in the current General Plan or Zoning Ordinances, leads to outcomes contrary to public desires, that policy is having consequences that are violative to the democratic process. One cost or benefit of a given level of growth is the degree to which it corresponds to people's wishes.

Our method for determining the cost or benefit of growth on this issue was to conduct a public opinion survey. We are quite aware of the range of criticisms that can be applied to any survey, and particularly to any survey conducted as a guide for policy making. We make only the minimal assumption that, at least to some degree, what people say they want is an indication of what they do in fact want, and to the degree to which they get something else, an important cost is ipso facto being paid. Thus, this measure of "now sentiment" is useful.

41

Survey Methods

A total of 192 phone interviews were conducted with residents of the city of Santa Barbara. Residents were asked the following questions:

1. We are interested in citizens' attitudes toward population growth in Santa Barbara. Do you think there should be (a) more people here, (b) fewer people here, or (c) about the same as now?[1]
2. How about in your own <u>neighborhood</u>? Would you like to see (a) more people there, (b) fewer people there, or (c) about the same as now?

Those interviewed were selected at random from phonebook listings in such a way that every listed household had an equal chance of being selected. There were 235 households selected, with 82 percent of those phoned willing and able to participate in a brief interview. Of those who did not participate, three spoke neither English nor Spanish, 23 simply refused, and 17 did not answer their phone despite four attempts over a number of weeks. Because the phone directory was used to draw the sample, those without phones and those with unlisted numbers were not represented. The use of phone directories is likely to lead to a slight underrepresentation of the poor and of young, single adults, but in comparing the characteristics of those interviewed with the citywide social profile, we find a reasonable correspondence between our sample and the characteristics of the city population generally. Of our sample, 22.8 percent consists of persons over 60, while 29 percent of all city residents are over 60. Blue-collar workers are underrepresented (15 percent in the sample, versus approximately 30 percent in the city's population).

Findings

A majority of the people of Santa Barbara are in favor of no-growth. Few surveys on any controversial issue provide so lopsided a set of results. Even granting the qualifications made previously regarding our sampling methodology, it is very doubtful that any methodological modification could change the direction of the results.
As shown in Table 3.1, more than 80 percent of all respondents either favored the current population level, or wanted fewer people in the area than are presently there. Answers to the same question phrased in terms of neighborhoods are also displayed in Table 3.1. They reveal an even stronger tendency to oppose growth. Only 2.6

percent of all respondents favored growth in their own neighborhood.
This means that of the minority that does favor substantial growth in
the area as a whole, very few people want any of that growth to occur
within their own residential area.

TABLE 3.1

Number and Percentage of City Residents with Various
Population Preferences

Preference	City		Neighborhood	
	Number	Percent	Number	Percent
More people	27	14.1	5	2.6
Fewer people	50	26.1	36	18.8
About the same	109	56.7	150	78.1
Other	6	3.1	1	0.5
Total	192	100.0	192	100.0

Source: Planning Task Force Survey.

A number of attempts were made to determine whether this no-
growth feeling was peculiar to any specific age or social group within
the city. Additional information gathered in the phone interviews permitted breakdowns by age, by sex, by length of residency in the Santa
Barbara area, by occupation, and between those who rented and those
who owned their homes. Across the board, the antigrowth sentiment
was pronounced, with no group favoring population gain. Variations
in growth sentiment among social groups indicates only minor tendencies, not any sharp differences between groups.[2]

Summary

Santa Barbara residents are generally opposed to further
growth; this antigrowth sentiment is shared among all social groups.
We thus find that the population levels implied in the General Plan,
or those permitted either under full Zoning or under the city's temporary Half-Density Ordinance are all higher than those preferred
by the majority of city residents. There is a minority that does
favor growth; these people tend to favor growth generally but not in
their own neighborhoods.

LAND USE AND HOUSING TYPE

A generation ago, Santa Barbara was almost exclusively a
single-family home area. In 1974 a slight majority of its approximately 28,660 dwelling units were single-family homes (56 percent).
But there will be substantial changes in the way the city's residents
use land as growth continues. With these changes, the nature of
Santa Barbara as a homeowners' city will be ended.

Under current zoning, the consequences of full development
will be most dramatic in the city neighborhoods currently adjoining
the downtown area. The commercial heart of the city will itself fill
in, become more intensely developed, and spread across the edges
of the nearby residential areas. In these adjoining residential areas
the current pattern of old houses, some of which have been converted
to low-density apartment use, will be altogether transformed. Apartment buildings will replace all of them eventually. For the city as a
whole, only one-third of the total number of dwelling units would remain single-family.

Under the General Plan PIPs, the apartment/single-family
house ratios would likely resemble those of full zoning, because the
general distribution of apartments and single-family houses is roughly comparable across the two documents.

The city's Half-Density Ordinance, however, being aimed exclusively at multiple units, has a major effect on this future ratio.
Under the maximum population growth permitted under the Half-
Density Ordinance, a majority of the city's dwelling units (about 54
percent) would remain single-family.[3]

The changes in land use implied by these figures are impacts
that will primarily affect those areas that are now disproportionately
made up of the elderly, the economically less well-off, and the city's
minorities. Because the outer neighborhoods of the city will generally remain the same (except for the elimination of open space and
some increase in traffic), the effect of growth will be to sharpen the
life-style differences between the two sorts of social groups: the urbanites and the exurbanites, the well-off and the less well-off. The
traditional difference between the living styles of social classes in
Santa Barbara was once seen in the size and condition of the house
and the amount of land surrounding it. Increasingly, under growth,
the difference will also be seen in the type of house. It is the current
housing supply of the poor and the middle class that will be replaced
by apartments; henceforth, those less well-off social classes will
raise their children under this new pattern, while the more well-to-
do continue to live in the single-family zones.

Population growth virtually guarantees these differences, regardless of city zoning policy, because of the rising costs of housing

and land relative to wages. Single-family housing in most U.S. cities increasingly becomes beyond the means of larger and larger proportions of the people. This represents a general decline in the U.S. standard of living that will be felt in Santa Barbara in the manner described: As the existing housing stock is shared by larger numbers of people, the most desirable units (the single-family houses) will go to the better-off, while the apartments that are built will be disproportionately reserved for the less well-to-do.

But it is also clear that this local tendency toward apartments is not merely due to national or statewide increases in building costs. In the six-year period from 1968 to 1973, single-family homes accounted for only 11.4 percent of residential construction in the city, compared to 44.7 percent statewide.[4] These figures indicate that the city of Santa Barbara is well on its way to becoming predominantly an apartment city and that it is moving in that direction faster than the statewide trend would predict.

PARKS

The Task Force analysis of the relationship between parks and growth suggests that the greatest impact on parks will be in those neighborhoods that share the characteristic of being heavily zoned for multiple dwellings. They not only have the highest population densities within the city but also have the potential to accommodate much of the new growth that is envisioned for each PIP. Yet it is precisely these areas that presently have the least per capita park space. For example, the Westside neighborhood has only 15 square feet of park space per capita, as compared to a citywide average of 512 square feet per capita.[5] West Downtown and Lower Westside lack any parks whatsoever.

The fact that population increases ranging between 20 and 130 percent can feasibly occur in these neighborhoods, coupled with an understanding of the probable increases in noise, congestion, and a decline in open space that would accompany this growth, makes these areas critically important for purposes of future park planning under any of the PIPs.

The impact of the continuous decline in available park space in the in-city areas becomes most impressive when one takes into account the population characteristics of these neighborhoods at present and at higher PIPs. There is currently a disproportionate number of poor and elderly that is expected to continue with population growth. These two segments of the city's population, particularly those residing in the in-town neighborhoods, are likely to lack automobile transportation and thus the means to travel to those outlying areas where the city's park acreage is now concentrated. Consequently, these people are forced to stay close to home and use whatever park and recreational facilities are available nearby. The consequences will be increased crowding of already inadequate parks and recreational facilities.

This situation is made more serious by the effects of growth on the children who will live in these neighborhoods. Although potentially more mobile, they will tend to stay close to home and make use of whatever vacant land they can find for recreation. As vacant land in these neighborhoods vanishes and the parks and recreational facilities become increasingly more crowded, the children will inevitably turn to the streets and the creek beds for their needs, increasing the dangers of traffic accidents, drownings, and health risks from ever-increasing levels of stream pollution.

Meanwhile, the lower-density neighborhoods of the city will experience little change within their parks and recreational facilities. They already have abundant regional-type park land, and they have sufficient means to take advantage of more distant park areas and private or quasi-public recreational facilities, such as the YMCA and country clubs.

These contrasts suggest that the effects of growth, as with housing types, will be to further sharpen the life-style differences between the urbanites and exurbanites, the well-off and the less well-off.

Besides the in-town neighborhoods, the city's beaches will be the other major stress point under all growth scenarios. Because beaches constitute a finite resource, increases in growth will lead unavoidably to heavier beach use and waterfront traffic. Based on available Park Division data, each Santa Barbara resident has some 48 square feet of beach space at today's population. This per capita beach space will decline by 26 percent at Half-Density Probable, 38 percent under Zoning Probable, and 56 percent at the Zoning Maximum PIPs. As the tourist industry expands, pressure on this finite resource will continue unabated.

Growth will also have an impact on the costs of maintaining beach quality. With growth, increased litter and demand for restroom facilities will cause substantial increases in capital improvements and maintenance costs and will make it difficult to preserve fragile plantings. Growth will permit the support of various amusements in the beach area, and these will in turn cause the need for future additional adjacent or on-site parking.

Some of these negative growth impacts can be ameliorated through acquisition and development of additional parks and recreational facilities. The costs of such a program, aimed at maintaining current per capita neighborhood park ratios at each PIP, are detailed in Chapter 6.

CIRCULATION*

In Santa Barbara the automobile has not always been predominant. It was the street railroad that first made possible the settlement of some suburban areas, and a private bus line remained profitable in the city until the beginning of the 1960s. But almost all the growth of the past 25 years, both residential and commercial, has been planned around the automobile, and presently, although bicycles and mass transit have begun to make inroads, 95 percent of all trips in the city's central business district (CBD) are still performed in cars.[6] And on the South Coast, as a measure of this dominance, the automobile--including its sale, service, fuel, parts, salvage, and roadway, but not its insurance)--accounted for a $20 million payroll in 1971 (Dodson et al. 1972).

There were 122,471 cars and trucks registered in Santa Barbara County in 1964, or 0.54 vehicles per capita.[7] By 1973 there were 173,341 vehicles, giving a per capita ratio of 0.63. It is widely assumed that this trend toward more and more cars will continue. The 1974 revision of the county's Comprehensive Traffic Plan, for example, foresees a car-to-person ratio of 0.66 in 1975, and 0.80 in 1980 (Comprehensive Plan 1974, p. 43).

Demographic factors will tend to push the ratio up even if individual usage habits remain the same. The declining number of children per capita foreseen in the area promises less strain on school facilities (see Chapter 6) but more on the highways, as a higher percentage of population comes of driving age.

But the ability of any area to absorb continually increasing numbers of automobiles is not infinite. The impact of higher population levels on roads, parking, mass transit, and city noise levels will now be discussed.

Effects on Road-Network Capacities

The Problem of Capacity

There are today 240 miles of paved public road in Santa Barbara, a network that makes it possible at most times of day to reach any point in the city from any other point in less than 15 minutes' time. But an increasing number of motor vehicles on this roadway will impose increasing restrictions on this mobility, particularly in a city where topography and tradition limit ability and willingness to build additional roadway.

---

*Eric Mankin is coauthor of this section.

The traffic problem begins at the two extremities of the city. Entering the city through the narrow slot between the Santa Ynez mountain foothills and the highlands of Hope Ranch are only four major through-routes: Foothill Road, State Street, U.S. Highway 101, and Modoc Road. Two others, Cliff Drive and Calle Real, exist but are awkwardly situated for handling through-traffic to and from Goleta and points north.

In the south the passage between the ocean and the foothills contains only three roads: Old Coast Highway, Highway 101, and Cabrillo Boulevard, with smaller low-capacity routes twisting around and over the inland ravines.

If lines, called "screenlines," are drawn between the ocean and the mountains in these locations, the problem can be quantified by counting and averaging the total number of cars crossing the line in either direction. In 1973, according to Santa Barbara County Transportation Study (SCOTS) measurements, an average of 122,000 vehicles per day crossed the northern, or "Arroyo Burro" screenline. There were 67,000 per day that crossed the southern, "Westmont" screenline.

Peak hour traffic is already unpleasantly congested at a number of locations around the city. To determine the impact of growth on this congestion, a two-step process was used. First, city staff determined the capacity of the existing road system at intersections making up the Arroyo Burro, Westmont, and four other screenlines across the city. Simultaneously, screenline traffic volumes corresponding to the PIP populations were determined, using SCOTS projections for 1990 traffic volumes. The screenlines are shown in Figure 3.1. The projected screenline volumes appear, along with their capacities as calculated, in Table 3.2.

The SCOTS projections assume an increase in total motor vehicles of 76 percent between 1970 and 1990 and an increase in population of 63 percent in the same period. The experience of the past 10 years in the county, however, is that motor vehicles are increasing about twice as fast as people--a 44 percent increase in cars over the past nine years, compared to a 22 percent increase in population. While there are indications that long-term economic trends are decreasing per capita car ownership, the effects will have to be very deep to change long-standing habits and the demographic effects discussed above. The values appearing in Table 3.2 are therefore believed to be, if anything, underestimates of screenline traffic at the PIPs. The capacity of the existing system is exceeded by the traffic generated even at the lowest PIP, Half-Density Probable, at all but the Laguna screenlines. (a solid-line border in Table 3.2 bounds points at which demand exceeds capacity.)

FIGURE 3.1

Screenline Map, City of Santa Barbara

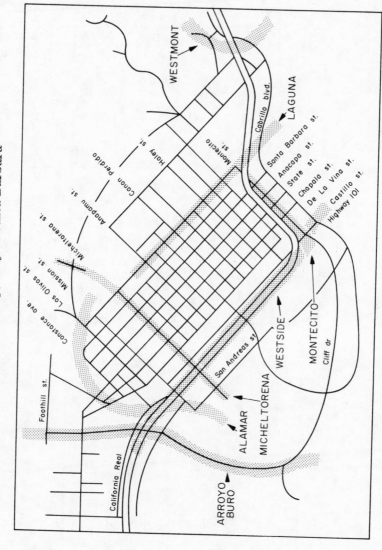

49

TABLE 3.2

Screenline Capacities and Demands

	City Population	Screenlines						
		Arroyo Burro	Westside	Alamar	Micheltorena	Montecito	Laguna	Westmont
*Capacity, existing[a]		155,000	117,000	155,000	172,000	†20,000	192,000	101,000
*Capacity, "reasonable improvement"[a]		206,000	137,000	215,000	266,000	51,000	262,000	120,000
1972	71,594	117,000[b]	66,000[b]	109,000[a]	115,000[a]	26,000[a]	152,000[a]	63,000[b]
Half-Density Probable[d]	93,555	179,000	87,000	182,000	207,000	43,000	168,000	115,000
General Plan Probable[c]	103,443	198,000	96,000	202,000	228,000	47,000	168,000	127,000
Half-Density Maximum[d]	117,486	226,000	109,000	229,000	260,000	54,000	191,000	144,000
Zoning Probable[d]	119,461	229,000	111,000	233,000	264,000	55,000	195,000	146,000
General Plan Maximum[d]	139,721	268,000	130,000	272,000	309,000	64,000	228,000	171,000
Zoning Maximum[d]	170,038	326,000	158,000	331,000	376,000	77,000	276,000	203,000

Key: *exceeds existing capacity   †exceeds expanded volume

*Capacities assume level of service B for single-family residential neighborhoods, C for multiple unit residential streets, and D for all others.
†Capacity based on present rush-hour signalization setting.
Sources: [a]Santa Barbara Department of Public Works, Transportation Division; [b]SCOTS 1972 Screenline Counts; [c]SCOTS 1990 Projections; [d]Santa Barbara Planning Task Force estimates.

50

For the individual motorist, the consequences of this excessive demand would include delay, inconvenience, increased gasoline consumption, and, in some cases, increased accidents. For the shop owner, resident, or pedestrian in the area, the consequences would include increased noise and concentrated auto emissions, increased neighborhood disruption, decreased pedestrian safety, and increased spillover of nonresidential through-traffic into residential neighborhoods.

The capacity of the road system can be increased by various "improvements." Relatively easy and cheap methods include the removal of onstreet parking, the installation of signals and special turn lanes, and the creation of one-way couplets (that is, two parallel one-way streets, going in opposite directions). More ambitious is street widening. With great expense, particularly in a mature urban area like Santa Barbara, entire new roads can be constructed.

The capacity of the Santa Barbara road system after installation of all improvements deemed "reasonable" by the City Transportation Department is shown in Table 3.2. All techniques except the last, the construction of new roads, were used to arrive at these figures. Table 3.2 also indicates the point at which this "reasonable improvement" capacity is exceeded. The criterion of reasonable improvement was based on social rather than on engineering considerations. Projects were deemed "unreasonable" (even if technically possible), if, in the opinion of the Transportation Department, they involved unacceptable costs in neighborhood dislocation or environmental damage.

Most of the increased capacity reflected in Table 3.2 comes from the reconstruction and widening to six lanes of the freeway from Milpas Street northward. Reconstruction of the downtown section of the freeway is currently contemplated regardless of city growth rate or plans, with acquisition of right-of-way scheduled to begin in July 1976, and construction to begin a year later. Widening of the freeway to six lanes is foreseen as a "reasonable" improvement, at a population of approximately 80,000. Both would be state projects, and city funding would not be involved.

At populations higher than approximately 100,000, additional capacity would be needed. Costs in 1974 dollars of this "reasonable" construction were determined in coordination with the Engineering Division of the City Public Works Department. They include costs of right-of-way acquisition, based on current land values, and amount to an estimated $3.985 million for four different projects.[8] These costs are reflected in the analysis of government costs of growth to be presented in Chapter 6.

Some federal or other outside agency money may be available to pay for part or all of these projects. Between 1968 and 1973, for

example, the city received $352,000 from the federal government as
part of the Traffic Operations Program to Improve Capacity and
Safety (TOPICS) effort. Under the Federal-Aid Urban program, the
city is presently entitled to a total of some $925,000 on an 80-20
matching basis over a period of three years.

However, particularly with the shifting of federal priorities
away from financing of automobile roadways, it cannot be assumed
that outside monies will be available when the road projects come to
be needed. Making the assumption that the city's normal allotment
of gas-tax subvention revenue is used for ongoing maintenance, routine reconstruction, and small-scale, high-priority improvements to
the existing road network, these costs have been budgeted as a separate capital expenditure that, it is assumed, would be begun soon
after the city should reach a population of approximately 100,000.

These costs are in an important sense conservatively estimated:
They provide additional capacity at the screenlines but not in the road
network into which they feed. Thus, for example, the widening of
Modoc Road to four lanes between Hollister and Las Positas would
have the effect of putting many more additional cars onto Modoc between Las Positas and Mission, generating pressure for the widening of this stretch of road--a much more expensive and destructive
project, ruled out of consideration. This project, if carried out,
would, in turn, have the effect of funneling more cars onto San Andres,
generating pressure to widen it, and so on. The process, once begun,
is difficult to stop; therefore, these "reasonable improvements," if
undertaken, can be viewed as only the first steps in a more costly
and disruptive process.

Additional capacity can be achieved in downtown areas by the
removal of onstreet parking to create (in the case of narrow streets)
one or (in the case of wider streets) two additional lanes of traffic.
We made the assumption that 18 streets could be widened in this manner. [9] In addition, two downtown streets could be made a one-way
couplet to provide additional carrying capacity.

Even with these alterations, however, demand still exceeds
capacity at all screenlines at the highest PIP (Zoning Maximum), and
at one screenline (Westmont) at populations below the General Plan
Probable PIP.

Consequences of Increased Auto Traffic

The kind of delays and traffic dislocations implied by growth
have several important effects beyond the obvious economic ones of
time loss and driver inconvenience and frustration. These include
increased gasoline consumption, increased air pollution, increased
accidents, property value changes, increased noise, and the adverse
impact on surrounding neighborhoods.

Increased Gasoline Consumption. Either cars are standing motion-
less in line with their motors running, wasting gasoline, or they are
attempting to bypass congestion by circuitous detours, wasting gasoline. To take an example, there is clearly a point at which, due to
congestion on State Street, it is faster to go from the intersection of
Las Positas and State to that of LaCumbre and State by way of Foothill Road (2.87 miles) than by way of State (0.94 miles), using (roughly) three times as much fuel. The point at which this becomes a common alternative is clearly not far in the future, because it is done
now on occasion.

Increased Air Pollution. Increasing delay means average speed goes
down. A pre-1968 car traveling one mile at 20 miles per hour emits
a total of 0.2 pounds of carbon monoxide. The same car traveling
the same distance at 10 miles per hour emits approximately 0.35
pounds--not quite a doubling. The increase is somewhat less marked
for newer cars, but is still present (Klein et al. 1971). Pignataro
(1973) states: "A motor vehicle produces its smallest concentration
of pollutants when it is in motion at uniform speed. It produces twice
the amount of pollution when it is decelerating to a stop (and approximately four times as much pollution when it is stopped and idling) as
it does when it is in motion."[10]

Increased Accidents. Increased urban traffic volumes tend to produce more accidents both relatively and absolutely. Wider, more
heavily traveled roads are more dangerous to pedestrians--and to
animals--than narrower, less-traveled ones. There are clearly exceptions to this rule: Signalization can increase safety, and a narrow,
little-traveled road can have hazardous, narrow shoulders or blind
curves. In few cases, however, does a street become safer by having more traffic upon it. This is particularly true in neighborhoods
in which, because of a lack of park space, streets are used by children as play areas. These are also the areas likely to experience
the highest increases in traffic flow.

Economic Impacts. Stores and other businesses on North State will
lose business, as former or potential customers are deterred by
traffic congestion from shopping in the area, and seek out less congested shopping facilities. According to Pignataro (1973): ". . .
there is little doubt that congestion can adversely affect the economic
life of a community. This is reflected by the detrimental effect on
downtown business activities and property values, neighborhood dis-
integration, and increased road user costs."
     All other things being equal, residences located on less-
traveled, less-noisy streets are considered more desirable. According to Klein et al. (1971), there is some evidence that such homes

would tend to command higher resale prices than those on heavily
traveled streets, although the findings are not conclusive. A corol-
lary to this rule would be that increasing traffic on a street leads to
the decreasing in value of properties on that street, or, more precisely, to their not increasing so much as comparable properties in
less-traveled locations.

Increased Noise. Klein et al. (1971) state: "At intersections, acceleration and braking noises predominate. Noise levels from stop and
go traffic consisting primarily of passenger vehicles are estimated
at 67 to 76 dBA at 100 feet."* By contrast, the movement of a continuous stream of vehicles, at a rate of 25,000 per day (corresponding to 2,500 per hour) is calculated by the same source as 64 dBA.
These figures do not include the sounding of auto horns, which similarly increases with congestion. Klein et al. (1971) set 70 dBA as a
"noise threshold," beyond which people become "annoyed" by noise.

Adverse Impact on Surrounding Neighborhoods. When traffic builds
up and congests on through-roads, motorists attempt to avoid the
traffic jams by detours that take them through residential communities. In the present instance, increasing traffic congestion on State
would send increasing numbers of cars onto such relatively quiet
arteries as San Remo Drive, Madrona Road, Calle Alamo and Calle
Noguera, Via Lucero and La Colina, Ontare and McCaw Roads.
        Dense and fast-moving streams of automobile traffic form a
barrier to human movement in an area. A widened or suddenly more
heavily traveled thoroughfare can divide what was once one neighborhood into two--as happened, for example, with the improvement of
Carrillo Street above the intersection with San Andres. In particular,
small children and older people are affected by this consequence of
traffic increase, and this acts to narrow their effective radius of independent travel and establishes a psychological "edge" to the neighborhood (see Lynch 1960).

Ameliorative Measures

        Congestion problems could be ameliorated by the following
measures.

Programs Encouraging Higher Levels of Car Occupancy. Currently,
according to City of Santa Barbara, Department of Public Works
(1974), the average car in the central business district carries only

_____

        *"dBA" is an abbreviation for decibels, a measure of noise in-
tensity.

1.24 persons. There is little reason to believe the ratio is higher
elsewhere. Furthermore, a trend toward increase in the number of
cars per person would most likely act to lower the average number
of riders per car, as more and more riders come to have cars of
their own. City measures to increase car occupancy might include
the following:

- Car pooling. Computer data banks could be used to match commuters in terms of home and work destinations. Programs of
  this sort have been attempted among county employees and at
  UCSB.
- Hitchhiking. Encouragement of hitchhiking by the establishment
  of pickup points coded by destination, such as now exist outside military bases and on Los Carneros Road in Isla Vista,
  is perhaps the easiest, cheapest, and most effective way of
  increasing vehicle occupancy and easing congestion at the city's
  disposal.
- Priority traffic lanes. Establishment of lanes on major city
  streets for the exclusive use of cars with two or more passen-
  gers would serve to encourage utilization of proposals previously mentioned above.
- A method of staggering trips to smooth out peaking effects.
  Roughly 20 percent of daily usage--and almost 100 percent of
  congestion problems--on most roads, comes in two rush hours.
  According to SCOTS data, 19 percent of all trips are trips between work and home, many of which tend to fall during these
  two hours. An additional 11 percent of trips are between home
and shopping--many of which join the evening rush hour, as stores
close at the same time as business. If travel peaks could be extended by the staggering of work openings, lunch breaks, and closings
by as little as an additional half hour, substantial relief could be experienced from congestion. Nonretail businesses, for example,
could be assigned by lot one of six opening times 15 minutes apart,
annually at the time of business-license renewals.

Buses, Bicycles, and Other Modes of Transportation. We will now
discuss programs aimed at producing a change in the present 95 to
99 percent dependence on the private car.

 1. Buses account for only 3.2 percent of rush-hour traffic in
the central city. For our various PIP populations, rough order-of-
magnitude calculations were performed to estimate the size of the
bus fleet that would be needed at rush hour to carry the excess of
demand over road capacity at each PIP.

 The method was first to calculate total rush-hour deficit of demand over capacity at the three border screenlines (Arroyo Burro,

Westmont, and Westside) ringing the city, taking rush-hour load as one-tenth of total daily traffic. This deficit was converted from vehicle crossings to person-trips using the 1.24 persons per vehicle occupancy factor found in the city survey. All of these deficit trips were then assigned to fully loaded 45-passenger buses. Each bus was assumed to cross a screenline twice during the rush hour.

This method, crude as it is, was able to backcast correctly the size of the existing bus system from current screenline counts and the 3.2 percent bus-ridership rate. An alternative version of the same analysis, more in keeping with current transit policy, was also carried out. Here, the same total trips deficit was divided between full-sized 45-passenger buses and 19-passenger minibuses. The results of the exercise are shown in Table 3.3.

The costs of acquiring and operating such a system would be borne by the all-South Coast Santa Barbara Metropolitan Transit District (SBMTD) and not exclusively by the city. Detailed accounting and forecast of these costs would therefore fall outside the scope of this study, though it may be of interest to note parenthetically that current cost of a 45-passenger bus is approximately $43,000. Of more immediate concern, perhaps, are measures the city might be called on to undertake to encourage that the buses, once bought, would be used. Some of the measures might include the following:

- Exclusive bus lanes on city streets
- Signalized intersections favoring buses
- City tax credits or other incentives to encourage retailers to home-deliver merchandise on a much larger scale than presently, to encourage bus use for shopping
- Restriction of Downtown parking

There are, however, severe disadvantages and limitations associated with buses. Some of these include the following:

- Environmental and neighborhood impacts. Present-model buses, owing to their size and design, are even noisier than a heavy stream of private cars; their fumes are objectionable to many; the presence of full-sized passenger buses in a residential neighborhood is a disruptive impact.
- Congestion. Unless buses have a separated right-of-way, they must use the public roads and are consequently affected by overall road congestion; the large size of buses and their frequent stops contribute disproportionately to this congestion, without special road design.
- Expense. Under prevailing present fare structures, with payment on a per-ride instead of a per-day, weekly, or monthly basis,

TABLE 3.3

Bus Requirements

PIP	Population (thousands)	With No Construction		With "Reasonable" Construction	
		45-Passenger Buses Only	Mixed (PB/MB)	45-Passenger Buses Only	Mixed (PB/MB)
Half-Density Probable	94	52	39/31	(no construction necessary)	
General Plan Probable	103	103	71/56	9	7/5
Half-Density Maximum	117	156	117/92	59	43/34
Zoning Probable	119	164	123/97	68	49/40
General Plan Maximum	140	270	202/159	155	116/91
Zoning Maximum	170	450	338/266	323	242/192

Note: "Mixed" means both 45-passenger buses (PB) and 19-passenger minibuses (MB).

Source: Santa Barbara Planning Task Force estimates.

out-of-pocket expenses for bus transportation are higher than
those for individual car use.

The effects of environmental/neighborhood impacts and congestion
can be mitigated somewhat through the use of minibuses, but with
considerably heavier expenses (at least twice as many drivers are
needed).

    2. The bicycle is capable of carrying far more than the pres-
ent 1.8 percent of all peak-hour trips that surveys indicate it now
carries. It is especially feasible in an area of mild climate with
little rainfall, such as Santa Barbara. The psychological ground-
work for its increased use seems already to have been laid. A survey of 405 nonowners of bicycles in the city found that two-thirds of
them believed that "the bicycle can become a reasonable alternative
to the automobile for travel within the city" (Bikeway Master Plan
1974, p. 26).

    The city has already embarked on an ambitious plan to encour-
age bicycle use through the planning of an extensive system of bike-
ways. To the extent that this system is implemented and used, relief from the congestion projected at higher population levels will be
experienced.

    3. A short-distance, intracity "people mover" serving the
downtown has been proposed by the Santa Barbara Redevelopment
Agency consultant. Such a system would in part be a park-and-ride
arrangement, where shoppers and others with business in the CBD
would be encouraged to leave their automobiles in a lot outside the
CBD while performing their business downtown, thus parking only
once instead of several times, moving from lot to lot (as is often
done). This system is also designed to interface with both the
SBMTD bus system and Amtrak long-distance passenger rail service at a unified transportation center. Again, to the extent that
such a system changes the present pattern of reliance on private
automobile transportation, it would improve congestion problems
characteristic of higher populations.

                               Parking

Capacity

    In addition to the problems of moving cars through an area,
there is also the problem of providing parking space for those who
need to stop or have business to transact. The dimensions of this
problem can be seen by studying the Downtown Santa Barbara area.

Unlike more recent development, the Santa Barbara Downtown area was not planned around parking lots. Any provision of additional parking must be at the expense of existing uses.

Presently, the Transportation Department estimates there are approximately 6,300 offstreet and about 3,500 onstreet parking spaces in the area bounded by the freeway on the south and west, by Laguna Street on the east, and by Sola Street on the north. Population growth to higher PIPs will eventually involve the loss of onstreet parking from all streets in this area with the exception of Bath and Castillo Streets, for reasons already described.

At the same time that the supply of parking will be dwindling, however, the demand for parking will be increasing. Table 3.4 sets forth estimates of parking demand at various population levels, based on current usage patterns, along with estimates of the amount of land necessary to supply this demand. (It should be remembered that if it is decided to widen roads to retain onstreet parking, the same amount of land will be required.)

TABLE 3.4

Space Demand for Downtown Parking at Various PIPs

Population (thousands)	Available Offstreet Spaces	Spaces Needed	Spaces Deficit	Acres Required
73,000	6,300	6,100	None	0
94,000	6,300	8,400	2,100	19.2
103,000	6,300	8,900	2,600	23.8
119,000	6,300	10,700	4,400	40.3
140,000	6,300	12,500	6,200	56.9
170,000	6,300	16,000	9,700	89.0

Note: The following have been assumed: no change in automobile use patterns; straightline increase of parking demand with population; no increase in per capita automobile ownership; removal of parking when street capacity is reached; no multistory parking structures.

Source: Transportation Division, Department of Public Works.

Mitigating Policies

In anticipation of additional parking demand the city could continue to use condemnation powers to acquire new land. The city can also continue to rely on taxing and bonding mechanisms for raising construction revenues for new parking lots and structures. The city's parking structures are currently self-supporting; with increasing parking demand in the future, it seems likely that they will continue to be so.

Other possible parking policies, aimed at reducing private automobile traffic, include the following:

• Elimination of onstreet parking (this is assumed for most central areas to provide road space for vehicle movement). The Bikeway Master Plan (1974), while considering some new construction of new bicycle right-of-ways, also calls for the use of what is presently onstreet parking space
• Increase of fees in existing offstreet parking
• Zoning or other regulation or prohibition of commercial parking facilities
• "Sticker" parking in residential neighborhoods abutting high parking demand districts, giving residents exclusive onstreet parking privileges
• Creation of "park and ride" lots served by bus or other transportation outside principal trip-destination areas
• Increase of fines for illegal parking
• Elimination of free parking in offstreet facilities

Some of these alternatives are economically discriminatory, falling more heavily on poorer car operators. Others imply what is for most people a very different life-style than has become customary. To the extent that measures such as those discussed are necessary, implemented, and perceived as onerous, growth has exacted a cost. None has worked to replace auto travel in any U.S. city thus far.

Area Impacts

At higher populations, the following areas could expect to receive significant traffic impacts.

Coast Village. Coast Village will experience some increase in traffic congestion, as traffic on the freeway increases, along with traffic on a widened Old Coast Highway.

Upper East. Substantially increased volume of through-traffic on
Laguna, Garden, State, and particularly Anacapa and Santa Barbara
Streets, mainly composed of through-traffic from or to Foothill Road,
seems likely below Los Olivos Street. Among cross streets, Mission, Los Olivos, and Micheltorena will receive increasing pressure.
The SCOTS 1990 study shows daily traffic demands on Micheltorena
of five times the present volume in the neighborhood of Alameda
Park--well beyond the capacity of the street to absorb. Widening is
proposed by the Comprehensive Transportation Action Plan on Los
Olivos between Laguna Street and Mission Creek. The 1971 proposed
revisions for the General Plan suggested a study of the feasibility of
extending Santa Barbara to link with Foothill. The study was never
performed, but if traffic volumes and congestion increase, pressure
would be generated to revive the plan. Onstreet parking would be
removed from through streets in this neighborhood at higher city
populations.[11]

Summary of Findings

First, assuming the continuation of current automobile patterns, key segments of the existing city road and parking system
would be inadequate to accommodate the traffic demands of the Half-
Density Probable (94,000) or higher population levels.

Second, again assuming present automobile-usage patterns, by
completion of certain construction, including the crosstown freeway,
the widening of the present freeway to six lanes between Milpas Street
and Turnpike Road, and the removal of onstreet parking from ar-
terials, traffic demands of population up to the level of the General
Plan Probable (103,000) could be accommodated at acceptable service levels. From the standpoint of costs and extremely adverse
neighborhood impacts, further improvements are not feasible.

Third, at population levels higher than the General Plan Probable, despite improvements, severe congestion and delay would be
experienced at numerous locations throughout the city. Onstreet
parking in the CBD would progressively become scarcer and totally
disappear well before the Zoning Maximum (170,000) population was
reached.

Fourth, a large number of neighborhoods will experience adverse impacts of increased noise and higher volumes of through-
traffic. These will tend to be the densest and lowest-income neighborhoods.

Finally, vigorous city measures to increase occupancy of cars,
stagger work hours, and encourage transit and bicycle ridership, if
successful, would ameliorate these effects.

SOCIAL CONSEQUENCES *

Life-Style and Social Tensions

A way of life, a day of routine activity, seems to change as cities grow from smaller to larger places. There is at least a folk-lore that argues that smaller places are characterized by a slower-paced, more friendly and personal relationship between individuals and a lower degree of suspicion and hostility toward one's fellow residents. These informal observations provide the basis of the classic literature in urban sociology (see Wirth 1938).

Space Disorganization

Rats, when confined at high densities in their habitats, are said to undergo breakdown of normal instinctual patterns (Calhoun 1963). From this it is sometimes concluded that population density, per se, is similarly the culprit in causing human social ills, such as poverty, divorce, and crime. A more sophisticated reading of this evidence, however, notes that human beings are not rats and that they have proven themselves quite able to live under extremely high densities without any of the consequences observed among the rats. The residents of Hong Kong live under densities dramatically higher than those experienced by the residents of Harlem, but they do not find themselves in comparable situations of family breakdown or high rates of juvenile delinquency. Other factors besides density are clearly at work, and the effects of density, per se, have not been clearly established.

We have found in our cross-city analysis that certain forms of crime, particularly murder and burglary, rise on a per capita basis with increases in population size. Similarly, these data indicate that there is a size-associated increase in liver cirrhosis, a disease used as an indicator of alcoholism. Other studies have shown that mental illness rates rise with the size of a city. Such rates increase with higher densities within a given city. This all adds up to a sordid portrayal of the effects of size and seems to support, once again, the idea of size and/or density causing social pathology.

But, again, there is an alternative interpretation. It may be that size and density do not cause these negative effects; rather, it may be that those afflicted with psychosis, or desperate poverty, or alcoholism, gravitate to the city precisely because it is a large place

---

*Eric Mankin is coauthor of this section.

where they can experience some sort of anonymity. Thus, what is a liability for many residents of a large place--the presence of larger numbers of deviants and their difficult habits--reflects the asset of such large places when viewed from the perspective of others. Some people need a large place for the anonymity it permits; other people simply enjoy the opportunity for such anonymity. The social stultification of small towns where everybody knows everybody is found quite undesirable by some people. For whatever good it does, anonymity does seem to increase with size of place, providing the dangers and the opportunities that go along with it.

Access to Local Institutions

The same smallness of scale that permits people to enjoy or suffer from personal knowledge of one another has the additional consequence of creating conditions under which citizens interact with persons who represent dominant social institutions on a more or less personal basis. Access to government, to civic groups, to local media, and to educational institutions seems easier and more direct in small places than in large.

To an appreciable degree, both the extent to which people cannot fight city hall and the extent to which people feel called on to do it depend upon city size. There are a number of reasons for this, most of them commonsense but important and significant nevertheless.

First, the number of elected officials in a city tends to increase only very slightly with increased city size. A city of 25,000 can and usually does have the same elected structure as a city of 50,000 or even 500,000--a mayor and four or six councilmembers being common. Each elected official thus comes, under growth, to represent a much larger number of constituents.

This reduces the likelihood that a citizen knows, on any kind of personal level, any of the elected officials who represent him or her. It also means, concomitantly, that local elections come increasingly to be decided on some other basis than personal contact--reportage in newspapers, television, and radio, through advertising on these media, through bulk mailing, blind telephone solicitation, and billboards.

All of these changes cause a shift in the character of local political campaigns. In smaller areas, the principal determinant of campaign effectiveness is the willingness of a candidate's friends and supporters to do volunteer work and the principal campaign expenditure traditionally is free food at various functions feting a candidate. As city size increases, money--for advertising and to pay a candidate's increasingly higher personal expenditures--becomes an increasingly critical factor. Elections become more expensive per vote and complicated enough to demand the intervention of professional campaign managers and publicists. All these factors tend to make elections and the people who run for office more remote from the average voter.

The fact that in a city the size of Santa Barbara any citizen can still be guaranteed the opportunity of speaking his or her mind at a meeting of the City Council, Planning Commission, or other government body is a demonstration of the size effect on the relationship between the governors and the governed. That people in Santa Barbara regularly take advantage of this opportunity is even more important evidence that they believe this relationship has real meaning and does not represent merely a pro forma waste of everyone's time.

Local Bureaucracies

It is with city employees and not with elected officials that most citizens deal when they come into contact with government. And it is these dealings that on occasion can create frustration when dealing with bureaucracies, often thought to become rigid and unresponsive due to increased size. The size effect upon bureaucracy emerges almost mathematically from the situation. In a small organization the people who set policy and the people who carry it out are, if not identical, at least in constant and intimate contact. As the size of the organization grows, however, to cope with increased load, an organizational hierarchy develops: Every three (or five or seven or whatever) additional workers require one supervisor; every five supervisors, a department head; every five department heads, an administrator. This process continues endlessly upward. A small department can work by seat-of-the-pants guidelines and rules of thumb; because of the small volume of cases, each one can be judged individually. In a large department there must be explicit guidelines, explicitly formulated to ensure uniformity among the actions of the many functionaries. In a small town a citizen can walk into a department and talk to the manager. In a small city, the citizen can make an appointment to see the manager. In a medium-sized city, the citizen can make an appointment to see one of the manager's assistants.

There is, of course, another side to the coin. A smaller organization may make up in arbitrariness what it lacks in red tape, using the lack of explicit rules to enforce whim or prejudice. Some small cities are run by feudal bosses, as unresponsive as the most massive bureaucracy to public opinion. This is still another reason why those who are different from the parochial majority may find small places stultifying, or downright repressive.

The same patterns persist across other civic institutions. The
police in small towns are not anonymous technicians; they must answer to a public that often either knows them or one of their superiors
personally or as neighbors. With larger size, one may know a friend
of a friend who knows those superiors. Similarly, police tend to have
more intimate knowledge of the people they serve and an authentic
sense of the social structure around them. They may be more dis-
posed to "sidewalk justice," in which they reprimand a teenager or
turn him over to his family, rather than to "filing a report" and thus
starting the chain of events that cranks up the criminal justice system. There is less due process when matters are handled on a personal basis, but perhaps the results are less damaging to the victims
over the long term.

Relations with media vary in a similar way. Small-town papers
give extensive coverage to local community news and every church
group, boys' club, and service organization is grist for the mill.
People read about their neighbors and have their own accomplish-
ments publicly celebrated. They seem to enjoy this. Again, there
is the other side to the coin: If one is arrested for drunken driving,
one may find oneself humiliated by coverage in the Santa Barbara
News-Press. If the same thing happens in Los Angeles, there will
not be room for one's transgression on the pages of the Los Angeles
Times or Herald-Examiner, unless one is a notable public figure.
Similarly, small-town residents have the opportunity of expressing
themselves through the letters column of their newspaper; in Santa
Barbara the News-Press and the News & Review actually print most
of the letters they receive. In larger cities this is not the case; to
have a letter printed becomes an accomplishment reserved for a
lucky few.

Segregation by Race and Income

With increases in size there tends to be increasing differentiation between social groups: rich and poor, black and white, Chicano
and Anglo. These differences certainly exist in all cities, and in
small places the discrimination against minorities and the poor may
even be more strongly felt because it takes a more personal form
than the bureaucratic. But in larger places the differentiation among
social groups comes increasingly to be reflected in geographic terms:
ghettos for the blacks and barrios for the Chicanos grow in size and
become increasingly remote from the nearest white or Anglo area.
These higher levels of segregation were found to be associated with
larger places in our cross-city analysis; in fact, size of place seems
to be a more striking explanation in variation in residential segregation

than any other variable, including whether the city is in the North or
the South (see Taeuber and Taeuber 1965).

In part, this increasing racial segregation of larger places is
purely a function of geometry. In a small city, there may still be a
ghetto, but by definition its absolute size will not be large. Hence,
a larger proportion of ghetto residents live at or near the boundary
of the area than would be the case in a larger city.

These proximities make for a number of social consequences,
beyond the mere fact of a resident's being able readily to cross
ghetto boundaries. It means that public facilities tend to be inte-
grated--and integrated merely by the force of arithmetic. There is
not a sufficiently large Black population in Santa Barbara to support
a Black shopping center with its own supermarket. In terms of routine daily activity (such as shopping), racial, ethnic, and income integration comes about "naturally," and there are some important
consequences, particularly for the poor and the minorities. There
is not the opportunity for ethnic market specialization that has developed in other cities in which low-income and minority areas find
their stores stocked with poorer-quality goods at higher prices (see
Caplovitz 1963). Of course, the other side of this coin is that there
is also a lack of specialization that would provide a wide selection of
some types of "ethnic" foods preferred by minority groups and people
of other ethnic extraction.

The relative lack of segregation in shopping facilities is paralleled by a similar pattern in other realms. Santa Barbara's schools
were relatively easy to integrate; the costs of integration, both
monetarily and socially, would have been far higher in larger places,
and perhaps altogether impossible. Similarly, the city's recreational facilities are integrated, both racially and economically. The
Palm Park beach areas are within walking distance of a wide variety
of economic and ethnic groups, and on any weekend members of all
groups can be found there enjoying the city's recreational facilities,
seemingly without stress. Although taken for granted here, this is
not common in large cities. (For actual counts of integrated recreation use in one large city, see Molotch 1972.)

Unless growth is accompanied by concomitant city expenditures
to maintain present per capita access to recreation facilities, the effect of growth will be the further increasing of segregation. With
decreasing quality of or access to public facilities, private clubs
are formed for the well-to-do. Members of the clubs lose incentive
to maintain the public facilities. As such private facilities prolifer-
ate, more and more influential citizens become members of such
clubs, and the public facilities become increasingly used only by
those who cannot afford an alternative. Without a constituency
among the more well-to-do, the facilities become increasingly

rundown and crowded, providing the basis for perpetuating a vicious cycle. (See Chapter 6 for an analysis of growth-induced parks costs.)

Range of Retail and Service Facilities

Although smallness may lead to the beneficial consequence of limiting segregation, it also has the rather detrimental effect of limiting the variety of stores and services that are available to a citizen. As a city grows, the number of retail stores and commercial service facilities expands as well. Large numbers of people mean the crossing of thresholds that are required by various forms of commercial and cultural facilities. In general, the more specialized the service, the larger the support base needed. Almost any settlement can support a grocery, because everyone eats, but only a large city can support an airplane upholstery specialist, because a very small portion of any population has use for one. City growth thus increases options and decreases the inconvenience and cost associated with importing goods from distant points for those with idiosyncratic needs and tastes.

By comparing the "yellow pages" of three urban areas, the effect of size can be more concretely understood. The three cities, and the population size served by the relevant yellow pages are Santa Barbara South Coast (162,000), Sacramento (805,000), and Los Angeles (3 million). The relevant population ratios are approximately 1:5:19. The telephone directories can be used to reveal the pattern of what is or is not present in Santa Barbara, as compared to larger places.

A couple with a marriage on the rocks can select from 301 counselors in Los Angeles, compared to 89 in Sacramento and 36 in the South Coast--a reasonable enough distribution, given the comparative population sizes.

There are ten race tracks in the Los Angeles area and three in Sacramento, but there is none on the South Coast. Los Angeles has 35 Turkish baths; Sacramento, nine; the South Coast, only one.

Those looking for an escort have their choice of eight different escort services in Los Angeles, while in Sacramento there is a monopoly, and there is none on the South Coast.

A Los Angeles businessman or official seeking to destroy confidential documents could find 11 competing companies specializing in records destruction, or 14 retailers selling shredding machines for those who prefer to do it themselves. In Sacramento, however, the choice is narrowed to five companies and two retailers, while in Santa Barbara there are no listings.

But the "size brings more" rule admits exceptions. A home builder in search of adobe bricks could patronize the sole supplier listed in Santa Barbara or the sole supplier listed in the Sacramento directory or the sole supplier listed in the Los Angeles directory. A bibliophile searching for a book would do better in Los Angeles, to be sure (roughly 1,000 listings) than in Sacramento (55), but not much better in Sacramento than in Santa Barbara (42).

In many areas the South Coast seems disproportionately supplied. There are 23 automobile customizers in Los Angeles, widely known as a home of that art. In Sacramento there is only one. But Santa Barbara supports five. Santa Barbara is well-stocked in restaurants (269 to Sacramento's 746) and art galleries (an equal number: 34), and stockbrokers (18 to 30).

The overall impression gained by comparing the Sacramento, Santa Barbara, and Los Angeles "yellow pages"--that this area is rather rich in retailers and services--is confirmed by a more rigorous methodology based in the 1967 U.S. Census of Business. By comparing the number of retail stores among all our 115 matched cities with the size of their population, we determined that the average for all cities is to have 0.0104 retail stores per resident. In Santa Barbara the average is 0.0148, or 42 percent more stores per capita. In terms of commercial service establishments, such as barber shops and restaurants, Santa Barbara's ratio was even more favorable: 0.0126 establishments per resident compared to 0.0075 in the United States, a 68 percent superiority in per capita service establishments. A clearer way of expressing this high level of service is to note that the city of Santa Barbara ranks fifth in terms of the number of retail stores per capita, while in terms of service establishments only West Palm Beach, Florida, and Reno, Nevada, have a higher number per capita.

We conclude that while the number and range of retail establishments generally rises with increasing population, there are many exceptions to the pattern and other forces at work. Santa Barbara reveals some of these other forces--particularly, tourism and the city's function as a market center. Santa Barbara's particular array of economic and population characteristics has brought a disproportionate endowment in facilities of this type. If Santa Barbara continues to grow and retains the present ratio of retailing and service establishments to population, the range of options open to its citizens should further increase. But it is also possible that growth may somehow cause this favorable ratio to change in the direction of the more prevalent national pattern. We have no way of knowing, but we note that the city currently has so much, for its size, that the gains that lie ahead through increased growth are likely quite marginal. There is likely little suffering or inconvenience now present

in Santa Barbara due to lack of access to goods and services that
would be changed by the population gains envisioned by our various
PIPs.

Freedom and Spontaneity

There is a quality of life, difficult to articulate, that many
visitors and newcomers associate with Santa Barbara: One can
typically go about one's day without tension, without hassles. The
environment is adaptable to a change in plans or a change in taste.
One does not have to scheme the day around a train schedule into
the city; one does not have to prearrange a parking space. Although
perhaps they are not what they once were, toilets in public places
tend to be available, free, clean, and unlocked. Dress is more informal, with bathing suits occasionally the mode of dress on the
main streets. Reservations tend not to be needed for many eating
places; lines at the movies tend to be short. One can park on the
street and not far from the place one wants to go. An escort to
avoid criminal assault is generally not needed in most parts of the
city. There is more freedom and more opportunity for spontaneous
activity.

Apart from the tendency of large-size places to increase the
range of commercial merchandise and services to which the residents have access, virtually all the other indicators of freedom
would seem to decline with increase in size. These changes occur
not only in the Downtown areas and in the parks and public places
but in the neighborhoods as well.

Horses and Dogs

The increasing stress recently developing in the city over
horses and dogs provides a case in point of the consequences of
growth upon a seemingly trivial detail of life, but one that large
numbers of people take very seriously.

It is quite clear that horses, and to a lesser but still very important extent, dogs, are inconsistent with more intensive forms of
land development. At the turn of the century, when virtually every
house in the city had substantial grounds attached, middle-class
families of quite limited means could maintain horses, and many
did, often, even then, as much as pets as for a means of transportation. As land value increased and average lot size diminished, the
horse was driven out of most of Santa Barbara. It still survives,
astonishing visitors from more densely settled localities, who come

upon it grazing in pastures well within the city limits. The cost, however, continually increases as human population grows, stables compete with apartments, more cars appear on formerly deserted roads to menace horses, and the open space that horses and their human friends need for enjoyment of each other becomes increasingly hard to get to. To the extent that the opportunity for horse ownership is valued by Santa Barbarans, growth is clearly undesirable.

Large dogs present a similar, but less intense problem. Any size dog can be a noise nuisance; as the city grows, there is increasing pressure for control, and there are increasing numbers of complaints to the police. Pressure for leash-law enforcement seems to rise with the number of people— and dogs— on a given block.

Dogs and people compete for use of area beaches. Surf birds, whose feeding the dogs interrupt and whose eggs the dogs steal, represent still another factor. There is a critical point--a critical number of dogs--at which all dogs must be banned from the beaches altogether, be exiled to a separate beach, or be kept on a leash.

In addition to these generalized difficulties, there are certain specific problems directly traceable to high dog populations in certain areas. Creeks in Santa Barbara have been showing increasingly high counts of coliform bacteria, rendering their waters hazardous for children and others playing in or near them. The source of the bacteria, tracers have discovered, is the intestines of the increasing number of dogs who live near the watershed of the creeks. To retain creeks for any human uses there must be either expensive rerouting of storm drains to flow into sewers (instead of into the creeks) or a limit on the number of dogs in a given area.

As such factors multiply, the area comes closer to that point at which restrictions become so onerous that people begin to ask themselves whether it is not cruel to keep their dogs. The thrust of all these restrictions, necessary though they be under higher densities, is to make dog ownership what horse ownership has already become: the preserve of the landed and relatively affluent. To the extent that this is perceived as not in the tradition or best interest of Santa Barbara, growth is contraindicated.

The impact of growth on dogs and horses is only an illustration; whenever more people crowd into smaller places, the need for mutual regulation and the establishment of orderly routines becomes increased. When one stays up all night, more people hear one's routine noises while they are trying to sleep; a ride on a motorcycle infringes on the peace and quiet of large numbers of people, especially as formerly remote areas become increasingly impinged upon by development. Nude swimming at the beaches, once out of range of those who might have objections, becomes impossible. Growth brings increasing regulation of life; regulation may bring additional tension. It

certainly eliminates some of the opportunity for spontaneous, unfet-
tered, and idiosyncratic joy. The new opportunities it does bring--
for example, more night spots and shopping facilities--are of a very
different sort.

NOTES

1. The survey schedule and response by age, occupation,
length of residence, and housing type are reported in Volume 3,
Appendix 4.1.

2. None of these differences is significant. Tables containing
the relevant data are presented in Volume 3, Appendix 4.2.

3. Although we cannot provide precise figures, the effect of
probable restriction on maximum development at the Half-Density
PIP would limit single-family houses and not apartments, the latter
generally being located on sites that are flat and suitable for development to at least half the density permitted under full zoning. Thus,
we anticipate that under the Half-Density Probable PIP, the proportion of the city's dwelling units given over to apartments will be
slightly higher than that specified under the Half-Density Maximum
PIP. Full-Density Probable PIP will, however, reflect restrictions
on both apartments and single-family houses; we thus assume the
ratio of housing types will remain rather much the same under both
the Maximum and the Probable Full-Density PIPs.

4. Data from Security Pacific Bank, Los Angeles, City Building Department.

5. Figure based on park land within the city boundaries.

6. Data from City of Santa Barbara Department of Public
Works, 1974. Santa Barbara County Transportation Study (SCOTS)
data indicate that the ratio is even higher outside the central business district, reaching levels above 99 percent.

7. Data from California State Department of Motor Vehicles.

8. A complete breakdown of costs for each project is contained in Volume 1, Table 4.5.

9. See Volume 1, Table 4.2.

10. The estimates of air pollution that appear in Chapter 4
could not take this factor into account in estimating PIP emission
levels.

11. Taken from Volume 1, which contains similar analyses
for each of the city's 26 neighborhoods and service areas.

4

ENVIRONMENTAL
EFFECTS OF GROWTH

AIR QUALITY

This chapter is an analysis of the impact of varying population levels on the air quality in the City of Santa Barbara and its vicinity. The objectives of this analysis are threefold: (a) to estimate the changes in air-pollutant emissions due to growth, (b) to assess the changes in geographical air-pollution distributions in Santa Barbara and the South Coast region with changing population, (c) to predict the air quality for three possible population levels through the year 2000.

Because future levels of emissions and air quality for the city are jointly dependent upon levels of emissions and air quality in the remainder of the South Coast region, this analysis treats the region as a single unit.[1] We thus use PIPS that correspond to the total South Coast area, calculated in the manner described in Chapter 1. Because of the roughness of some of the measurements upon which emissions data are based and the assumptions that have had to be made, given lack of certain information, it makes little sense to create emissions and air quality projections for population levels that are only marginally different. Thus, in order to secure a range of PIPs that provide enough variation to be useful, the analysis was restricted to the Probable Population under the city's Temporary Half-Density Zoning Ordinance (Low PIP) and the Probable Population

---

Coauthors of this chapter are Richard Nordsieck and Raul Martinez of Environmental Research and Technology, Inc., The project was carried out by General Research Corporation under a contract with the Task Force, utilizing Task Force staff for certain computation purposes.

under the city's Full-Density Zoning Ordinance (High PIP). For the South Coast population as a whole this provides a range of approximately 90,000 additional people between present population and the Low PIP and a range of approximately 75,000 additional people between that point and the population at the High PIP.[2] Both these growth PIPs are contrasted in the analysis with the emissions and air-quality results that would obtain in the future under the assumption of population frozen at its 1973 level.

Approaches to Emissions Analysis

For purposes of compilation and projection of an air-pollutant-emissions inventory, the primary air-contaminant sources are divided into mobile and stationary categories. The three primary (directly emitted) air contaminants to be evaluated here are reactive hydrocarbons (HC), oxides of nitrogen (NO_x), and carbon monoxide (CO). In this analysis, the mobile sources considered were automobiles, trucks, and aircraft. Emissions from sources such as railroad trains and off-road vehicles were neglected because they represent a relatively small total contribution. Stationary sources include petroleum (for example, gasoline distribution and service stations), organic solvent utilization (for example, surface coating, dry cleaning, and degreasing), and fuel combustion (as in power generation, power-driven machinery, and space heating).

Vehicular Emissions

We have characterized motor vehicle emissions as the product of daily vehicle miles traveled (VMT) in a prescribed area times the average vehicle emission factor per mile of operation. Gram-per-mile emissions of HC, NO_x and CO for an average California motor vehicle (assuming a vehicle population in which all but 5 percent of all miles are traveled by light vehicles of 6,000-pound gross vehicle weight or less) were obtained using methods outlined by Nordsieck (1975). Emission factors for future California vehicle mixes include the effects of the emission control requirements of the Federal Clean Air Act, with the conservative assumption that Congress will further delay enforcement of the final emissions standards until the 1978 model year, as is currently proposed.

Estimates of daily VMT for the study area were obtained from traffic network flow simulations of past and future traffic flows generated by the South Coast Transportation Study (SCOTS). These data (SCOTS 1967, 1969; Menchen 1974) obtained in the form of traffic counts and average speeds on each network link, were allocated

into 2 x 2 km. squares comprising a grid overlay of the South Coast
region of Santa Barbara County in order to assess the impact on the
City of Santa Barbara. The complete grid, shown in Figure 4.1 is
46 km. in an east-west direction and 14 km. in a north-south direction, extending from a point west of Ellwood to Rincon Point and
from the ocean to the mountain ridge.[3]

Because vehicle emission factors vary considerably between
stop-and-go and cruise-type driving, it was necessary to separate
the daily VMT in each square into surface street and freeway mile-
ages. The two complete network flow calculations provided by SCOTS
corresponded to the 1964 study area population of 120,036 (for which
the SCOTS network simulation was calibrated by extensive survey
work) and a future population of 289,681 representing the fulfillment
of the then-current General Plan expected in 1990.[4] We have assumed
that the traffic generated under these two scenarios is representative
of their respective total populations rather than of a particular year.[5]
Assuming a linear variation of daily VMT in each grid square with
changing population, we were then able to construct the geographical
distributions of freeway and surface street VMT for other population
levels of interest. These VMT maps are translated into distributions
of vehicular emissions of HC, NO_x, and CO by using the average
vehicle emission factors shown in Table 4.1.

Aircraft Emissions

The bulk of aircraft-pollutant emissions of concern to South
Coast residents occur during landing, takeoff, and taxiing of the aircraft at the Santa Barbara Municipal Airport in Goleta. Referring
to Figure 4.1, these emissions are allocated to squares (5,5), (6,5),
and (6,4) in proportion to land area devoted to actual airport operations as opposed to other commercial activities on airport land. We
estimate that in 1972 aircraft emissions amounted to 0.17 tons per
day of reactive HC, 0.13 tons per day of NO_x, and 2.28 tons per day
of CO.[6] (See Table 4.5 for a complete accounting of the total emissions in the study area.)

The volume of traffic and hence of aircraft emissions at the
airport is assumed to be roughly proportional to population; however,
this growth could eventually exceed the traffic-handling capacity of
the facilities. The airport's master plan (Pereira Associates 1970)
sets an upper limit of 375,000 flight operations per year, assuming
reactivation of a currently inactive runway and addition of some
taxiways. Under our population-scaling assumption, this predicts
airport saturation at a South Coast population of about 275,400. Thus,
accepting this definition of the Santa Barbara Airport's capacity, we
limited aircraft emissions at a constant value for populations exceeding

FIGURE 4.1

Two-by-Two Kilometer Grid Overlay for Geographical Distribution of Pollutant Emissions

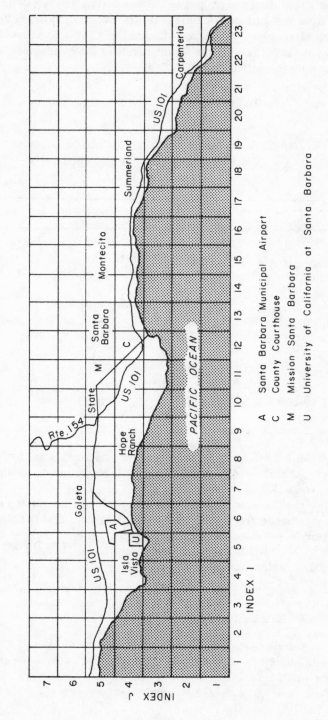

A   Santa Barbara Municipal Airport
C   County Courthouse
M   Mission Santa Barbara
U   University of California at Santa Barbara

Note: A: Santa Barbara Municipal Airport; C: County Courthouse; M: Mission Santa Barbara;
U: University of California at Santa Barbara.

275,400. Existing and proposed federal legislation regulating emissions from new and existing aircraft are expected to take effect
starting about 1980. We have estimated that for a fixed traffic level,
by the year 2000 these rules would result in the emissions changes
indicated by the ratios shown in Table 4.2.

TABLE 4.1

Pollutant Emission Factors for California Motor
Vehicles (5 Percent Heavy Duty Vehicle Mix)
(grams per mile)

	HC*	NO_x	CO
1972			
Surface streets	8.44	4.11	74.38
Freeways	2.71	6.00	21.46
1980			
Surface streets	2.05	1.61	21.00
Freeways	0.65	2.35	5.02
1990			
Surface streets	0.83	0.56	9.44
Freeways	0.27	0.82	2.12
2000			
Surface streets	0.83	0.55	9.39
Freeways	0.27	0.80	2.11

*The HC emission factors tabulated here are total hydrocar-
bons. Of these, 70.4 percent are considered reactive, contributing
to the production of ozone.

Note: These emission factors were derived using the data and
techniques presented in Nordsieck (1975), except that the final step
reduction in emission limits for light-duty vehicles (less than 6,000
pounds gross weight) has been delayed until the 1978 model year in
accordance with pending legislation.

Stationary Emissions

In order to extrapolate current estimates of stationary-source-
pollutant emissions to future years and population we have related
current emissions to current land use. This provides us with emission factors per unit area for each land-use category. Using South

Coast land-use maps for 1964 (Eisner, undated) and projected land
use from the 1967 General Plan (County of Santa Barbara) we have
assumed that the changes in land use occurring between 1964 and
development to General Plan densities will happen in proportion to
population growth.[7] The 1964 study-area population was 120,036.
The population associated with the General Plan is 289,681. Table
4.3 shows the resulting trends in the three basic land-use types used
to allocate pollutant emissions.

TABLE 4.2

Estimated Ratios of Emissions From Future Aircraft,
Year 2000, to Current Aircraft Emissions,
Year 1972

	HC	NO_x	CO
Turbojet and turboprop	0.30	0.50	0.40
General aviation (piston)	0.70	1.00	0.50

TABLE 4.3

Projected Land-Use Areas
(acres)

	1964	1972	?	?	?
Population	120,036	157,000	254,081	289,681	327,221
Industrial	900	784	478	366	248
Commercial	3,845	4,416	5,915	6,465	7,045
Residential	13,295	17,336	27,948	31,840	35,944
Total	18,040	22,536	34,341	38,671	43,237
Notes	Data base	Inter- polated	Low PIP	General Plan (1967)	High PIP

An apparent anomaly in Table 4.3 is that it indicates decreasing land areas designated for industrial use. The decrease was a
methodological consequence of the fact that the 1964 South Coast land-
use maps show substantially more land being used for industrial purposes than that designated for the long-term futures in the General

Plan. There are a number of different possible interpretations that
would make such a turn of events plausible. One can assume that as
a city grows its land area devoted to industry can actually shrink as
certain forms of manufacturing activity are removed from the locality
in response, perhaps, to increasing land costs that come with higher
levels of population and commercial densities. An example of this
is the current use of the city's East Beach area for industrial use--
a use that would be terminated under the General Plan. Certain
industrial uses, such as the Goleta quarry, will cease to exist when
the mineral resources are fully exploited. Under these scenarios,
industrial land use will decline and the consequent emissions will as
well, thus justifying use of these data in the present study.

On the other hand, it is possible for the amount of land used by
industry to decline, but the amount of emissions to remain stable or
to increase. Under this scenario increasing population and land
costs require that industrial uses be more densely concentrated. It
may be, for example, that under current conditions of relatively
cheap land industrial users have relatively little incentive to concentrate their operations--either in multistory structures or in
more efficient arrangements of service yards, storage facilities,
and so forth. Under this assumption, increased population levels
may be associated with decreasing industrial acreage, but the emissions from these stationary sources will rise concomitant with population. To the degree that this scenario is more nearly correct than
the former one, this chapter, which bases stationary emissions on
the land-use projections shown in Table 4.3, understates future
emissions from stationary sources by 13 and 29 percent for NO_x
and 7 and 24 percent for HC (for the Low and High PIP, respectively).

As with the vehicular emissions projections, it is necessary
to account for future policy decisions that will affect pollutant emissions from stationary sources. Under the Federal Clean Air Act of
1970 each state is required to submit a plan designed to control pollutant emissions sufficiently to bring the air quality in its air basins
into compliance with the national ambient air-quality standards
within three years. As a part of the Los Angeles Air-Quality-Control
Region, the South Coast of Santa Barbara County will be subject to
the controls specified in the California State Implementation Plan
(SIP) for that region.[8] With respect to stationary sources, these
controls will take the form of requirements for vapor-recovery devices to reduce greatly evaporative emissions from gasoline transfer
operations, substitution of less reactive organic solvents for those
currently used in degreasing and dry-cleaning operations, and in-
stitution of additional control measures affecting surface controls
proposed in the State Implementation Plan will be accepted by the
Environmental Protection Agency (EPA) and will have reached full

application by 1980. At full application, the stationary-source controls are expected to effect the reductions in reactive HC by varying amounts.[9]

Estimates of total HC and NO_x emissions from stationary sources in the Santa Barbara South Coast region were obtained from the California State Air Resources Board (ARB).[10] Table 4.4 shows the South Coast stationary source emissions inventory for 1972 and its allocation to the three basic land-use categories (industrial, commercial, and residential) with the numbers in parentheses included to indicate how application of the SIP would affect this inventory.

TABLE 4.4

Stationary-Source Emissions in the South Coast
Air Basin of Santa Barbara County, 1972
(tons per day)

	Total HC	Reactive* HC			NO_x		
		Ind.	Comm.	Res.	Ind.	Comm.	Res.
Petroleum marketing	2.9	--	0.97 (0.10)	1.93 (0.20)	--	--	--
Organic solvents users							
Degreasing	1.1	0.83 (0.0)	--	--	--	--	--
Surface coating	1.5	1.13 (0.74)	--	--	--	--	--
Dry cleaning	0.5	--	0.38 (0.02)	--	--	--	--
Fuel combustion							
Industrial	1.5	--	--	--	1.4	--	--
Domestic and commercial	0.1	--	--	--	--	0.10	0.20
Miscellaneous	0.3	--	0.07 (0.04)	0.13 (0.06)	--	--	--
Total		1.96 (0.74)	1.42 (0.16)	2.06 (0.26)	1.4	0.10	0.20

*Reactive hydrocarbons are defined here to include all HC except methane, ethane, propane, benzene, and acetylene. Numbers in parentheses are estimated emissions if SIP controls were currently in effect.

Results of Emissions Analysis

Following the assumptions and procedures outlined above, we have assembled geographical distributions of average daily primary pollutant emissions for the year 1972 (South Coast population = 157,000) and for the year 2000 PIPs of 254,081 and 327,221, respectively. In addition, we have obtained an estimate of emissions in the year 2000 under the assumption that the population remains constant at 1973 levels--that is, 160,000. This case has been added in an attempt to highlight the effect of the legislated controls on automotive and stationary-source emissions. Inclusion of this case allows us to visualize better the changes in emissions induced by the postulated increases in population versus the improvements brought about by emission controls.

A graphic representation of the likely geographic distribution of future emissions are contained in three-dimensional (isometric) pictures of the changes in emissions that occur between Low and High PIPs.[11] Figure 4.2 shows a 3-D view of the differences in distributions of NO_x over the South Coast area.[12]

Table 4.5 lists total emissions of each primary pollutant compiled by source type for 1972, 1980, 1990, and 2000, following the population growth to each of the two different PIPs resulting from the Half-Density Zoning Ordinance and Full-Density Zoning Ordinance, as well as estimates for the no-growth scenario. This table allows us to compare the relative total contributions of different source types but masks the effects of source density. For instance, in the square containing the airport, the CO emissions from aircraft are comparable to those in the squares containing the freeway. These represent emissions densely concentrated in a single geographic area.

An overall view of trends in total pollutant emissions in the South Coast area over the next 25 years is shown in Figures 4.3 and 4.4. Here we see the dramatic improvements expected from state and federal regulations eventually being overtaken by the effects of population growth after 1990. It should be noted that this upturn in emissions is a direct result of our assumption of linear population growth between 1974 and 2000. If we had assumed a constant annual percentage growth then the upturn would have been more pronounced.

Comparing the emissions shown in Table 4.5 for 1972 and for 2000 with the population level of 160,000 makes it apparent that the emission controls have the greatest effect on the vehicular emissions. As a result, it can be seen that if those controls were in effect today, the total NO_x emissions would be reduced by 75 percent, the total HC emissions by 85 percent, and the overall CO emissions by 86 percent. Compared with the population level of 160,000, a

FIGURE 4.2

Geographical Distribution of the Difference in NO$_x$ Emissions Between the High and Low PIPs in the Year 2000 (front view looking toward northeast)

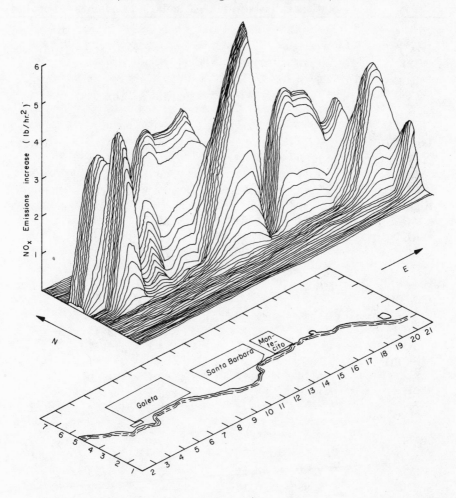

TABLE 4.5

Aggregated Pollutant Emissions by Source Type, for Year 2000
and Selected Intermediate Years
(tons per day)

	Stationary	Aircraft	Vehicular	Total Emissions	South Coast Population
1972					
Low PIP					157,000
NO_x	1.70	0.13	11.35	13.18	
RHC	5.44	0.17	8.26	13.87	
CO		2.28	100.39	102.67	
1980					
Low PIP					184,737
NO_x	1.59	0.08	5.40	7.07	
RHC	1.14	0.11	2.40	3.65	
CO		1.29	32.53	33.82	
High PIP					205,635
NO_x	1.54	0.08	5.95	7.57	
RHC	1.13	0.11	2.63	3.87	
CO		1.39	35.70	37.09	
1990					
Low PIP					219,409
NO_x	1.46	0.09	2.33	3.88	
RHC	1.11	0.13	1.21	2.45	
CO		1.53	17.74	19.27	
High PIP					266,428
NO_x	1.29	0.11	2.89	4,29	
RHC	1.08	0.15	1.49	2.72	
CO		1.83	21.79	23.62	
2000					
Low PIP					254,081
NO_x	1.31	0.11	2.76	4.18	
RHC	1.08	0.15	1.46	2.69	
CO		1.80	21.24	23.04	
High PIP					327,221
NO_x	1.26	0.11	3.71	5.08	
RHC	1.15	0.16	1.94	3.25	
CO		1.95	28.25	30.20	
No-Growth PIP					160,000
NO_x	1.68	0.07	1.55	3.30	
RHC	1.16	0.09	0.84	2.09	
CO		1.13	12.23	13.36	

population of 254,081 yields increases in NO_x, RHC, and CO of 27, 29, and 72 percent, respectively. The high population (327,221) causes emissions to increase by 53, 56, and 126 percent, respectively, for NO_x, RHC, and CO, relative to the population of 160,000.

FIGURE 4.3

Future Trends in Total Emission of NO_x
and Reactive HC

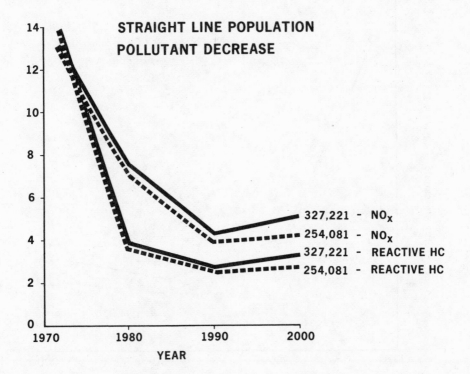

Present and Future Air Quality

The South Coast area currently has two air-quality monitoring stations that provide continuous measurements of CO and ozone (0_3). These stations (operated by the County Air Pollution Control District) are located in Santa Barbara and in the eastern end of Goleta. A review of the data obtained during 1973 showed that the highest hourly average ozone readings at both stations were 0.24 parts per million (ppm.) measured on May 28. (The National Ambient Air Quality

Standards require that hourly average readings of 0.08 ppm. of
ozone and 35 ppm. of CO, not be exceeded more than one hour per
year.) Overall, during 1973 the data show that the ozone standard
was exceeded for 314 hours at the Santa Barbara monitoring station
and 502 hours at the Goleta station.[13]

FIGURE 4.4

Future Trends in Total Emissions of CO

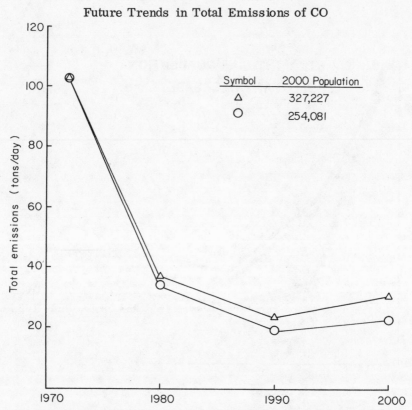

To estimate the worst-day ozone readings for future years we
simulated stagnant meteorological conditions in the GRC photochemical smog model (DIFKIN), using average pollutant fluxes in the area
surrounding the two monitoring stations (Martinez et al. 1973).
Lacking a detailed description of the microscale meteorology on our
worst case day (May 28, 1973), we assumed stable mixing conditions
under an inversion base height of 200 meters and slow, eddying air-
flows in the regions of interest. The randomly eddying flows were
assumed to result in mixing of the pollutant emissions over an area
of nine grid squares (13.9 mi^2) centered on the downtown station and

six grid squares (9.3 mi^2) surrounding the Goleta station. We first calibrated the model to reproduce the worst case readings of May 28, using the pollutant flux distributions obtained for 1973. Emissions for the Low and High PIPs were then introduced, and estimates of the corresponding worst case ozone values were calculated.

Table 4.6 summarizes the results of the DIFKIN simulation predictions of ozone levels, including the case where the population in the year 2000 has been assumed to be equal to that in 1973. The table shows that for Goleta the wide range of population levels has very little effect on ozone levels. The results also indicate that it is possible to increase the population and yet decrease the ozone peak. The reason is that the chemical processes that produce ozone depend critically on the ratio of emitted hydrocarbons to nitric oxide (HC/NO). In general, beyond a certain point the lower ratios yield lower ozone concentrations at a given place, for a constant times of reaction. In the case of Goleta, the HC/NO ratio decreases with increasing population, thus lowering the ozone level. We note that this situation is not necessarily typical of the whole area. Instead, it should be interpreted as being representative only of the area that surrounds the present monitoring station in Goleta.

TABLE 4.6

Current and Predicted Ozone Concentrations

| | Population | Worst Case (O_3, ppm.) | | Expected No. of Hr./Yr. Above Ambient Air-Quality Standard (0.08 ppm.) | |
		S.B.	Goleta	S.B.	Goleta
1973	160,000	0.24	0.24	314	502
2000	254,081	0.14	0.16	10–50	40–180
2000	327,221	0.14	0.15	10–50	30–140
2000	160,000	0.11	0.16	2–20	20–180

In 1973 the peak hourly average CO reading at the State Street station was 23 ppm. Assuming that local CO readings are directly proportional to local CO emission rates (since CO is nonreactive), we find that worst-case CO readings Downtown should be about 4.3 ppm. for the Low PIP and 5.5 ppm. for the High PIP. As mentioned above, the hourly ambient air-quality standard for CO is 35 ppm., not to be exceeded more than once a year.

Finally, we note that our calculations indicate that future concentrations of nitrogen dioxide will likely satisfy the air quality
standard of 0.05 ppm. annual mean.

Summary and Conclusions

Air pollutant emissions and air quality were investigated for
the City of Santa Barbara and its surrounding South Coast area.
Projections for the year 2000 were made for two different average
rates of growth between 1970 and 2000, and for a growth rate of zero.
Vehicle miles traveled formed that basis for mobile sources estimates and land use for stationary-source estimates. An atmospheric
computer simulation model provided air-quality predictions for the
monitoring station sites in Santa Barbara and Goleta. Because of
the scheduled controls on vehicular emissions, both population growth
rates gave lower photochemical smog indexes (ozone concentrations)
at the monitoring stations in the year 2000, compared to 1973. A
model case for the population frozen at 1973 level showed substantial
reductions in Santa Barbara ozone values but not in Goleta. Although
none of the cases meets the present national ambient air quality
standard for ozone, the frozen-growth case might meet it if the
calibration discrepancy in monitoring instruments were resolved in
favor of the lower alternative reading. These results tend to indicate that if there is population growth, the Santa Barbara area may
be forced to meet air-quality standards through other means, such
as substantially changing the transportation mode split in favor of
mass transit, or bicycles, or in some way lowering vehicle miles
traveled.

This preliminary analysis of future air quality in Santa Barbara
appears to indicate that significant improvements lie ahead, even in
the case of a rising South Coast population. However, these improvements would not be sufficient to bring the area into compliance with
the present National Standards for ozone by the year 2000, and subsequent population increases seem to spell a reversal in the trends
of improving air quality. It is important to note that we have estimated future air quality only at the existing measurement stations.
Although this is all that is required in a legalistic sense, since the
laws pertain only to those locations, it leaves unanswered the questions of interest to South Coast residents in outlying areas concerning the air quality in their neighborhoods. Unfortunately, a study of
sufficient scope to answer such questions is well beyond our current
budget limitations, and the basic background concentration and detailed meteorological analyses that would be required are non-
existent. With a concerted effort by the Santa Barbara County Air

Pollution Control District using their mobile unit, the fringe-area levels could be mapped out and correlations attempted with the fixed stations.

Lacking such a study, we can only estimate, based on experience, that while reduced pollutant concentrations may persist in Downtown locations, outlying areas downwind of these points may actually be suffering increased pollution levels such as occurs in Pasadena and Azusa relative to Downtown Los Angeles. Thus, if eddying wind patterns carry midday contaminants from Downtown areas back into the canyons behind Santa Barbara and Montecito, the added time for photochemical reaction may well produce relatively higher ozone concentrations in those areas than are indicated by the State Street readings. In the case of Los Angeles, the urbanization trend and the present control programs have pushed peak ozone areas farther and farther from the city center. It is plausible that this same trend could occur in the future in the Santa Barbara area.

With respect to CO concentrations, station locations are all-important. If a measurement station is too close to a busy roadway or street, then its readings are bound to approach or violate standards. At this point, the best indicators of relative CO levels in South Coast neighborhoods are the CO based on data from a measurement station in a high emission area (Downtown busy streets) and yet still show very minor air-quality effect, it can be concluded that, unlike ozone, CO dosages measured and expected in the Santa Barbara area do not constitute a health hazard.

NOISE

The state of the art on the subject of generating and interpreting noise-pollution data has been succinctly summarized in the following comment (Berry et al. 1974):

> Noise has been defined as unwanted sound. Scientifically-based standards for acceptable community noise levels have yet to be determined, and thus standards set in municipal ordinances vary greatly across the country. Most current research focuses upon source delineation and source emission measurement, yet because no agreement has been reached upon measurement for systems community noise levels, different types of noise emissions are measured by different agencies on different measurement scales. There is a total absence of detailed surveillance systems or workable data in the majority of cases.

Despite these problems, the thrust of the research literature to date indicates a series of general findings that are nevertheless useful:

1. Noise has tended to increase over time as more and more people come to utilize noise-producing modern devices, such as washing machines, automobiles, chain saws, gas lawnmowers, and motorcycles (Bolt, Beranek and Newman, Inc. 1970, as cited in Berry et al. 1974).
2. Increases in numbers of persons and in density of those persons causes higher levels of noise. Increasing population size almost inevitably brings increasing levels of noise (Dickerson et al. 1970).
3. Noise has detrimental effects on physical and mental health. Studies have indicated that high noise levels lead to circulation disorders, hearing loss, muscular tension, sweating, metabolic changes, reduced gastrointestinal activity, nausea, headache, tinnitus, and respiratory irregularities (Berry et al. 1974). Although temporary hearing loss can come about for some people simply through a long automobile ride, most individuals require higher noise levels at long exposures before even temporary loss occurs.
4. Noise affects different people in different ways. Those most subject, for example, to sleep losses caused by noise are the very young and the old. The less healthy are more susceptible than the healthy.

There are few, if any, examples of successful urban noise-control systems. Although many cities and states have noise-control ordinances, enforcement is difficult and often not attempted. Control of aircraft and automobile noise is potentially more effective (an exception to this was the banning of sonic booms enacted by the Santa Barbara City Council some years ago and still on the books).

Although there is no regular noise monitoring in the Santa Barbara area, a 1969 study was conducted by Norman Sanders, then of the UCSB Geography Department. Sanders found noise levels of 100 decibels adjacent to Highway 101, a level generally considered "dangerous" under conditions of prolonged exposure (see Chalupnik 1967, p. 107) and likely to lead eventually to hearing impairment (Dickerson et al. 1970, p. 22). Noise declined to 92 decibels with 40 feet of distance when trucks passed by and to 75 decibels for automobiles at a freeway on-ramp in Montecito (Daniel et al. 1969, p. 108). The quietest area of the city was Cielito (near Sheffield Reservoir) with a 40-decibel level. Other residential areas showed substantially higher noise levels (50 to 60 decibels on the Riviera).[14]

There is no way to specify with any certitude how increased population growth will affect these noise levels, except to predict with safety that they will increase, particularly as a function of the following:

1. Increased "people noise" from yelling, singing, talking
2. Increased traffic noise from larger numbers of cars, trucks, and motorcycles making more stops and starts (Klein et al. 1971, p. 204)
3. Increased number of dogs
4. Increased construction, street maintenance, and industrial activity
5. Larger numbers of people playing musical instruments, radios, and record players
6. More frequent sounding of police, fire, and ambulance sirens

Growth-induced noise would be lessened if any of the following circumstances were to occur:

1. Removal of Highway 101 traffic-light impediments (stops and starts create additional noise, particularly from trucks regaining speed after stopping at the intersections), heavy landscaping or depression of existing freeways (see Daniel et al. 1969, p. 41).

2. Changes in transportation technology, favoring extensive use of relatively quiet transit modes, such as electric cars, monorails, bicycles.

3. Legislation to require sound-proofing of existing buildings and future construction.

4. Increased legislation regulating passage of heavy trucks in residential districts, noise regulation of motorcycles, chain saws, and other high noise-producing devices (current city noise ordinances only cover amplified sounds).

URBAN HABITATS*

The city, particularly in its undeveloped land, is a habitat for life forms other than human beings. All remaining open space in the city was inventoried by field examination to determine the current state of the urban habitat, in order to evaluate the impacts of additional population upon the city's ability to sustain complex ecological networks.

---

*Lee Waian, Environmental Research and Technology, Inc., is coauthor of this section.

Maintaining a rich biological habitat in urban areas is significant not only in terms of the direct ecological benefits of enabling
species of plant and animal life to survive. It also has importance
for the spiritual and educational development of human beings, particularly, perhaps, of a city's children. Santa Barbara has not yet
developed a large, biologically sterile inner city, but continued population growth in both city and suburbs creates the ingredients for the
development of environments in which access to natural habitats is
denied to the majority of population.

The present effort attempts to determine how close this city is
to such a condition. The exposition is divided into three sections.
The first contains a description of the remaining habitats of the city,
displayed primarily through an ecological map of existing open areas.
We explain how the map was made and attempt to put what is revealed into historical perspective. The second section focuses on
the stream habitats of the city: the problems that they have under
current population and the prognosis under higher levels of population. Finally, in the third section we present a more detailed evaluation of three sample neighborhoods, chosen for their diversity, to
provide a guide to some of the potential ecological effects of population growth throughout the city.

Identifying, Classifying, and Ranking Open Space

For the purposes of this research we have defined "open space"
as the major undeveloped parks, parts of hillsides, cliffs along the
beach, and land along the creeks. We did not include the freeways,
the ocean, or the sandy or rocky beaches. However, areas down to
the size of city lots were considered open space, for these areas can
be biologically significant if they contain rare or unusual life forms
or are connected to a major habitat corridor, such as a stream.

A major aim was to determine the relative quality of the city's
various plant communities as habitats for all forms of native life.
Habitats were ranked numerically on the basis of the degree to which
they have retained their pristine state, and by the species diversity
they can support.[15]

We are painfully aware of the problems inherent in such a
simple ranking system--especially since the data upon which we relied to make our determinations were drawn from only one spring
session's field visits. Nonetheless, even this limited analysis iden-
tifies important habitats that are subject to destruction under current
land-use policies.

Table 4.7 compares the present total area of each habitat
classification with estimated totals of each prior to the arrival of

European man. Categorization of existing habitats was based on others developed for Los Angeles (see Los Angeles County 1972). As this table suggests, the only habitat that is near extinction is a small marsh area that was once part of the old estuary fed by Mission Creek. Only tiny remnants of the original marsh remain between the freeway and present sewer plant.

TABLE 4.7

Historical Comparison of Habitat Resources

	Current	Pristine	Percent Loss
Native grassland or foothill open oak woodland	676	6,780	90
Coast live oak forest	215	750	71
Soft chaparral	601	2,050	71
Hard chaparral	179	350	49
Marsh	10	958	99
Riparian	77	156	51
Total	1,758	11,044	84

Note: Pristine figures are approximate, based on extrapolation from limited descriptive information.

Sources: Current: Planning Task Force; Pristine: Santa Barbara Coast Survey Map 1852; Menzie 1924; Bolton 1927.

Marsh areas are among the most productive and diverse habitats because they act as spawning nurseries and feeding areas for commercially important ocean species. For these reasons the Coastal Commission is charged through Proposition 20 with the responsibility of restoring and preserving coastal marshland habitats. Although it is too late for "El Estero" to be restored, it is worth noting that if it had been allowed to remain, it would now represent 3 percent of the total remaining marshland in the state (Coastal Land Environment 1974).

The next most endangered habitat in Santa Barbara is an eight-acre area of native grassland (Stipa spp.) off Las Tunas Road in the Riviera neighborhood. This area has been evaluated for permanent preservation by the Nature Conservancy but is currently subject to development into single-family residences under current zoning.

In addition to its value as a native grassland preserve, the site is the habitat for a significant tarantula population. The entire habitat complex offers a unique opportunity for scientific investigation. In recent years classes from UCSB and staff from the Museum of Natural History have used this site for biological studies.

One other area containing remnants of native grassland is located in Lower Riviera. It is also zoned for residential development (E-1) under existing city policy. Most of the remaining high-ranking habitats are found at the city's periphery in the low-density neighborhoods along the foothills. Analysis of the distribution of habitats, by rankings, show that the high-density neighborhoods (lowest-income neighborhoods) have the least, and ecologically, the poorest quality open space. Conversely, those neighborhoods that are the least crowded (and highest-income) have the most and best-quality open space (Table 4.8).

Stream Environment

Existing Conditions

Each of the city's streams and their tributaries were examined for restrictive fencing, flood-control modifications, and possible pollution.

As recently as 40 years ago the city's principal creeks (Arroyo Burro, Mission, and Sycamore) carried water most of the year and supported significant steelhead (Salmo gardauri) runs. The "riparian" environments (the area directly affected by the stream) are second only to the marsh habitats in their biological diversity and productivity.

At present the streams are relatively unaltered for only approximately one-quarter of their length through the city. Most of these unaltered areas are located in the canyon sections of the city, while the areas of severe degradation are located where the creeks approach the ocean.

Because many structures were built prior to the enactment of a city ordinance that required a 25-foot setback for houses, offices, and garages, sections of the stream environment were "stabilized" by a variety of flood-control measures. The most severe of these "stabilization" projects was the channelization along Mission Creek between Canon Perdido and Arrellaga streets. These areas are nearly biologically sterile most of the year. Table 4.9 shows how "stabilization" has impacted and degraded the natural riparian zone and the creek bed.

TABLE 4.8

Comparative Habitat Resources of Four High-Income Neighborhoods and Four Low-Income Neighborhoods

	Median Income	Total Neighborhood Acres	Habitat Acres	Percent Habitat Acres of Total Acres	Percent Habitat Pristine or Near-Pristine
Affluent neighborhoods					
Riviera	17,765	633.6	90	14	46
Foothill	17,677	543.2	242	45	87
Cielito	14,971	1,249.3	807	65	91
Eucalyptus Hill	13,551	676.7	163	24	51
Lower-income neighborhoods					
Eastside	6,599	444.9	16	4	27
Laguna	6,286	330.4	9.3	3	3
West Downtown	5,117	197.6	7.5	4	0
Lower East	5,114	173.6	2	1	0

Source: Planning Task Force. Income data from 1970 Census as aggregated by Task Force (see Volume 3).

Stream "Stabilization" Modifications

TABLE 4.9

	Total Feet of Stream	Fencing	Walls	Sandbag Wall	Rockfill	Cement Channel
Arroyo Burro Creek						
Campanil	1,920	300	241	125	--	--
Hidden Valley	5,775	4,654	53	603	--	--
North State[a]	5,760	4,761	401	--	--	1,284
San Roque	3,720	1,177		1,141	--	--
Total	17,175	10,892	695	1,869	0	1,284
Percentage	--	63.4	4.0	10.8	0	7.5
Mission Creek						
West Downtown	12,000	5,276	1,466	1,242	--	1,302
Oak Park[b]	4,300	8,398	3,047	1,978	--	3,012
Upper East[c]	3,900	380	427		--	--
Total	20,200	14,054	4,940	3,220	0	4,314
Percentage	--	69.6	24.5	15.9	0	21.4
Sycamore Creek						
Waterfront	486	200	--	120	--	--
East Beach	1,200	999	450	189	374	--
East Side	4,380	2,279	689	573	--	--
Riviera	3,300	856	642	588	--	--
Total	9,366	4,334	1,781	1,470	374	0
Percentage	--	46.3	19.0	15.7	4.0	0

[a]Boundary between North State and North View.
[b]Partially as border on North State and Samarkand.
[c]Border between Upper East and East San Roque.
Source: Santa Barbara Planning Task Force.

In addition to the problems created by stabilization are those caused by the proximity of development and storm-drain runoff. Single tests conducted at several sites along the lower section of Mission and Sycamore Creeks indicated significant levels of pollution in the form of high coliform bacteria counts. Pollution from storm-drain runoff includes pet feces, biocides from gardens, and oils and other traffic-generated contaminants that are periodically washed off the streets.

To place perspective on the impact of these phenomena we can refer to data drawn from New York City. There, nearly 500,000 dogs contribute 5,000 to 20,000 tons of feces and 600,000 to 1 million gallons of urine to stream pollution through storm-drain runoff. Assuming direct comparability between New York City and Santa Barbara, Santa Barbara's 11,000 dogs could potentially contribute 440 tons of feces and 13,000 to 22,000 gallons of urine to stream pollution through runoff.

Despite the pollution problems, the creeks still support a variety of life and act as travel corridors for mammals and birds. An indication of the effect of pollution modification of Santa Barbara's creeks can be seen by comparing these creeks with the generally unspoiled Refugio Creek, 21 miles northwest of the city. Refugio Creek flows through untouched riparian habitat throughout its course and supports a diverse population of aquatic insects throughout its length. The creeks of the city reveal a dramatically different pattern. Each of the three creeks shows a significant reduction in the number and species of aquatic insects as the creeks pass through the city.[16] Aquatic insects are a basic source of food for larger animals in the riparian habitat. Degradation of the creek, reflected in decreasing species and quantities of these insects, has the effect of reducing the number of birds, mammals, and reptiles in the riparian zone.

Studies by the U.S. Government Bureau of Land Management and the State of California suggest that a 100-foot untouched natural riparian zone along creeks is necessary for healthy stream environments (Sadler 1970; Federal Water Pollution Control Administration 1970). By this standard the city's 25-foot setback requirement would appear to be inadequate.

Ameliorative Possibilities

By way of contrast, the city of Chico (population 21,000) maintains the 2,400-acre Bidwell Park that contains Chico Creek. The riparian zone along the creek's course through the city is fully protected and supports salmon and steelhead runs annually. Other native plants and animals abound, despite the fact that the park receives heavy use from the majority of residents within the city.

It is perhaps pertinent that Chico Creek passes through all income areas and is within walking distance of most of the city's residents.

If the population of Santa Barbara continues to increase, the
three city creeks are likely to suffer further degradation under current regulations. Only setting aside a corridor at least 100 feet on
each side of the stream as a natural open space and subsequent removal of unnecessary flood-control structures as part of a redevelopment plan would result in enhancement of the stream and stream-
side environment. However, much of the lower portions of the creeks
will continue to remain dry during the late spring, summer, and fall.

Specific Neighborhood Investigations

Three neighborhoods were chosen to provide a picture of the
range of ecological problems that will arise as population increases.
These include West Downtown, East Beach, and Cielito.

West Downtown

Existing Conditions. West Downtown contains 197.6 acres and a
current density of 17.2 people per acre. Existing open space consists of less than eight acres (all of it introduced grassland) of
poorest-quality habitat and 2.8 acres of the next-poorest-quality
habitat. This little remaining open space is on or near Mission
Creek.

Approximately 12,000 feet of Mission Creek flows through the
neighborhood. Most of its length is of poor ecological quality because of the channeling of the creek bed. The highest coliform
counts of the study were recorded in this section of Mission Creek.

Many of the older residential dwellings abut the creek; some
of them have small yards whose drainages are directed into the
creek bottom.

Despite the destruction of the riparian woodland, the creek
still supports a variety of wildlife consisting of two frog and one
toad species, and a variety of aquatic insects. Each year seeds
from many native and introduced species are washed downstream
and sprout on the creek bottom during the spring where they provide
an esthetically pleasing display of color as well as a food supply for
resident and migrant birds. A few patches of native riparian vegetation (primarily willows) offer perching, nestling, and feeding
habitats for birds; the creek is still used extensively as a travel
corridor for migrant bird species in the spring and fall.

Seasonal changes can be seen along this stretch of Mission Creek, perhaps more than anywhere else in the city. Each winter the creek flows steadily after the first major rainfall, sometimes to a depth of ten feet. These heavy flows scour its altered channel, washing out buried debris and depositing debris from upstream. The stream is relatively lifeless in winter and only an occasional errant steelhead enters the creek at present. The native vegetation is leafless, and a few birds such as White Crowned Sparrows move along the stream from tree patch to tree patch. Tree frogs in large numbers gather in all the pools where the bottom is not cemented, and their mating chorus can be heard for a block, drowning out the roar of the freeway.

By late spring, pollution inputs concentrate because of declining stream flow. Numbers of insect species diminish and become dominated by species, such as flies, that are tolerant of pollution. In late spring and early summer raccoon and possum tracks, in addition to many dog tracks, are often seen in the creek between Haley and de la Guerra streets. Bats and swallows gather emerging aquatic insects at dusk. By late summer most of the water in the creek is from street and yard runoff. The creek bed has gained an increasing array of junk. Flies are prevalent, and occasionally a Norway rat can be seen along the creek. In the fall birds migrate along the creek, and a bulldozer scrapes all the debris to the sides of the creek or piles it into a truck and carts it to the dump.

Impacts of Growth. An increase in population in West Downtown to any of the projected PIPs might destroy all the remaining open space not purchased for parks. The apartment-zoned areas of West Downtown are likely to experience a 42-percent population increase under current zoning, and this will cause further degradation of the single most important natural resource within the neighborhood: Mission Creek.

According to the City Pound personnel, most of Santa Barbara's dog problems are concentrated around apartment houses. Increases in "dog problems" will occur as more apartments are built and the human population increases. The neighborhood already has a significant population of "free-ranging" dogs—that is, dogs that run free most of the time but may belong to someone. (Beck [1973] calculated that approximately one-third of the dog population in Baltimore is "free-ranging.") The dogs tip over garbage, bite people, and their feces are a hazard to small children. Indirect problems caused by dogs, and to a lesser extent cats, are a proliferation of houseflies and fecal runoff into the creeks. Houseflies can spread a variety of diseases, including typhoid, cholera, dysentery, and tuberculosis.

At present, the back and front yards of the single-family residences contain mature vegetation supporting a variety of native birds.
As the neighborhood undergoes transformation from single-family
residences to apartments (under existing zoning and General Plan
designations), these areas will be lost, and bird populations will decrease. Like the rest of the city, however, the neighborhood has
many species of large trees lining the streets, and these will continue to support good nesting bird populations, including barn owls
and sparrow hawks.

Increased growth in West Downtown will result in further
degradation of Mission Creek, which already shows signs of being a
health danger.

East Beach

Existing Conditions. East Beach contains 377 acres, of which 15
percent (59 acres) are open spaces of introduced grassland and/or
other exotic plantings of relatively low-ranked habitats. This neighborhood now contains the only marsh areas left in the city (17 acres)
and the brackish Bird Refuge lagoon, with its nesting populations of
Black Crowned Night Herons and other water-associated bird species.

Despite their degraded correlation, the open areas near
Cabrillo Boulevard, with the remnant marsh areas, contain a rich
array of bird species. There were 34 species and 905 total birds
were seen in this area in 11.5 hours of observation from April 4 to
May 11, 1974.

Sycamore Creek passes through the neighborhood before entering the ocean at the waterfront. The stream has been severely
altered along its brief course (1,200 feet) through the neighborhood;
most of the creek has visible man-made alterations.

The rest of the neighborhood is a mixture of industrial areas
and houses with few trees or well-developed yards. Several large
old buildings stand vacant and are potential breeding areas for Norway rats, although there seems no severe rat problem at present.
"Free-ranging" dogs are a problem within this neighborhood. Killing
and harassment of animals has occurred at the Child's Estate zoo
for several years.[17]

Impacts of Growth. Development of the East Beach area, whether
for tourism, as suggested by the General Plan, or for manufacturing,
as permitted under zoning, will completely alter the habitat. Under
these conditions it is unlikely that any marsh areas will be preserved,
despite the charge of the Coastal Commission to "Preserve and re-
store" marsh habitats.

There are also preconditions that indicate that a significant
rat problem may develop in this neighborhood in the future. There
is a growing number of restaurants nearby, in addition to the
Child's Estate with its animal food and a feedstore near large old
buildings. If large Norway rat populations become established,
control is difficult (Field 1972). Norway rats, like houseflies, can
transmit a variety of diseases, including plague, endemic typhus,
rat bite fever, salmonellosis, and leptospirosis.

Cielito

Existing Conditions. Within Cielito's 1,249 acres are many steep
slopes and canyons with thin soils. The natural vegetation is dominated by hard and soft chaparral, and there is some open oak woodland on the gentler slopes. The majority of the upper neighborhood
is contiguous undeveloped habitats relatively free of roads and houses.

Three main branches of Sycamore Creek have their headwaters
in or near this neighborhood and portions of these branches have
water all year round in normal rain years.

Among the city's neighborhoods, Cielito has the lowest residential density and the next to least area devoted to roads. These
factors, coupled with the fact that the recently (1972) acquired 200
acre Parma property adjoins portions of the Sycamore Creek's
headwaters, make this neighborhood the best place in the city for
viewing large mammals, including on occasion black bears, bobcats,
deer, and mountain lions. Bird watching is good here as well, and,
during approximately 24 hours of observation scattered through
June 1974, 53 species of birds were identified in the neighborhood.

Although alteration of Sycamore Creek is relatively minor in
this neighborhood, a major problem exists in the steep headwaters,
where recent clearing of large portions of chaparral, oak forest,
and riparian woodland down to the stream edge has occurred.

Impacts of Growth. Steepness of slopes and inaccessibility of some
of the canyon areas may make building in some parts of this neighborhood economically unfeasible. However, continued advances in
construction techniques may allow construction of residences at the
projected maximum densities as population pressures increase.
Regardless of the increase in population (or in dwelling units per
acre), any additional building in the chaparral zone would result in
an increased fire hazard, because the more accessible the chaparral,
the more likely it is that fire will occur.

If the market for avocados continues to make it economically
advantageous, it is likely that chaparral areas above the Parma

property will continue to be cleared and planted. The unrestricted clearing of vegetation to the stream bed will result in silt degradation and possible flooding from increased runoff downstream from the cleared site. If significant amounts of rain fall during the first year after such clearing, this silting and flooding could affect every neighborhood along Sycamore Creek below the cleared area. The Parma property does not offer protection from the introduction of harmful agricultural practices upstream, nor does it prevent development along the upstream areas that could present dual problems of increased runoff to the streams and fire hazard.

Zoned and/or purchased buffer strips have been suggested for the chaparral slopes (City of Santa Barbara 1972). A Palo Alto study demonstrated that purchasing open space along the periphery of the city was cheaper than allowing development of these areas (Livingston and Blayney 1971).

Summary

In summary, the above site-specific examples seem to indicate three major points:

1. Degradation of riparian habitat is rapidly occurring due to lack of controls on construction, dogs, channelization, and creek contaminants.

2. Realization of PIP projections will greatly accelerate these problems and compound difficulties of preserving open space within the city of Santa Barbara.

3. Heavy population encroachments on the steep chaparral slopes and deep canyons will render these areas dangerously susceptible to areawide fires, flooding, erosion, and silation.

DISASTERS

Situated on an alluvial coastal valley in a region of active faulting, Santa Barbara has experienced severe ground shaking from earthquakes on several occasions. In addition to the threats from earthquakes, the city's chaparral-covered mountain backdrop is perennially subject to ravaging brushfires and the concomitant dangers from flooding and mudslides. Santa Barbara is also one of five areas in the county coastal region that could be subject to inundation from a seismic sea wave, or "tsunami," in the event of an earthquake. For these reasons, the city of Santa Barbara ranks high as an area of potential geologic hazards in the Geology Master Plan for the State of California.

Our aim is to delineate regions within the city where major
disaster potentials lie and to relate this knowledge to the distributive
patterns of future growth, thus determining the condition under which
future growth will aggravate disaster problems. Because the data
required to do a more thorough and detailed hazards/land-use correlation do not exist, we can merely point out those areas that deserve
special investigation in considering future population policies.

We will first outline the location of major hazards areas for
potential earthquake, fire, and flood disasters. For each of these
we will discuss those areas of the city that, because of their projected densities under the PIPs, could be most affected by natural
disasters.[18]

Disaster Impacts Due to Earthquakes

General Background

Damage from earthquakes in Santa Barbara has been well
documented by historians, research geologists, and seismologists.
Santa Barbara is located in a region of active faulting that in recent
history has experienced four significant earthquakes: the 1812, 1925,
and 1941 quakes in the Santa Barbara Channel, and the 1927 quake at
Point Arguello. In addition to these major disturbances, the Santa
Barbara Channel has experienced many series of low-magnitude
earthquakes, or earthquake "swarms."

The city is underlaid by three faults: the Lavigia, Mission
Ridge, and Mesa faults (see Figure 4.5). The Lavigia fault, which
is considered inactive, is located in the Campanil Hills and Alta
Mesa area.[19] The Mission Ridge fault, a potentially active one,
runs northeast through the city, passing through the La Cumbre
Plaza area and on to the Mission Ridge. The exact location of the
trace of the Mesa fault, which is suspected to be active, has not been
finally determined.[20] A fourth fault, known as the Red Mountain
fault, is located offshore in the Santa Barbara Channel; it is considered by some experts to be potentially more hazardous than any of
the others.[21]

Earthquakes can generate various seismic hazards, such as
ground shaking, liquefaction, compaction, landslides, or tsunami.
Of these hazards, ground shaking is considered the most serious
problem and the one most likely to cause damage to urbanized areas.
The intensity of ground shaking is dependent not so much on a proximity to the earthquake epicenter as it is to the nature of a region's
underlying soils and geologic formations. For example, areas of alluvial deposits with relatively unconsolidated sediments or formations

FIGURE 4.5

Disaster Map, City of Santa Barbara

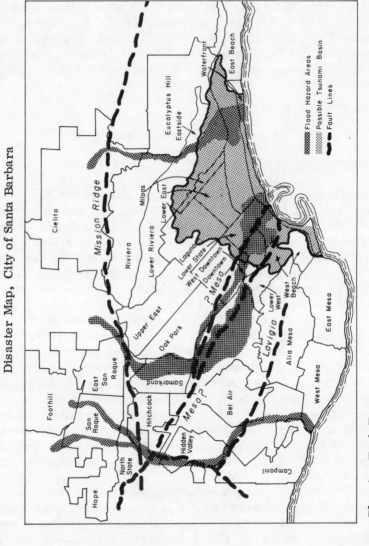

Source: Planning Task Force.

with high water content can magnify the shaking intensity of an earthquake.

Because Santa Barbara is situated on top of deep alluvial deposits between two fault blocks, it is particularly susceptible to
groundshaking.[22] Many portions of the city were formerly low-
drainage areas of swamps, estuaries, and streambeds that were
subsequently drained and filled, these low-lying areas are often
characterized by high groundwater table levels that make them most
susceptible to high-intensity ground shaking and additional complica-
tions, such as differential settling and liquefaction in the event of an
earthquake.[23] However, the degree to which these potential hazards
might occur would depend upon the magnitude of the earthquakes.

Location of Major Seismic Hazards

Although the entire city of Santa Barbara has a ground-shaking
intensity potential, available geological data and historical research
conducted on the 1925 earthquake point to large areas in the southeast region of the city as being particularly vulnerable (see Olsen
1972).

Areas particularly susceptible lie immediately below the mesa
and in the waterfront area stretching from the harbor to the bird
refuge (encompassing the neighborhoods of West Beach, portions of
Lower State, and East Beach). These regions could also experience
possible ground-failure hazards such as liquefaction (see Moore and
Tabor 1974).

Landslides as a result of an earthquake are most likely to occur
in the area along upper Sycamore Canyon Road and in the hillsides
between Las Positas Road and Las Palmas Drive (Moore and Tabor
1974). The coastal bluffs along the shoreline of the mesas, which
experienced landsliding during the 1925 earthquake, are also an area
prone to slides in the event of a major earthquake (Olsen 1972).

Areas situated on or immediately adjacent to the trace of an
active fault run increased risk of damage in the event of an earthquake; the areas bordering the suspected trace of the mesa fault fall
into such a category.

Impacts Due to Increased Population

In general, single-story, wood-framed structures can withstand the stresses of ground shaking and linear acceleration better
than can structures made of less-flexible building materials. Particularly susceptible are buildings constructed of unreinforced
masonry or brick, as found, for example, in many pre-1933 buildings
that still exist in Santa Barbara (Sage 1972). Although it is not well

understood, multistory buildings can experience the critical problem of resonance during an earthquake, due to the relationship of the building height and the thickness of underlying soils or alluvium. For example, a resonance may be created in a three-story building, whereas a four- or five-story building would not resonate, given its depth of foundation materials.

Therefore, those neighborhoods located in maximum earthquake intensity zones expected to undergo a transition from predominantly single-family to multiple dwelling units at higher population levels may experience increased risks from ground shaking and linear acceleration, if buildings constructed there are not adequately reinforced according to special Uniform Building Codes.[24]

Based on existing land-use policy, the high-density neighborhoods of West Downtown, Oak Park, Lower West, Laguna, East Side, West Beach, and Westside will be more vulnerable to greater risks. Of particular concern are the neighborhoods bordering the suspected trace of the Mesa fault. Some multistoried apartment buildings may have already been constructed on, or in close proximity to, this fault (Olsen 1972). The East Beach neighborhood should also anticipate severe ground shaking and possible ground failure problems in the event of an earthquake.

Tsunami Hazards

The State Geology Master Plan for California has designated Santa Barbara as a region having high tsunami probability in the event of an earthquake. The city harbor area is one of five along this coastal region that could experience inundation and damage from such a wave. Although the possibility of a major transoceanic tsunami inflicting damage to this area is slight (Sage 1972), a locally based tsunami (originating from a quake centered in the channel) could possibly have a serious effect on the low-lying areas of the city (Sage 1972; Moore and Taber 1974).

Estimates as to the size of such a wave or the extent of its potential damage are difficult to make because the historical record is incomplete and subject to controversy. There is only one well-documented account of a tsunami striking along the shoreline region of Santa Barbara and San Luis Obispo counties; it occurred during the 1927 Point Arguello quake, but the wave was of relatively small height. Based on existing geologic knowledge of the Santa Barbara area's seismic activity, ocean floor stability, and coastal configuration, it has been estimated that should the maximum anticipated earthquake occur in the channel, a potential tsunami generated by this quake might reach 12 feet in height with a possible 24-foot run-up

(Sage 1972).[25] Low-lying areas of Santa Barbara below an elevation of 40 feet could be subject to possible inundation (see Moore and Taber 1974).

Neighborhoods that would be particularly affected in the event of a major tsunami include portions of West Beach, Lower State, and East Beach. Because of the lack of historical records and geological evidence, there seems no justification for the removal of buildings or human activity from these areas. However, it should be noted that increased development in these areas due to growth would tend to magnify the damage resulting from a possible earthquake-generated tsunami.

Disaster Potential from Fire

The danger from wildfire is extreme. Although fire risks within the urbanized areas of Santa Barbara will not necessarily increase in proportion to population, the foothill areas of Santa Barbara, with their natural coverings of chaparral, will experience increased fire risks with population growth. Development of homes in these areas and the corresponding increase in through-traffic would lead to greater fire risks and damage potentials. This has proved the case in Los Angeles County, where development has taken place in areas of chaparral-covered foothills. There, damage due to fires and subsequent winter flooding and mudslides have been of disaster proportions.

Disaster Potential from Floods

Three major creeks traverse the City of Santa Barbara: Arroyo Burro, Mission, and Sycamore Canyon creeks. Areas bordering these creeks have been indicated as flood-hazard zones by the United States Army Corps of Engineers in a preliminary study (1973) for the Federal Flood Insurance Program. According to this study, these areas or zones encompass lands that could be subject to possible inundation from flooding, up to and including the "100-year" flood.[26] Additional areas have been demarcated as possible flood hazard zones by the County Flood Control Office, in particular, the area of Westside.

Further study of flood-disaster potential seems warranted in areas that are projected for density increases. Such areas lie along Sycamore Creek, with the neighborhoods of East Beach and East Side, and portions of Oak Park, West Downtown, and Westside bordering Mission Creeks.

Apart from direct hazards, there are potential economic considerations that involve the new Federal Flood Insurance Program. Under this program, homeowners living in areas designated as flood-hazard zones can qualify for federally subsidized flood insurance. However, once these zones have been formally delineated, the city must comply with federal regulations regarding setbacks and structural safety or lose eligibility for the program. Federal grants, loans, and guarantees of loans on property will not be allowed to homeowners residing in these areas unless their property is covered by National Flood Insurance.

Summary

The preliminary evidence in this chapter seems to indicate that the areas in the city slated for the most intense land uses at future population levels are also those areas most susceptible to potential disasters. It would seem warranted, therefore, that a more detailed and thorough investigation of these regions should be undertaken as part of implementing a population policy.

ESTHETICS

How beautiful! when the wood smoke goes up
straight, and the pepper trees stand unstirring,
and behind the screen of the tall Eucalyptus trees
the fallen sun glows, a long slow fire over the
sea, and the lavender color-mist rises between.
How beautiful, the mountains, behind us, remote
in that late light, a little unearthly!
      The loveliness of these evenings moves the
heart; and of the morning, shining, cool fragrant.
There is something in it all of that dream, as of
Paradise, which stirred the Italian painters in old
days. Well may it be sainted--San Ysidro, Santa
Barbara!

                                    --John Galsworthy--

The beauty of the city, from the very first days of its modern-era development, has been its most remarkable attribute, and it remains to this day the cornerstone of its economy, its international reputation, and the feeling of well-being of its residents. Whatever detracts from the beauty of Santa Barbara, detracts from everything else as well.

It is impossible to express in quantitative terms the significance of the city's esthetic assets, just as it is impossible to assign a dollar cost to a loss in esthetic value. There are no amounts of money that can express the loss of a poem, the lack of inspiration for a painting, a blissful moment not experienced, or merely a day made less pleasant. But we can note that Santa Barbarans are often people who have chosen to live there because of this beauty, and they sacrifice income and convenience to experience these qualities. Over the years then the population has tended to be selective of those kinds of people most appreciative of those assets. Hence, a decline in the city's esthetic values is particularly costly to this population.

The past decade has seen a number of assaults on the beauty of Santa Barbara, unparalleled both in their degree and in their intractability. In the late 1960s in the channel waters became the site of oil exploration and drillings; the horizon that once was a poetic inspiration came to be littered with oil platforms visible from every oceanfront vantage point. The spill itself was an esthetic horror, but it was only symptomatic of a larger development: The waters of Santa Barbara Channel had been converted from an esthetic and recreation resource into an area of industrial use. The year following the spill, the elite magazine Town and Country removed Santa Barbara from its list of the world's most fashionable watering spots.

It is also in the last decade that air pollution has come to Santa Barbara, increasingly visible as the years have gone by. Smog blocks the views, and the views are a crucial esthetic resource. As yet mild by Los Angeles standards, smog in Santa Barbara is still a blight; it is particularly important to the vacation and second-home choices of those who can afford to travel the world in search of the few remaining places that do have clean air.

A number of other negative developments have also occurred. The streams of the city, once natural and free flowing, have been badly degraded and artificially dammed and channeled. Public investments in landscape detailing, park maintenance, and some recreation facility upkeep have all declined. The city's Parks Department, for example, has doubled the amount of acreage under its control, but has remained constant in the size of its maintenance staff. The results are apparent throughout the city: The flower borders that once graced Cabrillo Boulevard are gone; playlot equipment is rusting and unsightly; street trees and park specimen plantings are ignored. Unwillingness to make investments in improvement or expansion of the sewer plant has resulted in polluted ocean beaches and foul smells in the heart of the tourist area.

Growth of the city has had the direct effect of turning natural hillsides into building sites, sometimes with esthetically benign effects, as on the Riviera, but sometimes with detrimental effects, as with several new projects in Eucalyptus Hill. Large expanses of the city's and the surrounding area's open spaces have come to be covered with tract homes and commercial shopping strips. The net effect has generally been to lessen the esthetic qualities of the area. Streets have had to be widened and have become increasingly clogged with traffic; lovely old houses have been replaced by undistinguished apartment buildings. Roadside plantings are removed, and rock walls are replaced by graffiti-covered concrete.

There have also been some positive esthetic developments in the city in recent years. Not all old buildings are beautiful, and some new construction has been more attractive than the structures that have been replaced. The creation of the State Street Mall added new lushness to the already-pleasant Downtown core; the city's new parking lots are profusely landscaped and attractively designed. Larger and larger areas of the city have come to be artifically landscaped--a development detrimental to nature, and especially so as the plantings mature, one that ameliorates some of the negative impacts of grading, road building, and commercial signs. Future creative use of public redevelopment can possibly have the effect of reclaiming streams, restoring or relocating old structures, and providing for a higher quality of architecture than would otherwise come about through the natural course of growth-induced private, unorganized redevelopment. Even through redevelopment, however, these goals are not easy to achieve.

We think that future growth in Santa Barbara is likely to continue the esthetic trends of the past--trends generally in a negative direction. The quality of the air, if state and federal standards are in fact enforced, may be improved, and thus the rate of deterioration we have seen in the past may be halted or even reversed (see air-quality discussion earlier in this chapter). But the other effects will be more difficult to reverse, particularly the consequences of traffic congestion and the destruction of the general small-scale charm and romance of the community that, because it is difficult even to describe adequately, is even more difficult to protect through legislation or policy.

Growth will bring widened streets and more parking lots, increased concentrations of litter, more wear and tear on public plantings, greater amounts of graffiti. As land becomes scarcer, the higher costs of developing steep sites will be paid to serve a growing housing market, and the sort of scarring that has recently occurred in Eucalyptus Hill will also occur in other areas with steep terrain. Wherever there is construction, there is the potential for disturbing views; seldom are they improved. Hillsides become less natural; the topography is obscured. The ocean is made more difficult to see from more and more places as low-lying buildings tend to be replaced with higher ones. The in-city areas, as seen from above, become increasingly made up of paving and large-scale flat-roofed structures replacing vegetation or small-scale variegated roof lines.

The city's architectural qualities are particularly vulnerable to growth. Of the various growth PIPs, only the lowest (the Half-Density Probable) would have the likely effect of saving a substantial number of interesting structures by reducing the financial induce-ment to replace old houses with apartments in those older areas of the city where both the General Plan and Zoning indicate higher-density usage. It is an unfortunate coincidence that it is just those areas of the city with the most remarkable architectural worth that also tend to be zoned for more intensive use.

Many of the city's interesting structures are thus unprotected, and even in El Pueblo Viejo buildings of great charm can be replaced at the whim of the marketplace. More than is generally realized, the great bulk of the city's Spanish Revival architecture was built within a very brief period immediately following the earthquake. It was the deliberate result not only of inspired citizens but also of a city council that gave an Architectural Board of Review the short-lived power to deny any construction not in conformity with the Spanish style as they interpreted it. Lacking such controls in force today, current construction costs being so high, the likelihood is slight that new construction will maintain the standards of the past. Thus, growth will increasingly dilute the impact of the city's heritage represented by the fine old construction. Rather than its being the architecture typical of the city, there is the danger that it will repre-sent only an enclave serving more as a museum for tourists than as the routine backdrop of everyday life.[27]

NOTES

1. The South Coast Region Study area is approximately bounded by the Santa Ynez Mountain ridge on the north, the Pacific Ocean on the south, Carpinteria on the east, and Ellwood on the west. The Task Force provided GRC with basic population figures that GRC used to obtain estimates of future emissions and air quality.

2. The actual figures used by GRC throughout this chapter vary negligibly from the final Task Force PIP estimates due to the fact that time did not permit GRC to await final adjustments. These differences are as follows: Low PIP, GRC: 251, 081; Low PIP, Task Force: 252,599; High PIP, GRC: 327,221; High PIP, Task Force, 322, 545. These differences are so small (0.6 and 1.5 per-cent) they would not affect study results.

3. The labor involved in this task was performed by regular
and volunteer members of the Task Force. The South Coast Transportation Study designation was changed to Santa Barbara County
Transportation Study in 1972.

4. The SCOTS study area corresponds closely to our South
Coast study area. The future-population figure, supplied by the
County Planning Department, is in contrast to the figure reported in
the SCOTS 1969 Progress Report of an anticipated 254,700 population
for the South Coast under the General Plan. We have not resolved
the discrepancy. To the extent that the reported SCOTS figure is
correct, the emissions estimates in the present study understate
actual emissions to occur at the various PIPs.

5. The resulting daily freeway and surface street VMT (in
thousands of miles) for the two SCOTS simulations keyed to the grid
in Figure 4.1 are presented in Vol. 3 as Figures 5.1.1 through 5.1.4.
No consideration is given to the higher emissions likely to develop as
traffic speed deteriorates at higher PIPs.

6. See Volume 3, appendix 5.1.

7. Although now superseded, this General Plan was the basis
for the SCOTS transportation projections and hence was used for the
sake of consistency between mobile- and stationary-emissions projections.

8. Federal Register 38, no. 14 (January 22, 1973), Pt. 2,
p. 2194; California Air Resources Board, "The State of California
Implementation Plan for Achieving and Maintaining the National
Ambient Air Quality Standards," Rev. 4 (December 31, 1973).

9. For a detailed breakdown, see Volume 1, Table 5.4.

10. Howard W. Linnard, California Air Resources Board,
private communication, May 1974.

11. Volume 3 contains, in Figures 5.1.5 through 5.1.13, the
emissions in pounds per hour in each grid square for these scenarios.

12. Additional isometrics for other pollutants and other views
of air pollutants are omitted from this book, but are contained in
Volume 1, Figures 5.2 through 5.7, and Volume 3, Figures 5.14
through 5.25.

13. At the time of this writing (1976) there is a disagreement
between the California Air Resources Board (CARB) and the Los
Angeles County Air Pollution Control District (LAAPCD) as to the
method of calibrating the oxidant instruments (see Los Angeles
Times, July 27, 1974). Since the health standards were set by
LAAPCD measurements, which are low if the state is correct, the
standard could be as high as 0.11 ppm. The Santa Barbara stations
are operated by CARB procedures. Thus, if LAAPCD procedures
are correct, all readings should be reduced by about 30 percent and
the air quality standard held at 0.8 ppm. The results in this report
are based on reported values and have not had any adjustment applied.

14. See "Quietest Place is the Reservoir," Santa Barbara News-Press, February 18, 1969.

15. A complete enumeration of habitat acreage for each city neighborhood--ranked into four categories for each of eight principal habitat types--is contained in Volume 1, Table 5.11. Maps for the city as a whole and for each neighborhood were also prepared to aid the city in locating these ranked habitats and are presented in Volume 1, Figures 5.13 through 5.21.

16. Histograms summarizing this information for Refugio Creek and for each of the three principal creeks that pass through the city, at various locations, are presented in Volume 1, Figures 5.11 and 5.12.

17. Personal communication from Curtis Globish, former zoo employee.

18. The special implications of these hazards for individual neighborhoods are discussed in Volume 1.

19. Faults are classified according to three categories of activity: active (movement in the past 11,000 years); potentially active (movement between the past 11,000 and 500,000 years); and inactive (no movement for more than 500,000 years).

20. In the preliminary Seismic Safety Element of the county Comprehensive Plan and Implementation program, geologic consultants Moore and Taber (1974) list the Mesa fault as active; they suggest this fault has the potential of a 6.4 maximum credible and 5.6 maximum probable magnitude earthquake (Richter scale). Moore and Taber also indicate two possible locations for the trace of the Mesa fault. Attempts to substantiate the location of the suspected trace of the fault have been made by Olsen (1972). Through this research, the southeast segment has been fairly well delineated, but the location of its northwest portion is still uncertain.

21. In their Wastewater Treatment Plant report for the City of Santa Barbara, Geotechnical Consultants, Inc. (1974) mention the Red Mountain fault as potentially dangerous to this area.

22. The preliminary Seismic Safety Element (Moore and Taber 1974) classifies the County of Santa Barbara into zones of relative ground-shaking intensity. The entire South Coast region, including the City of Santa Barbara, falls into Zone Category III (high ground-shaking probability).

23. Liquefaction occurs when soils, such as unconsolidated alluvial deposits, lose their cohesiveness during ground shaking, often causing structures built on them to sink or "float."

24. Recently, there has been debate on the adequacy of Uniform Building Codes. The San Fernando earthquake of 1971, where much more linear acceleration occurred than was anticipated, casts doubt on how much linear acceleration must be withstood by a building.

25. "Run-up" refers to the amplication of the wave height as it reaches shore, due to coastal configurations or tidal effects.

26. The "100-year flood" refers to the possibility of rainfall from a storm or storm system exceeding 20 inches in seven days, overloading the creekbed capacities. Such an outpouring in this area is expected to have a 1 percent probability of occurrence per year, which translates into one such storm per 100 years. However, the severity of Santa Barbara's flood hazards and the concept of a "100-year flood" potential are open to debate, given the relatively short recorded history of flooding in this area (see Kelley 1972).

5

ECONOMIC EFFECTS
OF GROWTH: THE
PRIVATE SECTOR

An important possible consequence of manipulating population levels is that the economic well-being of a city's citizens will somehow be affected. The most obvious result of limiting opportunities for growth is that the total income received by an individual city resident will be less than it otherwise would have been, as will be the total income of its citizens. More people translates as more dollars, both for local governments that seek rising property-tax assessment rolls and for a local business community that seeks increasingly higher levels of demand for consumer goods.

The problem with this line of reasoning is that it does not take into account the possibility that the larger amount of property added to the tax rolls may entail higher levels of government service to maintain it. Similarly, increases in the total dollar amount of local payrolls may merely reflect a larger number of people sharing the same proportionate total amount of income. And more customer dollars may bring the same proportionate gain in the number of competitors seeking it.

There is always a possible difference between economic well-being in the aggregate and economic well-being at the level of the individual. A city may be very rich as a totality, but many of its citizens may be individually very poor, and its costs of government may be high relative even to its vast tax base. The question to be answered is thus not whether growth leads to aggregate economic increase; it is clear that it does. Rather, the question is whether the individual citizen and the city government are better off economically with population growth.

Our discussion of the economic well-being of citizens is divided into two parts, reflecting the distinction often made between the public economy and the private economy. The public economy consists

113

of the revenues and the expenditures of government units, while the
private economy consists of the revenue and expenditure flows related to operation in the private sector. Evaluations of the way per
capita tax and revenues will fare (that is, the public economy) is reserved for Chapter 6. The present chapter will attempt to evaluate
the effects of growth on the economic well-being of the individual
citizen in terms of the private economy.

GROWTH AND THE INDIVIDUAL

Individual economic well-being can be conceived in a number
of ways. A common argument heard in the current growth controversy is that a city that does not grow will die, implying that a lack
of aggregate population growth will lead not merely to a lack of aggregate economic growth but to a decline in the individual economic
well-being of citizens as well. The contrary argument is sometimes
expressed, "The only thing that grows forever is a cancer," apparently implying that growth in itself leads to self-destruction, in economic as well as in other terms. We find both of these formulations
difficult to deal with because they lack any theoretical or empirical
base. We have attempted to examine the idea of economic well-being
to determine how its various components could be expected to fare
under various growth conditions. As directly as possible, we want
to measure the effect of growth upon the indicators that most closely
measure individual well-being. The most important of these indicators make up the bulk of our analysis. They are as follows:

● Median family income: What will be the likely effects of growth
    on the amount of money families receive in Santa Barbara?
● Local wealth: The well-being of citizens not only has to do with
    the monies they receive as reflected in family income, but
    also in the amount of wealth they have. Income reflects incom-
    ing money flows; wealth reflects resources, as are represented
    in stocks, bonds, savings accounts, land, and ownership of
    local businesses. For that portion of Santa Barbara's popula-
    tion that has significant holdings in these forms, the question
    can be asked whether or not growth will increase or decrease
    their financial resources.
● Unemployment: If the city grows, will there be a tendency for
    unemployment to increase or decrease? Will the number and
    proportion of citizens unfortunate enough to have no work what-
    ever grow larger or smaller?
● Cost of living: An increase in family income means nothing if it
    is associated with comparable increases in the cost of living.

Is there evidence to suggest that a city's cost of living would be affected by growth?

In the pages that follow we draw upon available studies and data sources to answer as many of these questions as we can. Taken together, these questions represent the concrete issues in the debate over the consequences of growth for the private economy.

PER CAPITA INCOME

Money comes to the residents of Santa Barbara from a number of sources. The percent of income coming to Santa Barbarans from the city's basic economic sources in 1970 was as follows (Keisker et al. 1970):

Property and pension income	31 percent
Tourism (visitor expenditures)	29 percent
Manufacturing (R & D)	20 percent
University	8 percent
All other elements	12 percent

The relationship between these income sources remained stable over the 1960-70 period, and we have no reason to doubt their continuity to the present and into the future.

Despite this stability in terms of income source, the median family income of Santa Barbarans has been on a continuous decline over the past decade, when compared to income changes in the country as a whole. That is, while incomes in both Santa Barbara and the country have been rising more or less continuously since 1960, they have risen in Santa Barbara much more slowly than elsewhere over the past decade. In other words, Santa Barbara has been "losing ground" relative to the rest of the country. Table 5.1 shows that while median family income in the city was considerably higher than that of the nation in 1950 and 1960, it was just below the national figure in 1970.

The fact that Santa Barbara's median family income is below that of the nation as a whole is all the more striking since the national figures do not control for marked regional differences in income; the South, for example, pulls down the national figures significantly. When Santa Barbara City is compared to the State of California, the 1970 ratio is still less favorable to Santa Barbara. Thus, for example, while 13.3 percent of Santa Barbarans were classified as living under poverty in the 1970 Census, only 11.1 percent of the residents of the state as a whole were so classified.

TABLE 5.1

Comparison of Median Family Income, Santa Barbara
and United States, 1950, 1960, and 1970

	Santa Barbara	United States	Ratio, Local:U.S.
1950	$3,466	$3,073	1.13
1960	6,477	5,660	1.14
1970	9,505	9,586	0.99

Source: United States, Department of Commerce, Bureau of
the Census, County and City Data Book, 1972 (Washington, D.C.:
U.S. Government Printing Office, 1973).

What is clear from these figures is that the growth of the city
and the rapid growth of its environs during the 1960-70 decade was
accompanied neither by an increase in the median family income of
Santa Barbarans relative to the rest of the country, nor by a reduction in poverty. The implication is quite the reverse. The rapid
growth of the period was accompanied by a lowering of city income
relative to the rest of the country. This does not, of course, "prove"
that growth was the cause of this income decline; it merely shows
that the two phenomena occurred together.

From our cross-city analysis (Chapter 2) there is evidence
that Santa Barbara's experience in this regard has been contrary to
comparably sized cities in the nation as a whole. There is a positive
relationship between size of place and median family income among
all urban areas, although this relationship disappears when one looks
only at urban areas outside the South. There is a positive relationship between urbanized-area growth and median family income.
Larger and more quickly growing places have higher median family
incomes than smaller and more slowly growing places. Consistent
with this finding, we learned that the proportion of the population living under conditions of poverty is generally unrelated to population
size; however, there is a tendency for more rapidly growing places
to have less poverty than more slowly growing places. This provides
a number of inconsistent findings to explain.

One major conceptual problem is to understand why median family income in Santa Barbara should have undergone relative decline
in the 1960-70 high-growth decade, while the experience of other
cities tends to imply the opposite kind of effect. We reconcile this
seeming contradiction by assuming that both in Santa Barbara and
elsewhere the key effect of growth on median family income data is

caused by the ratio of the income of the in-migrants relative to the
income of those already in residence.

In Santa Barbara, a city that had a population with a large,
wealthy aristocracy, increased growth primarily occurred through
increases in the tourist and R & D industries, whose net effect was
to bring into the city an occupational array that was less affluent
than that already present. R & D employees are of relatively high
income, and perhaps only in Santa Barbara could their addition to
the population (combined with other migrants) have had the consequence of lowering city income figures. For other cities of the country, however, growth would tend to have the opposite consequence:
Those industries undergoing most rapid growth tend to be higher paying (electronics, R & D), and accompanying population growth would
tend to be tied to these sorts of enterprises. The addition of these
sorts of industries in most cities would thus have the effect of increasing the overall income figures.

From this line of reasoning we conclude that city growth has
its effect on income through its effect of changing the types of people
who are in residence. Growth per se, we take it, does not greatly
affect the incomes of people already present, one way or the other.
We presume that it is the occupational type of the consumer, based
on the form of the economic expansion that created their migration,
that will have the greatest impact upon the income data of the area.

WEALTH

The income data we have presented on Santa Barbarans probably understate the economic well-being of the city's residents compared to the rest of the state and nation. Income data do not take
wealth into account, the financial resources that people have in terms
of savings, stocks, bonds, property, or family resources. There
are a number of reasons to believe that the city's residents have disproportionate amounts of wealth. First is the fact that so large a
proportion of the residents' income comes from property and pen-
sions--an amount that has remained constant as a proportion of local
income over the 1960-70 period. Some of this income is based in
wealth resources of the sort enumerated; persons with substantial
investments can show relatively low incomes, but they have the
wherewithal to sell off portions of those resources to make major
purchases at will. Similarly, the large number of students in the
area causes income data to decline but obscures the higher-income
spending styles that are characteristic of UCSB students. Evidence
for these propositions is contained in the fact that, according to our
cross-city analysis (Chapter 2), Santa Barbara has the country's

second median house value and is fifth highest in median gross rents paid among our 115 comparative cities. We interpret this, in light of the relatively less-impressive incomes of Santa Barbarans, as an indication of the existence of substantial wealth that allows relatively less-affluent people to live under relatively more-affluent conditions. Another possible interpretation is that Santa Barbarans are forced to purchase and rent more expensive housing than elsewhere and not that they have greater wealth. However, our same cross-city comparative data indicate that Santa Barbara residents live in housing with less overcrowding and fewer substandard units than those in other cities, indicating that people are actually spending more money for superior facilities.

There are certain area residents who are so situated that growth will increase their wealth. These are owners of property who would enjoy an increasing economic return on their holdings, should growth proceed at a rapid rate. These people would experience a wealth loss, should the population not grow and thereby cause the value of their properties to decline. It is important to note, however, that these potential wealth gains from growth derive from the expenditures of other Santa Barbarans. Rising land values and rents that bring wealth to some residents require other residents to pay increased amounts of money for housing. The total wealth of the citizens as a whole is thus unaffected: New wealth is not created; it is only redistributed. Perhaps for this reason, we find in our cross-city analysis that there is a weak tendency for the distribution of local wealth to become increasingly unequal (to be in the hands of proportionately fewer people) as the rate of population growth increases. What has been said of those with real property holdings is also true, to a more limited extent, of those in other businesses, particularly owners of construction companies.

There are no general cross-city data on the wealth resources of populations, and thus we are unable to compare cities in terms of the effects of growth on local wealth. But it is likely that even if there were such data, we would end up with the same kinds of problems in interpretation that we are faced with in the case of income, and we would be led to the same conclusions as those for income: Growth, per se, has little effect on wealth directly; rather, it is the types of people who come to a city, relative to those already present, that will determine the way the data on wealth correlate with growth over time. Thus, the apparent decline of Santa Barbara as a center for international high society would probably be reflected in a decline in wealth. The major effect on wealth would thus be due to the fact that a smaller proportion of current migrants is as rich as in the past. Growth is not likely, in itself, to make those individuals already there richer or poorer.

LOCAL RETAILING

As a city grows, all other things being equal, the increased number of inhabitants generates additional spending that comes to be reflected in increased local retail business activity. But growth not only brings additional spending, it also stimulates new entrants into the retailing field, thus increasing competition for a growing retail dollar. If population growth merely increases the number of business competitors in the same proportion as the increase in retailing dollars spent, there is no net gain to individual merchants. The gain is only to merchants in the aggregate.

Therefore, it is clear that the effect of growth on local merchants is more complex than ordinarily thought. Different business enterprises can be affected in quite different ways. The following are illustrations of some possible differential effects.

Monopoly Versus Competitive Business

In a few instances businesses have a virtual monopoly on a given type of service--a captive market that is not likely to be lost, even with continuous population growth. Thus, for example, since U.S. cities tend to have only one daily newspaper (or one newspaper company), continuous growth will not tend to create competition, except marginally at the suburban periphery. Under these circumstances, where the entry of a new competitor is quite difficult, growth becomes an important source of growing dollar volume for the business in question. Cable television is also an example of this situation. For those types of business in which new entries are relatively common, such as shoe stores, additional population growth will likely lead to additional entries, rather than additional dollar volume for existing businesses.

Skilled, Well-Financed Business
Versus Marginal Business

The creation of larger markets and increased retailing dollar flow does provide the opportunity for certain businesses to expand their volume and profits greatly, even if most will fail to do so. We would thus anticipate that those local businesses that are most able will prosper--perhaps well beyond their profitability under a slower growth scenario.

But this growth effect is a two-edged sword. Several illustrations appear in the history of Santa Barbara. The Santa Barbara

National Bank has, for example, expanded in both absolute and proportional terms as the city has grown in population, experiencing a
continuous increase in its share of local banking activity. On the
other hand, however, certain retail merchants, such as the city's
only home-owned department store (now defunct), have done less well
within the same period of growth. Sharpening of competition owing to
population growth may be a contributing factor to this lack of success.

"Unique" Versus Undifferentiated Establishments

Some businesses in Santa Barbara provide unique goods or services, found in very few cities in the world, or merchandise that is
particularly tied to the consumer styles of this area. Businesses of
this sort include art galleries, craft shops, and the retailing of
Spanish-American artifacts and building materials. The products
they offer are not easily replicable by new entrants. The city already
contains many fine galleries, accomplished craftspeople, and the like;
new entries with better financing or merchandising acumen probably
do not exist or would not have a strong competitive edge over existing businesses. On the other hand, merchants who sell manufactured
products, such as shoes, appliances, and mass-produced clothing,
can be more easily replaced by a new entry that possesses financial
or marketing superiority.

Local Ownership Versus Chain Stores, and CBD
Versus Outlying Shopping Centers

One source of new entries that provides especially acute competition is regional shopping centers and the chain stores they tend
to bring with them.
The development of regional shopping centers in outlying areas
has had a detrimental effect on Santa Barbara's CBD, just as it has
had on the CBD of virtually every U.S. city. Shopping centers, particularly the large-scale regional shopping centers, tend to accompany growth. They require a minimum threshold of population to
draw upon for their high-volume activity, and then tend not to enter
a market until that population base is either present or is anticipated
in the near future. Therefore, it is clear that population growth,
while producing increases in retailing activity, does not necessarily
secure a dominant CBD. As a proportion of total area retailing, the
CBD does not necessarily grow with increased population: The reverse may also occur.

There is evidence that the impact of Santa Barbara's one major shopping center, La Cumbre Plaza, has been less deleterious to the CBD than have the effects of similar projects on the CBDs of other cities. There are two reasons for this. First, Downtown Santa Barbara contains the types of unique shops that can hold their own against competition and with which regional shopping centers cannot or do not wish to compete. This partially has to do with tourist activity and the Downtown's proximity and special appeal to tourists. Second, La Cumbre Plaza seems to have added to the total retailing of primary shopping goods in the city, thus partially lessening the amount of business it might have taken away.[1] The increase was minimal, however, in terms of increased sales-tax revenue it generated, as indicated by the fact that city per capita sales-tax revenues did not substantially increase during this period (see Chapters 6 and 7 for documentation).

In 1967, before the development of La Cumbre Plaza, $26.63 million was transacted in the Downtown area. In its first year of operation, La Cumbre Plaza sales amounted to $21.6 million, while Downtown sales dropped to $22.7 million, a decline of 15 percent. Remaining city business locations experienced a similar decline of 14 percent (Keisker 1970, p. 48). This implies that La Cumbre Plaza increased the total amount of business done within the total city limits by $13.402 or 23 percent, apparently by drawing additional shoppers from elsewhere in the region or, alternatively, by inhibiting local residents from shopping out of town. Part of the net growth, however, is due to inflation (5.4 percent), per capita real-income growth (1.5 percent), and area population growth (1.1 percent). The real gain was thus closer to 15 percent.

Given the current judgment of several observers that "leakage" of current retail dollars continues to flow to Ventura and Goleta, an additional regional shopping center would likely have an effect similar to that created by the last one. Any potential increase in retail space would draw part of its business from existing merchants, no matter how much "leakage" it captured or how much new business it created. There would thus be a decline in the CBD and a rise in total retailing (if the project were located within the city limits). It is not possible to specify the magnitude involved.

A major new retail center not only has the effect of increasing total retail activity in the city; it also redistributes that activity. It redistributes retailing geographically from the traditional "strip" shopping streets to the new superblock centers. It also tends to redistribute business from locally owned independent "mom and pop" stores to chain outlets and franchises, and from a relatively large number of outlets to a relatively small number of outlets. Evidence for this is provided by a Task Force comparison of retail outlets in the La Cumbre Plaza with those presently in the Downtown core (defined as Sola to Ortega, Anacapa to Chapala). The results of this study are presented in Table 5.2.

TABLE 5.2

La Cumbre Plaza and Downtown Core:
Independents Versus Chain Stores

	Number of Stores	Total Dollar Volume of Stores	Percent Under Local Ownership	Percent Under Nonlocal Ownership
La Cumbre Plaza	60	21,600,000	48	52
Downtown Core	331	22,700,000	88	11

Sources: Santa Barbara Planning Task Force Downtown Survey; La Cumbre Plaza Management; Downtown Organization; Keisker (1970), p. 48.

A pattern emerges: Increased population growth induces increased shopping-center development, which leads to city capture of an increasing regional dollar volume of retail activity. But an increasing proportion of the total retailing activity comes to be dominated by nonlocal merchants who often supplant local ones.

La Cumbre Plaza has almost the same ratio of chains to independent stores as do regional shopping centers nationwide--an equal number of national chains and independent merchants. But the national figures reveal that as a proportion of sales in these centers, the chains do approximately five times the amount of business of the independents, using about five times the floor space (see Urban Land Institute 1972). We would assume that this pattern would hold even if the regional shopping center were to be located in the Downtown core itself. Many local merchants lack the capital and/or marketing capability required to compete with national chains located within the shopping centers. With the advent of a new Downtown regional complex, there would be two potential effects upon nearby merchants--effects that go in opposite directions. Increased business will be brought into the Downtown core as shopper traffic generated by the new stores "spills over" into adjacent retail areas. On the other hand, a proportion of the business now done in these adjacent retail areas will be "cannibalized" by the new stores. There is no way to know, given existing data, what the net effect will be on total retailing activity in the adjacent shopping areas. As a general guide, however, the effects will likely fall differentially in the pattern implied by previous discussions: Those shops that are of the "unique" variety, not easily duplicated in shopping centers, will tend not to be hurt, while those that provide goods and services more easily replicated in shopping centers and chain department stores will tend to be eroded.

Conclusion

Growth of population will lead to the following effects on local retail business:

1. Businesses with monopolies over a given product or service will tend to benefit from local growth;
2. Those businesses without such a monopoly position will tend to experience increased competition for the increased total area sales volume;
3. Businesses with unique services and merchandise, particularly those tied to the peculiarities of the Santa Barbara locale, will tend not to be eroded by increased competition, particularly from regional shopping centers;
4. Additional population growth leads to additional retailing activity, but the form of that activity changes from home-owned businesses on "strip" shopping streets to absentee-owned chain-store businesses in large-scale shopping centers.

UNEMPLOYMENT

Unemployment rates are both a measure of the economic well-being of citizens, and an indicator of the social ills that are likely to result should that level of well-being be particularly low. Economic growth and its consequent population growth through the creation of new jobs is often thought to be the means of ameliorating problems of unemployment. It is this notion that we now wish to test.

We have examined the 25 most quickly growing metropolitan areas in the United States to determine whether these places of rapid population growth experienced unemployment rates substantially lower than the national average. We found that the rates of unemployment in the most rapidly growing U.S. Standard Metropolitan Statistical Areas (SMSAs) are not different from the aggregate national

SMSA unemployment rate. Tables 5.3 and 5.4 list the 25 SMSAs that grew fastest during the 1950-60 and 1960-70 decades and the unemployment rates of those areas at the end of the respective decades.

In both cases, half of the most quickly growing areas had unemployment rates above the national figure for all SMSAs. More striking are the comparisons of growth and unemployment rates for all SMSAs in California during the 1960-66 period--a time of general boom in the state. Table 5.5 reveals that, taking all California metropolitan areas, there is virtually no relationship between 1960-66 growth rates and the 1966 unemployment rate (r = 0.09). Table 5.5 is also instructive in that it reveals that although there is wide diversity of growth rates across metropolitan areas, there is no comparable spread in the unemployment rates that all cluster within the relatively narrow range of 4.3 to 6.5 percent.

In our matched cities studies, we found that the size of cities and rate of unemployment show no relationship among the 115 places examined. When the relationship of rate of population growth was examined, we found that the unemployment rate actually shows a slight tendency to <u>increase</u> with high rates of population growth. We can only explain this finding by noting the possibility that places with expanding labor forces attract new migrants faster than the rate at which new jobs are created.

Still another way of measuring the impact of growth upon unemployment is to use rates not of population growth but of growth in the labor force. Using this measure we can test the idea that increases in job opportunities do not affect the unemployment rate. We found that for our 115 comparative cities there was no significant relationship between percent change in size of the labor force over the 1960-70 decade and the 1970 unemployment rates (r = 0.127).

The explanation for this pattern of findings is rather clear. Unemployment is a national problem rather than a local one. The country has continually experienced situations in which there are more people in the national labor pool seeking work than there are jobs.

The labor force is mobile and capable of taking advantage of emerging employment opportunities at points geographically distant. As jobs develop in a quickly growing area, the unemployed will be attracted from other areas to fill those developing vacancies, and in sufficient additional numbers to replenish the pool of the unemployed.

Growth of a given locality does not create jobs; it merely distributes them. The number of jobs in this society, whether in the building trades or in any other economic sector, will be determined by factors having to do with rates of investment return, federal decisions affecting the money supply, and other issues having very little

TABLE 5.3

Growth and Unemployment Rates of 25 Most
Quickly Growing SMSAs, 1950-60
(percentages)

Metropolitan Area	Growth 1950-60	Unemployment Rate, 1960
1. Fort Lauderdale-Hollywood, Fla.	297.9	4.7
2. Anaheim-Santa Ana-Garden Grove, Calif.	225.6	4.6
3. Las Vegas, Nev.	163.0	6.7*
4. Midland, Tex.	162.6	4.9
5. Orlando, Fla.	124.6	5.1
6. San Jose, Calif.	121.1	7.0*
7. Odessa, Tex.	116.1	5.6*
8. Phoenix, Ariz.	100.0	4.7
9. West Palm Beach, Fla.	98.9	4.8
10. Colorado Springs, Col.	92.9	6.1*
11. Miami, Fla.	88.9	7.3*
12. Tampa-St. Petersburg, Fla.	88.8	5.1
13. Tucson, Ariz.	88.1	5.9*
14. Albuquerque, N.M.	80.0	4.5
15. San Bernardino-Riverside-Ontario, Calif.	79.3	6.7*
16. Sacramento, Calif.	74.0	6.1*
17. Albany, Ga.	73.5	4.4
18. Santa Barbara, Calif.	72.0	3.6
19. Amarillo, Tex.	71.6	3.3
20. Reno, Nev.	68.8	6.1*
21. Lawton, Okla.	64.6	5.5*
22. Lake Charles, La.	62.3	7.8*
23. El Paso, Tex.	61.1	6.4*
24. Pensacola, Fla.	54.9	5.3*
25. Lubbock, Tex.	54.7	3.9
United States	26.4	5.2

Note: Oxnard-Ventura, Calif., and Middlesex County, N.J.,
although among the most quickly growing SMSAs, were omitted because 1960 unemployment rates are not published for these SMSAs.
    *Unemployment rate above SMSA national mean.
    Sources: United States, Department of Commerce, Bureau of
the Census, 1973a: tables 33 and 154.

TABLE 5.4

Growth and Unemployment Rates of 25 Most
Quickly Growing SMSAs, 1960-70
(percentages)

Metropolitan Area	Growth 1960-70	Unemployment Rate, 1970
1. Las Vegas, Nev.	115.2	5.2*
2. Anaheim-Santa Ana-Garden Grove, Calif.	101.8	5.4*
3. Oxnard-Ventura, Calif.	89.0	5.9*
4. Ft. Lauderdale-Hollywood, Fla.	85.7	3.4
5. San Jose, Calif.	65.8	5.8*
6. Colorado Springs, Colo.	64.2	5.5*
7. Santa Barbara, Calif.	56.4	6.4*
8. West Palm Beach, Fla.	52.9	3.0
9. Nashua, N.H.	47.8	2.8
10. Huntsville, Ala.	47.3	4.4*
11. Columbia, Mo.	46.6	2.4
12. Phoenix, Ariz.	45.8	3.9
13. Danbury, Conn.	44.3	4.2
14. Fayetteville, N.C.	42.9	5.2*
15. Reno, Nev.	42.9	6.2*
16. San Bernardino-Riverside-Ontario, Calif.	41.2	5.9*
17. Houston, Tex.	40.0	3.0
18. Austin, Tex.	39.3	3.1
19. Dallas, Tex.	39.0	3.0
20. Santa Rosa, Calif.	39.0	7.3*
21. Tallahassee, Fla.	38.8	3.0
22. Washington, D.C.	37.8	2.7
23. Atlanta, Ga.	36.7	3.0
24. Ann Arbor, Mich.	35.8	5.0*
25. Miami, Fla.	35.6	3.7
United States	16.6	4.3

*Unemployment rate above SMSA national mean.
Sources: United States, Department of Commerce, Bureau of
the Census, 1970 Census of Population, Vol. 1, Part 1 (Washington,
D.C.: 1973a), tables 32 and 186.

TABLE 5.5

Growth and Unemployment Rates of All
California SMSAs, 1960–66
(percentages)

California SMSAs	Growth 1960–66	Unemployment Rate, 1966
Anaheim–Santa Ana–Garden Grove	6.5	4.3
Bakersfield	11.1	5.2
Fresno	12.3	6.5
Los Angeles–Long Beach	11.9	4.5
Modesto	n.a.	n.a.
Oxnard–Ventura	68.8	6.0
Sacramento	20.0	5.2
Salinas–Monterey	15.9	6.1
San Bernardino–Riverside	27.9	6.2
San Diego	14.0	5.1
San Francisco–Oakland	11.1	4.4
San Jose	44.8	4.8
Santa Barbara	48.7	4.5
Santa Rosa	n.a.	n.a.
Stockton	12.5	6.3
Vellejo–Napa	20.6	4.4
California average	23.29	5.25

Note: n.a. = data are not available.

Sources: United States, Department of Commerce, Bureau of the Census, Estimates of the Population of Counties and Metropolitan Areas, July 1, 1966; A Summary Report, Current Population Reports, Population Estimates and Projections, Series p-25, no. 427 (Washington, D.C.: U.S. Government Printing Office, July 31, 1969), Table 2; State of California, California Statistical Abstract, 1970 (Sacramento, Calif.), Table C-10.

to do with local decision making. A locality can merely attempt to
guarantee that a certain proportion of newly created jobs will be in
the locality in question. Aggregate employment is unaffected by the
outcome of this competition among localities to "create" jobs and,
because of the mobility of the unemployed elsewhere, a locality can
do little about lowering its own rate of unemployment. Thus, as
Santa Barbara grows from one PIP to the next, the rate of unemployment will tend to parallel the general national rate and be unaffected
by local policies. A study completed for the city of Milpitas comes
to a similar general conclusion:

> There is a serious question as to whether a local
> jurisdiction should get involved with making its
> decisions on the basis of employment and income
> effects. Economists unanimously have argued
> that the only jurisdiction that should be concerned
> with the effect of its policies on the level of em-
> ployment is the Federal Government. Smaller
> jurisdictions do not have the power to effect sig-
> nificant changes in the level of unemployment.
> The local jurisdiction has no control over the
> level of unemployment through its policy actions.
> The local jurisdiction cannot control the policy
> actions of neighboring jurisdictions. Indeed, in
> a regional context, that is in the context of re-
> gional jobs and housing market, what goes on in
> one sub-part of a region is usually offset by bal-
> ancing actions elsewhere in the region. The
> total amount of activity for the region cannot be
> affected by local decisions. This policy pre-
> rogative is reserved for the Federal Govern-
> ment. [Levy and Arnold 1972a, p. 95]

Some peculiar impacts on Santa Barbara's rate of joblessness
in absolute terms would likely result if the city entered a period of
severe economic decline caused perhaps by a crash in one of its important basic industries, such as tourism. But nowhere in our data
is there an indication that stability would of itself lead to such a decline. In a stable economy everything would be likely to remain the
same.

EMPLOYMENT IN CONSTRUCTION: A SPECIAL CASE

One sector of the labor force--the construction sector--seems
particularly dependent upon high rates of growth for its employment.

This sector includes people who make their living in construction,
as well as those who manufacture or engage in the wholesale distribution of construction materials and those who service the needs of
the other groups (the multiplier effect). Although it is likely that it
has declined somewhat since then, the construction trades themselves
made up 5 percent of the city's total labor force in 1970.[2] Of this 5
percent (which we adopt as an approximation of the current figure),
a substantial proportion is engaged in work not dependent upon population growth, such as alterations, rehabilitation, maintenance, road
building, and so on (Buchalter et al. 1973). Also, the need for new
public facility construction continues regardless of growth: City
schools that fail to meet earthquake standards must be replaced;
UCSB continues to build new structures despite stable enrollment
(albeit at a slower pace); local hospitals continue to expand despite
decreasing total numbers of bed patients.

Our task is to determine the effect of a slowdown in construction, particularly residential construction, upon the rate of unemployment among persons engaged in the construction trades. Drawing upon the work of Buchalter et al. (1973), we have attempted a
"worst-case" analysis. We ask the question: What would happen if
all new residential construction in the city were to come to a complete and permanent halt? We made the following assumptions regarding other conditions during this halt: (a) there would be no
switch-over of construction workers into other trades; all those displaced would be unemployed; (b) there would be no out-migration of
construction workers to other cities as a result of their lack of work
in Santa Barbara; (c) there would be no compensating tendency for
residents to expand, remodel, or rehabilitate construction.

In order to determine the effect on the construction trades under
these worst-case conditions, we utilize the regression predictor developed by Buchalter et al. for their analysis of the effects of "no-
growth" on the construction industry of the entire county of Santa
Barbara. They determined that, with the exception of the lumber industry, major developers almost invariably purchase their building
materials from outside the county, and thus changes in the rate of
subdivision construction do not affect employment in construction supply firms. Supporting this proposition is the fact that, according to
Buchalter et al., the employment in wholesale building supplies has
not fluctuated with the substantial fluctuations in county building activity over the years. Thus, in their analysis, they restrict consideration almost exclusively to those engaged in construction work.
They use a multiplier effect of 1.25 (higher than that used in other
segments of this chapter) to generate the total number of workers
outside the construction trades who are at risk with changes in residential construction activity. Buchalter et al. developed an econo-

metric model capable of predicting 90 percent of the actual historical variation in the construction labor force. For every $1 million change in construction valuation loss, there is a consequent loss of 21 jobs in the construction sector and a loss of an additional 26 jobs in other sectors of the economy, according to their calculations. We have taken this ratio of 47 total jobs for every $1 million in construction and applied it to city building permit data.

Over the past five years, the average value of permits for new residential construction has been $11.57 million per year (computations based on City Building Department data). Given our adopted formula, this represents 243 jobs in the construction trades, or 17 percent of the jobs in that sector, representing 544 jobs, or 1.93 percent of the city's total labor force in a given year.

Under conditions of total no-growth in the residential sector, the maximum impact on the city's unemployment rate could be the addition of about 2 percent of the labor force. But we doubt that even this would happen. Construction labor is mobile and rises and falls in a given place with the rate of construction activity. It is also very unrealistic to assume, as we did, that the halting of new residential construction will not affect the rate of rehabilitation and additions to existing units. A good portion of the existing stock is currently left in poor condition precisely because it is being readied for demolition and replacement by new construction. Should the new construction not be possible, some rehabilitation would undoubtedly be induced.

On the other hand, to the degree that commercial and public facility construction were forced to come to a standstill along with residential construction, the result would be more severe. Averaging building permit valuations in the city over the past five years (1969-73), one arrives at the annual figure of $4,041,112 for representing such forms of construction. Again, by the same formula, this amounts to an additional 0.7 percent of the total city labor force that is pushed out of work, or an additional 6 percent of those in construction out of work. We find this result highly unlikely, given the virtual certainty that these forms of construction would persist to some degree, regardless of any growth control policy. Nevertheless, it provides some additional perspective on the possibilities, however remote.

We conclude from this exercise that a complete and total no-growth program, one that had the effect of terminating all new construction regardless of its type, could have the effect of eliminating the jobs of 23 percent of the construction sector and 2.6 percent of the jobs of the total city labor force. From these figures it appears that under a complete no-growth city land-use policy, 75 percent of the current construction workers would be unaffected. We assume that these are people who do routine maintenance, remodeling, and rehabilitation work (which is labor intensive) or who do their work in areas outside the city limits. For a number of reasons we think that under an actual policy of no-growth, the impacts would be far less substantial.

The traditional mobility of construction workers will in fact be reflected in migration to jobs elsewhere; the manual skills of some workers will be applied to new tasks in other occupations, such as fabrication work, and still other workers will find employment in the increased housing and commercial rehabilitation work that would follow a ban on new construction.

In the five years prior to the creation of the city's current Half-Density Ordinance, average city population growth was 656 persons per year. The current construction labor force is thus geared to the amount of new residential construction associated with that level of population growth. Since the lowest growth PIP (Half-Density Probable) is based on the addition of 785 new people each year until the year 2000, a land-use program based on that PIP would maintain the present construction labor force at its current strength for that entire period of time. Thus, building restrictions based on any of our growth PIPs will have no adverse effect on employment rates in the building trades. Only the no-growth alternative would have such an effect.

Again, we conclude by noting the possible impacts of regional effects: To the extent that construction workers living in the city work outside the city, it is land-use policies in other areas that will have the most impact upon their levels of employment.

COST OF LIVING: HOUSING AND OTHER EXPENSES

The other side of income is expenditures, and changes in cost of living have as great an impact on the economic well-being of the individual as have changes in income level. The U.S. Bureau of Labor Statistics (BLS) regularly gathers cost-of-living information for a series of cities and SMSAs in the United States, but Santa Barbara is not one of the places that falls within the BLS sample. There is thus no reliable information on the cost of living in the area, and we are not able to describe the way costs have changed in recent years, nor how costs there compare with those in other areas.

From the data gathered by the BLS, however, comparisons can be made among the places that are used in the sample. The questions can be asked: Do small places have higher or lower costs of living that bigger places? The BLS reports that the 25 small cities in the sample (all containing populations of 2,500 to 50,000) taken as a whole have costs of living that are significantly lower than that for other places. The BLS estimates that in these small places it would require $9,805 per year for a standardized "intermediate" budget for a four-person family in 1971. For larger areas--SMSAs with cities over 50,000 in population--the comparable figure is $11,232, or an extra 15 percent in costs. Similar differences are present for families on a lower budget standard.[3]

Among the 39 SMSAs used by the BLS, we find that there is a significant tendency for larger cities to have higher costs of living ($r = +0.38$) with the cost of both food ($r = +0.38$) and housing ($r = +0.48$) showing a significant increase with larger size. The strongest relevant findings from our cross-cities comparisons were the discovery of very strong tendencies for both house values and rent values to be higher among cities with the highest growth rates.

These findings are plausible on the assumption that housing costs are forced upward in big cities by the rising value of land associated with large numbers of people competing for scarce living and trading sites. Food may be cheaper in smaller places because consumers are closer to the farms that produce it. The only types of expenditures that perhaps are cheaper in the city are durable goods, such as televisions and cars, but these are not of sufficient magnitude to alter the general effects of the more important budget items.

This pattern of lower cost of living associated with smaller places is based on data gathered in the recent past and reflects costs and size relationships that have been created through natural market forces, rather than through artificial constraints of growth limitation. An effective program of growth limitation for a U.S. city is a new phenomenon and may result in cost-of-living effects not found in previous experience. While it is likely that costs of food and durables would not be influenced by the mode through which population size is affected, the same may not be true for housing.

On this issue the different means of population control (described in Chapter 9) become crucial in predicting consequences for housing costs. A population program that relies upon limiting residential construction, as, for example, through zoning restriction, will create a market situation of a fixed number of housing units for increasingly larger numbers of people. That is, because mere manipulation of residential housing supply does not itself control the amount of migration into the area (which may continue in response to growing economic opportunities), there comes to be increasing demand for housing in the face of a fixed supply. The results are basic to elementary economics: Prices are bid upward.

However, higher prices are not the only consequence. As costs rise, families do not simply expand the proportion of their income spent for housing. A plateau is likely reached at about one-third of income, with the rest reserved for food and other necessary expenditures. The poor and less well-to-do, already spending close to this proportion for housing, are particularly affected. One of the few alternatives for such families is to change the way they use the existing housing stock; they may double up, perhaps sharing facilities with parents and other relatives--in other words, they may use existing facilities more intensively than before. This circumstance of a fixed housing supply but increasing housing demand existed during World War II in most U.S. cities. The consequences were slums and sharply rising housing costs. Since the war, most U.S. cities have seen a continuous decrease in the amount of residential overcrowding. This trend would be reversed. (There are signs that it is already reversing in many cities--not in response to zoning changes but in response to higher interest rates and construction costs).

To summarize this scenario: Because nothing is done to restrict the number of persons migrating into the area, demand for housing continues to rise. But because residential construction is curtailed below a level consistent with this rise in demand, costs rise and overcrowding increases.

There are two assumptions made in this discussion that lead to these unhappy results. First is the assumption that population growth continues in spite of a lack of housing. To some extent, this may not be the result of residential restrictions in the case of a city like Santa Barbara. For example, moderate-income retirees may be less likely to move to Santa Barbara if housing opportunities become poorer than they are at present. The second and more critical assumption is that other parts of the Santa Barbara region (the South Coast commuting area) are not available to serve the "excess" city population. That is, since the South Coast is essentially a single labor and housing market, demand that is not met by housing construction in the city could be met through housing construction elsewhere within the region. When this occurs, the supply does rise to meet demand, and the consequence of controlled growth in a single place is to have no overall effect on prices in the regional market. Only if all jurisdictions in the region create similar restrictions on residential construction will prices, overall, be forced up. The price rise will increase rapidly as the supply ceiling is finally approached.

Although only such a regionwide response would lead to overall increases in costs, growth control in only one place (for example, Santa Barbara) would have certain pricing effects on housing within the city itself. Under the scenario of growth limitation in the city, but an open market elsewhere in the region, city housing will become scarcer relative to demand and thus expensive in relation to housing elsewhere in the region. Increases in costs in the city would be

compensated for, more or less, by decreasing (or by less rapidly
increasing) costs elsewhere. The long-term result of such a situation would be the city's increasingly becoming a place for well-to-do
residents (thus reversing past trends in the opposite direction), while
the other South Coast communities receive an increasing proportion
of the poor and the working class. This is the sort of land-use manipulation that raises moral questions and that, given recent court
decisions, may place the city at some legal risk as well (see Chapter 10).

HALF-DENSITY ORDINANCE EFFECTS

Under the city's temporary Half-Density Ordinance, there is
nothing close to a complete regional halt on residential construction:
There are few constraints on new construction in Carpinteria, and
building in the city is still possible; only the maximum allowable densities have been altered in the City of Santa Barbara's multiple-unit
zones. We can ask whether under these conditions, the city's Half-
Density Ordinance has had any of the possible effects envisioned.
Have the restrictions caused the pace of new residential construction to be slowed down? Has the lowering of the development potential of the land caused developers to build only high-priced units?

To answer these specific questions, as well as to provide more
general evidence for what can be expected to occur if allowable building densities are substantially decreased, we compared the pattern
of city building-permit activity before the Half-Density Ordinance
with the permit activity after it became effective.

Our results generally indicate that the effects of the Ordinance
have been rather minor. Table 5.6 displays the history of building
activity in the city of Santa Barbara and in the state of California.
This makes it possible to distinguish city trends from those affecting
the state in general. Examining residential construction over the
years, we find that the city building-permit pattern has generally followed that of state totals. Figure 5.1 displays the relationship over
time between the annual total residential valuation in the city compared to the annual total valuation in the state. It can be seen that
as building activity in the state slumped, an analogous slump occurred
in Santa Barbara. When it rose in the state, it rose in Santa Barbara. The pattern is not perfect: The state experienced a sharp
rise in construction permits in 1970; the corresponding rise in Santa
Barbara did not take hold until a year later. The sharp decline in
1972, however, occurred in both the city and the state and continued
through 1973 and 1974.

TABLE 5.6

Building Permit Activity: City and State, 1968-74

Year	State of California Valuation*	Number of Units	Valuation per Unit	City of Santa Barbara Valuation*	Number of Units	Valuation per Unit
1968	2,839,909	159,747	17,778	8,804	784	11,230
1969	3,148,139	184,230	17,088	12,006	892	13,460
1970	3,177,606	195,668	16,240	9,169	731	12,543
1971	4,526,476	256,676	17,635	8,795	672	13,088
1972	5,406,800	280,851	19,252	14,499	744	19,488
1973	4,549,626	216,933	20,973	13,385	757	17,682
1974	1,528,801	63,520	24,068	3,281	150	21,873
1973						
Jan.	410,988	21,481	19,133	1,881	175	10,749
Feb.	319,260	16,772	19,035	545	28	19,464
Mar.	456,051	22,714	20,078	324	10	32,400
Apr.	500,217	24,652	20,291	877	44	19,932
May	466,351	22,232	20,977	4,407	290	15,197
June	442,794	20,636	21,457	712	51	13,961
July	388,812	17,649	22,030	411	21	19,571
Aug.	398,043	18,150	21,931	2,628	87	30,207
Sept.	362,168	16,436	22,035	539	19	28,368
Oct.	297,097	13,353	22,250	193	9	21,444
Nov.	225,106	9,995	22,522	346	9	38,444
Dec.	282,739	12,863	21,981	522	14	37,286
1974						
Jan.	225,099	9,763	23,056	618	22	28,091
Feb.	211,515	9,351	22,620	766	17	45,059
Mar.	359,798	14,126	25,541	782	63	12,413
Apr.	383,643	15,978	24,011	469	14	33,500
May	348,746	14,302	24,384	646	34	19,000

*In thousands of dollars.

Sources: City of Santa Barbara Building Department; Security
Pacific Bank.

FIGURE 5.1

Total Valuation: Residential Building Permits, City and State, 1968-74 (thousands of dollars)

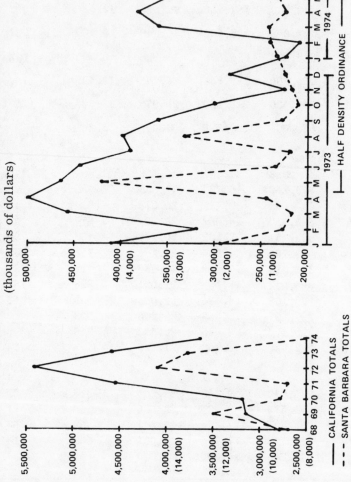

In the period following the effective date of the Half-Density
Ordinance (April 15, 1973) city and state building activity continued
to be in general conformity. The first full month of record after the
ordinance was enacted saw a sharp city rise in total valuation (from
$324,000 in March to $4.407 million in May 1973). Parallel to the
state pattern there was then a period of more or less continuous decline through the remainder of 1973. A gradual recovery began in
the city in October 1973, while state building-permit activity continued to decline for the next six months. Finally, in the most recent
period, state totals rose considerably (and began a slight decline),
while the city permit activity lagged. We conclude from these data
that the Half-Density Ordinance itself has had no effect on the total
valuation of building in the city. There have been declines, but they
appear to be more a response to changes in the state and national
economy than to the land-use policies of the city.

While it may be the case that the ordinance has not decreased
the amount of total permit valuation in the city, it may be that fewer
housing units are being constructed as a result of the ordinance, but
at a higher cost. This notion is tested in Figure 5.2, where the number of units over time are compared for the city and state. Again we
see the same pattern of parallel city and state activity with the same
minor variations seen in Figure 5.1. The most important single data
point is again the month immediately following the effective date of
the ordinance, and again there is a substantial surge, rather than decline, in number of units during that period.

Figure 5.3 provides further measure of the ordinance's effect.
It compares the average per unit valuation of new housing in the city
and state in the years since 1965 and in the months since 1973. We
see the same general pattern of the city and state performing the
same way over the years, with a generally continuous rise in the per
unit costs in both. Again, the ordinance has no perceptible impact;
city average valuation per unit rises and falls, but it proceeds in the
same general upward direction as the state valuation.

Still another approach to these data is to compute the average
valuation per unit in the period since the Half-Density Ordinance and
compare it to the period prior to the ordinance's effective date. The
results here indicate that in the period since the ordinance (April 15,
1973, to May 30, 1974) the average unit valuation in the city ($20,060)
was less than that of the state ($22,542). This low per unit city valua-
tion, relative to the state, is not unique to the post-ordinance period;
it has been the pattern in every year since 1968--except for 1972, the
year before the ordinance went into effect. The point is that the city
returned to its previous per unit relationship to the statewide figures,
despite the enactment of the ordinance.

FIGURE 5.2

Number of Units: Building Permits, City and State, 1968-74
(thousands of dollars)

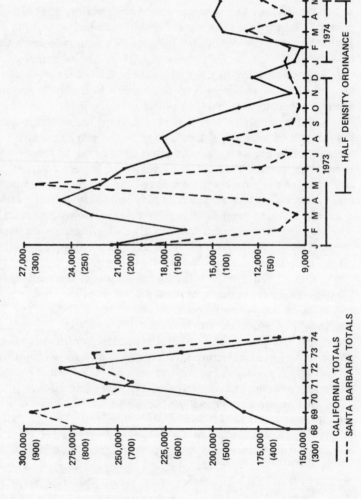

FIGURE 5.3

Valuation per Unit: Residential Building Permits, City and State, 1968-74
(thousands of dollars)

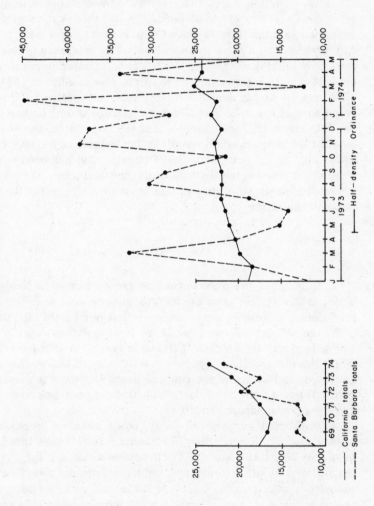

The only indication we find of an impact of the Half-Density Ordinance is in the ratio of single-family houses to multiple units. Since 1968, single-family houses have represented only from 9 to 16 percent of new residential units each year. During the first half of 1975, there was a sharp rise in the proportion of construction activity in single-family homes, which amounted to about two-fifths of all units. For the state, the rise in single-family dwellings was much less striking (47 to 55 percent), and this is the source of our suspicion that the Half-Density Ordinance may be having an effect. But the pattern is by no means clear. The existence of the ordinance for three-fourths of the year 1973 had no similar impact, and the amount of data represented by the first five months of 1974 may for some reason be atypical. Nevertheless, we point out the possible trend so that it can be looked for as additional data become available.

In summary, we conclude that the city's Half-Density Ordinance has had little or no effect on either the volume of housing construction in the city or the per unit value of housing that has been constructed. There is a recent sign that the ordinance may, however, have had the effect of changing the ratio of apartments to single-family housing, in favor of the latter.

SUMMARY

In general, we have found that growth per se is likely to have little, if any, effect upon the individual economic well-being of Santa Barbarans. There is some evidence that per capita incomes rise with size and growth rate, but there is also evidence for a compensating tendency of the cost of living to rise with size (see Chapter 2). While the income rise is probably a function of the wealth of the migrants, it is likely that the cost-of-living increase is due to size itself. Thus, existing residents can likely expect a decline in actual spending power under growth.

With a few exceptions, local growth does not increase or decrease the wealth resources of citizens. Businesses that have a monopoly on certain services will tend to acquire a larger share of the nation's wealth. Similarly, unique stores and services may tend to prosper with growth, but other Santa Barbara retailers will only see an increase in competition for the increased dollars spent by new residents. A larger proportion of the city's retail business will go to chain operations with greater capital and marketing resources than the locally owned shops. This wealth will flow outside the locality.

Unemployment is a national phenomenon, and it is unaffected by local growth patterns. So long as there are not absolute declines in employment and population, variations in the growth rate or ultimate population size will have no effect on the local unemployment rate. The major exception to this is in the construction industry, which, under the worst-case analysis runs the risk of a 23 percent unemployment rate if all new construction in the city comes to a halt.

In conclusion, the individual well-being of Santa Barbara residents is dependent upon the state of the national economy and not local policies.

NOTES

1. All figures dealing with retailing activity in this section refer to "primary shoppers' goods" (see Keisker 1970), representing 32 percent of total transactions in the city subject to the sales tax. Shoppers' goods include general merchandise, apparel, and other specialties.

2. The city labor force consists of 28,303 persons, 1,417 of whom work in construction (United States, Department of Commerce, 1973a, Table 87).

3. U.S. Bureau of Labor Statistics, Urban Family Budgets and Geographical Comparative Indexes, supplement to bulletin, 1970-75 (Washington, D.C.: U.S. Government Printing Office, Autumn 1971).

6

ECONOMIC EFFECTS OF GROWTH: THE PUBLIC SECTOR

The public sector is that part of the economy that exists to serve the needs of the general public, and is financed by funds generated from the general public by means of taxes, service charges, and special fees. For the purposes of this work, the public sector consists of the city government of Santa Barbara and the local school districts.

The public sector can be broken down into two general categories. The first consists of those services that are financed out of general tax revenues and are administered as a part of the city's General Fund (this includes police, fire, library services, park and recreation, and public works, as well as general administration). The second comprises those services financed through independent sources of funding, either through service charges (water and sanitation), or through separately levied property taxes (education).

In this chapter we will consider the impacts of growth on the public sector. How will growth affect the costs of administrating city services and the costs of education? If new revenues will be needed, what amount will be needed? What will it mean to the taxpayer? To answer these questions we will first analyze the different expenditures of each service financed through the General Fund; we will then analyze the sources of revenues available to the General Fund; finally, we will appraise the effects of growth upon the projected balance between costs and revenues.

We will then follow the same procedure for the remaining services (water, sanitation, and education): First, we will analyze expenditures; then we will analyze projected revenues; finally, we will appraise the effects of growth upon the net balance.

In the last section, we will summarize all our findings concerning the public sector and draw some conclusions concerning the aggregate effects of growth on all services combined.

Three assumptions are made in order to isolate most clearly the major effects of growth on the public sector: (a) assumptions of current standards, (b) assumptions of constant per capita costs and revenues, and (c) use of constant dollars.

First, we assume that for all projections, the current level and standards of service will be maintained throughout. For example, we project park requirements by assuming that the current acreage per capita will be maintained. Our estimates are thus intended to be taken as minimal estimates of capital costs that would be incurred in order to maintain the current standard of services under growth. Except when future projects aimed at improving existing standards are already being implemented by city departments (for example, the new sanitation plant), we have assumed that projects are undertaken only to serve additional population, at the lowest possible costs.

It must be emphasized that a decision to raise or lower the current standards of service is a political decision, and if changes are made in the standards of service, appropriate adjustments should be made in the projected impacts of growth. It is understood that when we are talking about future capital costs, these projections are not intended to reflect a complete capital program for the next 25 years. Such an effort would be well beyond the scope of the present work. Furthermore, for most services, the data base does not currently exist for such long-range planning. Rather, we include only those capital expenditures that would have to take place to keep pace with growing population, and of those, only projects visible now are possible to include.

Second, we assume constant per capita costs and revenues. From 1969-74 the total assessed value of property in Santa Barbara has averaged about $3,300 per resident; at various times it has been higher or lower. We assume that this ratio of assessed value to population remains constant in the future. We make the same assumption with regard to expenditures on the operating costs of the police division or public works or fire, and, in general, we make it with regard to all major expenditures and sources of revenue to local government. This assumption is made for reasons discussed in Chapter 1: No one can predict the future merely on the basis of past trends.

We make this assumption only with regard to certain types of costs: those incurred in the day-to-day operations of government. Such operating costs may increase or decrease in small amounts, depending on the level of the service. They generally consist primarily of wages and salaries of employees, and the materials used in daily work. On the other hand, there is another class of expenses that are not so flexible: capital costs. Thus, we assume that the costs of operating the city parks or the city libraries increase at approximately the same rate as that of the population, but we do not make the same assumption with regard to the capital costs of a parks program or school expansion.

As population grows, new parks will have to be added and new schools built. The current school system, without any physical expansion, is capable of serving the Santa Barbara population until that population reaches a certain level; then costly urban land must be bought, playing fields constructed, and buildings erected. Such capital costs are "lumpy": they occur at specific points in time and involve a major increase in expense over the day-to-day operating costs of running a school district or a parks division. Under this assumption we assume that such capital costs become the major sources of differences in the impact of growth to different population levels. To estimate the magnitude of such costs, we have asked the following questions: How much would it cost to maintain the current level of services, in the face of a growing population? What capital programs are already underway or would be required to accommodate growth at current standards? To answer these questions, we have gathered relevant information from various city agencies and have projected such capital costs for each of our PIPs. In the following sections of this chapter we estimate minimal capital requirements for libraries, parks and recreation, public works, schools, water, and wastewater treatment (sanitation).

Finally, we adopt the convention of expressing prices in constant dollars; that is, all information on past expenditures and revenues is expressed in 1974 dollar values. They are thus clearly underestimations of actual costs and revenues, but to the extent that expenditures and revenues experience the effects of inflation equally, the assumption can be made without altering the conclusions of the analysis.

THE GENERAL FUND: EXPENDITURES AND REVENUES

The city budget can be divided into two categories: General and Special Fund appropriations. The General Fund is currently 70 percent of the city's operating budget, excluding its capital program. The Special Funds are intended to provide revenues that are tied to specific expenditures; examples include water, sanitation, the airport, the parking district, and the harbor. The General Fund comprises the principal municipal services (fire, police, public works, parks and recreation, library), a number of lesser services, and the general administrative, fiscal, legal, and planning functions of government. It also includes expenditures on pensions for retired

municipal employees, which have averaged one-eighth of all General
Fund expenditures from 1969-74. We will exclude from our analysis
of General Fund appropriations any services whose costs are intended
to be directly met by transfer payments from the Special Funds: such
services generate their own revenues and thus do not constitute a new
"cost" to the General Fund. (Examples are costs associated with
sanitation, the harbor dredge, the municipal golf course, the county
libraries, and the parking district.) We will include as expenditures
all operating costs, including capital outlays funded by current revenues from the annual capital program (such outlays have averaged
about 4 percent of the total operating budget from 1969-74).

General Fund Expenditures at Future PIPs

We will discuss separately the following municipal services:
police, parks and recreation, public works, and the city library.
The costs of each service will be estimated for each year, for each
PIP. (All operating costs of each service, unless otherwise indicated, are based on the average per capita cost over 1969-74.) Operating and capital costs are estimated separately, the latter on the
basis of capital programs that would be required to accommodate
growth of each of the PIPs. Such programs were estimated with the
assistance of the heads of the appropriate city departments and divisions.

Police

Police costs per capita are generally among the highest of all
local governmental expenditures; Santa Barbarans pay more for
police than for any other single municipal service. Police protection
is also the service whose costs have shown the most dramatic--and
consistent--increase over time. In 1969 each resident of the community paid an average of $26 per year into the General Fund to sus-
tain the Police Department; today, the per resident cost has risen to
almost $34 (1974 dollars).
    The rising costs of police protection are usually attributed to
increasing crime rates; incidents in all categories have risen in past
years, nationally as well as locally. [1] We note these consistent increases in crimes and police expenditures over the past decade. In
our analysis, however, we shall project constant per capita costs of
police, based on the average of 1969-74 (about $30 per resident). If
police costs continue to rise at current rates, per capita police costs
will double in merely 25 years. It is highly unlikely, however, that
recent trends will continue. Changing drug laws, shifting emphasis

at the federal level away from "law and order" (and the police-
support programs that presently accompany such emphasis), or continuing budgetary difficulties at the municipal level could all serve to
halt the current rise of police expenditures. There are no major
capital expenditures associated with the police function.[2] Because
of the size of the overall police budget and the labor intensity of the
service, capital equipment costs are absorbed into operating costs
and reflected in the five-year average of operating expenditures on
which we base our projections.

Fire

Our historical study of the Fire Department indicates that the
per capita noncapital costs of fire protection rose more than $4 over
1960-74 (in 1974 dollars). However, this increase appears to be
more the result of the shortened work week for Fire Department personnel than it was of the 25 percent increase in population experienced
during this period. For example, although the number of Fire Department employees rose from 77 in 1958 to 97 in 1973, no new positions were created in this period. In fact, according to the fire chief,
no new positions were created in the Fire Department for the 25 years
preceding 1973.

Because fire protection is such a labor-intensive city service
(currently more than 95 percent of Fire Department expenditures is
for salaries), and based on the observation that the trend toward
shorter work week has leveled off, we should expect the constant
dollar per capita cost of fire protection to remain stable over the
period we are examining.

There is a possibility that the shifting density patterns associated with population growth might require capital expenditures for
some fire-station relocations in order to maintain the current Class
III standards of the department (that is, to maintain a constant level
of service). However, the Fire Department has already requested
that the city allocate funds to make two such changes (see City of
Santa Barbara 1974a), and, in the opinion of the fire chief, if these
relocations are implemented, the distribution of station houses
should be adequate for the density patterns under consideration in
this work. Because these relocation expenditures are clearly the
result of shifting density patterns that precede the period of our work,
they are not included in our projection of fire-protection expenses
caused by population growth. The reader should note that the actual
expenditures on fire protection over the first few years of our projections are understated to this extent.

According to the fire chief, no additional capital expenditures
would appear to be necessary to serve the population levels of each

PIP. Therefore, no bonded capital projects are explicitly entered
into our projections. However, because the five-year average we
use to project operating expenditures includes two years that experienced some special capital expenditures, a moderate level of
capital projects is implied in our projections. This amount should
suffice to cover the ordinary capital replacement associated with
fire protection services.

City Library

The current library facilities of the city include a central library Downtown and one branch library located on the East Side.
The central library also functions as the area library for the South
Coast, and in fact, the county has been contracting with the city library for several years to operate several branch libraries in the
unincorporated areas adjacent to the city.

Although these county-paid facilities are excluded from the
present analysis, the central library in Santa Barbara attempts to
maintain one employee and 1,000 square feet of service area for
each 2,000 residents of the city. Currently, the number of employees is adequate to meet these standards, but the present useable
square footage of the central library falls substantially below the
norm. The current plans of the city are to construct a 13,000-
square-foot addition to the central library in the next year or two.
This addition will bring the facilities up to the square foot requirements of a population of 78,000 in the city and 100,000 in the balance
of the South Coast. Since such plans are already in the "pipeline,"
we are including this minimal expansion program in our analysis.
Such expansion is therefore incorporated in our definition of current
standards; it will impact all seven PIPs, including No-Growth.

The East Side branch was opened in 1973, with a service area
of 6,500 square feet. Branch libraries are expected to have one employee and 1,000 square feet of service area for each 2,000 people
in its district. By this standard the capacity of the current East
Side facility will be exhausted when the district reaches 13,000. The
present population of the East Side district is just over 11,000.

A 9,000-square-foot North Side branch is slated for construction in the near future. It is intended to service a district population
of 18,000. The current population of the West Side library district
is just under 17,000.

A West Side branch has not yet appeared in any of the city's
Five-Year Capital Program publications, although the 1969 Master
Plan referred to above calls for a 8,000-square-foot building to
serve a population of 16,000. The current population of the West
Side library district is just under 14,000.

<u>Analysis</u>. The analysis of library services proceeds by establishing
the number of employees as a function of population on the basis of
the library's stated policy of one employee for each 2,000 people in
each library district that has a library, with one additional employee
for each 20,000 residents of the South Coast exclusive of the city.
Average operating costs per employee are taken from the 1974/75
City Operating Budget, and this is extended to each PIP.·

The construction schedule of branch libraries and presumed
additions to the central library can be found in Table 6.1.[3] Additions to the central library are assumed to be of 13,000 square feet
each and to occur in the year that lies halfway between the exhaustion
of the existing facility and the exhaustion of the addition then constructed.

The North Side branch is assumed to be constructed in the year
during which its district population reaches 18,000, while the West
Side branch is assumed to be constructed when the West Side district
passes 15,000 residents. Branch library additions are assumed to
be constructed in increments of 2,000 square feet (with the exception
of the first addition to the North Side branch, which the Master Plan
indicates will be 3,000 square feet). The year of construction is in
each case determined in the same manner as for the central library.

For purposes of calculating the costs of construction in current dollars, a figure of $55 per square foot is used on the advice of
the library director. The purchase price of the land for the North
Side and West Side branches is based on the estimate in the 1974
<u>Five-Year Capital Program</u> for the North Side branch. An initial
capital cost of stocking each branch with books is included, but in
all other instances the purchase costs of books are presumed to be
included in the estimates of operating costs.

The No-Growth alternative also includes some construction
activity, because, in the opinion of the library director, the projected addition to the central library is necessary even if the population of the city stops growing, and the North Side branch would
probably be built within the next five or six years without any further
additions to the North Side population. On the other hand, a West
Side branch would probably not be constructed if that district's population were to stabilize at the current 13,728.

All construction costs are expressed in terms of yearly repayments on 25-year bonds at a 6 percent annual interest rate. In most
cases, projected constructions falling within a span of three to four
years were grouped together in a single bond. The annual cost of
the projected capital program is presented in Table 6.2.

<u>Conclusions</u>. The current expansion of the city library, with the
additional employees and capital expenditures it envisions, will

TABLE 6.1

Library Construction Schedule, 1975–2000, Half-Density PIPs
(square feet and thousands of dollars)

Year	Maximum					Probable				
	Central	East	North	West	Expenditures	Central	East	North	West	Expenditures
1975	--	--	--	--	--	--	--	--	--	--
1976	13,000	--	9,000	--	1,681	13,000	--	--	--	710
1977	--	--	--	8,000	810	--	--	--	--	--
1978	--	--	--	--	--	--	--	--	--	--
1979	--	--	--	--	--	--	--	--	--	--
1980	--	--	--	--	--	--	--	--	8,000	810
1981	--	--	--	--	--	--	--	--	--	--
1982	--	--	--	--	--	--	--	9,000	--	971
1983	13,000	--	--	--	715	--	--	--	--	--
1984	--	--	3,000	2,000	275	--	--	--	--	--
1985	--	--	--	--	--	--	--	--	--	--
1986	--	--	--	--	--	--	--	--	--	--
1987	--	--	--	--	--	--	--	--	--	--
1988	--	--	--	--	--	--	--	--	--	--
1989	--	--	--	--	--	--	--	--	--	--
1990	--	--	--	--	--	--	--	--	--	--
1991	--	--	--	--	--	--	--	--	--	--
1992	--	2,000	--	--	--	--	--	--	--	--
1993	--	--	--	--	110	13,000	--	--	--	715
1994	--	--	--	2,000	110	--	--	--	--	--
1995	13,000	--	--	--	715	--	2,000	--	--	110
1996	--	--	2,000	--	110	--	--	--	2,000	110
1997	--	--	--	--	--	--	--	--	--	--
1998	--	--	--	--	--	--	--	--	--	--
1999	--	--	--	--	--	--	--	--	--	--
2000	--	--	--	--	--	--	--	--	--	--

TABLE 6.2

City Library Bond Costs, 1974–2000
(1974 dollars)

Year	No-Growth	Half-Density		General Plan		Zoning	
		Maximum	Probable	Maximum	Probable	Maximum	Probable
1974	0	0	0	0	0	0	0
1975	0	0	0	0	0	0	0
1976	56,000	195,000	56,000	195,000	56,000	195,000	195,000
1977	56,000	195,000	56,000	195,000	56,000	195,000	195,000
1978	56,000	195,000	56,000	195,000	56,000	195,000	195,000
1979	56,000	195,000	56,000	195,000	56,000	281,000	195,000
1980	132,000	195,000	195,000	195,000	56,000	281,000	195,000
1981	132,000	195,000	195,000	260,000	195,000	281,000	195,000
1982	132,000	195,000	195,000	260,000	195,000	281,000	195,000
1983	132,000	272,000	195,000	260,000	195,000	281,000	251,000
1984	132,000	272,000	195,000	260,000	195,000	281,000	251,000
1985	132,000	272,000	195,000	346,000	195,000	419,000	251,000
1986	132,000	272,000	195,000	346,000	260,000	419,000	251,000
1987	132,000	272,000	195,000	346,000	260,000	419,000	251,000
1988	132,000	272,000	195,000	346,000	260,000	419,000	337,000
1989	132,000	272,000	195,000	346,000	260,000	419,000	337,000
1990	132,000	272,000	195,000	346,000	260,000	419,000	337,000
1991	132,000	272,000	195,000	346,000	260,000	419,000	337,000
1992	132,000	272,000	195,000	346,000	260,000	501,000	337,000
1993	132,000	354,000	268,000	346,000	260,000	501,000	337,000
1994	132,000	354,000	268,000	419,000	260,000	501,000	337,000
1995	132,000	354,000	268,000	419,000	260,000	501,000	337,000
1996	132,000	354,000	268,000	419,000	260,000	501,000	337,000
1997	132,000	354,000	268,000	419,000	260,000	501,000	337,000
1998	132,000	354,000	268,000	419,000	260,000	501,000	337,000
1999	132,000	354,000	268,000	419,000	260,000	518,000	337,000
2000	132,000	354,000	268,000	419,000	260,000	518,000	337,000

Source: Santa Barbara Planning Task Force.

involve moderate increases in per capita costs under all our PIPs.
These increases are least under No-Growth (about $13 per resident),
but not substantially less than those required by growth (the range is
$15 to $16 for all PIPs). The present library is understaffed and
undersized according to its own standards, and the development plans
that will increase floor space and employees to acceptable levels will
occur regardless of growth. The per capita cost of expansion to
meet minimal standards is by far the larger part of the total expansion envisioned under any of our PIPs. Thus, to the extent that this
expansion does not occur (that is, to the extent the city "makes do"
with current facilities considered inadequate), to that extent do the
lower costs associated with lower population growth become relatively greater.

An analysis considering only dollar costs of library services
ignores at least one significant benefit of library expansion: A library for a larger city, assuming it is funded at the same level per
capita, would have a proportionately wider selection of books and
materials from which users could draw.

Parks and Recreation

Background. Santa Barbara has approximately 1,860 acres of land
used or reserved for parks and recreation. Of this total, some
1,000 acres are currently undeveloped and located in rugged terrain
outside the city limits.

Historical records indicate that most park land within the city
limits was acquired between the turn of the century and 1940. An
unusually large number of parcels were acquired in the period between Santa Barbara's great earthquake and the trough of the Depression (1924-35), a time that has since come to be known as Santa Barbara's "planning renaissance." During that period, Santa Barbara
hired some of the best planners, architects, and landscape architects
in the country to develop long-range plans for the purchase and construction of a comprehensive park system designed to serve Santa
Barbara far into the future. The Depression unfortunately cut short
this vision. Even so, the city managed to acquire more than a dozen
major parks within a single decade.

Since that time, parkland acquisitions have become less concentrated and have tended to move in the direction of the purchase of
larger parcels of land at the city's periphery or of county land annexed for park purposes. The general topography and isolation of
these parcels suggests that they are more appropriate for open-
space uses, such as hiking and riding trails, than for diversified
public uses. Much of this land has been donated to the city because
it is only marginally useful for development.

The Recreation Division of the Community Services Department
offers a wide variety of public recreation programs in the areas of
aquatics, summer play for children, child development, cultural
arts, sports, and adult recreation. A majority of Santa Barbara
residents and a comparable number from outside the city are served
by these programs.

Although for purposes of analysis it was necessary to make
certain simplifying assumptions about the future of public recreation
under various PIPs, it should be noted beforehand that there are important dimensions to recreation that lie outside the scope of this
work. Among the most significant are the recreation programs that
are offered by nongovernmental organizations, such as the YMCA,
the Boys Clubs, the Girl Scouts, the Boy Scouts, and the Cub Scouts.
In addition to these, there are activities available through the Continuing Education Division of Santa Barbara City College and UCSB
that must also be considered as an integral part of public recreation
in Santa Barbara. However, since these sectors lie outside the city's
sphere, they have not been considered in the following analysis.

Assumptions and Methodology. It is assumed for purposes of projecting the costs of parks and recreational facilities that the same
per capita level of services will be maintained at all PIPs. The estimates of needs are thus derived from standards reflecting the current situation. With regard to recreation, three further assumptions
are made that minimize the projected costs of recreational facilities.
First, it is assumed that the city continues to coordinate its program
with those of nongovernmental agencies and the public school system.
For example, the Recreation Division makes use of school play-
grounds and other school facilities for public recreation after school
hours. In so doing, it maximizes the use of existing facilities while
minimizing expenditures on capital improvements. Second, it is assumed that the city will continue its current policy of making new
recreation programs, such as scuba diving and karate, more self-
supporting. Finally, it is assumed that all capital improvement
costs for recreation are subsumed in the per acre acquisition and
development estimates for future parks. If, for some reason, additional recreation facilities cannot be provided in new parks, additional land-acquisition costs will result.

The Parks Division of the Community Services Department. Parks
are classified according to their size, location, and function. Of the
total 1,860 acres, some 43 acres are classified as neighborhood and
mini-parks, 46 acres as community parks, 95 acres as citywide
parks, 158 acres as special-use facilities (that is, tennis courts,
municipal golf courses, and so on), and 731 acres as regional parks.

In addition to these categories, the city owns 768 acres of open space, and the Parks Division maintains 18 acres of boulevards, buildings, and plazas, as well as other locations for which no acreage figures are available.[4]

Following is an explanation of the means by which future park needs and costs were projected. Definitions of park classifications were arrived at in conjunction with the Parks Division of the Community Services Department. Although not all existing parks in a given classification meet the acreage criteria stated, it is hoped that such definitions will provide some guidance in the future.

1. Neighborhood and mini-parks. Mini-parks are usually less than two acres, while neighborhood parks generally range between two and ten acres. For purposes of this work these two park types have been considered together. There are presently 0.59 acres of park land under these classifications for every 1,000 residents in the city. In projecting the future needs of neighborhood and miniparks for each PIP, it is assumed that this will be maintained. Park needs for all neighborhoods were computed using this ratio, and neighborhoods with needs of fewer than two acres for any of the PIPs were combined with adjacent neighborhoods to meet the appropriate acreage and service requirements of a neighborhood park. These were developed in such a way that the Parks Division, in preparing a park plan, could use these acreage needs in locating potential park properties.

a. Acquisition costs. For purposes of projecting site acquisition costs it was assumed that the least-cost property (that is, that which is either vacant or overzoned, meaning it is used less intensively than zoning permits) will be purchased. Market value of such land was then estimated at 5.3 times the current assessment value; this formula compensates for the current under-assessment of city land and hence reflects current market value. If the number of vacant acres in a given area were significantly greater than what is required for parks, overzones land costs were not included in computing acquisition estimates.

b. Development costs. The average development costs for neighborhood and mini-parks was assumed to be $24,000 per acre, based on City Parks Division estimates.

2. Community parks. These generally range from 10 to 15 acres, serve larger populations, and provide generally for more diversified activities than neighborhood or mini-parks.

a. Acquisition costs. It was assumed that community parks will be developed on vacant land. Cost estimates were developed as follows: Neighborhoods were identified that contain parcels of land of sufficient size and topography to render them suitable for

community-park use. The average assessed value of these parcels was then computed and used as a basis for calculating current market values. These values were then totaled and averaged
to produce an average land cost per square foot. Using those criteria, six neighborhoods were found to contain land that is appropriate for community-park use. The average market value of
this land is approximately $0.72 per square foot, or $29,185 per
acre.

b. Development costs. It was assumed that the City Parks
Division standard of $43,000 per acre will apply to the develop-
ment of new community parks. [5]

3. Citywide parks. These are usually larger than 15 acres
and are designed to serve all segments of the city's populace.

a. Acquisition costs. Cost estimates for citywide parks
were computed in the same manner as those for community parks.
In some cases there is insufficient land within the city limits to
accommodate citywide parks, after providing for community-park
acquisition. Because of this situation, it is assumed that land
currently under county jurisdiction might be purchased by the city
or acquired jointly with the county. Those neighborhoods that
contain sufficient land or are adjacent to suitable county land for
citywide parks include Eucalyptus Hill, Foothill, Campanil, and
Hope. Average vacant land costs in these neighborhoods is estimated at $0.24 per square foot, or $10,454 per acre. [6]

b. Development costs. Based on City Parks Division estimates, $50,000 per acre will be needed for the construction of
new citywide parks.

4. Buildings, boulevards, and plazas. Landscaping along
boulevards such as Cabrillo and State Street, around public buildings
such as City Hall and the Public Works Building, and small plazas
and walkways such as de la Guerra Plaza provide an additional 18
acres of land that are classified as "park" by the Parks Division of
the Community Services Department. Because boulevards and
plazas are "fixed" into the city's infrastructure, it cannot be assumed
that their acreage will increase proportionately with growth. No cost
estimates were made for the acquisition-costs classification.

5. Special-use facilities. These include tennis courts, municipal pools, golf courses, baseball diamonds, and soccer fields.

a. Acquisition costs. Costs associated with special-use
facilities are higher than those for any other type of park because
of the unique requirements in this category. Special-use facilities
must be located on flat land near residential areas. Because of
the relative scarcity of undeveloped land of this type, it was necessary to assume that two-thirds of the land for such facilities will
be acquired from residentially used land, and one-third from

vacant parcels. The estimated cost is $2.57 per square foot, or
$112,000 per acre.

      b. Development costs. Special-use facilities require high-
intensity development, and thus costs are higher than those for
other park types. The Parks Division has estimated these costs
at $60,000 per acre.[7]

      6. Regional parks. These generally require a minimum of 50
acres and are designed to serve an area larger than the city. Rattle-
snake Canyon (452 acres) and the city's beach system (about 83 acres)
are included in this classification. It was assumed that no additional
inland areas will be purchased for regional parks. Park officials believe that present noncoastal sites are adequate to serve populations
at all PIPs.

      Growth could have a significant effect on the regional beach-
park system. Because the city owns most of its coastal beaches,
this resource must be considered fixed at its present acreage. On
a per capita basis there are presently some 48 square feet of beach
per resident, exclusive of tourist use. This ratio would decline to
as little as 21 square feet in the year 2000 for the Zoning Maximum
PIP. The Half-Density Probable PIP, which approximates recent
growth trends in the city, would result in a reduction to 38 square
feet per resident in that year.

      This decline in per capita beach space would be compounded by
increased tourism within the city and additional growth in the neighboring Goleta and Carpinteria Valleys. Crowding would be further
aggravated by the need to expand parking facilities for these new
beach users. Unless measures were taken to provide alternate
modes of transportation to the beach areas, the city would have to
acquire and develop new land for parking purposes. Our estimates
of additional parking-space requirements are based on current
ratios, which, it should be noted, are considered substandard by the
city's Community Services Department. The total acreage to be acquired for each PIP is estimated as follows: Half-Density Maximum,
8.3 acres; Half-Density Probable, 3.7 acres; General Plan Maximum,
12.4 acres; General Plan Probable, 5.6 acres; Zoning Maximum,
18.0 acres; Zoning Probable, 8.6 acres.

      Assuming that existing beach land is not used to accommodate
new parking facilities, the city would have to acquire land valued between $4 and $6 per square foot. Using $4 per square foot as a
standard, land-acquisition costs for beach parking would range from
about $661,000 for the Half-Density Probable population to approxi-
mately $3.1 million under the Zoning Maximum. These costs in-
clude land, but not development, which is conservatively estimated
at $3 per square foot.

7. Park financing. It has been assumed that all land needed for neighborhood, community, and citywide parks under each PIP would be acquired under a bond floated in 1976. Purchasing park land well in advance of needs would be beneficial for several reasons; the city would avoid appreciably higher purchase costs associated with having to buy land already developed, and it would avoid the objectionable task of condemning lands for this use at future dates. The present ratio of the cost of developed land to vacant land (10:1, according to the County Assessor's analysis of city property values) makes it clear that the costs will be far greater than those shown in this work, if early acquisition is not undertaken. It has further been assumed that park development will occur after land acquisition, as the need occurs. Thus, park improvements will be financed as part of five-year capital-improvement programs. The annual costs of these programs were computed by assuming that 25-year 6-percent interest bonds would be floated to finance each program.

Tables 6.3 and 6.4 summarize the impact of population growth on total park-acreage requirements and on the costs of acquiring land and developing facilities. The figures represent the amount of land and the total costs that would be required for the population projections in the year 2000.[8]

The Recreation Division of the Community Services Department. As indicated previously, it is assumed that the cost of recreational facilities is included in the acquisition and development costs previously detailed in the discussion of city parks. The future requirements for recreational services, in order to maintain current standards, were determined to be the following:

1. Adult recreation centers. A population increase approximating that of Half-Density Probable (1 percent per year) will result in the need for a new adult recreation center in the general area of the East Side neighborhood. A second facility will be needed if the city comes close to the General Plan Maximum population, and a third if the city approached the Zoning Maximum level. A larger facility will be needed in the San Roque/Samarkand area if the city's population surpasses 100,000. The cost of each of these adult recreation centers will range from between $350,000 and $500,000 based on an estimated $35 to $40 per square foot construction-cost figure supplied by the Parks Division and local contractors.

2. Special-use facilities. Development of a major sports facility can be justified currently, but it will become a necessity if the city approaches a population of 100,000. If the population increases to approximately 150,000, another major sports complex will be required to maintain current standards. Such facilities would include

TABLE 6.3

Impact of Population on Park Acreage Requirements

Type	Present Acres*	Present Sq. Feet Per Person	Half-Density		General Plan		Zoning	
			Maximum	Probable	Maximum	Probable	Maximum	Probable
Neighborhood	43.5	25.9	69.0	55.9	84.0	62.1	99.5	71.5
Community	46.1	27.4	74.0	58.9	88.0	65.2	107.1	75.3
Citywide	95.2	56.7	152.9	121.8	181.8	134.6	221.2	155.4
Special use	158.2	94.2	254.0	202.3	302.0	223.7	367.5	258.3
Regional and beaches	731.0	435.4	731.0	731.0	731.0	731.0	731.0	731.0
Beach parking	13.6	8.1	21.8	17.4	26.0	19.2	31.6	22.2
Open space	768.0	457.5	768.0	768.0	768.0	768.0	768.0	768.0
Plazas, city buildings, and boulevard	18.0	10.7	18.0	18.0	18.0	18.0	18.0	18.0
Totals	1,873.6	1,115.9	2,088.7	1,973.3	2,198.8	2,021.8	2,343.9	2,099.7
Total additional acreage to be acquired	--	--	215.1	99.7	325.2	148.2	470.3	226.1

*Total park acreage figures referred to in text do not include acres of beach-related parking.

Source: Santa Barbara Planning Task Force estimates.

TABLE 6.4

Costs of Land and Development for Parks at Each PIP
(1974 dollars)

	Average Cost per Acre	Half-Density		General Plan		Zoning	
		Maximum	Probable	Maximum	Probable	Maximum	Probable
Land acquisition[a]							
Neighborhood	Varies	771,440	465,765	1,999,051	911,068	2,583,234	1,356,970
Community	31,363	876,282	403,642	1,315,678	599,033	1,914,711	915,486
Citywide	10,454	602,882	277,554	904,898	411,992	1,316,995	629,540
Special use	112,000	10,730,720	4,940,320	16,108,960	7,332,640	23,443,840	11,207,840
Beach parking	174,240	1,437,070	661,705	2,157,451	982,076	3,139,754	1,501,027
Subtotal	--	14,418,394	6,748,986	22,486,038	10,236,009	32,398,534	15,610,863
Land development[b]							
Neighborhood	24,000	612,240	298,560	971,280	447,120	1,344,960	672,720
Community	43,000	1,201,420	553,410	1,003,050	821,300	2,625,150	1,255,170
Citywide	50,000	2,883,500	1,327,500	4,328,000	1,970,500	6,299,000	3,011,000
Special use	60,000	5,748,600	2,646,600	8,629,800	3,928,200	12,559,200	6,004,200
Beach parking	130,680	1,077,802	496,279	1,618,088	736,557	2,354,816	1,125,770
Subtotal	--	11,523,562	5,322,349	17,351,018	7,903,677	25,183,126	12,068,860
Total costs	--	25,941,956	12,071,335	39,837,056	18,140,486	57,581,660	27,679,723

[a]Does not include financing costs.

[b]All development costs are based on Parks Division, Community Services Department estimates, with the exception of beach-related parking, which was derived from Traffic and Parking Division, Public Works Department, and Parks Division estimates.

Source: Santa Barbara Planning Task Force.

lighted athletic fields, picnic areas, pathways, and parking, and they would require between 20 and 25 acres of relatively flat land for each such project. Development of a special-use facility is estimated at about $300,000 to $500,000, exclusive of land costs, which were taken into account in the previous estimates.

3. Tennis courts. Approximately four new public tennis courts will need to be constructed for each population increase of 10,000 to maintain the city's present ratio of 3.9 courts per 10,000 residents.[9] Per court costs are estimated at $25,000.[10]

4. Aquatics. City pools are the most capital-intensive aspect of the city's aquatic program. Santa Barbara owns and operates one pool, and relies heavily on the use of high school pools to meet present aquatic recreation needs. Another public pool will have to be constructed if the city reaches a population of 100,000, and a third pool will become necessary if population goes beyond 150,000. In addition to swimming pools, the Recreation Division of the Community Services Department maintains four wading pools for children. Based on today's standard, a new pool will be needed for each population increase of 20,000. Wading-pool costs are estimated at $50,000 each.

5. Lawn bowling. There are presently four lawn bowling greens in the city. It is assumed that the present ratio of 1.04 bowling greens per 20,000 persons will be maintained for each increase of 20,000 persons. Costs of each green are estimated at $25,000.

Projecting Park and Recreation Requirements to the PIPs. Under the growth policies analyzed in this book, the city will need to make substantial investments in land acquisition and development if it desires to maintain its current ratio of population to park acreage. Total acreage to be acquired, for each PIP, is presented on the bottom line of Table 6.3.

Depending upon the population level ultimately reached, costs of land acquisition will range from $6.7 million to $32.4 million (excluding financing costs). Total costs for land acquisition and development (excluding financing) are presented on the bottom line of Table 6.4.

The annual capital costs (25-year bonds at 6 percent annual interest) of the required programs for parks and recreation, for each PIP, are presented in Table 6.5. It is apparent that maintaining the city's current standards with regard to parks and recreation will require substantial investment under even modest population increases. When operating costs, as well as capital costs, are included, the yearly per capita costs of all such programs, for the year 2000, amount to almost $8 for the slowest-growth scenario (Half-Density Probable) and $21 for the highest (Zoning Maximum).

TABLE 6.5

Parks and Recreation Bond Costs, 1974–2000

(1974 dollars)

Year	No-Growth	Half-Density		General Plan		Zoning	
		Maximum	Probable	Maximum	Probable	Maximum	Probable
1974	0	0	0	0	0	0	0
1975	0	0	0	0	0	0	0
1976	0	586,540	279,328	946,272	430,859	1,351,582	655,719
1977	0	586,540	279,328	946,272	430,859	1,351,582	655,719
1978	0	586,540	279,328	946,272	430,859	1,351,582	655,719
1979	0	586,540	279,328	946,272	430,859	1,351,582	655,719
1980	0	586,540	279,328	946,272	430,859	1,351,582	655,719
1981	0	835,023	393,743	1,319,260	600,639	1,895,207	915,209
1982	0	835,023	393,743	1,319,260	600,639	1,895,207	915,209
1983	0	835,023	393,743	1,319,260	600,639	1,895,207	915,209
1984	0	835,023	393,743	1,319,260	600,639	1,895,207	915,209
1985	0	835,023	393,743	1,319,260	600,639	1,895,207	915,209
1986	0	1,083,506	508,158	1,692,248	770,419	2,438,832	1,174,699
1987	0	1,083,506	508,158	1,692,248	770,419	2,438,832	1,174,699
1988	0	1,083,506	508,158	1,692,248	770,419	2,438,832	1,174,699
1989	0	1,083,506	508,158	1,692,248	770,419	2,438,832	1,174,699
1990	0	1,083,506	508,158	1,692,248	770,419	2,438,832	1,174,699
1991	0	1,331,401	622,886	2,066,326	940,910	2,980,576	1,434,862
1992	0	1,331,401	622,886	2,066,326	940,910	2,980,576	1,434,862
1993	0	1,331,401	622,886	2,066,326	940,910	2,980,576	1,434,862
1994	0	1,331,401	622,886	2,066,326	940,910	2,980,576	1,434,862
1995	0	1,331,401	622,886	2,066,326	940,910	2,980,576	1,434,862
1996	0	1,579,296	737,614	2,440,404	1,111,401	3,522,320	1,695,025
1997	0	1,579,296	737,614	2,440,404	1,111,401	3,522,320	1,695,025
1998	0	1,579,296	737,614	2,440,404	1,111,401	3,522,320	1,695,025
1999	0	1,579,296	737,614	2,440,404	1,111,401	3,522,320	1,695,025
2000	0	1,579,296	737,614	2,440,404	1,111,401	3,522,320	1,695,025

Source: Santa Barbara Planning Task Force.

Public Works: Streets and Highways

Chapter 3 contains the analysis of holding capacities and feasible improvements that can be made at each PIP. Here, we merely summarize the minimum costs involved, as estimated in consultation with the city's Engineering Division. A total of $4 million was estimated for four basic road-widening projects.

Assuming that gas-tax subventions are spent for routine maintenance and reconstruction of existing roads and small-scale improvements, the cost of these improvements has been budgeted as a separate capital expenditure. The yearly repayments will amount to $312,000 on the total projected capital programs (see Table 6.6).

The road network, even with these improvements, would be unequal to projected traffic demand at numerous locations considerably before city population reaches the Zoning Probable PIP (119,000). Nevertheless, further capital expenditures for higher PIPs are not projected, because, in the view of city traffic planners, the improvements necessary to accommodate the traffic resulting from such population growth (assuming current car-usage patterns) would involve unacceptable environmental costs.

Instead, massive investments in some form of mass-transit system would be indicated. These investments, however, would be made not by the city, but by the Metropolitan Transit District, and a detailed accounting of them lies outside the scope of this work (an estimate of the magnitude, however, appears in Chapter 3).Because population growth will lead inevitably to higher transit costs (whether for mass transit subsidy or road improvement), the omission from analysis of these high-PIP expenses leads to a major understatement of the costs of growth.

Overview: Total General
Fund Expenditures

Table 6.7 summarizes the cost of municipal services from 1968/69 to 1972/73 per resident of the city. The single most expensive service is police, which has averaged almost one-fifth of the city's operating budget over the period; the costs of fire protection and public works make up the remainder of the first-half of the budget. Altogether, total General Fund expenditures have averaged $161 per city resident over the period.

Table 6.8 projects the total costs (operating and capital) of all General Fund expenditures combined, for each of our PIPs. Most of the increase in costs, under our assumptions, result from capital expenditures on library expansion, street widening, park acquisition, and the provision of recreational facilities, for all population-growth

TABLE 6.6

Public Works (Streets and Highways) Bond Costs, 1974-2000
(1974 dollars)

Year	No-Growth	Half-Density		General Plan		Zoning	
		Maximum	Probable	Maximum	Probable	Maximum	Probable
1974	0	0	0	0	0	0	0
1975	0	0	0	0	0	0	0
1976	0	0	0	0	0	0	0
1977	0	0	0	0	0	0	0
1978	0	0	0	0	0	0	0
1979	0	0	0	0	0	0	0
1980	0	0	0	0	0	0	0
1981	0	0	0	0	0	312,000	0
1982	0	0	0	0	0	312,000	0
1983	0	0	0	0	0	312,000	0
1984	0	0	0	312,000	0	312,000	0
1985	0	0	0	312,000	0	312,000	0
1986	0	0	0	312,000	0	312,000	0
1987	0	0	0	312,000	0	312,000	0
1988	0	0	0	312,000	0	312,000	0
1989	0	0	0	312,000	0	312,000	312,000
1990	0	312,000	0	312,000	0	312,000	312,000
1991	0	312,000	0	312,000	0	312,000	312,000
1992	0	312,000	0	312,000	0	312,000	312,000
1993	0	312,000	0	312,000	0	312,000	312,000
1994	0	312,000	0	312,000	0	312,000	312,000
1995	0	312,000	0	312,000	0	312,000	312,000
1996	0	312,000	0	312,000	0	312,000	312,000
1997	0	312,000	0	312,000	0	312,000	312,000
1998	0	312,000	0	312,000	0	312,000	312,000
1999	0	312,000	0	312,000	0	312,000	312,000
2000	0	312,000	0	312,000	0	312,000	312,000

Source: Santa Barbara Planning Task Force.

TABLE 6.7

Costs of Municipal Services per Resident, City of Santa Barbara,
1968/69 Through 1972/73, and Five-Year Average
(1974 dollars)

Service	1968/69	1969/70	1970/71	1971/72	1972/73	Five-Year Average	
						Average	Percent of Total
Library	8.19	8.45	7.92	10.08	12.26	9.38	5.8
Parks and recreation	16.79	19.48	18.83	17.80	19.95	18.57	11.5
Parks	10.43	12.08	11.55	11.50	13.87	11.89	7.4
Recreation	6.36	7.40	7.28	6.30	6.08	6.68	4.1
Police	26.08	29.19	29.74	32.15	32.55	29.33	18.5
Fire	20.85	22.36	22.89	22.44	21.72	22.05	13.7
Public works	24.79	26.69	23.08	27.97	23.41	25.19	15.6
Streets	14.24	15.94	12.67	10.50	10.30	12.73	7.9
Traffic	2.18	2.40	2.22	2.25	2.23	2.26	1.4
Electrical maintenance	3.41	3.67	3.62	3.68	3.67	3.61	2.2
Engineering/administration	4.95	4.68	4.56	11.54	7.22	6.59	4.1
Subtotal	96.65	106.17	102.46	110.44	109.88	105.12	65.1
All other	54.89	57.17	57.50	56.44	55.06	56.21	34.9
Total	151.54	163.34	159.97	166.89	164.95	161.39	100.0

Source: City of Santa Barbara, Annual Report, 1972–73 (1973).

TABLE 6.8

Total Costs, Operating Plus Capital, for Each PIP, 1974-2000

Year	No-Growth	Half-Density Maximum	Half-Density Probable	General Plan Maximum	General Plan Probable	Zoning Maximum	Zoning Probable
1974	11,786,913	11,786,913	11,786,913	11,786,913	11,786,913	11,786,913	11,786,913
1975	11,786,913	12,067,276	11,916,008	12,207,812	11,978,508	12,399,459	12,079,756
1976	11,842,913	13,259,679	12,380,429	13,769,994	12,656,975	14,790,587	13,223,318
1977	11,842,913	13,641,552	12,509,521	14,321,402	12,848,571	15,403,135	13,516,161
1978	11,842,913	13,921,916	12,638,614	14,843,814	13,040,178	16,015,682	13,939,506
1979	11,842,913	14,202,279	12,767,709	15,264,721	13,231,772	16,714,229	14,333,847
1980	12,049,413	14,482,653	13,035,802	15,685,632	13,423,379	17,326,774	14,626,691
1981	12,049,413	15,011,499	13,380,809	16,544,519	14,054,257	18,794,946	15,179,034
1982	12,049,413	15,291,873	13,640,403	16,965,428	14,347,361	19,407,492	15,471,878
1983	12,049,413	15,649,236	13,769,497	17,386,337	14,538,957	20,020,039	15,820,720
1984	12,049,413	15,929,598	13,898,590	18,119,247	14,730,565	20,632,586	16,113,564
1985	12,049,413	16,209,973	14,027,683	18,626,156	14,922,160	21,383,131	16,406,407
1986	12,049,413	16,738,819	14,271,192	19,420,052	15,348,547	22,539,304	16,958,742
1987	12,049,413	17,019,181	14,400,286	19,840,952	15,540,142	23,151,851	17,251,584
1988	12,049,413	17,299,555	14,529,379	20,261,862	15,731,747	23,764,408	17,544,438
1989	12,049,413	17,579,919	14,658,471	20,682,770	15,923,356	24,376,953	18,235,280
1990	12,049,413	18,172,292	14,787,565	21,103,681	16,114,951	24,989,501	18,528,125
1991	12,049,413	18,700,550	15,031,387	21,898,668	16,477,048	26,143,790	19,081,130
1992	12,049,413	18,980,912	15,160,481	22,319,578	16,668,644	26,838,338	19,373,971
1993	12,049,413	19,343,288	15,362,574	22,740,488	16,860,251	27,450,885	19,666,816
1994	12,049,413	19,623,650	15,491,667	23,234,386	17,051,846	28,063,429	19,959,668
1995	12,049,413	19,904,023	15,620,760	23,655,296	17,243,452	28,675,976	20,252,514
1996	12,049,413	20,432,282	15,864,582	24,450,282	17,605,541	29,830,267	20,805,518
1997	12,049,413	20,712,645	15,993,676	24,871,193	17,797,147	30,442,815	21,098,361
1998	12,049,413	20,993,018	16,122,769	25,292,101	17,988,743	31,055,361	21,391,204
1999	12,049,413	21,273,381	16,251,862	25,713,011	18,180,349	31,684,906	21,684,048
2000	12,049,413	21,553,745	16,380,957	26,133,910	18,371,946	32,297,454	21,976,891

Source: Santa Barbara Planning Task Force.

164

scenarios except No-Growth. Parkland is extremely costly, and we assume that needed land is assembled and bought at the beginning of the study period, in anticipation of future growth; land costs are thus minimized.[11]

Having projected General Fund expenditures to our PIPs, we now turn to the other side of the ledger: anticipated General Fund revenues under future population levels.

General Fund Revenues at Future PIPs

Property-Tax Revenues

Taxes on real property provide one-quarter of the city's General Fund revenues and three-quarters of all revenues in both the elementary and the high school districts. The city currently taxes property at the rate of $1.46 per $100 of assessed valuation; $1.34 of this is used to generate revenues for the General Fund, while the remaining $0.12 is currently used for debt service.

Assumptions on the Effects of Population Growth on the Property Tax. Just as we assumed that present per capita operating expenditures would persist on the cost side, so we now make the analogous assumption that per capita revenues from property taxes will, all other things being equal, continue at their present rate.

The historical comparison of population growth and assessed valuation reveals that assessment has been a rather clear-cut reflection of population numbers.[12] Each person added to the population is thus assumed to add a constant amount of assessed valuation to the tax rolls.[13] It is people who use their income to bid up land prices and cause improvements to be built and who produce increments in valuation. Those increments in valuation generally grow in proportion to numbers.

We therefore employ the average per capita assessed value over 1969-74 as a predictor of the additional revenue base created by each new resident. This amounts to $3,295 per person in 1974 dollars, or $48 in revenues at the current tax rate of $1.46 per $100 of assessed valuation (of which $44 goes into the city's General Fund, and the remaining $4--equivalent to a tax rate of $0.12--is used for debt service).

The No-Growth Scenario. Although the assumption of constant per capita property valuation provides a way to project property tax revenues under our growth PIPs, it does not provide a way to predict property tax revenues under No-Growth. The crucial question

is whether government revenues will fall as a result of No-Growth
policies. With regard to the value of property, it is widely assumed
that much of the value of property represents speculative--that is,
anticipated--use. If such future use is denied through growth controls, it is then argued, the value of property will drop.

1. No-Growth through downzoning: A worst-case analysis.
A possible No-Growth scenario would be one in which all land in the
city is downzoned such that its current use becomes its legal maximum use. [14] An analysis of the consequences of such approach
should thus serve to indicate property-value losses that might result
from such extreme measures, and thus constitutes a worst-case
analysis. It does not assume that such measures are either desirable or legal.

The County Assessor has speculated that any loss in land value
of improved properties would be compensated for by a corresponding
increase in the value of the improvement. This would be true, the
argument goes, because currently the structures on "overzoned" parcels of land tend to be considered primarily as impediments to more
intensive development. Should such development become impossible
because of downzoning, the value of the land would decline, but the
improvement value would rise. Thus, according to the County Assessor, any loss that would come about from a downzoning policy in
the total assessed valuation of the city land would result from the
loss of speculative value of presently unimproved (vacant) land.

We undertook two studies relevant to this issue. First, we examined the land values of all vacant lots in the city and studied the
effects on property-tax revenues that would be caused by the removal
of all value from such land. Second, we examined all residential
parcels in the city that are zoned for a more intensive use than they
currently possess--for example, parcels zoned for apartments that
currently have old single-family houses. We compared the value of
such lots (land only) with the value of nearby land actually zoned for
single-family homes; the value of the latter is expected to be the
"floor" to which land values of overzoned lots will fall if downzoned
to single-family residential.

a. The effects of downzoning unimproved (vacant) lots.
To estimate the dollar loss of a policy that would eliminate all
value from unimproved land, we inventoried all such parcels in
the city, noting the value of each. We estimate the total assessed
values of unimproved parcels at $5.324 million, which represents
2.4 percent of the current assessed valuation of the city. At current tax rates, this provides the city with only $77,730, amount-
ing to 0.7 percent of total General Fund receipts (for the high
school district revenues derived from this land amount to 0.8

percent of total operating revenues; for the elementary school district the figure is 2.3 percent). We shall therefore reduce the projected assessed value of the city for No-Growth by $5.3 million, and that of the school districts by appropriate amounts. This means we assume this land has lost 100 percent of its market value.

      b. The effect of downzoning on "overzoned" lots. What would be the revenue loss from developed land currently being used at less than its legal maximum but having value because of its legal development potential? To estimate the speculative value of such land in the city we had the following procedure.

First, we assumed that a good indicator of the results of downzoning such land to single-family use would be the current value of lots that are presently used for single-family homes and that are zoned only for such use. We selected a random sample of single-family lots (R-1) from all such lots in the city, weighting the sample to achieve appropriate locational representation.[15] The average assessed valuation of each parcel was determined, and the summary results are presented in Table 6.9.

Second, all "overzoned" lots in the city were inventoried. That is, we looked at all lots in the city zoned for high-residential density (R-3 or R-4) or commercial use (C) that presently contain either single-family dwellings or duplexes. (Present city policy permits the development of high-density residential structures in commercially zoned areas.) Again, average land values per square foot were calculated; the results are summarized in Table 6.9. From this table, several facts emerge.

First, the current use of the land--that is, whether it presently contains a single-family house or a duplex--is inconsequential to the value of the land itself. The second fact that may be noted is that there is a significant difference in land value between overzoned land carrying high-density residential zoning (R-3 or R-4) and such land with commercial (C) zoning. The difference is some $0.18 per square foot on the average: $0.45 per square foot for R-3/R-4 versus $0.63 per square foot for C zones. It is likely that this is due to locational differences; the high-density residentially zoned land is scattered throughout the city, in both desirable and undesirable locations, whereas commercially zoned land is concentrated in central areas that are generally already commercially developed. It was decided to drop commercial land from the analysis on the judgment that its speculative value is based primarily on its location and potential commercial use rather than on its potential residential use (though residential development is legally possible). Since downzoning would only indirectly affect this further commercial use, the effect of removing

TABLE 6.9

Comparative Values of Overzoned R-3/R-4 Areas and Proximate R-1 Areas: Tax Loss Due to Downzoning

R-3/R-4 Neighborhoods	Number of Overzoned R-3/R-4 Lots Inventoried	Average Assessed Value		Tax Loss from Downzoning R-3/R-4 to R-1 Value		
		Overzoned R-3/R-4 Lot (¢/Ft²)	Nearby R-1 Lot (¢/Ft²)	City of Santa Barbara ($)	Santa Barbara Elementary School District ($)	Santa Barbara High School District ($)
Laguna, Upper East, Downtown	373	55.95	44.94	3,852.52	10,432.93	6,886.77
West Downtown, Oak Park	788	44.71	44.94	--	--	--
Westside, Lower West, West Beach	587	38.18	32.01	3,171.27	8,588.07	5,668.98
East Beach, East Side	155	37.24	31.22[a]	782.51	2,119.10	1,398.10
Total	1,903	44.29	--	7,806.30[b]	21,140.10[c]	13,953.85[d]

[a]No nearby R-1 area for comparison--therefore, the assumption was made that the percentage drop in value would be approximately equal to the average drop in those sections with comparable areas.

[b]0.2 percent of city's property-tax revenue.

[c]0.3 percent of tax revenue of district.

[d]0.1 percent of tax revenue of district.

Source: Santa Barbara Planning Task Force estimates, derived from 1973-74 Secured Assessment Rolls.

further residential use would likely be insignificant. In any event, the number of such lots is not large (256), relative to the total number of overzoned lots in the city (2,159).

In order to determine the effects of downzoning apartment zones (R-3/R-4), proximate sections of such zones were grouped together, and the values of these large sections of overzoned land were compared to the values of the nearest parcels of single-family zoned (R-1) and used land. In Table 6.9 it may be seen that in three of the areas there would be a slight revenue loss associated with downzoning to single-family use. In the fourth the average overzoned (R-3/R-4) lot and the corresponding single-family (R-1) lot are virtually identical in value. For all areas, the total losses would amount to 0.2 percent of the City of Santa Barbara's tax revenues, 0.3 percent of those of the Santa Barbara elementary school district, and 0.1 percent of those of the Santa Barbara high school district.

We may conclude that the speculative value of residential property lies in its location, not in its zoning. A change in the zone, by itself, is likely to have little effect on land value, and hence city revenues from this source. To the extent that downzoning would have the compensating effects of raising the value of improvements (as the County Assessor has suggested), even the minor revenue losses indicated by our data would not develop.

We do not include such possible compensating effects in our calculations. It reveals that the maximum losses of downzoning would amount to $5.3 million to the city, necessitating a $0.03 rise in the property tax rate to maintain constant revenues from this source.

2. No Growth through limitation of migration opportunities. In restricting the housing supply one does not necessarily restrict population growth; if persons continue to migrate to Santa Barbara, attracted, for example, by employment opportunities, they will compete with one another for the limited housing supply available. While severe housing shortages in the long run may restrict the number of persons that can find housing in Santa Barbara, other consequences are also probable: A higher proportion of the more-desirable housing will become occupied by upper-income persons, who can better afford the rising cost of such housing in a scarcity market, and the remaining housing will become increasingly crowded as low- and moderate-income persons double up in order to afford the rent. Housing restrictions entail minimal fiscal costs to the governing bodies that depend on property tax revenues, but they do result in severe and regressive financial burdens to residents (Buchalter et al. 1973). It is for these reasons that we now consider effects of the second sort of growth-limitation policies.

The market value of property lies to some extent in its expected future uses--what is often termed its speculative value. In the previous section it was demonstrated that the speculative value conferred on property by zoning itself is negligible in Santa Barbara. There is a further component of speculative value that has not yet been considered, however: the value that comes from anticipated general population growth, and the demand for property that such growth will entail. It is plausible that the value of land in rapidly growing areas of the city reflects the expectation of owners and buyers that higher-density housing will be built in the future, thereby appreciating the total property value substantially.

The two most rapidly growing neighborhoods in the city are Oak Park, the population of which increased by 9 to 10 percent over 1969-74, and Lower West, which increased by more than 17 percent. The average assessed value per square foot of overzoned residential land in these two neighborhoods is $0.44 and $0.40, respectively--about the same as the citywide average ($0.44). They do not apparently enjoy inflated property values because of their growth patterns. Rather than expected future residential use based on past growth trends, it is location and expected commercial use that apparently determine the value of land; the most expensive overzoned land in the city is either in the higher-income residential neighborhoods (Laguna and Upper East) or in the neighborhoods with the greatest commercial potential (Downtown, East Beach, and West Beach).

While neighborhoods that are in the process of rapidly converting from single-family houses to apartments may indeed experience high speculative land values, there is no evidence that this has happened in Santa Barbara. Lower West, West Downtown, and Oak Park are all extensively overzoned neighborhoods that are currently undergoing conversions of this sort. Furthermore, they are areas in which the General Plan calls for substantial densification. Yet the value of overzoned land in these three neighborhoods is not significantly different from the city average.

We may thus conclude that the value of residentially zoned land in Santa Barbara is not generally inflated in anticipation of future, more intensive uses. With the exception of undeveloped land, which might indeed lose substantial value under extreme land use measures, no significant drop in land value would result from growth policies that resulted in a reduction of immigration to the city. This is reasonable, in light of the extremely modest growth rates the city has experienced since the mid-1960s--only about 1 percent per annum. Measures that limit growth through influencing immigration, such as those measures that restrict the supply of housing, will not reduce the tax base of the city, beyond those minimal losses resulting from potential loss of development rights on currently open land.

Revenues from All Other Sources

Revenues to the city's General Fund from other sources (not based on assessed valuations) can be classified as follows.

1. Revenues that are more or less directly tied to the number of people. Included in this category are property taxes; state subventions, such as gasoline and motor vehicle taxes; park and recreation fees; cigarette taxes; and special taxes on utility use. Revenues from such taxes are expected to increase at the same rate as that of the population.

2. Revenues that are tied to building activity and thus indirectly to the number of people. Examples include building permit fees, and service charges by certain city agencies (Building Department, Planning, and Public Works). While building activity may fluctuate in the short run, in the long run it is assumed that such activity is a consequence of the number of people.

3. Revenues that are a function of total sales in the city. The principal revenue of this sort is the sales-tax subvention (the city government receives $0.0095 in taxes for every dollar of sales in the city); business license and general franchise taxes are also of this sort. These revenues also reflect population to some degree, but will increase faster than population to the extent that total business activity outstrips population growth.

4. Revenues that are largely independent of population. The "bed tax"--levied on hotel-motel users--is the principal example. Revenues from this tax are a function of the number of hotel-motel units and the general state of the tourist industry.

Table 6.10 summarizes the principal nonproperty tax categories of revenue, per person, for the period 1963-73. All sources of revenue listed have averaged about 56 percent of total revenues to the General Fund over 1968/69-1972/73 (property taxes, not listed in this table, amount to an additional 27 percent). The three principal sources of revenue exhibit a similar pattern: The amounts per city resident increased slightly during the 1960s and have fallen off sharply since. City government has met its increasing costs not out of existing sources of revenue but by adding additional ones; the three relatively new taxes listed in Table 6.10 (bed tax, utility users' tax, and cigarette tax) currently add almost $20 per person to the General Fund (line VI). In forecasting General Fund revenues from these sources, we employ the average per capita receipts for all sources over 1969-74.

Our assumptions that per capita receipts from sales taxes will remain constant in the future is at variance with the assumption of

TABLE 6.10

Per Capita Revenues from Principal Sources to the General Fund, Excluding Property Taxes, 1963-73

(1974 dollars)

Line	Source of Revenue	1963/64	1964/65	1965/66	1966/67	1967/68	1968/69	1969/70	1970/71	1971/72	1972/73	5-Year Average 1968/69-1972/73	Percent of Total General Fund Expenditures ($161.40 = 100%)
I	Revenues tied directly to population[a]	21.8	26.6	24.7	24.2	23.6	22.3	21.2	21.5	21.4	20.4	21.4	13.3
II	Revenues tied to building activity[b]	4.3	4.7	2.9	2.9	4.1	4.2	4.3	3.2	3.4	3.6	3.7	2.3
III	Revenues tied to sales: total[c]	52.7	53.5	49.3	53.8	52.4	55.2	51.4	46.4	47.5	49.1	49.9	30.9
IV	Sales tax	44.7	44.9	41.9	43.8	45.3	43.8	43.9	38.9	39.9	41.3	41.6	25.8
V	Principal sources of revenue throughout period: subtotal	78.7	84.8	76.9	80.9	80.1	81.7	76.9	71.1	72.3	73.1	75.0	46.5
VI	Principal revenue sources added since 1963: total	--	2.0	4.1	4.4	10.0	11.8	10.5	15.4	19.2	19.1	15.2	9.4
VII	Bed tax	--	2.0	4.1	4.4	4.4	5.1	4.5	4.1	4.6	4.8	4.6	2.9
VIII	Cigarette tax	--	--	--	--	5.6	6.7	6.0	5.6	5.4	4.9	5.7	3.5
IX	Utility-user's tax	--	--	--	--	--	--	--	5.7	9.2	9.4	(8.1)	(5.0)
X	Total	78.7	86.8	81.0	85.3	90.1	93.5	87.4	86.5	91.5	92.2	90.2	55.9

[a]Gasoline tax, motor vehicle in lieu tax, alcoholic-beverage license fees, park and recreation charges. About half is the gasoline tax, which can be used for the construction and maintenance of streets and highways.

[b]Building, electricity, and plumbing permits; building, planning and public works service charges; public safety charges.

[c]Sales tax, general-franchise tax, business-license fees.

Source: City of Santa Barbara, Annual Report, 1972-73 (1973).

rising per capita sales often made by economists (for example, Gruen and Gruen 1974). For sales per resident to rise, one or both of two conditions are usually fulfilled: "Disposable" incomes must rise, and/or the city must "capture" an increasing amount of local trade. The latter will occur if the city becomes more attractive to shoppers (for example, by building a major shopping center) so that fewer residents shop elsewhere, and more nonresidents go to the city to shop.

Neither of these conditions can be predicted with certainty to occur. Although real incomes rose by an average of 1.5 percent per annum during much of the 1960s, they have since leveled off and even declined. Santa Barbara's per capita receipts from sales taxes have, on the whole, remained steady since the mid-1960s. We do not build into our model the optimistic revenue picture that would result from assuming continually rising incomes at rates characteristic of some prosperous periods of the recent past.

Nor do we believe that a growing Santa Barbara will necessarily "capture" a greater share of the southland retail market. That is certainly a possibility; but it is equally possible that other areas will build shopping centers to compete with those likely to attend growth in the city. A growing city, in the context of a growing South Coast, will not inevitably increase its share of trade--particularly in the absence of regional planning to promote such an end.

The data from the cross-cities analysis (see Chapter 2) support these assumptions: Large and growing cities are not fiscally better off than smaller ones; they do not necessarily receive increased per capita revenues from sales taxes, property taxes, or any other sources.

To the extent we have understated future sales-tax revenues attributable to ever-rising purchasing power, sales-tax revenues at all PIPs (including No-Growth) have been understated.

Table 6.11 projects total revenues to each of our population levels, on the basis of assumptions specified earlier: with the exception of No-Growth, where the total amount of property taxes is expected to drop somewhat, all other revenues are in direct proportion to population.

Net Effects of Growth on the General Fund

We are now in a position to compare future General Fund revenues with future expenditures, for each PIP. The difference between revenues and costs in any year is a measure of the increased cost (or savings) that will result from growth.

TABLE 6.11

Total Revenues for Each PIP, 1974–2000

(1974 dollars)

Year	No-Growth	Half-Density		General Plan		Zoning	
		Maximum	Probable	Maximum	Probable	Maximum	Probable
1974	11,727,115	11,798,457	11,798,457	11,798,457	11,798,457	11,798,457	11,798,457
1975	11,727,115	12,073,677	11,925,183	12,211,635	11,986,538	12,399,767	12,085,929
1976	11,727,115	12,348,898	12,051,908	12,624,823	12,174,630	13,001,078	12,373,400
1977	11,727,115	12,624,128	12,178,633	13,038,013	12,362,712	13,602,386	12,660,871
1978	11,727,115	12,899,349	12,305,359	13,451,199	12,550,804	14,203,698	12,948,343
1979	11,727,115	13,174,569	12,432,083	13,864,389	12,738,885	14,805,009	13,235,814
1980	11,727,115	13,449,800	12,558,810	14,277,577	12,926,976	15,406,320	13,523,284
1981	11,727,115	13,725,020	12,685,535	14,690,756	13,115,059	16,007,634	13,810,767
1982	11,727,115	14,000,250	12,812,260	15,103,947	13,303,150	16,608,940	14,098,240
1983	11,727,115	14,275,470	12,938,986	15,517,134	13,491,230	17,210,252	14,385,709
1984	11,727,115	14,550,693	13,065,711	15,930,325	13,679,321	17,811,562	14,673,182
1985	11,717,115	14,825,923	13,192,435	16,343,512	13,867,402	18,412,874	14,960,655
1986	11,717,115	15,101,143	13,319,160	16,756,699	14,055,497	19,014,185	15,248,123
1987	11,717,115	15,376,362	13,445,888	17,169,879	14,243,578	19,615,496	15,535,596
1988	11,717,115	15,651,592	13,572,613	17,583,070	14,431,670	20,216,817	15,823,078
1989	11,717,115	15,926,816	13,699,338	17,996,257	14,619,761	20,818,128	16,110,550
1990	11,717,115	16,202,046	13,826,062	18,409,448	14,807,842	21,419,439	16,398,022
1991	11,717,115	16,477,266	13,952,787	18,822,634	14,995,932	22,020,750	16,685,495
1992	11,717,115	16,752,485	14,079,515	19,235,825	15,184,018	22,622,062	16,972,964
1993	11,717,115	17,027,716	14,206,239	19,649,012	15,372,109	23,223,372	17,260,437
1994	11,717,115	17,302,939	14,332,965	20,062,193	15,560,190	23,824,684	17,547,916
1995	11,717,115	17,578,169	14,459,688	20,475,380	15,748,280	24,425,994	17,835,390
1996	11,717,115	17,853,389	14,586,417	20,888,571	15,936,362	25,027,305	18,122,863
1997	11,717,115	18,128,608	14,713,141	21,301,757	16,124,453	25,628,616	18,410,333
1998	11,717,115	18,403,839	14,839,866	21,714,947	16,312,537	26,229,927	18,697,805
1999	11,717,115	18,679,062	14,966,591	22,128,135	16,500,628	26,831,238	18,985,277
2000	11,727,115	18,954,281	15,093,319	22,541,315	16,688,709	27,432,548	19,272,747

Source: Santa Barbara Planning Task Force.

174

When we compare the balance sheet between revenues and expenditures, we will follow two procedures. First, we will indicate the total difference between costs and revenues for each PIP over the 26 years between 1974 and the year 2000. Second, we will express annual differences for specific years as an increase in the tax rate of average service charge over present levels.[16] The latter analysis is of direct interest to the individual citizen, because it provides an indication of how much more he or she will be paying in the future (in today's dollars) for a level of services the same as the current level, at different population levels.

One way to express the total difference between costs and revenues over the entire period 1974-2000 would be simply to add up the annual differences for each growth scenario and compare the totals. The larger the total difference, the larger the net cost (or benefit, should revenues generally exceed costs). While this approach makes good common sense, one serious objection can be raised. If costs exceed revenues by $100,000 in 1974, that is a very serious matter; $100,000 must be raised immediately if the costs are to be met. If costs exceed revenues by $100,000 in a hypothetical budget for 1984, however, that is less serious; money could have been put away in 1974 (invested), so that it would grow to a value of $100,000 in ten years. The present value of $100,000 in 1984--the amount of money that one would have to have invested in 1974 to realize a value of $100,000 in ten years--is only $56,000.[17] That is, the farther away in the future the deficit, the less costly it is to us now. Present-value analysis is a technique used to discount future values to reflect their lesser importance to us today, and we make use of it to facilitate the comparison of differences between costs and revenues that result from growth.

Our procedure in estimating the present value of future costs is as follows. First, for each growth scenario we compute the annual difference between projected revenues and expenditures. Next, we add up these differences, after first discounting each one in terms of its present value. A difference of $100,000 in 1974 is just that: $100,000 (for 1974). So we proceed, year by year, until we have added together the discounted differences for all 26 years up to the year 2000. The sum total of these differences is the total present value of all future differences; it is thus a summary measure of the net effect of each growth scenario.[18]

We have previously estimated average General Fund expenditures over 1969-74 at $161 per resident of the city. We have seen that these expenditures are met by $44 in property taxes (per person), $42 in sales taxes, and the remainder from numerous other sources.[19] In employing a five-year average as the baseline for our projections, we avoid tying ourselves to the actual budget of a specific year; such a budget may contain expenditures for a given service that are "atypical" (for example, a one-time major outlay on a library expansion).

The difference between revenues and expenditures is presented in Table 6.12. We find that the present value of total costs exceeds that of total excess of expenditures over revenues for all PIPs, but the larger the population, the greater the discrepancy. The present value of the total excess of expenditures over revenues for No-Growth, is $3.33 million for the 26-year period.[20] For our highest growth rate (Zoning Maximum) the population is 2.3 times greater by the year 2000 than the current (No-Growth) population; yet the present value of revenues less expenditures for Zoning Maximum is almost 11 times greater ($36.6 million). For the Half-Density Probable PIP (94,000) the present value of the total excess of costs over expenditures is $9.4 million, or almost three times as great as that under No-Growth. It is clear that the cumulative effect of the excess of costs over revenues associated with even modest increases in population is substantial.

What does this mean to the individual? We can express these differences as per capita differences or as tax rates or a moderately priced home (say $30,000). These results, for selected years, are presented in Table 6.13. Under No-Growth, taxes on a $30,000 home will increase by a little more than $8 by 1995. The increased annual costs of government amount to $4.41 per resident. Under the modest growth rate implied by Half-Density Probable (1.1 percent per year), annual taxes rise by $22.42, and per capita costs by almost $13. The General Plan Probable PIP, entailing an average annual population increase of 1.6 percent, will cost an additional $26.45 in taxes on a moderately priced home; the per person increase amounts to $15. Finally, for the Zoning Probable PIP (average annual population rate increase of 2.4 percent), the increase in taxes is projected at $37.95, with per capita costs rising by almost $22. It should be remembered that these increases are the results of only three capital programs: expanding the central library and building three branches, widening four streets, and maintaining the current ratio of park and recreation facilities to population. As such, these increases should be regarded as very conservative estimates.

SPECIALLY FUNDED SERVICES

A number of municipal services generate their own sources of revenue, either through property taxes or through service charges. In the following sections we consider three such services: education, water, and wastewater reclamation (sanitation). Each service will be taken up in turn, with an examination of the impact of growth upon their expenditures and revenues.

TABLE 6.12

Net Revenues (Revenues Less Costs) for Each PIP, 1974-2000

(1974 dollars)

Year	No-Growth	Half-Density Maximum	Half-Density Probable	General Plan Maximum	General Plan Probable	Zoning Maximum	Zoning Probable
1974	- 59,798	11,544	11,544	11,544	11,544	11,544	11,544
1975	- 59,798	6,401	9,175	3,823	8,030	308	6,173
1976	-115,798	910,781	328,521	-1,145,171	482,345	-1,789,509	849,918
1977	-115,798	-1,017,424	330,888	-1,283,389	485,859	-1,800,749	855,290
1978	-115,798	-1,022,567	333,255	-1,392,615	489,374	-1,811,984	991,163
1979	-115,798	-1,027,710	335,626	-1,400,332	492,887	-1,909,220	-1,098,033
1980	-322,298	-1,032,853	476,992	-1,408,055	496,403	-1,920,454	-1,103,407
1981	-322,298	-1,286,479	695,274	-1,853,763	939,198	-1,787,315	-1,368,267
1982	-322,298	-1,291,623	828,143	-1,861,481	-1,044,211	-2,798,552	-1,373,638
1983	-322,298	-1,373,766	830,511	-1,869,203	-1,047,727	-2,809,787	-1,435,011
1984	-322,298	-1,378,905	832,879	-2,188,922	-1,051,244	-2,821,024	-1,440,382
1985	-322,298	-1,384,050	835,248	-2,282,644	-1,054,758	-2,970,257	-1,445,752
1986	-322,298	-1,637,676	952,032	-2,663,353	-1,293,050	-3,525,119	-1,710,619
1987	-322,298	-1,642,819	954,398	-2,671,073	-1,296,564	-3,536,355	-1,715,988
1988	-322,298	-1,647,963	956,766	-2,678,792	-1,300,077	-3,547,591	-1,721,360
1989	-322,298	-1,653,103	959,133	-2,686,513	-1,303,595	-3,558,825	-2,124,730
1990	-322,298	-1,970,246	961,503	-2,694,233	-1,307,109	-3,570,062	-2,130,103
1991	-322,298	-2,223,284	-1,078,600	-3,076,034	-1,481,116	-4,123,040	-2,395,635
1992	-322,298	-2,228,427	-1,080,966	-3,083,753	-1,484,626	-4,216,276	-2,401,007
1993	-322,298	-2,315,572	-1,156,335	-3,091,476	-1,488,142	-4,227,513	-2,406,379
1994	-322,298	-2,320,711	-1,158,702	-3,172,193	-1,491,656	-4,238,745	-2,411,752
1995	-322,298	-2,325,854	-1,161,072	-3,179,916	-1,495,172	-4,249,982	-2,417,124
1996	-322,298	-2,578,893	-1,278,165	-3,561,711	-1,669,179	-4,802,962	-2,682,655
1997	-322,298	-2,584,037	-1,280,535	-3,569,436	-1,672,694	-4,814,199	-2,688,028
1998	-322,298	-2,589,179	-1,282,903	-3,577,154	-1,676,206	-4,825,434	-2,693,399
1999	-322,298	-2,594,319	-1,285,271	-3,584,876	-1,679,721	-4,853,668	-2,698,771
2000	-322,298	-2,599,464	-1,287,638	-3,592,595	-1,683,237	-4,864,906	-2,704,144
Discounted present value of the annual stream at r = 6 percent	-3,328,020	-18,696,880	-9,355,759	-26,698,304	-12,394,018	-36,553,152	-19,494,688

Source: Santa Barbara Planning Task Force.

177

TABLE 6.13

Change in Property Tax on a $30,000 Home, for Different PIPs, Selected Years
(1974 dollars)

	No-Growth	Half-Density		General Plan		Zoning	
		Maximum	Probable	Maximum	Probable	Maximum	Probable
1975							
Per resident	0.82	- 0.09	- 0.12	- 0.05	- 0.11	0.00	- 0.08
Increase in property taxes	1.72	- 0.15	- 0.22	- 0.09	- 0.19	- 0.01	- 0.14
Increase in rate	0.03	0	0	0	0	0	0
1985							
Per resident	4.41	15.06	10.21	22.53	12.27	26.02	15.59
Increase in property taxes	8.05	26.45	17.82	39.10	21.27	45.42	27.02
Increase in rate	0.14	0.46	0.31	0.68	0.37	0.79	0.47
1995							
Per resident	4.41	21.35	12.95	25.06	15.32	28.07	21.86
Increase in property taxes	8.05	37.37	22.42	43.70	26.45	48.87	37.95
Increase in rate	0.14	0.65	0.39	0.76	0.46	0.85	0.66

Note: Taxes computed on a $30,000 home assessed at $7,500, with $1,750 homeowner's exemption. Negative numbers indicate excess of revenues over expenditures for the growth PIPs in 1975, resulting from higher property values (no loss to open-space downzoning) and from the fact that capital programs are begun in 1976.
Source: Santa Barbara Planning Task Force.

Education

Population Growth and School Requirements:
The Recent Experience

Both the Santa Barbara high school district and the elementary school district are relatively wealthy. In the elementary school district, for example, there is $35,000 in property tax assessments for each pupil in attendance, compared with only $19,000 in assessments for the "average" elementary school district in the State of California. Historically, Santa Barbara has been able to finance superior schools, largely out of local property tax revenues. In 1972-73, for example, 84 percent of revenues in both school districts were funded out of local sources, almost entirely property taxes. The statewide average was 61 percent.

From 1962/63 to 1972/73 the elementary school district increased moderately through 1968/69, then began a long-term period of decline that reflects nationwide trends toward fewer children and smaller families. This decline is expected to continue well into the future; it is for the first time affecting high school enrollments, which are projected to decline in the future as well (Dodson and Fox 1973). Operating expenditures per pupil over the ten-year period have increased one-quarter in the high school district and one-half in the elementary school district. [21] These increasing per pupil expenditures were made possible by rising property values in Santa Barbara, which enabled the school districts to maintain programs in the face of rising costs. While taxes have risen in both districts, tax-rate increases reflect in part a shifting burden of financing from the state to the locality and in part the need to bring school buildings up to Field Act (earthquake) standards. While taxes may appear high, they are far higher in other localities that are nonetheless unable to afford the quality programs characteristic of the local school districts.

Can increasing expenditures on education be expected to continue into the future? Because of recent legislation, the answer is a qualified no. Both Senate Bill 90 and the Serrano-Priest decision have shifted the basis for finance from property assessment to enrollment, or average daily attendance (ADA). In the past, school districts with rising property value and declining enrollments automatically experienced rising per pupil expenditures without increasing the property-tax rate; wealthy districts were thus at an advantage. Since 1973, however, wealthy school districts are no longer free to increase their expenditures per student. Under Senate Bill 90 (Chapter 1406, Statutes of 1972), a "revenue limit" per pupil is calculated for each school district. In order to surpass this limit, tax-rate increases must be approved by a majority of those voting at a district tax-rate limit-increase election. Yearly increases in the revenue limit are determined for each district by the state Board of Education. Such increases are intended to cover inflation; poorer districts are allowed larger increases than are wealthier.

Thus, allowing for inflation, revenues (and hence expenditures) per pupil in Santa Barbara will stabilize at recent levels. Since total expenditures are calculated by multiplying the per ADA revenue limit by the number of pupils, declining enrollments will result in declining total expenditures, and corresponding decreases in the tax rate. The effect of the new legislation on the Santa Barbara schools is still unclear. According to Norman B. Scharer, superintendent of schools: "It appears virtually inevitable that this formula, and possible future legislation in response to the Serrano-Priest decision, will force a reduced rate of growth in Santa Barbara's investment in education" (Santa Barbara School District 1973, p. 1).

To what extent can enrollments be expected to decline in the future, thereby forcing reduced expenditures and a reduction in property tax rates? The answer to this question is a complex one, for it depends on two interrelated factors: fertility (that is, the number of children per family) and the characteristics of immigrants to the Santa Barbara area.

More children being born means more children entering school. Recent studies suggest that in the past few years, "completed fertility"--the number of children a woman will have during her lifetime-- has dropped to 1.7 or below in the South Coast area (see Dodson and Fox 1973).

The city itself differs from the South Coast in two important respects. First, it has a high and increasing proportion of elderly persons. Those over 65 currently comprise 18 percent of the city population, twice the statewide average. On the other hand, a substantial proportion of the city population (18 percent) is Chicano. Fertility among Chicanos is higher than the average, which currently compensates for the lower fertility resulting from the presence of elderly persons. Nevertheless, there is evidence that while fertility in the city is still somewhat higher than in the South Coast area, it is rapidly declining to levels of the surrounding area.

Earlier in this chapter we have argued that the value of property is directly proportional to the number of people, when income and inflation are taken into account. The proportion of the population in elementary schools has been declining steadily for several years; it is currently about 7 percent of the total population, and we estimate further declines to about 6 percent. The high schools will experience all their decline in the future; we estimate that the proportion will fall from the present 8 percent to about 5 percent. Thus,

even with some population increase, the local tax base can be expected to rise faster than the number of students. The result, under
current legislation, will be substantial tax relief through lower
property-tax rates.

Estimating the Costs of Education:
Methods and Assumptions

Operating Costs. School costs can be broken down into two categories: current, or operating expenses; and capital costs of development.
Operating expenses are the day-to-day costs of education: teachers'
salaries, materials and supplies, and the expenditures on equipment.
As indicated previously, since the passage of Senate Bill 90, such
costs have been tied to enrollment: The state establishes a limit for
each school district on the total amount of such costs per pupil. Capital expenses are expenses associated with long-term expansion of
facilities: constructing new wings on existing buildings, buying land,
and constructing new schools.

Since, under current legislation, operating expenses per pupil
will remain constant (except for inflation), in our projections we will
employ the current per pupil revenue limit. In the current year that
limit is set at $1,386 for each high school pupil and at $1,155 for
each elementary school pupil.[22] Of this amount, the state makes a
"basic aid" grant of $125 per pupil (ADA).[23] The state also estab-
lishes a "foundation" program for each school district. This foundation is intended to insure adequate education for all students (the
foundation level in Santa Barbara is considerably below the current
revenue limit). If local districts cannot raise sufficient revenues
through property taxes to make up the difference between "basic aid"
and the foundation program, the state will make up the difference
through "equalization aid."[24] Because of the relative wealth of the
Santa Barbara school districts (as measured by total property value
per pupil), they are not eligible for equalization aid: Virtually all
revenues beyond the first $125 per pupil are raised through local
property taxes.

In our projections we assume that local funding will continue to
provide all but the first $125 per pupil of revenues for education. The
total operating costs per pupil, to local taxpayers, can then be estimated at $1,030 ($1,155 minus $125) for the elementary school dis-
trict, and $1,261 ($1,386 minus $125) for the high school district.

The total cost to taxpayers is estimated by multiplying the difference between the current revenue limit and the basic grant by the
number of pupils. This amount will be expressed as a tax rate per
$100 of assessed valuation. This tax rate can be expected to decline
over time, regardless of growth, since the total population (and hence

total property value) is increasing faster than the number of students (and hence than operating costs). Thus, property taxes for operating expenses will decline for all our PIPs in amounts to be summarized in a subsequent section.[25]

Capital Costs. As the absolute number of students increases, new facilities must be provided: Classrooms and auditoriums are added; new schools must be built; increasingly expensive land must be acquired. The capital program required will reflect in part the total number of pupils to be served and in part the capacity of the existing facilities to serve additional students without incurring major capital costs.

TABLE 6.14

Selected Characteristics of Schools,
Santa Barbara School Districts

	Elementary	Junior High	Senior High
Existing schools			
Number	11	4	3
Average acres[a]	6.6	24.4	40.7
Average enrollment	466	1,410	2,354
Average square feet of buildings	25,749	98,761	189,307
Average square feet per student	55.2	70.0	80.4
Average cost per student at $40 per square foot	$2,208	$2,800	$3,217
Projected schools			
Optimal acres	11	24	46
Optimal enrollment	600	1,400	2,400
Cost ($ thousand)			
Development	1,325	4,390[b]	8,647[b]
Land	1,914	288	522
Total	3,239	4,678	9,169

[a]Under state standards, the average Santa Barbara elementary school site should occupy 9.6 acres; junior high school, 24.1 acres; senior high school, 42.2 acres.

[b]Includes 12 percent increase over internal square-foot cost to allow for external facilities, such as development of playing fields, swimming pools, and so on.

Source: Santa Barbara School District, Master Planning for the Future (1969).

To estimate the costs of capital programs we have established the existing standards of service and assumed that these standards are maintained in the future (see Table 6.14). Capital costs are met out of property tax revenues.[26] Accordingly, it is possible to express capital costs as a property-tax rate and to add this to the tax rate for current costs. The total of the two rates represents the total projected cost of education to the taxpayer. In this section we shall detail the assumptions made with respect to capital expansion. We shall discuss the elementary and high school districts separately, detailing the costs of expansion according to the following schema, which portrays the program of school-system adaptation to higher enrollments that has been used in estimating capital costs:

1. Expansion within existing facilities, at no additional capital cost (surplus classrooms, extra periods)

2. Addition of new wings to existing schools (estimated construction costs: $35 per square foot)

3. Construction of new schools on property already owned by the school district or received in trade for property already owned (estimated construction costs: $40 per square foot)

4. Acquisition of new sites and construction of new schools (estimated construction costs: $40 per square foot; estimated land costs: varies according to location)

Construction costs are derived from several sources, including the Office of Local Assistance Handbook; Santa Barbara School District, Business and Accounting Offices; and Arendt, Mosher, and Grant (a local architectural firm that contracts with the school districts). Relying upon these data, we estimated costs to the school districts that would be associated with each PIP.

1. Elementary school expansion

    a. Expansion within existing facilities. Under state standards, very little expansion is possible within the existing plant, beyond the surplus of classrooms that currently exists. Of the 210 district classrooms, 24 were classified as surplus for 1974-75; at 25 pupils per classroom, 600 additional students could thus be served with the existing plant.

    b. Addition of wings to existing schools. Despite size limitations, it is estimated by the district business manager that only 15 percent more students could be served by the addition of new wings to several of the present schools. Assuming the present ratio of 55.2 square feet per student, costs are estimated as follows: 15 percent x 5,205 (current enrollment) = 780 students; 780 students x 55.2 square feet per student x $35 per.square foot = $1,506,960.

c. Construction of new schools on district-owned property. The district currently owns two parcels of land suitable for schools. Consistent with the Master Plan, new schools are assumed to have a capacity of 600 students. Costs are estimated as follows: 600 students x 55.2 square feet per student x $40 per square foot = $1,324,800

d. Purchase of land. Additional schools, required for the two highest population levels considered, will entail the purchase of land. We assume that sites will be of optimal acreage (11 acres) and will be the least-costly sites available, consistent with locational requirements. The schools will be built in the neighborhoods that experience the greatest population increase, such as Oak Park, East Side, Laguna, Lower West. Since there are very few areas in the most rapidly growing neighborhoods where large parcels of undeveloped land exist, we assume that purchase will be of the cheapest developed land--for example, land that is currently over-zoned relative to use. The average value of such property (land and improvements) is estimated at $174,000 per acre; each 11-acre school site will thus cost $1.914 million.

These estimates are undoubtedly low, since the value of land in the city will certainly rise if population increases to higher levels where such land acquisition will be necessary. On the other hand, to the extent that school site purchase can be coordinated with other public-sector needs (for example, Parks Department acquisition of sites for community parks), costs to the school district may be reduced.

2.   High school expansion

a. Expansion within existing facilities. While some schools in the district currently possess excess capacity, for the district as a whole there is none. The district estimates that an additional class period would be feasible as a long-term option, under conditions of expanding enrollment. Extending the school day from six to seven full periods would increase the capacity of the school district by 17 percent, or 2,159 students (based on 1973/74 enrollments).

b. Additions of wings to existing schools. It is estimated that 15 percent more students could be served by adding new wings to existing school buildings: 846 in the junior high schools and 1,059 in the senior high schools (based on 1973/74 enrollments), or a total of 1,905 students. Assuming current ratios of 70 square feet per student in junior high and 80.4 square feet per student in senior high, costs are estimated as follows: Junior high school: 846 students x 70 square feet per student x $35 per square foot = $2.072 million; senior high school: 1,059 students x 80.4 square feet per student x $35 per square foot = $2,980,026.

c. Construction of new schools on district-owned property.
The district currently owns one 23-acre site suitable for a junior
high school; it owns an additional 27 acres of land that will not be
used for schools. We assume that one junior high school will be
constructed on the 23-acre site, should the need arise. We further assume that the remaining 30 acres will be sold, and the proceeds used to defray the acquisition costs of another high school,
should one become necessary. The difference between the 46
acres required and the 30 available for sale constitutes a net cost
that must be borne by the high school district; at $12,000 per
acre, this amounts to $192,000. Costs are then estimated as
follows: Junior high school: 1,400 students x 70 square feet per
student x $40 per square foot x 1.12 = $4.39 million; senior high
school: 2,400 students x 80.4 square feet per student x $40 x
1.12 = $8.647 + $192,000 (additional land) = $8.839 million. (For
the 1.12 figure, see Table 6.14, note b.)
    d. Purchase of land. Sites for a junior and senior high school
will have to be purchased to accommodate growth to the highest
population levels considered. It is assumed that undeveloped
property outside the city limits will be acquired for these schools;
such property is currently valued at about $12,000 per acre (as-
suming availability of water). The optimal 24-acre site for a
junior high school will thus cost $288,000; the optimal 46-acre
site for a senior high school will cost $552,000.

    This capital expansion program is summarized in Table 6.15.
It is assumed that the less-expensive options are exhausted before
the more-expensive ones are begun. We further assume that expansion is begun in the year prior to the shortage.

3.   Impacts on education at each PIP
    The demand for education facilities accompanying growth is
presented in Tables 6.16 and 6.17, which project enrollments in the
two school districts for each PIP. Under No-Growth, enrollment
drops over time, reflecting declining fertility, while it rises under
the other PIP assumptions. It does not rise, however, as quickly
as population (for example, while South Coast population almost
triples under Zoning Maximum, high school enrollments only double).
Current costs of education rise directly in proportion to enrollments, while property values rise in proportion to population; tax
rates hence decline for all growth scenarios.
    The potential thus exists for substantial increase in enroll-
ments in both school districts before it will be necessary to incur
capital costs; some 12 percent more students (600 students) can be
accommodated within the elementary schools through the utilization

TABLE 6.15

Program for Expansion of School Capacity: Current and Total Costs

Method (in Order of Use)	Additional Capacity Beyond Current Number of Enrollments (Students)			Total Cost ($ thousand)		
	Elementary	Junior	Senior	Elementary	Junior	Senior
1. Fully utilize existing rooms	600	--	--	None	--	--
2. Go from six to seven full periods per day	--	958	1,200	--	None	None
3. 15 percent expansion existing schools	780	846	1,059	1,507	2,073	2,980
4. Build new schools on district property*	1,200	1,400	2,400	2,650	4,390	8,839
Subtotal: costs and capacity before extensive land acquisition becomes necessary	2,580	3,204	4,659	4,157	6,463	11,819
5. Acquire new land, build school (single school estimate)	600	1,400	2,400	3,239	4,678	9,169

*The school district currently possesses two elementary school sites and two junior high school sites, one of which will be sold to offset costs of acquiring land for the senior high school (see text).

Source: Santa Barbara Planning Task Force, based on Santa Barbara school district estimates.

TABLE 6.16

Elementary Schools, Total Average Daily Attendance, 1974-2000

Year	No-Growth	Half-Density Maximum	Half-Density Probable	General Plan Maximum	General Plan Probable	Zoning Maximum	Zoning Probable
1974	5,206	5,206	5,206	5,206	5,206	5,206	5,206
1975	5,148	5,268	5,203	5,328	5,230	5,410	5,273
1976	5,089	5,327	5,199	5,446	5,252	5,608	5,338
1977	5,031	5,383	5,193	5,560	5,272	5,800[a]	5,399
1978	4,972	5,436	5,186	5,669	5,290	5,986	5,457
1979	4,914	5,487	5,178	5,775[a]	5,306	6,166	5,513
1980	4,855	5,535	5,168	5,876	5,320	6,340	5,565
1981	4,797	5,580	5,158	5,973	5,332	6,508[b]	5,615
1982	4,738	5,623	5,146	6,066	5,343	6,671	5,662
1983	4,680	5,663	5,132	6,155	5,351	6,827	5,706
1984	4,621	5,700	5,118	6,240	5,358	6,977	5,748
1985	4,563	5,734	5,102	6,321	5,363	7,121[b]	5,786[a]
1986	4,504	5,765[a]	5,085	6,398	5,366	7,260	5,822
1987	4,504	5,871	5,133	6,555[b]	5,438	7,489	5,931
1988	4,504	5,976	5,182	6,713	5,510	7,719[c]	6,041
1989	4,504	6,081	5,230	6,871	5,582	7,948	6,151
1990	4,504	6,186	5,279	7,029	5,653	8,178	6,261
1991	4,504	6,291	5,327	7,186[b]	5,725	8,408	6,370
1992	4,504	6,396	5,375	7,344	5,797[a]	8,637	6,480[b]
1993	4,504	6,501	5,424	7,502	5,869	8,867[c]	6,590
1994	4,479	6,569[b]	5,442	7,617	5,908	9,046	6,662
1995	4,454	6,637	5,459	7,730[c]	5,946	9,222	6,734
1996	4,429	6,703	5,476	7,842	5,983	9,396	6,804
1997	4,404	6,767	5,492	7,952	6,019	9,567[c]	6,873
1998	4,379	6,831	5,508	8,060	6,055	9,736	6,940
1999	4,354	6,893	5,523	8,166	6,089	9,902	6,006
2000	4,329	6,955	5,538	8,271	6,123	10,066	7,072

[a]Building new wings on existing facilities: Total cost = $1.5 million (15 percent expansion).
[b]Building a new building on district property: Total cost = $1.3 million per school.
[c]Acquire land, build new school: Total cost = $3.2 million per school.

TABLE 6.17

High School District, Average Daily Attendance, 1974-2000

Year	No-Growth	Half-Density		General Plan		Zoning	
		Maximum	Probable	Maximum	Probable	Maximum	Probable
1974	12,491	12,491	12,491	12,491	12,491	12,491	12,491
1975	12,234	12,624	12,469	12,768	12,533	12,965	12,637
1976	11,981	12,750	12,443	13,035	12,570	13,423	12,775
1977	11,732	12,868	12,414	13,290	12,602	13,866	12,906
1978	11,487	12,980	12,382	13,535	12,629	14,292	13,029
1979	11,246	13,084	12,346	13,769	12,651	14,703	13,145
1980	11,009	13,181	12,307	13,992	12,668	15,098	13,253
1981	10,922	13,450	12,432	14,397[a]	12,853	15,687	13,534
1982	10,836	13,720	12,556	14,802[b]	13,037	16,277[c]	13,816
1983	10,752	13,990	12,680	15,207	13,221	16,866[d]	14,098
1984	10,668	14,260	12,804	15,612	13,406	17,455	14,380
1985	10,587	14,529[a]	12,928	16,017	13,590	18,045	14,661[a]
1986	10,506	14,799	13,053	16,421[c,d]	13,774	18,634	14,943[b]
1987	10,427	15,069	13,177	16,826	13,959	19,223	15,225
1988	10,148	15,041	13,043	16,897	13,869	19,429	15,206
1989	9,873	15,003	12,905	16,953	13,772	19,611	15,176
1990	9,603	14,955	12,762	16,993	13,668	19,771	15,136
1991	9,336	14,896	12,614	17,017	13,557	19,908	15,084
1992	9,074	14,827	12,461	17,025	13,439	20,022	15,022
1993	8,815	14,747	12,304	17,018	13,313	20,113[e]	14,949
1994	8,752	14,986[b]	12,413	17,375	13,476	20,634[f]	15,198
1995	8,689	15,224	12,523	17,733	13,639	21,155	15,447
1996	8,628	15,462	12,633	18,091	13,802	21,676	15,696
1997	8,567	15,701	12,743	18,449	13,965	22,197	15,945
1998	8,507	15,939	12,852	18,807	14,128	22,717	16,194
1999	8,448	16,178	12,962	19,165	14,291	23,238	16,443
2000	8,390	16,416	13,072	19,523	14,454	23,759	16,692

[a]Build new wings, etc.: Total cost = $3 million (15 percent expansion).
[b]Expansion: Total cost = $2.1 million (15 percent expansion).
[c]Building new school on land acquired through trading district-owned property: Total cost = $8.8 million.
[d]Build on district property: Total cost = $4.4 million.
[e]New school, acquire new property: Total cost = $9.2 million.
[f]New school, acquire property: Total cost = $4.7 million.
Source: Santa Barbara Planning Task Force.

of surplus classrooms, and 17 percent more in the high school district through extending the school day one full period on a full-time basis. Accordingly, capital costs for necessary expansion in the elementary school district can be deferred according to the schedule shown in Table 6.18.[27]

It is clear that capital programs can be deferred substantially under all but our highest PIPs. The population size that can be served by the existing schools depends on the growth rate, since the proportion of the population in school declines relatively constantly over time. For example, at current growth rates (1 percent per annum) a population level of well over 95,000--reached in year 2000-- can be served without the need for elementary school expansion; at the highest growth rate, on the other hand, existing capacity is exhausted as early as 1977 with a population of only 84,000.

Because of declining fertility and substantial capacity for expansion within existing facilities, both school districts can sustain substantial increases in population without having recourse to major capital programs. Even under the most rapid growth conditions, only limited capital costs are incurred. To reach the Zoning Maximum PIP of 170,000 for the city (459,000 for the South Coast), representing an average annual rate of 5.1 percent, the high school district would require a total capital program in the year 2000 of $32 million involving annual repayments by that time of $2.5 million. Such a program would provide 15 percent expansion of existing facilities and the construction of two new junior and senior high schools, the former on property already owned by the district. Yet property values would be sufficient at that population level to require an additional bond tax rate of only $0.19 on the dollar. The elementary school district would require six new schools, four of them on costly urban land that would have to be acquired by the district; the total cost of elementary school expansion to serve the population under Zoning Maximum is $17.1 million in the year 2000, with annual bond payments of $1.3 million, yet the required tax rate to redeem such bonds would amount to only $0.29. It is clear that because of the combination of considerable capacity within existing schools and declining fertility in the population, the effects of growth on the costs of education are minor.[28]

What are the comparative costs of growth at the different PIPs? To answer this question we project revenues under the existing tax rate structure, and costs under the several growth scenarios. The difference between costs and revenues over the period is a measure of the fiscal impact of growth on education. The results of such an analysis for the elementary school district are presented in Table 6.19.[29] It is apparent that revenues far exceed costs for all of the population scenarios. Furthermore, because revenues increase in

TABLE 6.18

Capital Costs: Elementary Schools, Projected Capital Outlays, 1974–2000
(1974 dollars)

Year	No-Growth	Half-Density Maximum	Half-Density Probable	General Plan Maximum	General Plan Probable	Zoning Maximum	Zoning Probable
1974	0	0	0	0	0	0	0
1975	0	0	0	0	0	0	0
1976	0	0	0	0	0	0	0
1977	0	0	0	0	0	118,000	0
1978	0	0	0	0	0	118,000	0
1979	0	0	0	118,000	0	118,000	0
1980	0	0	0	118,000	0	118,000	0
1981	0	0	0	118,000	0	118,000	0
1982	0	0	0	118,000	0	222,000	0
1983	0	0	0	118,000	0	222,000	0
1984	0	0	0	118,000	0	222,000	0
1985	0	0	0	118,000	0	222,000	0
1986	0	118,000	0	118,000	0	326,000	118,000
1987	0	118,000	0	222,000	0	326,000	118,000
1988	0	118,000	0	222,000	0	326,000	118,000
1989	0	118,000	0	222,000	0	579,000	118,000
1990	0	118,000	0	222,000	0	579,000	118,000
1991	0	118,000	0	326,000	0	579,000	118,000
1992	0	118,000	0	326,000	48,000	832,000	118,000
1993	0	118,000	0	326,000	48,000	832,000	222,000
1994	0	222,000	0	326,000	48,000	1,085,000	222,000
1995	0	222,000	0	579,000	48,000	1,085,000	222,000
1996	0	222,000	0	579,000	48,000	1,085,000	222,000
1997	0	222,000	0	579,000	48,000	1,338,000	222,000
1998	0	222,000	0	579,000	48,000	1,338,000	222,000
1999	0	222,000	0	579,000	48,000	1,338,000	222,000
2000	0	222,000	0	579,000	48,000	1,338,000	222,000

Note: A similar schedule for the high school district is presented in Volume 1, Table 7.35.
Source: Santa Barbara Planning Task Force.

TABLE 6.19

Elementary Schools, Revenue Less Costs for Each PIP, 1974–2000
(1974 dollars)

Year	No-Growth	Half-Density Maximum	Half-Density Probable	General Plan Maximum	General Plan Probable	Zoning Maximum	Zoning Probable
1974	60,691	115,383	115,383	115,383	115,383	115,383	115,383
1975	23,464	211,658	205,121	217,734	207,823	226,014	212,199
1976	107,624	311,584	296,540	325,561	302,755	344,622	312,826
1977	192,784	416,155	390,633	439,861	401,178	354,190	418,257
1978	276,939	523,373	485,412	558,636	501,094	488,729	526,502
1979	377,094	650,227	597,856	580,879	619,496	647,224	654,546
1980	462,254	765,735	696,990	711,608	725,399	798,693	771,410
1981	546,409	883,897	796,807	846,803	832,791	853,123	891,078
1982	611,569	986,695	879,295	968,474	923,677	1,000,529	995,555
1983	735,729	1,152,144	1,022,465	1,154,624	1,076,052	1,214,897	1,162,842
1984	825,878	1,287,232	1,133,310	1,312,229	1,196,911	1,403,232	1,299,929
1985	880,038	1,389,972	1,209,836	1,439,327	1,284,270	1,459,533	1,286,828
1986	965,193	1,409,361	1,319,043	1,602,891	1,405,118	1,658,801	1,426,543
1987	970,193	1,446,535	1,338,857	1,552,194	1,432,108	1,734,097	1,465,146
1988	969,193	1,477,709	1,352,671	1,599,493	1,453,098	1,550,386	1,497,748
1989	976,193	1,516,882	1,374,486	1,654,801	1,482,083	1,627,685	1,538,355
1990	983,193	1,556,050	1,396,301	1,710,100	1,511,073	1,704,981	1,578,960
1991	1,141,193	1,746,223	1,569,115	1,812,407	1,691,064	1,680,276	1,770,569
1992	1,203,193	1,840,398	1,645,930	1,922,711	1,727,047	1,812,572	1,762,172
1993	1,203,193	1,872,574	1,660,744	1,971,010	1,749,038	1,629,861	1,795,781
1994	1,236,689	1,849,873	1,716,246	2,076,266	1,815,200	1,767,796	1,879,208
1995	1,270,186	1,932,736	1,772,474	1,930,871	1,882,429	1,909,140	1,964,259
1996	1,303,682	2,017,155	1,829,422	2,040,828	1,950,726	2,053,900	2,050,955
1997	1,337,179	2,103,146	1,887,084	2,153,120	2,020,097	1,949,079	2,139,273
1998	1,370,675	2,190,695	1,945,466	2,267,772	2,090,533	2,100,665	2,229,234
1999	1,404,172	2,279,806	2,004,573	2,384,755	2,162,029	2,255,657	2,320,814
2000	1,437,663	2,370,476	2,064,397	2,504,096	2,234,599	2,414,075	2,414,036
Discounted present value of the annual stream at r = 6 percent	9,006,877	14,760,830	13,352,933	15,308,463	14,142,203	15,072,454	14,809,603

Note: Similar results for the high school district are presented in Volume 1, Table 7.37.

Source: Santa Barbara Planning Task Force, derived from information provided by County Assessor's Office.

ratio to total population, while costs are based on enrollments (relative to total population), the excess of revenues over costs increases over time and is higher for the higher population levels.

A summary measure of the magnitude of difference in the revenues-expenditure balance for the different PIPs is the present-value figure at the bottom of each column. The present value of all savings over the 26-year period is greater, the higher the final population for the reasons indicated; population (and hence property value) increases faster than expenditures because of the decline in the proportion of population in school. The savings in the operating costs that are realized as a result of these trends are more than sufficient to offset the capital expenditures that result from growth.

Combining the results for both school districts, the effects of growth on the present value of total savings over the 26-year period amounts to $19.5 million for No-Growth, $27.7 million for growth to Half-Density Probable, $29.8 million for growth to General Plan Probable, and $34.3 million for growth to Zoning Maximum. Yet how large are these savings to the taxpayer? While the present value of total savings for Zoning Maximum is one and three-quarters times the amount realized under No-Growth, the final population at Zoning Maximum is two and one-third times greater; thus, per capita savings actually decline with growth.

One way to estimate the significance of these differences to the individual citizen is to express them as property-tax rates. We can compute the tax rate that would be necessary to finance all school costs (capital and operating) for our different growth scenarios, and then estimate the difference in taxes on a moderately priced home.[30] In both school districts tax rates decline dramatically over time, by as much as 40 percent in the high school district and 20 percent in the elementary school district. The declines are greater for lower PIPs than for higher ones, although differences between PIPs are minor relative to overall declines, regardless of growth.

Table 6.20 summarizes the findings concerning the effects of growth on school finances in both school districts combined. In this table, the difference between revenues (at current tax rates) and projected expenditures is expressed in three ways: (a) as a per capita savings, obtained by dividing each year's net savings by the population in that year, (b) as a tax rate, obtained by summing the rates for both school districts, and (c) as savings in property taxes on a $30,000 home (at present rates such taxes for both school districts would amount to $358). Tax rate reductions (and hence tax savings) are comparable for most PIPs: only the two highest growth rates, General Plan and Zoning Maximum, result in substantially lower reductions than the others. With the exception of these two highest PIPs, tax rates drop by 1995 by around $1.60 per $100 of assessed valuation,

TABLE 6.20

Change in Property Tax on a $30,000 Home, for Combined
Santa Barbara School Districts at Different PIPs
(1974 dollars)

	No-Growth	Half-Density Maximum	Half-Density Probable	General Plan Maximum	General Plan Probable	Zoning Maximum	Zoning Probable
1975							
Per resident	0.71	4.93	4.59	5.23	4.73	5.63	4.45
Tax decrease	1.72	9.77	9.20	10.35	9.20	10.92	9.77
Rate decrease	0.03	0.17	0.16	0.18	0.16	0.19	0.17
1985							
Per resident	24.02	30.44	29.78	29.65	30.50	25.47	28.38
Tax decrease	46.00	57.50	56.35	55.77	58.07	48.30	53.47
Rate decrease	0.80	1.00	0.98	0.97	1.01	0.84	0.93
1995							
Per resident	46.89	47.45	50.65	41.52	50.22	36.70	47.34
Tax decrease	89.70	89.70	95.45	78.20	94.87	69.00	89.12
Rate decrease	1.56	1.56	1.66	1.36	1.65	1.20	1.55

Notes: Revenues based on current tax rates, as explained in the text. The combined current tax rate of both school districts for 1973-74--excluding override taxes--was $6.22 per $100 of assessed valuation. Tax estimates assume a 25 percent assessment ratio and $1,750 homeowners' exemption.

Separate figures for each school district, presenting estimated tax rates for each PIP in each year from 1974 to 2000, are presented in Volume 1, Tables 7.38 and 7.39.

Source: Santa Barbara Planning Task Force.

and taxes on a moderately priced home decline by as much as $95.
Expressed as a per capita value, net savings amount to about $37
under Zoning Maximum, $42 under General Plan Maximum, and from
$47 to $50 for all other PIPs. These patterns of savings are under-
standable in light of recent fertility declines, combined with the considerable excess capacity that exists within current school facilities
before any major capital expansion must occur. Under all but the
very highest growth rates, the schools can accommodate the projected
enrollments without major capital expenditures. With the least amount
of growth there will be greatest per capita savings. [31]

Water

In recent years the greatest single deterrent to growth along
the South Coast has been the lack of water. Because of water shortages, moratoria on new water hook-ups have been declared in the
Goleta Valley and Montecito areas, bringing to a virtual halt all new
development in these areas. Today, the city of Santa Barbara finds
itself in a position similar to that experienced by Goleta and Montecito
several years earlier; they had to resort to moratoria. There is still
a small water surplus, but the situation is rapidly nearing equilibrium
between supply and demand.

In the relatively short time that remains until this "balance" is
reached, Santa Barbara must decide on a course for supplementing
its water supply. What this course will be depends a great deal upon
the population policy it chooses to follow.

In this section an attempt is made to clarify Santa Barbara's
current water-supply situation and to develop estimates of the cost of
providing the water to the city at populations of up to 170,000.

It must be emphasized that these estimates are tentative and
that further information is needed to determine the feasibility of the
supplemental water sources discussed here.

All the growth PIPs will require the city to augment its water
supply within the next few years. Precisely what supplemental
sources will be developed, and what the cost will be, can only tenta-
tively be considered in this analysis. The city government presently
lacks the information to provide more than approximate answers to
these questions.

Present Supply

The city of Santa Barbara is currently consuming approximately 15,000 acre feet (a.f.) of water annually against a firm yield supply of 15,380 a.f. [32] This water is drawn from five sources: Cachuma

Reservoir (8,280 a.f.), Gibraltar Reservoir (3,700 a.f.), ground-
water (2,000 a.f.), Mission Tunnel (1,100 a.f.), and the Montecito
County Water District (300 a.f.).

Basis for Determining Water Requirements
and Costs Resulting from Growth

For purposes of projecting the demand and costs of supplying
water as a result of growth, we developed a supplemental water-
development model based on information provided by the Water Resources Division of the Public Works Department and additional
material drawn from the Brown and Caldwell Study (1969) and Toups
(1974). The model is based on the following information and assumptions.

Water Demand. Demand was derived from estimates developed by
the Water Division of the Public Works Department. These estimates
assume that per capita water consumption will follow the historical
pattern of increasing as a function of advances in technology--for example, automatic devices, such as washing machines, whirlpool
baths, and so forth. A per capita per day figure of 183 gallons was
established for the years between 1975 and 1980; this figure represents commercial, industrial, institutional, agricultural, and residential uses. In the period 1980-90 per capita consumption is expected to increase to 189 gallons per day (gpd). A further increase
to 193 gpd is expected in 1990. These figures, as expressed in a.f.
per year, were multiplied by total population in each year to estimate
total demand in a.f. [33] Figure 6.1 estimates what the water requirement will be for the seven PIPs.

Costs: Supplemental Sources of Supply and Bond Obligations. According to the Water Resources Division of the Public Works Department
there are five potential sources for supplemental water available to
the city. These include wastewater irrigation, Cachuma conjunctive
use, wastewater injection, State Project water, and Cachuma enlarge-
ment. Estimates of amounts these sources can supply and costs per
a.f. appear in Table 6.21.

In developing the model it was assumed that these sources represent viable options for supplemental water and that the costs associated with each will remain proportionate throughout the study period.
It was also assumed that the city would develop these sources in order
of their estimated cost per a.f., utilizing the least-expensive alternatives first. Following this logic, wastewater irrigation would be the
first developed supplemental source, and expansion of Cachuma Reservoir would be the last.

FIGURE 6.1

Comparative Demand for Supplemental Water

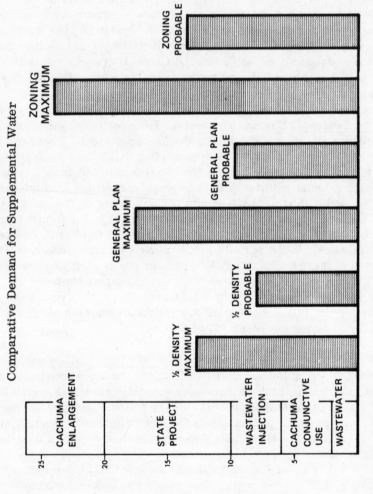

Source: Santa Barbara Planning Task Force.

TABLE 6.21

Supplemental Sources of Water and Incremental Costs

Source	Acre-Feet	Cost per Acre-Foot ($)
Present firm yield	15,000	50
Wastewater irrigation	2,000	100
Cachuma conjunctive use (includes Phase I)	4,000	150
Wastewater injection	4,000	250
State project	10,000	300
Cachuma enlargement	2,800+	400

Note: The above costs are to be considered approximate and do not include additional supply and distribution costs, which are treated separately. Costs are for individual sources only, and include construction, operation, and maintenance of each supplemental source plus treatment. Costs are expressed in 1974 dollars and assume full utilization of each supplemental source.

Supply and distribution costs associated with growth were arrived at through discussions with the Water Division of the Department of Public Works and from information provided by Brown and Caldwell (1969). The latter was designed to serve as a long-range planning guide for the development of supplemental water sources and the delivery system needed to supply an anticipated population of about 120,000.

1. State project water option. Included in the estimates of water costs related to growth is the city's share in maintenance costs of the state water project. Whether or not Santa Barbara exercises its option on the water, its residents are contractually obligated to pay a portion of its maintenance and operating costs up to the coastal terminus (option of the Santa Barbara County Public Works Department). Based on discussions with the County Department of Public Works, these costs were estimated at $110,000 per year.[34] They were assumed as a "constant" for all PIPs, including No-Growth.

2. Past and current bond obligations. The city has one outstanding bond related to the construction of the Cater Filtration Plant, which is scheduled to be paid off in fiscal year 1982/83.[35]

Payment on another bond, known as the "Water Revenue Bonds of 1974" ($3.8 million) will begin in 1975, and payments will continue to the year 2001. Amortization and interest payments for both bonds were assumed as "fixed" costs in computing annual water costs for all PIPs.[36]

3. Transmission pipeline. According to the Water Resources Division of the Department of Public Works, a new 36-inch diameter transmission pipeline will be required to serve populations of 98,000 or more. The projected costs for expanding the capacity of this transmission line to serve additional people is estimated at $1.3 million. For populations in excess of 98,000 it was assumed that a capital-improvement bond in this amount would be floated.

Methods of Computing Costs. Total annual water costs were computed in the following manner:

1. Population by year for each PIP
2. Projected water demand each year for each PIP
3. Projected supply for each year for each PIP, taking into account a 104-a.f. annual decline in Gibraltar Reservoir supply because of siltation (which is estimated at 104 a.f. annually)
4. Cost of present water supply
5. Cost of supplemental water by source, introduced in order of increasing cost.

The costs of floating bonds for developing water were included in the a.f. cost estimates supplied by the Public Works Department.

Costs related to storage and distribution were developed by isolating capital improvements needed to accommodate growth. These improvement costs were then totaled in 1964 dollars and updated to 1974 dollars by applying the Engineering News Record (ENR) Index of 2,000. A contingency of 30 percent--the same as that used in Brown and Caldwell (1969)--assumed a population of approximately 120,000; certain simplifying assumptions had to be made for population levels greater than 120,000. For Zoning Maximum it was assumed that storage and distribution costs would double those specified in Brown and Caldwell (1969), based on the fact that the population difference between Zoning Maximum and 120,000 is approximately one-third greater than the costs at 120,000, following the same logic.

For populations less than 120,000 sufficient information was supplied in Brown and Caldwell to determine the improvements that could be omitted from consideration.

Bonds for improving the distribution and storage systems were assumed to be floated in two and three stages, respectively, as was

·recommended in Brown and Caldwell. They assume a 6 percent interest rate.

Estimated projections of annual water demand and the annual costs of supply for the one PIP approximating recent growth trends (Half-Density Probable) are presented in Table 6.22 for illustrative purposes.[37]

Methods of Computing Revenues. Revenues are projected by applying the current rate structure to projected water consumption.

Revenue estimates are based on projected water sales, connection fees, and miscellaneous charges.

Water sales account for more than 90 percent of the city's annual water revenue. Sales revenues for each PIP were computed by multiplying the current sales rate of $148 per a.f. by the projected demand in a.f. for each year for each PIP.

Connection charges were computed by projecting the number of single-family and multiple units that could be accommodated for each PIP. The number of each was then multiplied by an average current meter charge of about $250 for single-family units and $500 for each multiple unit to produce estimated connection charges for each PIP (costs include commercial and industrial connections). The number of these connections is assumed to be constant. For each year under each PIP, and in all PIPs, the ratio of residential to commercial and industrial uses is assumed to be fixed.

Miscellaneous charges, such as penalty payments and reconnection costs, currently amount to approximately $100,000 per year, or about $1.35 per capita. This ratio of $1.35 per capita was multiplied by the annual population under each PIP to produce "miscellaneous" revenues.

Analysis: The Costs of Water. If we subtract projected expenditures on water from estimated revenues under the present rate structure, we can get an idea of the increase in cost for additional use of water; the results of this analysis are summarized in Table 6.23. It is clear that water costs rise appreciably faster than revenues under all growth scenarios, and that the faster the growth, the greater the deficit between expenditures and revenues.

Unlike many other services, the costs of water also rise appreciably under No-Growth. This is because increased per capita consumption is assumed to occur over time, while available surpluses are expected to decrease owing to the natural siltation of the Gibraltar Reservoir. As a result, even under a No-Growth policy the city will have to make use of more costly supplemental sources. By the year 2000 such costs will exceed projected revenues by more than $600,000. The differences in that year for the other PIPs are considerably higher,

TABLE 6.22

Water: Demand and Costs, Half-Density Probable, 1974-2000

(1974 dollars)

Year	Projected Demand (a.f.)	Available Supply (a.f.)	Demand for Supplemental Water (a.f.)	Fixed Distribution Costs ($)	Current + Supplemental Operating Costs ($)	Supplemental Distribution Costs ($)	Total Costs ($)	Total Costs per Capita ($)
1974	15,000	15,380	0	1,500,000	737,940	127,200	2,365,140	32.34
1975	15,159	15,276	0	1,515,900	734,680	581,260	2,831,840	37.87
1976	15,327	15,172	155	1,532,700	760,320	578,760	2,871,780	37.94
1977	15,494	15,068	426	1,549,400	785,860	576,010	2,911,270	38.10
1978	15,662	14,964	698	1,566,200	811,500	643,260	3,020,960	39.12
1979	15,829	14,860	969	1,589,200	837,040	641,485	3,067,725	39.31
1980	16,520	14,756	1,764	1,652,000	914,980	639,422	3,206,402	40.66
1981	16,693	14,652	2,041	1,669,300	943,170	851,623	3,464,093	43.48
1982	16,866	14,548	2,318	1,686,600	983,160	848,935	3,518,695	43.71
1983	17,039	24,444	2,595	1,703,900	1,023,150	850,960	3,578,010	44.45
1984	17,212	14,340	2,872	1,721,200	1,063,140	747,410	3,531,750	43.43
1985	17,384	14,236	3,148	1,738,400	1,102,980	751,373	3,592,753	43.75
1986	17,557	14,132	3,425	1,755,700	1,142,970	750,623	3,649,293	44.00
1987	17,730	14,028	3,702	1,773,000	1,182,960	754,983	3,710,943	44.30
1988	17,903	13,924	3,979	1,790,300	1,222,950	753,808	3,767,058	44.54
1989	18,076	13,820	4,256	1,807,600	1,262,940	757,395	3,827,935	44.83
1990	18,461	13,716	4,745	1,846,100	1,334,730	755,290	3,936,120	45.66
1991	18,814	13,612	5,202	1,881,400	1,401,720	1,014,640	4,297,760	49.38
1992	18,990	13,508	5,482	1,899,000	1,442,160	1,016,640	4,357,800	49.61
1993	19,167	13,404	5,763	1,916,700	1,482,750	1,018,140	4,417,590	49.82
1994	19,344	13,300	6,044	1,934,400	1,527,740	1,019,140	4,481,280	50.08
1995	19,520	13,196	6,324	1,952,000	1,596,180	1,019,450	4,567,630	50.58
1996	19,597	13,092	6,605	1,969,700	1,664,870	1,024,250	4,658,820	51.13
1997	19,874	12,988	6,886	1,987,400	1,733,560	1,028,285	4,749,245	51.66
1998	20,050	12,884	7,166	2,005,000	1,802,000	1,026,555	4,833,555	52.11
1999	20,227	12,780	7,447	2,022,700	1,870,690	1,029,075	4,922,465	52.61
2000	20,404	12,676	7,728	2,040,400	1,939,380	766,215	4,745,995	50.28

Source: Santa Barbara Planning Task Force.

TABLE 6.23

Water: Revenues Less Costs, 1974-2000
(1974 dollars)

Year	No-Growth	Half-Density Maximum	Half-Density Probable	General Plan Maximum	General Plan Probable	Zoning Maximum	Zoning Probable
1974	- 38,972	- 46,412	- 46,412	- 46,412	- 46,412	- 46,412	- 46,412
1975	-232,072	- 284,840	- 388,478	- 407,540	- 359,765	- 349,192	- 286,151
1976	-233,212	- 306,980	- 402,457	- 371,880	- 378,880	- 390,229	- 309,797
1977	-234,102	- 328,970	- 416,121	- 401,770	- 395,870	- 441,815	- 333,141
1978	-308,592	- 420,960	- 499,844	- 508,060	- 472,860	- 596,002	- 426,538
1979	-320,857	- 441,675	- 520,790	- 570,475	- 500,825	- 681,164	- 452,557
1980	-332,836	- 540,252	- 556,096	- 692,952	- 556,652	- 831,317	- 566,519
1981	-345,475	- 801,043	- 787,080	-1,150,493	- 806,543	-1,484,905	- 822,240
1982	-356,827	- 846,845	- 814,975	-1,113,645	- 841,545	-1,661,003	- 871,172
1983	-372,992	- 897,460	- 847,538	-1,181,610	- 881,326	-1,841,815	- 924,818
1984	-333,382	- 842,650	- 774,616	-1,520,453	- 851,150	-1,917,051	- 872,888
1985	-351,385	- 895,103	- 809,060	-1,436,753	- 856,903	-2,099,801	- 928,472
1986	-354,275	- 942,843	- 838,893	-1,566,543	- 893,743	-2,318,737	- 985,842
1987	-383,075	-1,010,693	- 873,836	-1,701,343	- 935,693	-2,546,624	-1,111,522
1988	-395,940	-1,104,608	- 903,244	-1,730,608	- 972,208	-2,768,795	-1,292,853
1989	-413,568	-1,406,845	- 937,415	-1,964,635	-1,013,585	-2,995,279	-1,398,575
1990	-425,502	-1,570,632	- 987,517	-2,244,570	-1,104,020	-3,367,595	-1,591,114
1991	-472,792	-1,927,170	-1,295,810	-2,876,960	-1,519,110	-4,275,365	-2,035,603
1992	-488,832	-2,019,360	-1,328,699	-3,044,500	-1,604,400	-4,505,086	-2,140,539
1993	-504,372	-2,128,450	-1,361,190	-3,211,840	-1,670,790	-4,734,307	-2,247,026
1994	-519,412	-2,221,740	-1,397,581	-3,378,580	-1,740,530	-4,963,027	-2,375,712
1995	-533,762	-2,336,790	-1,456,780	-3,544,530	-1,819,080	-5,190,805	-2,504,460
1996	-552,602	-2,461,630	-1,520,731	-3,715,070	-1,999,620	-5,467,926	-2,637,447
1997	-570,678	-2,586,005	-1,583,797	-3,884,945	-2,077,495	-5,790,681	-2,769,668
1998	-582,988	-2,704,615	-1,640,956	-4,048,955	-2,149,505	-6,107,672	-2,896,124
1999	-599,547	-2,827,475	-1,702,567	-4,218,015	-2,225,765	-6,428,561	-3,027,083
2000	-615,328	-2,684,955	-1,498,794	-4,022,701	-2,036,745	-6,220,166	-2,892,900
Present value	-4,851,580	-13,866,400	-10,927,800	-20,438,300	-12,211,900	-29,316,300	-14,596,800

Source: Santa Barbara Planning Task Force.

ranging from $1.5 million for Half-Density Probable (the closest ap-
proximation to the city's growth trajectory of 1966-74) to $6.2 mil-
lion for Zoning Maximum.

The present value of the sum of yearly differences between
revenues and expenditures over the 26-year period is presented at
the bottom of Table 6.23 for each PIP. While the figure for No-
Growth is a substantial -$4.9 million, the figure for the lowest
growth rate is more than twice as great (-$10.9 million for Half-
Density Probable), and that for our highest projection exceeds the
No-Growth estimate by a factor of six (-$29.3 million for Zoning
Maximum).[38] These amounts represent a substantial burden to local
users over the 26-year period. The difference between No-Growth
and a 1-percent average annual growth rate is $4.6 million in the
present value of the total projected deficit of expenditures over revenues, and, in general, each 1 percent increase in the average rate of
population growth is equivalent to a $4.6 million increase in the pres-
ent value of the total projected deficit for the 26-year period.

How significant are these differences in terms of the cost of
water to the individual? It is not possible to estimate the actual rate
increases that will be necessary to make up the projected deficits,
since different classes of users (residential, commercial, and industrial) will be affected differently. Nonetheless, we can get an idea
of the magnitude of overall rate increases by expressing the total
yearly deficits as per capita figures that are presented in Table 6.24.

TABLE 6.24

Water: Per Capita Net Revenues Less Costs, Selected Years
($ per year)

Year	No-Growth	Half-Density		General Plan		Zoning	
		Maximum	Probable	Maximum	Probable	Maximum	Probable
1975	-3.17	- 3.81	- 5.26	- 5.38	- 4.48	- 4.45	- 3.82
1985	-4.80	- 9.74	- 9.89	-14.18	- 9.97	-18.40	-10.01
1995	-7.30	.-21.45	-16.25	-27.93	-18.64	-34.28	-22.65
2000	-8.41	-22.85	-16.02	-28.79	-19.69	-36.58	-24.21

Source: Santa Barbara Planning Task Force.

Interpretation of Net Costs
per Resident for Five PIPs

We can illustrate the per capita costs consequences of growth
in terms of the specific causes of higher water costs at each of the
five selected PIPs.

1. No-Growth. Water costs rise under No-Growth, although to a lesser degree than under the growth scenarios. Per capita net increases (costs over revenues) amount to $4.80 by 1985 and to $7.30 by 1995--the latter figure representing a 24-percent increase over 1974 per capita costs.

2. Half-Density Probable (1.1-percent annual growth). Net increases under this moderate rate of population growth rise to $9.89 per capita in 1985 and to $16.25 in 1995--the latter representing a 50-percent increase over 1974 levels. The rise in costs is due to increased dependence on supplemental sources of water.[39]

3. General Plan Probable (1.6-percent annual growth). Cost under a General Plan Probable policy shows a marked increase above No-Growth estimates, especially during the period after 1990. The principal reasons for these increased costs are greater reliance on more costly supplemental sources and the necessary expansion of the 36-inch transmission line, which has a capacity for a population of about 98,000. Per capita net increases amount to $9.97 in 1985 and $18.64 by 1995, a 58-percent increase over current levels in the latter year.

4. Zoning Probable (2.4-percent annual growth). Under Zoning Probable, a substantial increase in water demand above General Plan estimates results in the need for state project water in addition to the costly wastewater injection. The per capita net increase amounts to about $10 in 1985 and $22.65 in 1995; the latter is a 70-percent increase over current rates. This is however, an understatement of actual costs, because it is based on the cost assumptions involved in the city using its full state water project allotment. Under this PIP, the city would be using less than its full allotment, and per capita costs would therefore be higher than the figures presented here.

5. Zoning Maximum (5.1-percent annual growth). Zoning Maximum estimates reflect (by the year 2000) a fourfold increase in costs above a No-Growth policy and more than a twofold increase above General Plan Probable estimates. These substantial increases result from the need for the development of Cachuma Reservoir in addition to all other supplemental water options. Net per capita increases under Zoning Maximum are high. They total $18.40 in 1985 and $34.28 in 1995; the latter represents a doubling of current average per capita water rates.

Conclusion

Although further studies will have to be made of Santa Barbara's supplemental water options before more reliable supply and cost figures can be developed, this preliminary investigation suggests that

the deficit of water costs over revenues per capita vary by as much
as 128 percent in the year 2000, under the various growth alternatives.
The principal reason for these substantial increases in cost is the fact
that all of Santa Barbara's supplemental water options are expensive
by today's standards. The approximate population and approximate
year in which existing surplus water (including Phase I conjunctive
use) would run out at the various growth rates suggested by our PIPs
are presented in Table 6.25. Beyond these estimated dates, the city
will need to meet projected water demand by using a number of increasingly costly sources.

TABLE 6.25

Year and Population at Which Supplemental Water
Will Be Needed, at Various PIPs

PIP	Year	Population
No-Growth	1981	73,132
Half-Density Maximum	1978	79,955
Half-Density Probable	1979	77,059
General Plan Maximum	1976	78,254
General Plan Probable	1978	77,795
Zoning Maximum	1976	80,586
Zoning Probable	1978	80,259

Source: Santa Barbara Planning Task Force.

The costs developed in this preliminary investigation suggest
that annual expenditures for water could increase as little as $20.15
by 1995 for the average four-person family (under No-Growth) to as
much as $94.61 (under Zoning Maximum).[40] Certainly, for persons
on fixed incomes, as for families in the low-to-middle-income area,
an increase of these proportions cannot be dismissed lightly, nor can
the fact that increases in water costs of these magnitudes may affect
the quality of life that extends beyond the family dwelling to home
gardens, city landscaping, and parks.

Apart from these concerns one should not overlook the fact that
the cost projections for water in this report likely represent a "best
case" appraisal of future costs. If supplemental sources, such as
wastewater irrigation or Cachuma Reservoir expansion, prove unfeasible, then the city will have to begin supplementing its water supply with state project water. This will mean appreciably higher

annual and per capita costs at earlier dates than those shown in this analysis. More importantly, it may mean that adequate water for higher populations, such as Zoning Maximum, are an impossibility.

In addition there is a self-fulfilling-prophecy aspect to water decisions that is often overlooked in the traditional growth analysis. Water is the second largest and most capital-intensive of the city's services, and a large part of capital expenditures is made on long-range investments.

Such long-term capital expenditures are much more sensitive to requirement projections than are more labor-intensive ones. For instance, the Police Department spends 90 percent of its annual budget on salaries; therefore, it increases its expenditures incrementally and would not be substantially affected by a sudden stop in population growth ten years from now. However, if the city commits itself to water importation or other supply facilities based on a high projection, and if the city does not in fact realize that assumed growth, the unit cost of water will increase by a large factor over what was anticipated. Therefore, commitments based on high growth-rate projections might reinforce those projections to a certain extent, by making it economically beneficial to increase population to water capacity levels as quickly as possible. This effect, while it may be of considerable weight, must of course be measured in light of the other countervailing growth costs developed in other parts of this work.

Wastewater

In this section we consider the impacts of growth on the costs of sanitation. The costs of wastewater treatment will increase substantially over the next few years, regardless of growth. The city's present wastewater treatment plant is inadequate under state standards, and as a consequence a new plant is scheduled for construction in 1978 adjacent to the existing facility. While the current plant is operating at its design capacity of 8 million gallons per day (gpd) of wastewater, the new facility will have a capacity of 11 million gpd with the capability of expanding to 16 million at a later date. The new plant will thus upgrade the current standard of service, while providing for substantial additional capacity.

This additional capacity--and the added capital cost it entails--will be borne by current users in the form of substantial rate increases when the plant becomes operational. The total cost of the plant is presently estimated at $30 million, but current rates of inflation drive up construction costs daily. Although state and federal grants will pay for 87.5 percent of the total construction costs, the balance must be met by city residents, who recently passed a $6.9 million revenue bond to pay for Santa Barbara's share. [41]

Because of this substantial capital outlay, wastewater-treatment costs will not rise so fast as population for moderate rates of population increase. While costs are partly proportional to use (flow), they are also to a large extent fixed regardless of use: The bonds must be paid whether use increases or declines. For this reason, we shall see that per capita wastewater costs are lower under moderate growth than they are for No-Growth, at least over the time period to the year 2000.

Projecting Expenditures and Revenues

Estimates of Treatment Plant Flow. First, we estimated the wastewater flow through the treatment plant expected under the population-growth rates implied by each PIP. We have included the increased per capita consumption estimates from Engineering-Science, Inc. (1971, pp. II-3, 5) and have presumed that all of this increase in per user consumption is attributable to residential uses. [42]

Treatment Plant Capacity. The capacity limit of the new treatment plant is 11 million gpd, a capacity below eventual flow volumes for all growth PIPs. Some treatment plant expansion will therefore be necessary over the 26-year projection period. A 5 million gpd expansion to the new plant is technically possible and is expected to cost approximately $4.5 million. A rather small investment increment will add 45-percent capacity to the treatment system, because some of the $30 million spent for the new 11 million gpd plant is intended to make its expansion less expensive. Table 6.26 presents the years for each PIP when we estimate that capacity will be reached for both of these flow levels.

To gain the capacity beyond 16 million gpd required eventually at the highest PIPs, it would be necessary to construct four satellite treatment plants at a cost of $14 million, to provide an additional 4 million gpd capacity. Beyond 20 million gpd, however, as required under Zoning Maximum, the planning range of all existing studies is exhausted. We make the conservative assumption that to expand an additional 4 million gpd would cost the same as adding four satellite plants--another $14 million.

Other major system expansion costs would no doubt result from the levels of population associated with General Plan and Zoning PIPs, but they are not included here because we lack accurate cost information. For example, although the Public Works Department felt that some of the present sewers would have to be redeveloped to serve the densities anticipated under population levels over 125,000, they

were unable to provide a cost estimate of these projects. Thus, the
emphasis of our study has been on treatment-plant expansion and
total costs of growth are understated to the extent that growth would
also require changes in the city's sewers.

TABLE 6.26

Wastewater: Population and Year of Capacity, Limits of
New 11 Million gpd Treatment Plant

PIP	Year	Population
No-Growth	*	73,132
Half-Density Maximum	1985	91,897
Half-Density Probable	1991	86,485
General Plan Maximum	1982	93,620
General Plan Probable	1988	89,453
Zoning Maximum	1980	95,495
Zoning Probable	1984	90,950

*After year 2000, not within scope of study period.
Source: Santa Barbara Planning Task Force.

Expenditures Estimates. Operating costs, including salaries, materials, and operating capital expenditures, are estimated. These
estimates are based on Brown and Caldwell (1973), prepared for the
city in order to establish the user service charges to meet added revenue requirements under the new treatment plant. One difference between our estimates and those in Brown and Caldwell (1973) is that we
have included the $200,000 collection system maintenance program
that was added to the Public Works Department after the Brown and
Caldwell report was commissioned. All other differences are essentially the result of the higher-than-expected construction costs under
most recent estimates.

Table 6.27 provides cost estimates of annual operating expenditures in 1975 and in 1978 when the new plant is assumed to be operational. These, the bases for the projections of annual expenditures
that are to be applied to each PIP, can be broken down as follows:

1. Salaries and materials. In fiscal year 1973/74 total salaries per employee amounted to $11,800. This is used throughout
as a basis for projecting salary costs. Current plans call for the
addition of five employees when the new 11 million gpd treatment

plant opens. From Brown and Caldwell (1973) we assume no additional employees are required to run the 16 million gpd plant when
it opens. No additional maintenance or disposal employees are included for either the 11 million or the 16 million gpd plant. Fringe
benefits are estimated to be 30 percent of salaries.

Under the new 11 million gpd plant the costs of electricity and
chemicals become dependent on the level of flow through the plant
each year. Starting with the Brown and Caldwell estimates for
these costs, we adjusted their inflation and flow calculations to the
appropriate years.

TABLE 6.27

Wastewater: Estimated Annual Operating
Expenditures, 1974/75 and 1977/78
(1974 dollars)

Expenditure	1974/75	1977/78[a]
Salaries	306,800	365,800
Benefits	92,000	110,000
Electricity	22,000	128,154[b]
Chemicals	38,000	46,278[b]
Other materials	603,000	603,000
Maintenance	200,000	200,000
Depreciation	--	598,668[b]
Bond repayment	473,100	588,100
Total	1,734,900	1,866,900
		+ 773,100[c]
		2,640,000

[a]Based on current growth rate of Half-Density Probable: 1.1
percent per annum.

[b]These expenditures were estimated by multiplying the average yearly per million gpd cost by 8.9, the number of million gpd
extrapolated for 1977/78.

[c]We have added on the cost of $86,869 per million gpd, or
$773,100 for the year.

Sources: Santa Barbara Planning Task Force estimate based
on Brown and Caldwell (1973); City of Santa Barbara, 1974/75;
interviews with City Public Works Department officials.

2. Operating capital. From the five-year capital program, 1974/75 to 1978/79, we include $200,000 per year for maintenance and special projects.

3. System expansion. The Public Works Department estimates the cost of expanding the 11 million gpd to 16 million gpd at $4.333 million (1974 dollars), and the cost of constructing four satellite plants with an additional million gpd capacity at $14 million. [43]

4. Depreciation fund. Under the conditions of the federal/state grant (which paid more than 80 percent of the actual costs of constructing the new treatment plant and outfall), once the new plant opens, rates must be increased to cover a depreciation item that will provide enough income to replace the treatment plant entirely at the end of its useful life (assumed to be outside the period of the study). Although the city government has not yet decided the kind of depreciation fund it will establish, we followed the recommendation expenditure on a units-of-production basis. The Brown and Caldwell estimate for a plant costing $23 million was $129.86 per million gallons of wastewater treated in each year of the useful life of the plant. We have appreciated this according to the most recent estimates of plant cost ($30 million) to arrive at $184.30 per million gallons per year. This figure must be multiplied by the total gallons of wastewater treated in each year under the flow estimates of each PIP. For example, the depreciation fund for the 1974 flow estimate of 8,288,049 gpd would be $557,533 ($184.30 million gpd x 365 days x 8.22 million gpd).

The depreciation fund is to be covered by service charges to wastewater consumers and is treated in our analysis as an expenditure item. To maintain the new plant, 20 percent of this fund can be used each year, while 40 percent can be placed in a sinking fund toward replacing the treatment plant when its useful life is over; the other 40 percent can be used to add to treatment-plant capacity as needed. [44] We assume that it will draw 7 percent over the years and that the amount available for plant expansion will be used when appropriate, thus providing a source of capital for future expansion. Expansion costs beyond what is available in this depreciation fund are assumed to be paid for by 25-year revenue bonds at 6 percent. Table 6.28 shows these expansions and the additional bonding required.

Expenditures increase annually up to the year 2000 under all growth options. This is because some expenditures, such as power and chemicals, are directly dependent on the level of flow through the treatment plant; under the five higher PIPs there are also increasing expenditures due to the bonded indebtedness required to fund system expansions. Table 6.32 (presented subsequently) illustrates our estimates of expenditures for one PIP, Half-Density Probable. [45]

TABLE 6.28

Schedule of Wastewater Treatment Plant Expansion Under Each PIP, 1974–2000
(thousands of 1974 dollars)

PIP	Expansion to 16 Million gpd (year)	Expansion to 20 Million gpd (year)	Expansion Beyond 20 Million gpd (year)	Project Cost	Available from Depreciation Fund	Annual Payment on 25-Year 6 Percent Revenue Bond
No-Growth	0	0	0	0	0	0
Half-Density Maximum	1984			4,500	2,344	169
Half-Density Probable	1990			4,500	5,261	0
General Plan Maximum						
(1)	1981			4,500	1,225	256
(2)		1993		14,000	6,312	601
General Plan Probable	1987			4,500	3,676	64
Zoning Maximum						
(1)	1979			4,500	586	306
(2)		1988		14,000	4,256	762
(3)			1994	14,000	3,384	830
Zoning Probable						
(1)	1983			4,500	1,926	201
(2)		1999		14,000	9,700	336

Source: Santa Barbara Planning Task Force calculations under the assumption that expansion occurs in year prior to capacity being reached.

Under the No-Growth option (with no additional users) expenditures increase 3 percent from the opening of the new plant in 1978 to the end of the study period. This is in part because of the assumed per capita increase in consumption over time. Under the Half-Density Probable PIP growth path (which involves no bonded system expansions) there is an 11-percent rise in total expenditures between 1978 and 2000. This higher percentage cost increase, as compared to the No-Growth option, is the result of the increased numbers of users implied by a positive population growth rate. It is interesting to note that the rise in expenditures under Half-Density Probable is less than half the percentage increase in population (11 versus 28 percent). Increase in rate of expenditures is smaller than increase in per capita use because of the high proportion of fixed costs.

The five highest growth rates all involve substantial system expansion capital requiring bonding. Thus, there is a noticeable jump in expenditures in each year a new bond is passed. The greatest jumps are noticed when the design limit of the plant currently being constructed is reached (16 million gpd), and it is necessary to add the four satellite plants at a construction cost of $14 million.

Revenue Estimates. Estimating revenues is dependent on first establishing the number of users to which average user rates can be applied. We estimate that of the 30,580 users in 1974, there were 22,928 low-density residential, 5,732 high-density residential, 1,869 commercial, and 51 industrial users.

Table 6.29 indicates our estimates of the number of users by each user class in 1974 and in the year 2000 under all the PIPs. Note that we have included a transition away from the present predominance of low-density users (80 percent) toward high-density users. This is the expected result of population growth--higher population densities and more multiple units, as determined by the various growth policies under consideration.

Revenue estimates are based on present rates (effective March 1, 1974). Table 6.30 shows the current average user charges for the four user classes (high- and low-density residential, commercial, and industrial). Because of the increased per capita usage over time, we assume that all residential users will be paying the maximum rates by 1978.

Our results show that except for the No-Growth option, annual revenues under all PIPs steadily increase from the present to the year 2000 (see Table 6.32 for an illustration of these trends).[46] However, the percentage increase in revenue over the present is consistently less than the percentage population increase for growth, as is indicated in Table 6.31.

TABLE 6.29

Wastewater: Estimated Number of Users, by Class,
in Year 2000, for Each PIP

PIP	Low-Density Residential	High-Density Residential	Commercial	Industrial
No-Growth	22,928	5,732	1,869	51
Half-Density Maximum	29,768	11,857	3,008	82
Half-Density Probable	26,348	7,774	2,395	65
General Plan Maximum	27,128	26,212	3,577	98
General Plan Probable	25,028	14,453	2,648	72
Zoning Maximum	29,288	36,054	4,353	119
Zoning Probable	26,228	20,116	3,058	84

Source: Santa Barbara Planning Task Force estimate.

TABLE 6.30

Wastewater: Current Revenue, by User Class

| | Average | | | |
	Month	Year	Number of Users	Revenue
Low-density residential	3.21	38.52	22,928	883,187
High-density residential	2.06	24.72	5,732	141,695
Commercial	19.41	232.92	1,869	435,327
Industrial	25.69	308.28	51	15,722
Total (1973/74)				1,475,931

Sources: City of Santa Barbara (1974b); Santa Barbara Planning
Task Force calculations. For other sources, see Volume 3.

TABLE 6.31

Wastewater: Percent Changes in Revenue, Population, and
per Capita Revenue for Each PIP, 1974-2000
(percentages)

	Percent Rise in Total Revenue	Percent Rise in Population	Percent Decline in per Capita Revenue
No–Growth	0	0	0
Half–Density Maximum	47	61	9
Half–Density Probable	21	28	5
General Plan Maximum	73	91	10
General Plan Probable	30	41	8
Zoning Maximum	107	133	11
Zoning Probable	52	63	7

Notes: Per capita revenues for each PIP, for the year 2000,
are as follows: No-Growth, $20.37; Half-Density Maximum, $18.59;
Half-Density Probable, $19.25; General Plan Maximum, $18.42;
General Plan Probable, $18.70; Zoning Maximum, $18.16; Zoning
Probable, $18.94.
Source: Santa Barbara Planning Task Force.

This decline in per capita revenue with growth results from the
fact that there is a maximum flat service charge for residential users.
As the number of such users grows over time, per capita revenues
will necessarily decline under the assumed increases in per capita
user consumption. This effect is reinforced by the assumed growth
in high-density, lower-rate residential users relative to low-density,
higher-rate users.[47] Growth, under the current rate structure, will
thus lead to a decline in per capita revenues.

Net Effects of Growth: Expenditures/
Revenue Synthesis

The results of contrasting estimated expenditures and revenues
for the PIP that most closely approximates recent trends (Half-
Density Probable) is presented in Table 6.32. [48] All the options indicate that once the new plant begins operation, there will be a substantial annual deficit for the rest of the study period. This result was
anticipated by Brown and Caldwell (1973).

As might be expected, we observe that for all the positive
growth rates considered, the higher ones have the higher deficits,
and the lower ones have the lower deficits. A comparison of the
present values of the difference between revenues and expenditures,
over the study period for all PIPs, indicates the extent to which higher growth rates cost more on balance. The present value of revenues
less expenditures over the 26 years, for each of the seven PIPS, is
as follows: No-Growth, $12.1 million; Half-Density Maximum, $11.9
million; Half-Density Probable, $11.6 million; General Plan Maximum,
$15.1 million; General Plan Probable, $11.7 million; Zoning Maximum,
$19.9 million; Zoning Probable, $12.1 million.

Figure 6.2 shows the percentage revenue deficits that would result if the present rate structure were to continue over the study
period. It is apparent that a user-rate increase sufficient to increase
total annual revenue more than 50 percent will be necessary once the
new treatment plant begins operation, because at that time expenditures will increase more than 50 percent over 1977, while revenues
will increase by only 1 to 4 percent. The increase in revenues required to meet costs ranges from a minimum of 59 percent to a maximum of 75 percent of the projected 1978 revenues, and on a per capita
basis from $10 to $15 for each resident of the city. The major reason
for these increases in revenue requirements is the addition of the depreciation fund (more than $500,000 per year), and an increase of
more than $100,000 in the annual bond repayment on the new treat-
ment plant. In addition, the new plant involves some expenditures
that increase with flow increases--and these amounts begin to show
in the 1977/78 expenditure estimates.

Summary and Conclusion

We find that wastewater expenditures increase each year
throughout the study period. This is because some expenditures depend on the level of wastewater flow through the treatment plant,
which is expected to increase annually even without any increase in
the population on the basis of higher per capita usage. Of course,
because of the increased number of users associated with higher population levels, such costs increase more under the higher PIPs.

TABLE 6.32

Half-Density Probable Wastewater Analysis: Expenditures, Revenues, and per Capita Deficit, 1974-2000
(1974 dollars)

Year	Operating Expenditures	Bonds (in thousands)	Total Expenditures (in thousands)	Total Revenues (in thousands)	Per Capita Deficit
1974	1,262	--	1,262	1,490	n.a.
1975	1,262	473	1,735	1,502	n.a.*
1976	1,262	473	1,735	1,514	n.a.*
1977	1,262	473	1,735	1,526	- 2.83
1978	2,052	588	2,640	1,538	-14.45
1979	2,065	585	2,650	1,550	-14.28
1980	2,079	587	2,666	1,562	-14.18
1981	2,092	583	2,675	1,574	-14.01
1982	2,107	583	2,690	1,586	-13.90
1983	2,120	583	2,703	1,597	-13.79
1984	2,135	582	2,717	1,609	-13.67
1985	2,148	581	2,729	1,621	-13.55
1986	2,163	579	2,742	1,633	-13.43
1987	2,175	577	2,755	1,645	-13.31
1988	2,192	580	2,772	1,657	-13.25
1989	2,206	576	2,782	1,669	-13.11
1990	2,221	576	2,797	1,681	-13.02
1991	2,236	575	2,811	1,693	-12.93
1992	2,251	568	2,819	1,705	-12.77
1993	2,266	571	2,837	1,717	-12.72
1994	2,281	567	2,848	1,729	-12.60
1995	2,297	566	2,863	1,741	-12.52
1996	2,313	564	2,377	1,753	-12.43
1997	2,328	561	2,889	1,765	-12.33
1998	2,343	557	2,900	1,777	-12.21
1999	2,359	556	2,915	1,789	-12.14
2000	2,375	548	2,923	1,801	-11.99

*Deficits in 1975 and 1976 covered by 1974 surplus.

Source: Santa Barbara Planning Task Force estimates based on 1974 user service charges.

FIGURE 6.2

Wastewater Revenue Requirements for Each PIP, 1977-2000

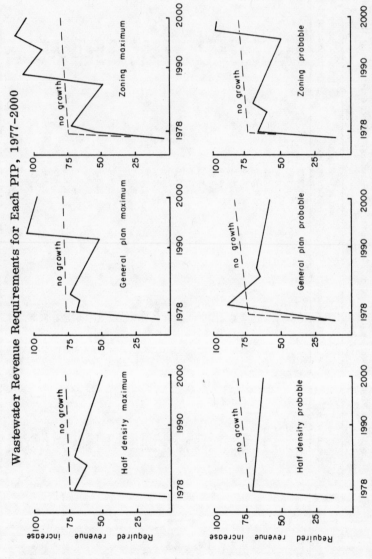

Note: Annual revenue deficits as a percent of projected revenues under present user charges.

216

Population growth rates implied by all PIPs, except for No-Growth, involve expansion of the new wastewater treatment plant, but only under the slowest positive growth rate (Half-Density Probable) does the Depreciation Fund accumulate income fast enough to finance all required expansions fully within the years covered by our study. The levels of bonding required to fund expansion of the treatment plant beyond the 16-million-gpd design limit are especially expensive.

Revenues from user sales under the current rate structure tend to increase only as the number of users increases--that is, as population increases. This has the result of requiring rate increases as expenditures rise, even if the increase in expenditures is only the result of increased per capita usage (and/or inflation), and not because of an expanded level of service.

The current rate structure will lead to a decline in revenue per capita as the city's population grows, because the housing mix will shift toward the user class (high-density residential) with the lowest rate per user.

The new 11 million gpd treatment plant scheduled to be completed in 1978 will have to be expanded to its design limit of 16 million gpd under all PIPs except for No-Growth, sometime between 1980 and 1991. The population limits for the new 11 million gpd plant range between 86,000 and 95,000--depending on both the population growth rate (which determines the number of users) and the yearly expansion of per capita consumption of wastewater expected on the part of residential users. The capacity of the 16 million gpd expansion is exceeded at a population of approximately 120,000 under the highest PIPs. At the lower PIPs that capacity would be exceeded by the smaller populations sometime after the year 2000, if per capita increases in usage were to continue unabated.

The apparent contradiction between the slowest positive growth rate (Half-Density Probable) being the least expensive option, while the No-Growth is more expensive, is resolved by the recognition that there is no increase in revenue through the years under the No-Growth option because there is no increase in the number of users. Total expenditures, on the other hand, continue to increase each year even without an increase in the number of city residents. As a result, under the No-Growth option, the gap between expenditures and revenues continually increases--it is the only population option under which this occurs. Only if per capita wastewater consumption were to stabilize would constant dollar expenditures stabilize in a No-Growth scenario.

And finally, the present value analysis allows us to state that five of the options are not significantly different from the viewpoint of cost. These are the five lowest PIPs, including the No-Growth option. It would appear that, over the 26 years of this study, to a population of up to 115,000, not growing at all is about as expensive as growing, and staying under 100,000 population for the 26-year period is the least expensive of all growth options considered.

In conclusion, the impacts of growth on the costs of wastewater services are the increasing of the costs of services by the decreasing of the amount of revenue raised per capita and by the continued need to expand system capacity. Lower growth rates decrease the costs of these expansions, and if Santa Barbara were to grow at the Half-Density Probable rate of about 1.1 percent per year, there would appear to be no growth costs per se over the study period.

SUMMARY OF PUBLIC SECTOR ANALYSIS

We have examined the impacts of growth on the city's General Fund expenditures, on two municipal services, and on public education. We have seen that the city's General Fund expenditures will rise substantially higher than revenues under all growth scenarios, increasing the tax rate almost two-thirds under the highest PIP. On the other hand, city property tax increases will be offset by declining tax rates for education, the costs of which fall in proportion to declining enrollments relative to total population. The costs of water increase substantially with growth, doubling at the highest PIP; at the same time, wastewater costs will be higher under all growth scenarios (including No-Growth), because the wastewater district is already committed to construction of a $30 million wastewater treatment plant capable of serving a population of between 86,000 and 95,000, depending upon how fast the population grows.

What are the effects of growth, in light of all these findings? We will summarize the results of the public sector analysis three ways. First, we shall consider the impact of growth on property taxes for the city's General Fund expenditures and for education. Next, we will examine revenue increases required for water and wastewater--increases that will be paid for in higher service charges. Finally, we will consider a summary measure that enables us to estimate the combined impact of all public sector expenditures, the present value of all projected revenues less expenditures.

The Effects of Growth on Property Taxes

Although the costs of municipal services rise with increasing population, declining enrollments in the public schools will result in overall reductions in the property tax. City, school, and total tax rate changes by 1995 are summarized in Table 6.33. City tax rate increases are as high as 63 percent under Zoning Maximum. For Half-Density Probable--representing minimal growth in our analysis--increases are almost 30 percent over current levels. In terms of city finances, therefore, we can conclude that even modest increases in population translate into significant revenue shortfalls. When one includes the costs of education in the analysis, however, the picture changes considerably, for under current legislation, if present demographic trends continue, we may expect substantial declines in school property tax rates. [49]

TABLE 6.33

Change in Property Tax Rates for Combined School Districts
and City of Santa Barbara, 1995
(1974 dollars)

PIP	City of Santa Barbara	School Districts	Combined Effect
No-Growth	0.14	-1.56	-1.42
Half-Density Maximum	0.65	-1.56	-0.91
Half-Density Probable	0.39	-1.66	-1.27
General Plan Maximum	0.75	-1.36	-0.60
General Plan Probable	0.46	-1.65	-1.19
Zoning Maximum	0.85	-1.20	-0.35
Zoning Probable	0.66	-1.55	-0.89
Current tax rate (per $100)	1.34[a]		6.22[b]

[a]Excluding debt service.
[b]Excluding overrides.
Source: Santa Barbara Planning Task Force.

The overall declines are largest under No-Growth, amounting to $1.42 for the combined city and school tax rates; this decline is equivalent to a one-fifth reduction in taxes to these two entities, a savings of $82 in taxes on a $30,000 home. As population increases, the net savings declines proportionately. The comparable tax savings amount to $73 under Half-Density Probable, $68 under General Plan Probable, and only $20 under Zoning Maximum.

While it is useful to combine city and school taxes for purposes of summarizing effects, it is recognized that in fact the two jurisdictions are independent of one another. Tax reductions in the school

districts, while no doubt appreciated by taxpayers, will not make
those taxpayers any more willing to award the city compensating tax
increases. Under our assumptions, a No-Growth policy will see the
city tax rate rise from its present $1.46 per $100 of assessed valuation (including debt service) to $1.60; a continuation of the present
growth rate will see it rise to $1.85; and a high growth rate (to Zon-
ing Maximum) will be accompanied by an increase to $2.31.

The Effects of Growth on Revenue Requirements
for Water and Wastewater

For water and wastewater reclamation, we can estimate revenue increases that will be required to service the different population
levels.[50] Table 6.34 presents the percentage of revenue increases
required for water and wastewater at the year 1995, at each PIP.
Our estimates for water indicate that under the present rate structure, even allowing for the higher revenues that will result from increasing usage, an additional 22 percent will be required in 1995 to
meet projected expenses under No-Growth. This is because higher
per capita residential usage and siltation of Gibraltar Reservoir will
result in the need for additional more costly supplemental water.
Under the growth PIPs, revenue increases are substantial. Should
Santa Barbara continue to grow at present rates (Half-Density Probable), required revenue increases will be nearly 50 percent. Our
highest PIP (Zoning Maximum) will see a near doubling in revenue
requirements. These will be met with a proportional increase in
water rates.

TABLE 6.34

Projected Revenue Increases Required,
Water and Wastewater, 1995
(percentage increase over current revenues)

PIP	Water	Wastewater
No-Growth	22	80
Half-Density Maximum	61	59
Half-Density Probable	47	64
General Plan Maximum	79	107
General Plan Probable	54	63
Zoning Maximum	95	63
Zoning Probable	123	56

Sources: Santa Barbara Planning Task Force estimates based
on city Water Department information and on Brown and Caldwell (1969).

The projections for wastewater reclamation offer a somewhat different picture. Unlike water, whose major cost increases will result from costly future options that will result from growth, wastewater costs will increase substantially regardless of population trends. The new $30 million wastewater plant could serve a population substantially greater than the present one; yet it must be paid for, even if it is not used to capacity. Since total revenues are tied to the number of users, they will be lower under lower population levels. Thus, because expenditures for wastewater service increase with wastewater flow, revenue requirements must be shared by fewer people. The result is that additional revenue requirements are higher under No-Growth (80 percent) than under all but our two highest PIPs. Supplemental revenues requirements in the year 1995 would appear to be lowest for the Zoning Probable population in that year of approximately 110,000. However, under this growth trajectory, an expensive system expansion would be required in 1998, raising the per capita cost by more than $2. Therefore, our projections indicate that a 1995 population of about 90,000 (Half-Density Probable) would be the least expensive option available within the period of the study. The required revenue increases for wastewater reclamation for almost all PIPs far outweigh the differences resulting from growth differentials.[51]

Overall Conclusions

We have considered services funded out of property taxes and users' charges. How may we combine these estimates into a single measure for purposes of comparison across the PIPs? One approach is to sum the projected expenditures for all services in each year, and subtract this figure from the sum of projected revenues (under current rate structures) for the same year. If this figure is negative, it means that total expenditures exceed total revenues; if it is positive, the reverse is true. If we then compute the present value of this revenue-expenditure difference, and total all present-value figures over the 26-year period, we have a summary measure that will enable us to make comparisons across PIPs.

The results of such an analysis are presented in Table 6.35. For all PIPs the figures are negative, indicating that if differences between revenues and expenditures over the entire 26-year period are considered, the present value of expenditures exceeds that of revenues. The present value figure for No-Growth is the smallest ($774,000), approximating a "breakeven" point: Savings in education nearly balance losses in other areas over the entire period. For the other PIPs, the present value figures increase with population. The figure for the lowest scenario (Half-Density Probable) is almost

$4 million, five times that for No-Growth; the Zoning Maximum estimate ($51.5 million) is almost 67 times greater than the No-Growth scenario.

TABLE 6.35

Present Value of Revenue Requirements (Revenues Less Costs)
for All Services, 1974-2000
(thousand 1974 dollars)

	General Fund	Education	Water	Waste-water	Total
No-Growth Half-Density	- 3,328	+19,473	- 4,852	-12,067	- 774
Maximum Half-Density	-18,697	+31,774	-13,866	-11,946	-12,735
Probable General Plan	- 9,356	+27,867	-10,928	-11,573	- 3,990
Maximum General Plan	-26,698	+32,517	-20,438	-15,111	-29,730
Probable Zoning	-12,394	+29,774	-12,212	-11,725	- 6,557
Maximum Zoning	-36,553	+34,285	-29,316	-19,905	-51,489
Probable	-19,495	+31,803	-14,597	-12,125	-14,414

Note: Plus (+) indicates that overall revenues exceed costs;
minus (-) indicates that overall costs exceed revenues.
Source: Santa Barbara Planning Task Force.

It is clear that at least in terms of present-value analysis, growth does not pay in the public sector. For each thousand persons added to the city population, the present value of yearly revenues-less-expenditures is reduced by more than $500,000.[52] In choosing a growth policy, the nonfiscal benefits and costs of growth must be weighed against these aggregate public costs.

NOTES

1. It is possible that there is a relationship between police expenditures per capita and city size, although the evidence is ambiguous. Our cross-cities study found no relationship between city size and the number of police officers per 10,000 population: There is a positive relationship between city size and per capita expenditures on police personnel among all cities, but this relationship ceases to be significant when it is only cities of approximately the same income as Santa Barbara's that are considered.

2. A lack of new housing facilities in the form of parking areas, garages, and station houses, in the face of increasing population, seems likely to us, but because no such sources are projected by the Police Department, even under population growth, we did not include any such capital outlays in this analysis.

3. Figures are presented only for the two Half-Density PIPs; for other PIPs, see Volume 1.

4. A complete listing of city parks, including the acreage for each, is contained in Volume 1, Table 6.7; the location of each park is presented in Volume 1, Figure 7.2.

5. Higher per acre development costs for community parks are due in part to the inclusion of recreation facilities (that is, adult recreation centers).

6. Average values per square foot are based on neighborhood-wide surveys and not on a specific parcel.

7. Development costs assume the inclusion of recreation facilities.

8. It is possible that some of the costs of acquiring and developing new park plans will be met from sources other than the city, such as the state and federal governments.

9. The current number of public courts is considered substandard by many.

10. Court cost estimates are based on lighted courts built in units of four to six at a time.

11. Doubling the population on a given amount of land should, as a first approximation, double the price of that land. Thus, an acre of potential parkland in the areas that most require such parkland under growth--the densely-zoned areas--will cost considerably more at higher population levels.

12. In this work, "assessed value" is the value of all property in the city for the purpose of generating tax revenues, whether such revenues come in the form of property taxes or in the form of reimbursements to the state for tax exemptions. Assessed value is thus computed by summing the value of the secured-, unsecured-,

and utility-tax polls, including homeowners' and business-inventory exemption. Property in California is assessed at 25 percent of its market value.

13. This assumes that real income (and hence purchasing power for housing) remains at current levels. The assumption of constant per capita real income is consistent with past trends: Real income did rise during the 1960s, but it has leveled off and declined in recent years. We are unwilling to make the assumption that real incomes will resume the 1.5-percent annual increase they exhibited during the 1960s (Gruen and Gruen 1974), although that is certainly a possibility; it is also possible, however, that real incomes will stagnate in the future, decline, or exhibit some mixture of patterns.

14. It is assumed that this policy (downzoning) would exclude commercial zones to allow commercial expansion. However, commercial zoning would be made to disallow residential expansion.

15. There are five sections of R-1 land in the city. The sample was drawn such that the percentage of the sample selected from each section was equal to the percentage of all R-1 lots in the city that each section contained. For example, 45 percent of all R-1 lots in the city are on the Mesa; therefore 45 percent of the sample was drawn from this area. The sample size was 100.

16. All increases are beyond what is due to inflation, the effects of which are controlled.

17. We assume an annual interest rate of 6 percent.

18. If we assume an interest rate r, then the formula for present value over period of n years is given by the following: Present Value $= V + V_1 + V_2/(1 + r) + V_3/(1 + r)^2 + V_4/(1 + r)^3 + \ldots + V_n/(1 + r)^{n-1}$.

19. In this study we assume a "balanced budget" in the first year of our projections (1974). We do so by setting revenues equal to expenditures. We are interested in noting how projected trends diverge, under our different growth assumptions, from this balanced budget.

20. The increase under the No-Growth PIP is due to a 2.2 percent overall decline in property assessments resulting from the downzoning of currently undeveloped land and the fact that some library expansion is currently planned to occur regardless of population growth.

21. School financing is discussed in a later section. By "operating expenditures" we refer to noncapital costs of education.

22. The actual formulas are somewhat more complicated than indicated here, taking into account the effects of inflation and changes in district assessment; the final effect is as described. Elementary schools are kindergarten through sixth grade, and high schools are seventh through twelfth grades. Under Senate Bill 90, the elementary

school districts are responsible for raising revenues for seventh-
and eighth-grade students; these revenues are then transferred to
the high school district. Such transfers are taken into account in
our projections of costs for each school district. The "revenue
limit" was initially set at the per pupil expenditure level in each district as of the time of passage of Senate Bill 90; it has since been increased to compensate for inflation. (See memorandum from Edwin
H. Harper, deputy superintendant of public instruction for administration, state Department of Education, "Recalculation of the 1973-74
Revenue Limit," July 11, 1974).

    23. "ADA" refers to average daily attendance. It is the figure
on which all calculations are based. We use the more familiar term
"enrollments" in the text, although technically they are not the same.
ADA is about 97 to 98 percent of enrollment.

    24. The state provides a formula for computing a theoretical
tax rate per $100 of assessed valuation. If a school district cannot
raise the difference between its basic aid and its foundation program
by applying this tax rate, it receives equalization aid.

    25. Detailed findings are presented in Volume 3.

    26. School districts are also eligible for long-term, low-
interest state loans, provided that they are bonded to capacity (5 percent of assessed valuation) and can show a need for capital expansion.
The Santa Barbara school districts are not eligible for such loans;
even under our highest PIP, the bonding required will not approach
5 percent of assessed valuation.

    27. All capital programs are presumed funded by 25-year,
6 percent general obligation bonds paid out of property taxes. Programs are initiated in the year prior to becoming "necessary" in
terms of shortages. The total capital program includes bonds that
are currently outstanding; tax rates for debt service currently
amount to 0.15 in the high school district and 0.16 in the elementary school district. Total cost of capital programs, including existing debt service, is presented in Volume 3.

    28. This capacity is, of course, predicated on full utilization
of all classrooms in the elementary school district, including some
35 portables currently in use; it also assumes that a seven-period
day will be utilized in the junior and senior high schools. These
assumptions are consistent with the views expressed by the districts
in the Master Plan and those of the district business manager.
Should the decision be made to terminate the use of portable classrooms, or retain the present six-period day, as much as one additional school at each level might be required at the high growth rate.

    29. The net revenue estimates for the entire South Coast high
school district were multiplied by the proportion of South Coast population each year that resides within the city limits.

30. We have excluded special override taxes from this analysis. Rates are initially higher under No-Growth because of the estimated loss in assessed value due to the downzoning of currently undeveloped land.

31. It is possible that under the conditions imposed by Senate Bill 90 the school districts will be forced to hold tax rate elections more frequently than in the past. This year, for example, the state granted a statewide salary increase to teachers that was twice as great as the revenue limit increase allotted in the Santa Barbara school districts. Since ADA declined during the same period, school revenues (tied to ADA, with a modest increase to allow for inflation) will not rise as quickly next year as expenditures (75 percent of which are used for teaching). The "pinch" will force the school districts to cut costs elsewhere. Under the new law, a higher revenue limit can be set locally only by a general election.

32. "City" in the present discussion refers to the area served by the Water Resources Division of the Department of Public Works.

33. One a.f. equals 325,000 gallons (approximately).

34. Costs vary with the operating and maintenance costs of the state water project.

35. See 1963 water bonds payment schedule.

36. The repayment schedule for such bonds is presented in Volume 3.

37. Comparable tables for all PIPs are presented in Volume 1, Tables 7.43 to 7.49.

38. The minus sign preceding the present (1974) value estimate indicates that local expenditures exceed revenues.

39. The cost of providing supplemental water under the Half-Density Probable population level could be appreciably higher than indicated because the city would not be making full use of wastewater injection.

40. This assumes residential users will use 69 percent of total water as projected in Brown and Caldwell (1969) and will pay the proportional amount.

41. This includes all costs of land acquisition and new ocean-outfall construction, as well as 12.5 percent of treatment plan construction costs. Payments began in 1975 and are to be completed by 2003.

42. See Volume 1, Table 7.53, for the resultant calculations of treatment plant flow at each PIP for each year from 1975 to 2000.

43. For a detailed breakdown of the estimates, see Volume 3.

44. A yearly schedule of depreciation funds available under each PIP is presented in Volume 3.

45. Similar tables for the remaining five PIPs are contained in Volume 1, Tables 7.62, 7.63, and 7.65 to 7.68.

46. Tables for the other PIPs are contained in Volume 1.

47. Residential use is estimated as billed at the maximum
service rate in 80 percent of cases in 1974. The proportion of maximum bills will rise toward 100 percent as per capita consumption increases. Therefore, we do not consider residential rates to be variable with flow.

48. Tables for additional PIPs are presented in Volume 1.
See note 45.

49. Under present conditions, to maintain even a constant tax
rate into the future will require tax rate elections; our analysis
makes it clear that, under the current revenue limits, tax rates will
decline automatically.

50. A revenue increase is the amount current revenues would
have to be increased in order to meet projected costs. When expressed as a percentage, it is equal to the required revenue incre-
ment divided by current revenues. "Current revenues" are estimated by applying the current rate structure to projected use.

51. This is not true of the two highest PIPs, where requirements for plant expansion and the construction of satellite facilities
result in substantial additional capital outlays. Our estimates for
such major expansion, however, must be regarded as highly tentative in the absence of a major study concerning wastewater requirements at city population levels in excess of 120,000.

52. This is the regression of present value on population in
the year 2000. The actual decrease is $545,434 per 1,000-person
increase.

SALIENT COSTS AND BENEFITS

The preceding chapters have dealt with the general costs and benefits of growth and were based on the assumption that the city's economic and demographic structure would be maintained in its present state; that is, the city's commercial base would only grow larger, not change qualitatively. By holding the economic mix constant, the effects of growth per se could be seen more clearly.

But the city not only has the option of deciding how much to grow, it can also choose in what way it will grow. We attempt here to give some indication of the relative costs and benefits that might be expected if the economic base of the city were to change along with its population level. Our concern here is with the mode of expansion and with the particular costs and benefits associated with each mode.

Relevant Costs and Benefits

Any manufacturing, service or retailing enterprise creates both direct and indirect costs and benefits. Direct costs and benefits are those that are generated by the project itself. A new factory, for instance, generates direct government revenues in the form of property taxes levied on the plant's assessed value, and also in the form of the business license fee that is paid. On the other hand, it also creates direct costs, such as loss of land that could be used for

----

Linda Lillow and Steve Logan are coauthors of this chapter.

other purposes, possible pollution of the air and water, increased
traffic congestion in the immediate area, or damage to another industry, such as tourism.

The indirect costs and benefits associated with a project are
those that are derived from the population growth the project generates. Any project that generates employment also generates growth.
New people generate benefits, in the form of property and sales taxes
and the like, and costs, such as denser residential land use, increase
of general traffic, and new expenditures related to schools and to
police and fire protection. In addition, they require other residents
to service their needs for food, clothing, and shelter--residents who
then migrate and who in their turn attract still others who generate
similar costs and benefits to the city in the well-known multiplier
effect. The indirect costs associated with a given economic sector
will vary with the character of the particular population that it causes
to migrate: their numbers, income levels, and their tastes and
habits.

Typically, cost-revenue studies examine only the costs and
revenues associated with the employment generator itself--that is,
the direct costs and benefits associated with the economic enterprise.
The employment a project generates is ordinarily treated merely as
another benefit of the project and is not recognized as a potential
source of both costs and benefits. It is usually assumed that, because of the existence of unemployment in a city, any new jobs
created will be taken by people already in the local population, and
thus each new project is assumed, in itself, not to be growth producing. For this reason, cost-revenue analyses of industrial and
commercial projects almost invariably show strong net benefits (see
Stuart and Teska 1971; Silverman, undated). For the same reasons,
cost-benefit studies of residential projects, where the people who
work in the economy have to live, usually show either losses or only
very minor gains (see, for example, City of Newport Beach 1972).
The policy implications of such "findings" would be for every city to
build the means of work, but not places for the workers to live. But
people who work in a locality must also live somewhere reasonably
nearby, and thus the costs and benefits associated with new residents
and residential land use must be included with the costs and benefits
associated with the commercial or industrial uses that generate them.
When both the direct and indirect costs and benefits associated with
a particular land-use project are considered, the result is a more
realistic picture of the project's total impact. We will take both the
direct and indirect costs and benefits into account in evaluating the
sorts of economic expansion that will increase or decrease the costs
of growth.

Choice of Economic Scenarios

It would be impossible to analyze all conceivable economic mixes for the city and describe their differential consequences. However, we can get an idea of what the future might hold by examining the way in which the components of the present economic mix are currently contributing to the city's fiscal, social, and environmental well-being. From these data we can project the impact of an increase or decrease in the proportion of the city's economic base derived from one source or another.

Among the major components of the city's current productive capacity, we selected for analysis: (a) retailing, (b) R & D, (c) technical manufacturing, (d) light manufacturing, and (e) hotel-motel industry (tourism). Each of these components was chosen not only because it was present in the current economic mix of the city, but also because the city seems to possess realistic options for expanding its population through any one of them. We first present the revenues associated with each economic sector, expressed in terms of net revenues generated per employee.[1] We examined only those sources of revenue that are financially most important and that would most reasonably be expected to vary with economic sector.

Retailing

Retailing is not ordinarily treated as a basic industry; no products are created and, typically, no wealth that is not already present is brought into an area. Retailing is thus not ordinarily growth inducing; it only provides for the consumption needs of those who have been brought to the area previously through labor-force growth in the basic industries.

Nevertheless, under certain conditions retailing does bring in new wealth, thus generating increases in the labor force and hence in population. The City of Santa Barbara generates sales from outside its boundaries in two ways: It is a market center for a much larger region, encompassing much of Santa Barbara and parts of San Luis Obispo counties, and it is a tourist center that captures retail dollars that people would otherwise spend in their home towns or in other vacation spots. To the extent that the city acts to increase retail trade from these sources, and to the extent that it acts to capture the "leakage" of the city residents' dollars into other areas, such as Ventura, Montecito, and Goleta, it can use retailing to build additional revenues, if it is willing to pay the costs associated with those revenues. This section of the study is thus analytically oriented toward what is only a segment of retail trade:

that portion of business that could be captured and added to the already existing volume of activity.

Our study of retailing is based on a case analysis of La Cumbre
Plaza, the city's only regional shopping center. A regional shopping
center is more appropriate for this analysis than other forms of retailing in that it typically draws some of its shoppers from outside
the immediate area--shoppers who might otherwise spend their
money elsewhere. The pattern in this city, as elsewhere, shows
an increasing proportion of overall retail activity taking place in
such centers. Given the fact that the city now faces the decision of
whether or not to encourage such a center within its boundaries, the
regional center seems a useful focus of study.

Direct Revenue Benefits. Retail stores provide the city with three
primary sources of direct revenue: (a) property tax on the structures housing them (b) a portion (0.95 percent) of the taxable sales
made with them, and (c) business license fees.

The following revenues expressed on a per employee basis are
estimated to accrue to the city's General Fund from the presence of
La Cumbre Plaza:

City property tax	$ 46.52
Sales tax subvention	380.00
Business-license fees	13.52
Total direct revenues	$440.04

Indirect Revenue Benefits.[2] The kinds of taxes that residents pay
that would most reasonably be expected to vary significantly by industry type are the property tax and the sales tax. These are also
the two most significant revenue sources that make up the city's
General Fund. Wealthy people pay more--in absolute terms--in
both forms of taxes, and the wealth of employees varies significantly
by economic sector. Based on the relatively low wages of retail
employees, the following estimates were made of indirect tax revenues that derive from La Cumbre Plaza on a per employee basis:

City property tax per employee (whether owner or renter)[3]	$ 21.31
Sales-tax subvention per employee/resident[4]	19.91
Total indirect revenues per employee/resident	41.22
Total major revenues, direct and indirect, per employee/resident	$481.26

Research and Development

R & D firms, varieties of which are sometimes called "think
tanks," are distinguished from other businesses in that they are involved in basic and applied research operations, rather than in the
production of a product for retail or wholesale distribution.

A sample of six Santa Barbara R & D firms, drawn from the
Technical and Services Directory for 1974 (published by the Science
and Engineering Council of Santa Barbara) was used to generate much
of the data used in the following analysis. These particular firms
were chosen on the basis of their primary activity being R & D, as
determined by their classification for business-license fee purposes
as "professional," as opposed to "manufacturing." Virtually all
firms fulfilling these conditions are in the sample. Of the employees
working in these companies, 68.2 percent consisted of scientific and
engineering personnel, the highest percentage of professional, executive, or management employment in the economic sectors examined,
and consequently also having the highest average income per employee. Most of these firms are located in either individual or
multistory office buildings.

Direct Revenue Benefits. The city's R & D firms provide direct
revenues to the city in the form of property taxes paid on the buildings that house them and in business-license fees. There are no
sales-taxable products. Direct revenues per employee are estimated
to be as follows:

City property tax	$19.44
Business-license fee	17.30
Total direct revenues	$36.74

Indirect Revenue Benefits. Employees in all economic sectors generate the same kinds of indirect revenues to the city as do those
engaged in retailing. Indirect revenues from these sources on a
per employee/resident basis for the sector are as follows:

City property tax	$126.80
Sales tax subvention	31.67
Total indirect revenues	158.47
Total major revenues, direct and indirect	$195.21

Technical Manufacturing

The technical manufacturing concerns surveyed in this report
also carry on R & D activities, but in addition are involved in the

manufacture and production of various products, such as surgical, optical, electronic, film, video supplies and equipment, and the like. They are thus classified for business license-fee purposes as "manufacturing" concerns. As for the R & D firms, their choice of plant location is largely independent of the economic factors that frequently govern other industrial plant-locational decisions. However, unlike the primarily research-oriented firms, they are not found typically in office-type buildings, but rather tend to locate in more conventional industrial areas and buildings. As might be expected, these technical-manufacturing concerns employ a much smaller proportion of professional, executive, or management personnel (21.7 percent) than do firms that are purely research-oriented. Similarly, the average income per employee in these industries tends to be lower. The nine technical-manufacturing concerns used in this survey were also selected from the Technical and Services Directory for 1974 and represent 80 percent of listed firms employing ten or more persons engaged in technical manufacturing.

The same types of direct and indirect revenue sources as for the R & D sector apply to the technical-manufacturing sector:

Direct Revenue Benefits

City property tax per employee	$ 8.35
Business-license fee per employee	6.64
Total direct revenues per employee	$ 14.99

Indirect Revenue Benefits

City property tax per employee/resident	$ 72.17
Sales-tax subvention per employee/resident	24.84
Total indirect revenues per employee/resident	97.01
Total salient revenues, direct and indirect, per employee/resident	$112.00

Light Manufacturing

The manufacturing concerns selected for study were drawn from the Santa Barbara Industrial Directory compiled by the Santa Barbara Chamber of Commerce (March 1973). All those selected were (a) involved primarily in the manufacture of a tangible product of a nontechnical variety, (b) had more than five employees, and (c) were located in the Lower East Side area of the city. These firms manufacture such products as diving equipment, paint, water-treatment systems, model sailboats, lampshades, paper boxes, and burial vaults. They do not manufacture the type of product reserved for a local market. Approximately 75 percent of the sample export their products, sometimes to foreign markets. More than 80 percent of the firms that fit the outlined criteria were included in our sample; those that were omitted were firms for which data were not readily available. As might be expected, the percentage of professional, executive, or management personnel is relatively low in these sectors (22.2 percent), with a concomitantly low average income.

These firms generate direct revenues to the city from the same sources as the R & D and technical-manufacturing sectors, but in addition they generate sales-tax subventions from a small portion of production that is retailed locally.

Direct Revenue Benefits

Property tax per employee	$13.46
Sales-tax subvention per employee	10.47
Business-license fee per employee	9.24
Total direct revenues per employee	$33.17

Indirect Revenue Benefits

City property tax per employee/resident	$37.63
Sales tax subventions per employee/resident	23.87
Total indirect revenues per employee/ resident	61.50
Total salient revenues, direct and indirect, per employee/resident	$94.67

Hotel-Motel Industry

Revenue data for the hotel-motel industry are based on data relevant to all hotels and motels in the city that cater to visitors. Day visitors who do not spend the night in the city, or visitors who stay with friends or relatives are not considered in this part of the study because their presence in the city is not based in any land use set aside for the purpose of housing them. These people do generate revenue to the city, but they would generate such revenue regardless of the existence of city hotels and motels or any policy to promote or inhibit them.

In addition to the revenues generated through city property taxes and business license fees, the hotel-motel industry generates revenue through the city bed tax. A portion of the bed tax is earmarked for city-promotion purposes, and so we have based our calculations only on the remaining revenue, which goes into the city's General Fund for other purposes. Because tourists shop, subventions that come to the city as a result of hotel-motel guest expenditure in the city are listed as well. (This means, however, that this revenue is double-counted, because it was also included as a revenue benefit from retailing.)

Direct Revenue Benefits

City property tax per employee	$129.32
Sales-tax subvention per employee	264.34
Business-license fee per employee	7.76
City bed tax per employee	266.88
Total direct revenues per employee	$668.30

Indirect Revenue Benefits

City property tax per employee/resident	$ 16.39
Sales-tax subvention per employee/resident	15.30
Total indirect revenues per employee/resident	31.69
Total major revenues, direct and indirect,	
per employee/resident	$669.99

Summary: Direct and Indirect Salient Revenue Benefits

As can be seen from the results portrayed in Table 7.1, hotel-motel and retailing are the city's most lucrative industries in terms of revenues generated per employee; they are followed by R & D, technical manufacturing, and light manufacturing, in that order. This indication that tourism and retailing are the city's most lucrative revenue sources is all the more significant, given the fact that they are the two industries of the group that are the most interdependent. That is, many people come as tourists to the city, but then spend money in the shops; others come to shop (particularly at the art galleries and craft and specialty shops) and thus become part of the hotel-motel support base. Another way of expressing the significance of tourism to sales-tax subvention revenues is to note that tourist dollars account for approximately 5 percent of retail sales volume in the city.[5] The significance of this 5 percent is that it represents subvention income the city would not otherwise receive; it is therefore income coming from outside of the area, based on the relatively few employee/residents needed to produce it.

In terms of city policy choice, retailing revenue of this sort can be maximized in the following ways: by capturing sales from regional shoppers outside the city, by stopping the "leakage" of city residents' dollars to other parts of the region, and by luring tourists who will spend money in the city. If the general costs of growth seem worth it, the hotel-motel sector would then seem a crucial way to minimize the attendant revenue costs of growth. On

TABLE 7.1

City Revenues per Employee, by Economic Sector

Revenue Source	Retail	R & D	Technical Manufacturing	Light Manufacturing	Hotel-Motel
Direct revenues, per employee					
Property tax	46.52	19.44	8.35	13.46	129.32
Sales tax	380.20	0	0	10.47	264.34
Business-license fee	13.52	17.30	6.64	9.24	7.76
Bed tax	0	0	0	0	266.88
Subtotals	440.24	36.74	14.99	33.17	668.28
Indirect revenues, per employee/resident					
Property tax	21.31	126.80	72.17	37.63	16.39
Sales tax	19.91	31.67	24.84	23.87	15.30
Subtotals	41.22	158.47	97.01	61.50	31.69
Grand totals	481.46	195.21	112.00	94.67	699.99

Source: Santa Barbara Planning Task Force.

the other hand, the benefits of tourism are sharply inflated by our decision to not count the tourists themselves as residents who use resources as do other residents. Tourists do in fact require police and fire protection, and they do contribute to traffic congestion, although not to school overcrowding or welfare services. If the tourists themselves were to be added to the employees of the sector, the advantages of the industry would be seen as much less.

Another way of comparing the revenue benefits of each of the economic sectors is to ask this question of each: If every member of the current labor force were engaged in work in the given sector, would the city be better or worse off than it is at present under these various assumptions? This is, of course, a highly unrealistic question. Workers of a variety of sorts are needed to make a city function, and complete homogeneity in economic base may make a city especially vulnerable to economic crises, should its only industry suffer a reversal. But, as an exercise, the question can yield important information.

For each economic sector, the total amount of revenue generated per employee was multiplied by the size of the city's labor force (18,926). The product represents revenues to the General Fund that would follow if all the city's workers were engaged in the given sector. Since revenues from the taxes we have studied represent 56 percent of the city's General Fund, and on the assumption that all economic sector groups share equally in the remaining 44 percent, the product was divided by 0.56 to yield the total revenue that would come into the General Fund, should all such revenue be dependent upon the economic sector in question. The resulting amount was compared with the amount of the fiscal year 1973/74 General Fund to gain an estimate of the surplus or loss that would result. This surplus or loss was then expressed as a percentage of the total current General Fund. The results for each economic sector are given in Table 7.2.

Again, the results are clear: Relative to other sectors, the tourist sector produces most revenues per employee. This would be the case, even if the sales generated by tourism were removed from consideration. It must be emphasized that we have not demonstrated, for example, that the city would make a "profit" by, say, 47 percent, if its retailing sector grew above what it currently is, because nowhere in these data have the costs of growth, either in general or for a particular sector, been calculated. The costs of population growth that would be associated with revenue gain in any economic sector are spelled out in the preceding chapters of this work. The present exercise only estimates the fiscal effects of making all current members of the population dependent upon the

economic sector in question. Thus, those data allow determination
of the economic sector from which the city currently receives relatively more or less of its revenues, not of the net effects that would
attend the addition of extra people to the population of a given sector.

TABLE 7.2

Total Revenue for General Fund, If Entire Labor Force
Were of a Given Sector, by Each Sector

Sector	Total General Fund Yield ($)	Percent Change from Current General Fund*
Retailing	16,271,628	+47
R & D	6,590,306	-40
Technical manufacturing	3,785,200	-66
Light manufacturing	3,199,507	-71
Hotel-motel	23,623,703	+113

*Current city General Fund (base data): $11,057,086.

SPECIAL STUDIES: TWO PROPOSED PROJECTS

The city now faces the prospect of adding two new major projects to the city: a luxury resort hotel (in the form of the Las Positas
Inn or the Hyatt Regency), and a Downtown regional shopping center.
We have made analyses, analogous to those above, of these two
types of projects to estimate the degree to which the addition of a
new tourist or retail center would result in findings different from
those derived from use of the aggregate data used in the preceding
analysis.

New Resort Hotel

Santa Barbara currently has no hotel or motel of the size of
those being proposed as the Las Positas Inn or the Hyatt Regency.
Either would thus be a unique addition to the city and would have
economic consequences for the city different from associated with
the existing hotel-motel stock.

We have calculated the direct and indirect revenue benefits associated with these projects by combining data drawn from their respective environmental impact reports, and as necessary, introducing supplemental data derived in the same manner as was followed in the preceding revenue analyses:

Direct Revenue Benefits

City property tax per employee	$190.72
Sales-tax subvention per employee	165.98
Business-license fee per employee	3.28
City bed tax per employee	304.35
Total direct revenues per employee	$664.33

Indirect Revenue Benefits

City property tax per employee/resident	$ 16.39
Sales-tax subvention per employee/resident	15.30
Total indirect revenues per employee/ resident	31.69
Total major revenues, direct and indirect per employee/resident	$696.02

The new hotel will generate approximately the same revenues per employee as do existing motels.

New Downtown Regional Shopping Center

The new regional shopping center being proposed for Downtown Santa Barbara would have approximately 600,000 square feet of floor space, would contain 25 percent more store area than does La Cumbre Plaza, and would be slightly under the median size for regional shopping centers in the Far West (Urban Land Institute 1972). Like La Cumbre Plaza, the new Downtown center is expected to contain two major department stores and a mixture of other smaller shops and variety stores. La Cumbre Plaza averages 0.19 employee per 100 square feet of retail floor space, so a new center of this size might be expected to employ around 1,140 persons. Our analysis of the fiscal impact of such a center on the city is parallel to that for La Cumbre Plaza, except that a slightly lower level of sales per square foot of retail floor space is assumed. This assumption is made because La Cumbre Plaza currently generates a sales volume substantially higher than do either the national or Far West average for regional shopping centers, and it was felt that a certain amount of the new center's business would be at the expense

of La Cumbre Plaza, bringing it in closer approximation to the Far
West average for a regional center:

Direct Revenue Benefits

City property tax per employee	$ 46.11
Sales-tax subvention per employee	303.20
Business-license fee per employee	11.88
Total direct revenue benefits per employee	$361.19

Indirect Revenue Benefits

City property tax per employee/resident	$ 21.31
Sales-tax subvention per employee/resident	19.91
Total indirect revenues per employee/ resident	41.22
Total salient revenues, direct and indirect, per employee/resident	$402.41

The results indicate that although the new center would generate revenues at a slightly lower level than the existing regional center, it would nevertheless generate substantially greater revenue
than would the R & D, technical-manufacturing, or light-manufactur-
ing sectors.

RELATIVE COSTS OF ECONOMIC SECTORS

Although it has been possible to enumerate the major revenues
associated with various economic sectors, albeit with important
assumptions and approximations along the way, the relative costs
associated with those revenue benefits is much more difficult to
express, particularly in quantitative terms. This is an important
asymmetry; it means that since benefits are easy to stipulate and
costs are not, cost-benefit analyses run the risk of being merely
benefit analyses.

The problems in enumerating costs derive from a number of
sources. First, the city agencies administering the services that
are drawn upon by a project do not keep records in terms of the
economic sectors served. There is no separate police force, for
example, for the retail sector as opposed to the industrial; nor are
there separate budgets within the Parks Department for tourists as
opposed to other users. Understandably, city department heads
find it impossible to describe the degree to which one kind of development as opposed to another draws upon their department's resources. Studies that have nevertheless attempted to distribute costs

in a quantitative way from one economic sector to another are based on the kind of guesswork we wish to avoid; as the city's late staff auditor, T. Geoffrey Moore, once reminded the city, such studies tend to represent the "swallowing of many camels while straining at many gnats."[6]

In addition to the problems posed by a sheer lack of information, there are difficulties deriving from the problem of "unused capacities." Unused capacities refer to the fact that certain city facilities may be able, at the decision point, to tolerate a project's additional burden without incurring immediate capital costs. If, on the other hand, there is little such unused capacity, the cost of the same additional burden can be very great. Thus, for example, a given project may increase water use by only a small percentage, but, because water demand is already close to supply, the project's realization will accelerate appreciably the day that more expensive water options have to be taken, and thus its ultimate economic burden to the city may be much greater than was at first indicated. Similarly, at one site a project might involve heavy costs of road construction; at another site the same project could be built with only marginal effects on the existing road system. In such instances, a given project's cost has not so much to do with the economic sector that it represents as it has to do with the unused capacities associated with the citywide resources it will draw upon, as well as with the unused capacities of the specific site it will occupy.

In the previous chapters on the effects of growth upon city and neighborhood resources we provided a general framework for examining any specific project. We will now provide a discussion of the relative impacts on the city of growth for each specific economic sector. Necessarily, the discussion is general, and often left deliberately inexact. Wherever possible, our assessments are based upon quantitative information; where such data do not exist, we draw upon our own understandings of the city at least to raise issues that typically might otherwise be overlooked when land-use decisions that affect the city's economy are made.

We list these costs with the knowledge that a specific given project may not follow the general rule. Whereas factories typically use more water than retail stores, a given factory may use less than a given store. Similarly, an economic sector that we may evaluate as having negative esthetic consequences may in a specific case be quite beautiful. Particularly on more subjective matters, such as esthetic consequences, our own judgment is not the only relevant one; the reader is encouraged to substitute his or her own viewpoint as appropriate and alter our conclusions accordingly.

Retailing

Retailing is a major generator of traffic; to the degree to which a city functions as a market center for a larger area (as in fact Santa Barbara does), and to the degree to which it attracts tourist-shoppers who use automobiles to get there and move around within the city, retailing is very costly as a source of traffic congestion and of associated emissions of air pollutants. Insofar as retailing serves the local public (and thus is not a basic economic sector at all), it has a greater tendency to serve people who may walk, use mass transit, or travel relatively short distances. If a regional shopping center's location is not chosen with maximum traffic efficiency in mind (as La Cumbre Plaza was not), then circulation impacts can be extremely negative. Additional monetary costs associated with road widening, signalization, and so forth may similarly be incurred along with social costs in neighborhood disruption. Noise levels, which rise with traffic congestion, are also rather high.

Retail centers use relatively little water: only that amount needed for building maintenance, sanitary facilities, eating places (if any), and irrigation of rudimentary landscaping. The kinds of business activities found in regional shopping centers were estimated to use an average of 0.075 a.f. per employee per year (see Mercer and Morgan 1973).

On the assumption that land not used to provide for an economic base can be used for esthetic or recreational opportunities, it becomes significant that retailing is not an intense user of land, per resident generated. The ratio of acres to employees in a regional shopping center is 0.036 employees per acre (traditional shopping areas use more land per employee).

Retailing has only minor effects on sewers, and its impact on parks and recreation facilities is not noteworthy.

The esthetic impacts of retailing depend upon the skill of the project's architect and the resources placed at his or her disposal. In the Santa Barbara area, though standards are generally higher than those for most areas, results have in too many cases been disappointing. The primary esthetic liability of most retail facilities is the sea of parking lot that surrounds the stores.

Other city services (schools, police, fire, and so on) are moderately affected by retail expansion. Retailing centers, because of the problems of theft and crowd coordination, tend to draw rather heavily on police services, as "high-value areas" receive extra care in fire protection, and their employees tend to draw heavily on police service.[7]

Research and Development

R & D firms generate relatively little direct traffic, since they merely require employees to travel within the local area to and from their place of work. Somewhat disproportionate indirect-traffic and air-pollution effects are generated through the greater number of cars per household and general avoidance of mass transit that tend to be characteristic of higher-income people.

Water use by the R & D sector is usually quite small, though occasionally of some significance if the R & D facility is located in a campus environment that requires extensive irrigation. On the average, R & D water use is estimated at 0.044 a.f. per employee per year (Mercer and Morgan 1973). The relatively high income level of R & D employees, however, probably means greater home water usage, primarily for landscape irrigation of the larger lots they tend to maintain.

R & D adds relatively little noise, either directly or indirectly. Because R & D firms can be "stacked" in multistory office buildings, and because little or no major equipment is required, R & D uses relatively little land area directly.

Impacts on sewers are minimal, as are impacts on parks and recreational facilities. Esthetic impacts are relatively positive; R & D firms can generally adapt to any design restrictions possible to impose on office buildings. Impacts on other city services are also minor.

It is worth noting that the growth impacts of a given R & D firm are slightly higher than the size of the employee roster would imply. Because of the R & D employee's higher spending capacity, the multiplier effect on population growth is likely to be higher than for other economic sectors. This rather minor effect was not taken into account in our previous calculations.

Technical Manufacturing

Relatively minor traffic and air pollution problems arise from technical manufacturing; travel is merely to and from work, with no traffic induced from outside the urban area. Stationary emissions from plants engaged in technical manufacturing are not appreciably higher than those from office or R & D structures. Water usage is usually minor, averaging 0.065 a.f. per employee per year (Mercer and Morgan 1973). Land is used more extensively than in R & D operations, due to the frequent need for single-story operations with some space-demanding equipment. Effects on sewage systems are typically minor, as are demands on parks and recreational facilities.

Esthetic impacts vary greatly, but physical plants are generally architecturally inferior to R & D establishments, although they are perhaps the equal of regional shopping centers. Demands on other city services are somewhat higher than those of R & D firms, due to the less affluent incomes of technical manufacturing employees.

Light Manufacturing

Depending upon the form that it takes, light manufacturing activities can generate high levels of air pollutants, such as dust, truck exhausts, fluid evaporation, and chimney smoke. Traffic generated is not usually great, except for instances in which truck transportation to markets and from raw-material sources is required. Similarly, depending upon the nature of the production process, water may or may not be a major requirement. On the average, light manufacturing concerns are rather heavy water users: 0.110 a.f. per employee per year (Mercer and Morgan 1973). Again, noise levels depend on the particular manufacturing process, but they are often high. Land requirements can be high, space being required for large pieces of equipment, as well as for storage of raw materials, warehousing of finished products, and/or operations related to receipt and dispatch of trucks. Sewage requirements may also be high and may involve the treatment of effluents that are environmentally toxic and/or destructive of the city's sewage system and treatment facilities. Esthetic impacts are on balance somewhat negative. Use of other city services are relatively high because of the greater indirect demands generated by low-income workers and their families. Impacts on parks and recreational facilities are slight.

Tourism

The dependence of the tourist industry on out-of-town travelers who arrive at and travel within the city by car makes tourism costly to the city in terms of the traffic and air pollution that it generates. Henningson et al. (1974) estimated that the Las Positas Inn project would generate 1,432 automobile trips per day. If other hotel-motel units in the city were assumed to generate analogous automobile traffic, the citywide total would amount to 12,230 trips per day. This is equivalent to the total automobile movements generated within the entire community of Isla Vista (Isla Vista Planning Commission 1971). Traffic and air pollution impacts can be expected to be great. Water usage is also typically high, generated by the routine needs of extra users brought from outside the city. It is particularly high in the case of the proposed luxury projects that require much landscape irrigation, such as that required for a golf course. Average annual water use of the existing hotel-motel facilities is 0.196 a.f. per employee (Mercer and Morgan 1973), the highest of any sector. A major luxury resort hotel like the Las Positas Inn would use much more: an estimated 0.619 a.f. per employee (Henningson et al. 1974).

Noise generated by tourism is moderate, a reflection of excess traffic and congestion. Land is also sometimes used rather extensively for tourist accommodations, averaging 0.086 acres per employee for the existing stock. Sewage effects are moderate again, a function of the routine needs of an "imported" temporary population.

Impacts on parks and recreational facilities are great. The tourist is not present in the city to work and live there with a routine round of obligations; he or she goes to the city with the express purpose of enjoying the local environment and consequently is a heavy user of the city's parks and beaches. These facilities, in fact, can be considered as the publicly owned and maintained overhead that is the basis of a private-business sector.

Attempts have been made to discover the extent to which non-residents use the park resources. The city's Recreation Department found for example, that of the 24 major accidents that occurred on Santa Barbara beaches during the 1971-73 period, 13 percent of the victims were not residents of either the city or the county. In a survey of dog-bite victims at the beaches, 28 percent of the victims were neither city nor county residents. In a third study, it was found that 13 percent of the boats moored in the harbor belonged to persons who resided neither in the city nor the county. Finally, in an examination of boat-launching permits at the city harbor, it was found that 10 percent of those using city facilities were neither city nor county residents.

The best data on the subject come from a random survey of 552 beach users (from East Beach to Leadbetter Beach) in August 1972 (Gold and Sonquist 1973). It was found that almost half the beach users (46 percent) were from outside the Santa Barbara Coast region. (Some of these out-of-towners are one-day visitors and would no doubt use the beaches regardless of the existnece of local hotels and motels.) In the light of the fact that tourists account for only 7 to 10 percent of the city's total daytime population, these studies support the conclusion that their use of at least certain recreational facilities is far disproportionate to their numbers.[8] This usage falls unevenly on certain of the city's facilities, with Palm Park, East Beach, West Beach, the Bird Refuge, and the Harbor area likely receiving the most impact.

Relative to other economic sectors, tourism brings certain nonquantifiable benefits to the city. Tourists patronize cultural and entertainment events heavily and shop for exotic and unique merchandise. Because they inflate the city's market for these sorts of goods and services, the range of such services available to the residents of the city is expanded. The kinds of merchandise and entertainment that prosper in Santa Barbara are partially dependent upon the type of tourist that is attracted. Those visiting Santa Barbara are different from those visiting other places; the kinds of tourist attractions peculiar to this city create this difference, and the kinds of visitors who come to Santa Barbara as a result act, through their own merchandise and entertainment tastes, to perpetuate it. The current types of benefits that residents gain from the tourist industry will continue only if the quality of present tourism attractions is maintained.

A NOTE ON PROPERTY AND PENSIONS INCOME

The substantial amount of wealth that comes to the city when residents who are not productive--that is, those who are retired or otherwise living primarily from dividends, property, interest or inherited wealth--has not been included in this analysis for a number of reasons. In Santa Barbara this sector represents a sizable number of persons; their incomes no doubt represent a substantial portion of the 31 percent of local wealth that comes from such sources (Keisker 1973, Table 4). But since these people are not in the labor force, there are no readily available data on their incomes, age, household size, or other relevant characteristics. Given that there are no direct costs and benefits associated with this group, it is their economic and social characteristics that will determine their total impact on the city. The lack of such data relevant to these indirect costs and benefits thus precludes analysis. We suggest, however, a simple principle relevant to this group: The more wealthy a person in this sector, the more that person will pay to the city in sales-tax subventions and property taxes but will have little countertendency to require additional city services from police, schools, or fire service.

SUMMARY

Table 7.3 allows a rough comparison to be made among the costs to be associated with growth in one economic sector as opposed to another. We have ranked each sector on a scale of 1 to 4, with 1

representing the most benign effect and 4 representing the most deleterious effect. We have revealed our reasoning in the paragraphs
above; to the extent that they are flawed in some subject areas, such
as esthetics, the reader can substitute his or her own ranking and
thus change the values in the matrix at will. It is also important to
reiterate that any given project may not conform to the general pattern usually found in its sector, and thus may not conform to the
matrix.

TABLE 7.3

Impacts of Various Economic Sectors on the City
(1 = best; 4 = worst)

Variable	Retail	R & D	Technical Manufac- turing	Light Manu- facturing	Hotel- Motel
Noise	3	1	1	4	2
Revenue	2	3	4	4	1
Traffic	4	1	1	2	4
Air pollution	4	1	1	3	4
Water	1	2	1	3	4
Sewers	1	1	1	3	2
Parks and recreation	1	1	1	1	4
Esthetics	2	1	3	4	2
Other services (police, fire, schools, etc.)	2	1	2	3	4

Source: Santa Barbara Task Force analysis; basic data from
sources provided in text.

The city can use these comparative data in two different ways.
If it is determined, on the basis of the analysis in previous chapters,
that population growth is desirable, the city can use the information
in this chapter to choose that method of economic growth that will be
of most benefit or of least cost. Alternatively, if the city chooses
not to grow at all, it can endeavor to change the current economic
base mix in order to maximize benefits and to lower costs. Finally,
the city can mix strategies: attempt to grow, with a certain favored

economic mix and also endeavor to change the current mix by decreasing or increasing a given economic sector below or above its
current level.

As a final caution, we emphasize that the data in this chapter
cannot be used to demonstrate that growth in any given economic
sector will benefit the city, either in net budgetary terms or in
quality-of-life terms. Nor does it demonstrate that expansion of any
one of them is possible or likely. The city does not have total freedom to create any mix it desires; growth in one sector may ipso facto
preclude growth in another. Expansion of tourism, for example, may
be choked off by the decreasing amenities caused by increased population from another sector.

NOTES

1. Because we assumed that the multiplier effect would be approximately the same for all sectors, we generally ignored them in
this comparative analysis.

2. Methods used in computing the figures in this chapter are
contained in Volume 3, pp. 123-50.

3. Derived by applying tax rate to housing values of units occupied by this income group as revealed in Dodson et al. (1972) and
in Buchalter et al. (1973).

4. Approximately 1 percent of the sales price collected by the
State of California as sales tax is returned to the city in which it is
spent. Reported income has taken into account spending capacities
of employee type, according to state franchise tax data (see Volume
3, pp. 124, 125).

5. Based on Chamber of Commerce estimates for average
tourist expenditures, compared with the retail sales in the city,
based on 1973 subvention totals.

6. T. Geoffrey Moore, "Cost Revenue Study--R1 vs R3 Zoning," unpublished memo to Carl J. Ellis, City Director of Finance.

7. To the degree to which the large number of part-time women
employees are "second earners" who would be residents even without
their jobs, these effects are overstated. The increased use of police
by lower-income people is not thought of here as being due to crime;
it is due to use of police for emergency transportation, and other
noncrime-related functions that actually make up the bulk of police
force activity.

8. Tourist percentages calculated on the basis of Chamber of
Commerce data that estimate that there are 11,914 tourists, including day visitors, per day in the South Coast area, and 159,875 in the
South Coast population. The resulting 7.5 percent figure is taken to
be conservative.

8

SUMMARY OF FINDINGS:
POPULATION EFFECTS
AT EACH PIP

It is clear from the analysis of the social, environmental, and economic effects of growth, presented in previous chapters of this volume, that any substantial population increase in the City of Santa Barbara and the South Coast region will have a significant impact on the quality of life of the existing population. We have not answered all questions that conceivably could be raised about the effects of growth. We were forced, for example, in our study of the experience of other cities to analyze only those variables for which comparable data are available for virtually all U.S. cities. Thus, we have learned the effects of growth upon infant mortality rates and crime but not those upon incidence of cancer and political corruption. Other topics, certainly interesting for a study such as this, were bypassed (for example, a study of the effects of growth on energy usage), because sufficient data could not be produced, given the resources at our disposal.

Nevertheless, there exists an assemblage of data that is sufficient in detail to chart the city's course on the basis of sound information, rather than on the basis of vague slogan.

As explained in some detail in Chapter 1, our method has been to use a number of different population levels, based on alternative specified land-use policies, as the point of departure for our analysis. These PIPs specify not only a level of future population for both the city and the South Coast but also a specific rate at which these populations will be reached, all horizoning at the year 2000. This is particularly relevant to our economic analysis of public-sector costs, where rate of growth is as crucial a determinant of costs as the eventual number of people reached.

Eric Mankin is coauthor of this chapter.

As indicated on several occasions in this volume, we are not in an adversary role for or against any level of population growth. However, two points are of such significance that they warrant special mention. The first is that many of the negative impacts of growth upon the quality of life in Santa Barbara have the additional consequence of undermining the economy of the area as well. That is, while our analysis has generally treated economic effects as a separate topic from the social and environmental impacts, the three topics are, in fact, intimately related. Tourism is not only among the most important components of the city's economic base in terms of dollar volume; it is also, our analysis indicates, the most lucrative from the standpoint of public revenues. This city is thus in an unusual circumstance: Whatever decreases the quality of a number of social and environmental features of the area, such as esthetics, noise, traffic, park access, air quality, and crime, also acts to undermine its economic base.

The second point, closely related, is that it is by no means the case, in terms of our actual findings, that there is any opposition between "environmental values," on the one hand, and "economic values," on the other. Instead, we have found that certain of the PIPs tend to maximize both sorts of values when compared to alternative population levels.

THE SOCIAL EFFECTS

Public Opinion. According to the results of our survey of citizens' attitudes, increased population in Santa Barbara runs counter to the expressed wishes of a majority of the city's residents. Although our subsamples were small, we could find no social, economic, or age grouping that preferred population increase.

Land Use. Increased population will lead to a decline in the proportion of the city's housing occupied by homeowners and a concomitant rise in the proportion of tenants. At higher PIPs the greater majority of the city's residents will be housed in apartments, rather than in single-family dwellings. Industrial and commercial uses will also increase. With the exception of parks, the amount of open land in the city will steadily decrease and eventually be reduced to a small fraction of the present acreage.

The neighborhoods experiencing the heaviest increases in population density will be Oak Park, West Downtown, and Lower West. More than one-third of the total population growth of the city from the present to the Zoning or General Plan Probable PIPs would occur in these three areas.

Other neighborhoods that will experience substantial increases in population density include Lower Riviera, East Side, Laguna, Upper East, Westside, and East Mesa. Elsewhere in the city, population will grow primarily from the filling in of vacant properties, and, while population density will rise, the increase will not be as substantial.

Circulation. Increasing constraints on mobility, both in the form of governmental regulation and in the form of congestion, will be placed on automotive movement in the city. Traffic at Half-Density Maximum and higher PIPs exceeds the capacity of large sections of the traffic network, even with all road improvements deemed "reasonable" by city traffic planners (assuming continuation of present automobile-use patterns).

This portends, for higher populations, either extremely expensive and destructive road building, extremely costly mass transit systems, large-scale congestion, or combinations of all three.

Even at moderate PIPs, certain residential neighborhoods will experience disruption from incursions of increasing volumes of traffic.

Parks and Recreation. Beach space per Santa Barbara resident will decline. Heavy expenditures will be necessary to meet increasing park demand at present standards.

Crime. Crime, both against persons and against property, and expenditures on police increase with population per capita. Police expenditures increase with the rate of growth.

Segregation. Segregation, both by race and by income, generally intensifies at higher population levels.

Health. As indicated by the rate of deaths from liver cirrhosis, alcoholism increases with size. A similar pattern seems to occur with infant mortality, and, there is evidence that suicide rates rise with population growth. Death rates from respiratory diseases show no patterned effects with population size.

Access to Government. Officials, both elected and appointed, generally become less accessible to citizens at higher populations. Campaign costs increase, thus increasing politicians' dependency on large contributions and sophisticated campaign organizations.

Government Regulation of Daily Life. With increased size, the number of rules governing citizens' lives generally increases, with a

lessening degree of spontaneity possible in daily living. Parking
and auto-travel restrictions increase, as do rules governing use of
public facilities, such as beaches and parks. Government regulation
of animals, particularly dogs and horses, also increases, thus raising the burden associated with pet ownership.

Shopping and Cultural Variety. A greater selection of goods and
services generally becomes available to citizens at higher city
population levels.

THE ENVIRONMENTAL EFFECTS

Air Quality. Provided that scheduled federal and state emissions
controls are implemented and prove effective, air quality in Santa
Barbara will substantially improve from present levels at all PIPs.
Relative improvement, however, will be less at higher populations.
Only under No-Growth is there a likelihood of meeting current air-
quality standards.

Noise. Noise from all sources generally increases at higher population levels, primarily from increased traffic and sirens of emergency vehicles.

Natural Habitats. Natural habitats in Santa Barbara will be increasingly subject to destruction as open space is developed. Increasing dog and cat populations will place increasing pressure on
wild forms and contribute to increasing pollution of streams. A
number of areas of major ecological significance are threatened with
obliteration.

Disasters. Higher populations in vulnerable areas of Santa Barbara
increases possible losses in the event of floods, earthquakes, or
other natural catastrophes. The neighborhoods on the lower tier of
the city are particularly susceptible to these impacts, and these are
zoned for highest future densities.

Esthetic Qualities. Architectural qualities of Santa Barbara may
decline as historically significant and visually interesting structures
are replaced with new buildings of varying degrees of attractiveness.
Open-space hillside development, with the potential of scarring and
disruption of views, seems likely.

THE ECONOMIC EFFECTS

Personal Economic Well-being

Median Family Income. The median family income of Santa Barbarans, compared to the rest of the nation, has declined with growth, but the more general pattern across the country is for median family incomes to show an increase with higher levels of population.

Cost of Living. The cost of living increases with city size, thus partially offsetting whatever higher wages may result from increases in population size. In Santa Barbara, the cost of housing is more likely to be a result of the way in which population is controlled, rather than of the degree to which it is controlled. Personal resources not derived from wages--that is, personal wealth--is likely unaffected by changes in population size.

Our general conclusion is that there is no evidence that personal economic well-being of the average citizen is significantly affected by growth, one way or the other.

The Private Economy

Unemployment. Due to labor-force mobility, overall unemployment is generally unaffected by growth rate or shows a slight tendency to increase at high growth rates.

Employment in Construction. Under a No-Growth plan that could lead to a complete stoppage of all new-unit residential and commercial construction in the city, an estimated maximum of 545 jobs in construction and other fields could be lost. Half-Density Probable and all higher PIPs would have no effect on employment rates in construction.

Retail Business. Businesses in Santa Barbara that have maintained and could maintain monopolies or near-monopolies in the city marketplace would add sales and profits proportionately under higher populations. Other merchants would experience proportionately increased competition and thus are likely to experience no overall net effect. The proportion of total retail sales done by national marketing chains in the city would rise, to the likely detriment of some locally based merchants, and with the effect that a greater proportion of retail-generated profits would leave the community.

Economic Mix. For any given population, different economic bases
produce somewhat different effects on the environment and public
revenues. An economy based on retailing and tourism produces more
revenue for the city, but causes more significant environmental impacts and generates higher needs for city services. An economy
based on R & D or technical manufacturing produces lower public
revenue, but has lower city-service demands and less marked environmental impacts. Light manufacturing as an economic base com-
bines rather high service demands and environmental impacts with
low public revenues.

Public Expenditures and Taxes

City Tax Rates. City tax rates will increase continuously as a consequence of growth, primarily to provide for necessary capital improvements needed to maintain current standards of park and library
services. The tax rate will show a particularly large jump with city
growth, moving beyond the General Plan Probable PIP (103,443).
The lowest tax rates would be obtained under No-Growth.

School Taxes. School taxes will decrease under all growth scenarios;
the greatest decreases are under moderate growth. The lowest
school tax rate would result from growth to the Half-Density Probable
PIP (93,555).

Water Costs. Water costs per capita will increase continuously under
growth with particularly large jumps with any substantial growth beyond the city's present level of population. After the Half-Density
Probable PIP is reached, costs will continue to rise at a more gradual
pace but then increase sharply again beyond the General Plan Maximum
PIP (139,721). The lowest water costs would be obtained under No-
Growth.

Wastewater Costs. Wastewater costs per capita are somewhat lower
with moderate population growth. The least expensive population alternative, in terms of net present value, is the Half-Density Probable
PIP (93,555).

Summary. A summary of the effects of each major government cost
that can be expected as a result of growth is presented in Table 8.1.
In combination--that is, when anticipated tax rates are combined with
costs involving the major government services--it turns out that per
capita expenditures will rise continuously due to growth. The increase will be particularly severe if the lower PIPs (Half-Density
Probable and General Plan Probable) are surpassed. Much beyond

TABLE 8.1

The Public Sector: Net Effects of Growth, by PIP
(1974 dollars)

	No-Growth	Half-Density Probable (93,555)	General Plan Probable (103,444)	Half-Density Maximum (117,487)	Zoning Probable (139,721)	General Plan Maximum (139,721)	Zoning Maximum (170,089)
General Fund							
Total capital program, 1970-2000 ($ millions)	1.7	19.9	30.5	42.0	62.4	93.2	145.3
Estimated city tax rate, 2000 ($)[a]	1.60[b]	1.88	1.95	2.13	2.15	2.24	2.33
Education							
Estimated tax rate, combined school districts, 2000 ($)	4.51[b]	4.43	4.45	4.53	4.54	4.71	4.91
Water							
Excess of costs over revenues, per resident, 2000 ($)	8.41	16.02	19.69	22.85	24.21	28.79	36.58
Wastewater							
Excess of costs over revenues, per resident, 2000 ($)	16.32	11.99	11.31	10.11	12.58	12.51	19.90
Total, present value, excess of costs over revenues, 1974-2000 ($)	0.8	4.0	6.6	12.7	14.4	29.7	51.5

Note: Present city tax rate is $1.46, including debt service. Present combined tax rate for Santa Barbara elementary and high school districts if $6.22, excluding overrides.

[a]Assumes all needed additional revenues are obtained through property tax increases.

[b]Assumes zero value for all presently undeveloped land, due to implementation of No-Growth policies.

Source: Santa Barbara Planning Task Force (see Chapter 6 for further reference).

TABLE 8.2

PIP Ratings for Each Growth Variable
(1 = best; 7 = worst; 0 = no effect)

	No-Growth (73,132)	Half-Density Probable (93,555)	General Plan Probable (103,444)	Half-Density Maximum (117,489)	Zoning Probable (119,461)	General Plan Maximum (139,721)	Zoning Maximum (170,039)
Social Environment							
Conformity with public opinion	1	2	3	4	5	6	7
Segregation	1	2	3	4	5	6	7
Parks and recreation access	1	2	3	4	5	6	7
Circulation: ease of auto movement	1	2	3	4	5	6	7
Crime rates	1	2	3	4	5	6	7
Range of shopping and amusements	7	6	5	4	3	2	1
Freedom from miscellaneous restrictions	1	2	3	4	5	6	7
Alcoholism	1	2	3	4	5	6	7
Emphysema	0	0	0	0	0	0	0
Library: range of selections	7	6	5	4	3	2	0
Library: proximity to residence	2	1	1	1	1	1	1
Natural Environment							
Air quality	1	2	3	4	5	6	7
Noise	1	2	3	4	5	6	7
Habitat preservation	1	2	3	4	5	6	7
Disaster risk	1	2	3	4	5	6	7
Esthetic qualities	1	2	3	4	5	6	7
Private Economy							
Per capita income	7	6	5	4	3	2	1
Cost of living	1	2	3	4	5	6	7
Unemployment rate	0	0	0	0	0	0	0
Unemployment in construction	7	0	0	0	0	0	0
Local wealth, per capita	0	0	0	0	0	0	0
Public Economy							
City General Fund (present values)	1	2	3	4	5	6	7
Water: least cost (present values)	1	2	3	4	5	6	7
Education: least cost (present values)	7	6	5	4	3	2	1
Wastewater: least cost (present values)	4	1	2	3	5	6	7
Summary: public services and General Fund (present values)	1	2	3	4	5	6	7

<u>Source:</u> Santa Barbara Planning Task Force estimates.

these populations, the per capita economies that derive from the city using its new wastewater facility and school buildings to fuller capacity is increasingly diluted and eventually reversed. Thus high growth rates will be more expensive than slow growth rates. No growth, however, will result in the least costs of all PIP alternatives.

The basic factor underlying these patterns is that, while assessed valuation and other forms of city revenue increase, at best, by a constant per capita amount with population growth, the expenditures associated with population growth tend to rise much more rapidly due to capital expenditures needed when the "unused capacities" of the city's various facilities--for example, roads, water source, and school plant--are exhausted.

CHOICES

In Table 8.2 we "score" the PIPs according to various costs and benefits. We rate each of the seven PIPs on each variable, using a scale of 1 to 7, with a 1 representing the optimum population level on that variable, and a 7 representing the least-optimum alternative. We use a 0 to indicate that a given population level will have no effect one way or the other.

Whenever monetary costs were involved, total per capita present values to the year 2000 were used as the basis for the rankings, with the least expensive PIP receiving a 1, and the others graded upward according to expense.

We make no overall rating of the PIPs. We provide this analysis, and the ranking that accompanies it here, so that others--policy makers and citizens--can weigh the consequences for themselves and determine, on the basis of the information we have provided, the optimum population of their city. In the chapters that follow, we discuss a range of possible population growth strategies available to the city and elaborate the consequences--social, economic, and legal-- of using one mechanism as opposed to another.

We return to the first principles with which we began this book. Given that there is no way to know the future population of the area, we will be concerned with the number of people that ought to be there in the future. In Chapter 8 we provided a summary of the consequences that follow city growth to different population levels. In this chapter we will compare general strategies through which a desired population level can be achieved through deliberate control of growth. Of course, if the city does not wish to restrain growth, it can maintain the land-use policies prescribed by the General Plan and existing Zoning Ordinances or even increase permitted densities above those designated levels.

HOUSING INTERVENTION

The use of residential restrictions as a means to control population levels is fraught with problems. Limiting residential construction to levels below that demanded by natural market forces will inevitably have the effect of bidding up prices and cause overcrowding. If jobs are being added to the local economy, people will still come to Santa Barbara for employment, and these people will find housing somewhere. Thus we will have many of the disadvantages of growth (more people on the streets and cars on the road, higher demands for services), even though some of the land is kept from development that otherwise would see new residential construction. But the net effect will be a rather high price in terms of the standard of living of the population, especially for the poor and less well-to-do, who do not currently own property, and whose rent will rise steeply as a result.

These negative consequences are ameliorated if growth control should occur in the City of Santa Barbara but not elsewhere within the South Coast region. As long as there is an "open valve" within the region that can keep pace with growing demand, there is likely to be decreased net consequence on housing markets caused by residential restriction in the city. Under this scenario, additional migrants would distribute themselves such that the more well-to-do will locate in the City of Santa Barbara, where a stable supply of housing is available to those people who can afford it. Santa Barbara, under these conditions, would reverse its current role of holding a disproportionately large proportion of the region's less well-to-do and become an increasingly well-off residential portion of the South Coast.

If such a valve were closed--by indefinite continuation of the water moratorium, for example--and all areas of the South Coast should engage in the same restrictive housing policy, the plight of the poor in terms of housing needs could be ameliorated through programs of public housing, including a number of innovative approaches in co-op construction, perhaps financed by the city (see Chapter 10 for additional discussion). But such programs would only be palliative; the basic reality of increasing numbers of people and relatively fixed supply of housing would not be altered, and hence the living standards of the population, in terms of housing, would have to go down.

Rent Control

Still another compensatory device is simply to remove the existing housing stock from the market in order to isolate costs from the pressures caused by rising demand in the face of fixed supply. Rent control is one such mechanism for controlling costs of apartments. Under rent control, the city government would establish a rental schedule based on a fair market return to the owner, based on maintenance costs and the condition of the structure. Rent control eliminates both increasing costs to residents and profit windfalls to landlords caused by the public decision to restrict the supply of housing.

Rent control does not, however, create the additional housing that an expanding population requires. Crowding will continue with or without rent control, and this represents a definite loss to the quality of life. In addition, rent control requires careful and extensive administrative capability in order to discourage illegal bonus payments from housing-starved tenants, in the form of "key money" or other payments to landlords. Particularly in New York, where

rent control was practiced extensively for many years, there was a
tendency for building owners to practice poor management technique
and low levels of service. The resulting tensions are intense and
often lead to court adjudication.

The key quality-of-life advantage of rent control is that, although it does not lead to quality housing, it keeps the costs low,
thus providing renters with cash to spend on other consumer goods.
In this way, perhaps, residents' total economic well-being is not
lowered to the extent it would be if their rents were allowed to rise
while the housing supply remained fixed.

Price Control

Any attempt to isolate single-family houses from market processes would raise similar problems to those related to rent control.
While there are precedents for rent control in U.S. cities, there
are virtually no precedents for the control of selling prices of owner-
occupied single-family houses. A number of (legally untested) possibilities do exist. There could be limitations set on the price of
housing, much in the manner of the federal wage and price controls.
As for rent control, administration would be extremely complex.
Even if the rule were simply that no house could be sold for a higher
price than that paid by its owner, there would have to be a means to
compensate owners for improvements they made, and prices would
also take into account factors such as inflation and the level of an
owner's previous standards of maintenance.

As with rent control, there is the possibility that owners
would allow their property to deteriorate once the incentive for
higher resale value were eliminated, and, again, the potential for
high administrative costs and corrupt abuse of the law would be
present. Potential purchasers could make side payments to owners
of desirable houses, just as they could pay landlords to get apartments. The results would be socially very undesirable.

Tax Methods

Another approach to the single-family-house market would be
to allow housing prices to float to market value and then to capture
a substantial portion of that increased value for public purposes.
Such a property-transfer tax, unlike the tax presently in force in
the city, would be based primarily on increases in value caused by
governmental restrictions on new housing: The higher the profit,
the higher the tax. In this way, substantial portions of the capital

gained by the private owner through a public action could be recaptured by the public.

This money could then be used to lower other taxes or to expand the level of public services by providing the public with services not now available--for example, free public transportation. Here, again, there would be a way of compensating the public for the deterioration in the quality of their housing under growth control, by improving the quality of their lives in other respects. This is perhaps not an ideal solution, but it is an ameliorating device.

But the major point remains: Restriction of residential construction does not stop population growth; it only stops housing growth. The results thus tend to be undesirable for the living standards of residents. When practiced in a single city, the results are not nearly as detrimental as when practiced in an entire region.

LABOR-FORCE INTERVENTION

The alternative method of achieving a given rate of population growth or level population is to simulate the conditions that have occurred in the significant number of cities around the world that have not, in fact, grown at the most rapid rate that market forces could be made to create. They grow only in relation to the job-producing capacity of their local economies. By controlling the job-producing capacity of the local economy, one controls much of the potential for population growth. As we have reiterated a number of times through this work, the population of an urban area increases primarily in response to growth of its basic economic base.

The often-heard argument that cities must grow in population in order to grow economically is thus fallacious because the dynamic is the other way around. People follow jobs; jobs do not follow people. There are exceptions to this generalization, to be sure, but even in Santa Barbara, one of the few cities with an appreciable amount of nonjob-related migration, it is the growth of the local basic economy that is the engine of the population growth we have seen over the last generation.

A method for controlling population is thus the controlling of labor-force expansion. This means that, to the degree to which population control is desired, any developments should be discouraged that will create jobs and hence migration. There is an important point to be made here: Virtually any project that adds to the labor force, that adds jobs to the economy, is growth inducing. As was argued in Chapter 5, even if there are presently available workers who can fill the openings created by any one specific project, that project acts as a vacuum to draw migrants from other areas, some of whom will merely take the place among the unemployed left vacant by those hired for the project. Each project in itself never seems to be growth inducing, but all the projects together create the great bulk of population growth in almost any city or region.

Controlling the size of the labor force is thus a means for controlling demand for housing. This demand control leads to none of the negative effects associated with limiting residential construction. Because housing supply is not restricted relative to demand, growth control through this mechanism has no effect whatsoever on the cost of housing, except to provide for the generally lower housing costs we found to be a tendency in smaller and/or more slowly growing cities.

There are a number of specific techniques that can be used to decrease the rate of labor-force growth and hence to control demand for local housing.

Zoning Methods to Decrease Labor-Force Growth

Reducing Acreage in Manufacturing

Zoning can more effectively be used as a tool, not for restricting residential construction but for restricting industrial expansion. By limiting the amount of land available for industrial purposes, the remaining available land will rise in value and discourage the location of new industrial facilities in the area.

Decreasing Commercial Zones

Because commercial zones can be used for hotel-motel development as well as for R & D and kindred industries (under current zoning regulations) a limitation of such zone areas is needed to the extent that additional labor force growth in this sector is deemed undesirable. Because retailing is generally not a basic industry, it is inappropriate to attempt to manipulate the local labor force by limiting land available for retail purposes. Retailing primarily provides services for residents who are in the city for other purposes and is thus usually irrelevant to a growth-control program. (This does not hold true for large retail centers that draw customers from nonlocal sources or for tourist-oriented facilities.)

Inhibiting Growth-Inducing Residential Construction

The one form of residential construction that is growth inducing consists of housing that is built for the retired, or as second-

home development for the well-to-do. These units tend to import
people from other regions. Their growth-inducing characteristics
are not always clearly apparent, but some indicators of these sorts
of projects are as follows:

1. Developments that advertise for customers outside the
Santa Barbara area (a check of the Sunday Los Angeles _Times_ real
estate section can reveal the type involved);
2. Projects that are extremely specialized in their markets,
when there are too few people in the relevant economic category in
the Santa Barbara area to absorb all available vacancies;
3. Projects marketed as second homes. One indication of
such projects are rules against children, presence of self-contained
recreation facilities, and arrangements whereby owners can rent
out their units while not in residence.

Retaining Modest Interregional
Transportation Facilities

To the degree that Santa Barbara comes to be efficiently linked
with other cities in the state and with other parts of the country, the
area will grow. This will happen in two different ways. High speed,
economical rail transit to Los Angeles, quite within the range of
current technology and practice, can put Santa Barbarans nearer to
Los Angeles than Long Island commuters presently are to New York
City. A commute pattern based on 90-mile distances is well within
current-day practicality; only the present poor service and high cost
precludes the rapid growth of Santa Barbara through this avenue.

To the extent that Santa Barbara is efficiently linked in air
travel to other cities, it is more attractive as a place of industrial
activity, particularly for firms that rely on air freight and air travel
for personnel. The recent addition to Santa Barbara airport of
direct (via Los Angeles) flights to Chicago is a step in the growth
direction.

Policies opposing any improvement in rail service between
Santa Barbara and Los Angeles are antigrowth policies; actions to
improve such service are pro-growth policies. Programs to improve the ability of Santa Barbara's residents to move efficiently by
air from city to city are similarly, but to a smaller degree, growth
inducing.

Restraining City Promotion

Programs aimed at "selling" Santa Barbara, as a place to visit,
to spend one's retirement, or in which to locate a business, all have

the impact of encouraging growth. Indeed, that is why most of them
were developed in the first place. The current use of the city bed
tax to finance many such activities is thus part of a policy of growth
inducement. Whether used for newspaper advertisements, "booster"
films, or city delegations to participate in parades or other public
displays, such actions have the effect of luring more people to the
city on a permanent basis by expanding one of its basic industries.

Nonexpansion of Public Institutions

Some growth-inducing employment centers are public institutions, and the decision to locate them in the city was in part a response to a local desire for growth. The establishment of UCSB is
the conspicuous case in point. The pressure that was used to generate the establishment and continuous growth of the campus at Santa
Barbara could be reversed. The university regents, partly in response to pressure from citizens of Santa Cruz, have scaled down
future development of that campus. Should less growth be desired
in Santa Barbara, attempts could similarly be made to modulate the
growth of UCSB to whatever level were deemed consistent with the
city's optimum growth choice.

There are other decisions of public bodies that are potentially
growth inducing and that might prove responsive to local government
influence. The County of Santa Barbara operates numerous agencies
in the city, some of which must be there but others of which could
operate efficiently elsewhere in the county. Whenever county government location decisions are being made, opportunities exist to place
employment-generating facilities outside the city and South Coast.
A number of state agencies now located in the South Coast could similarly locate in other areas at little cost in administrative efficiency.
At the present time, such civil-service employment amounts to a
trivial proportion of the labor force; the policy implication, however,
would be to discourage any change in this situation. An analogous
policy would follow regarding the establishment of federal government administrative units in Santa Barbara.

EVALUATING SPECIFIC PROJECTS

Listing these techniques of growth control is not meant as a
recommendation that all be used on every possible occasion of their
availability. This research has involved much effort to specify the
costs of growth so that a decision to accept a growth-inducing project
can be made with full information of the quality-of-life losses it may
entail.

Certain projects may be deemed worth the costs. Thus, for example, the presence of a major university, with its attendant cultural and educational resources, may be considered so beneficial on these grounds that it is worth the costs in traffic congestion, air-quality deterioration, and open-space loss. Similarly, a specialized medical center that may wish to move to Santa Barbara would be an important life-saving resource for local citizens; again, it may be deemed worth the costs. The trade-offs are always there to be made; whether or not they will be made in favor of a growth-inducing project will depend upon the values and interests of people as they are played out in the political marketplace.

It follows from this discussion that it might be desirable to establish a system whereby each project can be judged on its own merits, with the benefits it would bring to the people of Santa Barbara weighed against the costs of growth generally and the specific costs related to the given project. Some cities have already experimented with a point system, ranking possible proposed uses of land in terms of their economic, esthetic, habitat, and other impacts. Those with the highest "score" are approved for development. Such methods may involve legal problems for the city, a point discussed at some length in Chapter 10.

A possible alternative scheme is the method of variance or conditional-use permit. A variance or conditional-use permit could be granted for a specific purpose, for example, a growth-inducing medical facility, even if such a use was somewhat inconsistent with the less intense land use permitted under zoning. It could only be justified in terms of larger public needs of health, safety, or the general well-being. A further safeguard could be created in which specified categories of variance could be permitted only when approved through a vote of the people. Thus, the public would be able to decide directly whether or not the trade-offs were such that net benefits outweighed net liabilities of the project in question.

At present in Santa Barbara, as in other California cities, variances or conditional-use permits are granted by planning commissions and city councils and are sometimes overturned by referendum (or court decision). The strategy envisioned here would reverse this process and, perhaps by building land-use limitations into the city charter (much as the building-height limitation currently is), requiring votes of the people to allow more intensive use. When the benefits were clearly worth the costs in terms of the quality-of-life improvements that would come about, it is assumed the people would vote favorably. The background of legal precedents facing this or any other growth-limitation strategy are contained in Chapter 10.

NEED FOR COORDINATION

With the strategy of demand control, as with the strategy of residential construction limitation, the city is faced with the problem of regional cooperation. Two different consequences would follow, depending on whether the city acts alone or in conjunction with other governmental units.

If the city alone followed a policy of demand control, but the rest of the South Coast did what it could to lure additional industry, the consequences for the city would be the loss of tax base that such facilities would bring (property tax, business-license fee, and possibly bed- and sales-tax revenues),and the city might still suffer some of the disadvantages of growth, including increased pressure on the existing housing stock and strain on the circulation network.

If the city allowed residential construction to proceed in response to the general economic boom in other parts of the South Coast, all the detrimental revenue and quality-of-life effects of population growth would follow, but some of the positive revenue effects would be absent. To keep things close to a balanced position, the city might have to limit residential construction, too, and force the new migrants attracted to the South Coast by expanding industry to live elsewhere in the area. In that way, the government units that collected the tax revenues from the stores, plants, and motels would also have to carry the burden of providing municipal services, and those units would also bear much of the burden of the increases in traffic and other forms of congestion.

Alternatively, as another response to a lack of coordination among South Coast jurisdictions, the city could adopt a more thoroughly competitive and selfish outlook. It could attempt to locate the job-producing facilities in the city of Santa Barbara but discourage residential development there. That would mean Santa Barbara would get the revenues but a less-than-proportionate share of the service liabilities that come with additional residents.

To be sure, the general growth of the South Coast would inevitably impact unfavorably in certain ways upon life in the city, even if all residential construction were banned. Simply the increased traffic from commuters coming into the city would be an extra burden, for example. But, in a context of noncoordination, this strategy of discouraging residential use and encouraging employment use would represent the better trade-off, particularly in terms of the city's finances.

However, such a course of action by the city would probably motivate the other area jurisdictions to pursue a similar policy of attracting the high-payoff uses (industry) and discouraging the low-payoff uses (the people who work in the industry). This competition among areas, each engaged in its own selfish strategy, can lead to destructive consequences.

The result could be the very undesirable scenario previously discussed, wherein more and more people are brought into the South Coast region to work, but under conditions of restricted housing supplies. There could be a situation of complete restricted growth, where each jurisdiction competes with the other for industrial/ commercial uses and then feels obliged to provide housing in whatever way the market dictates. This is the reasoning that lies behind our claim, previously argued in other chapters, that unless there is a regionwide program of planned land use, there is a real danger that there will be no planned land use at all.

We now add the additional proviso that any attempt to manage growth through this coordinated, planned land-use program must be based in demand control, oriented toward limiting the growth of the labor force as its cornerstone. Otherwise there will be a lower quality of life for the people, either because housing costs will rise steeply or because uncontrolled growth will occur regardless of the people's wishes.

The possibilities we have raised in this chapter for demand control within the context of regionwide planning represent merely a reversal of past growth policies. The city has traditionally had a growth limitation program on paper, as contained in its zoning laws and its General Plan, but it has pursued, formally and informally, a program of growth inducement, using the reverse of many of the mechanisms described in this chapter. Similarly, although there has been formal talk of regionwide planning, land-use decisions get made on the basis of competition for increases in the tax base.

The location of UCSB, the development of the tourist business, the luring of R & D firms, the attracting of retirees--these have been a result of hard work on the part of many people, some in government, some indirectly supported by public funds, and some working as private citizens. The private citizens will always be free to act as their interests and taste dictate. But public officials and those supported by public funds can be motivated to follow growth policies in keeping with the public good, as interpreted by the people.

We have tried to lay the basis for the development of such policies. We hope they result in a land-use program and a demand-control program that are mutually consistent and thus effective mechanisms of maximizing the quality of life over the next generation of the city's history.

10

MANAGING GROWTH:
LEGAL ISSUES
AND TOOLS

The law on many issues related to controlling or managing population growth is at an early stage. Neither the United States Supreme Court nor the California Supreme Court has considered or ruled upon many of the key issues in any comprehensive manner. The city has the option therefore either to pioneer in this area of the law, as did the City of Petaluma, California, or to "play it safe" by following planning procedures that have the highest degree of legal safety.

Most of the legal problems faced by communities attempting to control population growth are related to the prevention of residential development of open and undeveloped land. Typically, these efforts have occurred in communities that are suburbs of large metropolitan complexes--for example, Petaluma and Livermore. Santa Barbara as the core urban community of its own small metropolitan complex is not faced with this particular problem to any great degree.

This work indicates that the bulk of future population growth here would occur by the conversion of single-family residences to multiple dwellings in areas zoned for multiple dwellings. The city is not faced with many of the growth pains and problems associated with "leap-frog" subdivision growth. Instead, it is faced with the pains and problems of a city slowly changing its character from a community of primarily single-family dwellings to one with a high percentage of apartments and multiple dwellings.

In broad outline, the thrust of court decisions so far has been as follows:

Philip Marking is coauthor of this chapter.

- Growth can be restrained temporarily if not permanently by the city so long as a valid public health, safety, or welfare reason is demonstrated for the effort. Growth and land-use restrictions can be justified on the basis of maintenance of the local economy, provision of adequate water supply, sewer service, schools, transportation systems, and other demonstrably necessary facilities.

- The city is obliged to make a bona fide and reasonable attempt to provide all of the foregoing public necessities. The city, however, has no obligation to let population growth proceed at such a pace as to overburden these facilities or to destroy the qualities that make the city a pleasing place to inhabit.

- The city's basic legal obligation is to strike the proper balance between many competing interests. These interests include the "freedom to travel" held by every U.S. citizen. To an extent not yet fully defined by the courts, this includes the freedom to settle and reside in the community of that citizen's choice. Competing with this is the right of a community to exercise its police power in protection of "compelling State interest" based upon the public health, safety, and welfare. Real threats to these interests may be restricted by restrictions on the rate of population growth and the ultimate population size of the community.

- Any effort by a community to restrict population growth unavoidably raises problems as to the provision of adequate low- and moderate-income housing. These problems are both legal and social, and in many ways they are the hardest to deal with.

- Any population growth plan must consider more than merely the numbers of people in the city. It must also consider the dispersal of the people throughout the city and the dispersal of the types of dwellings that they will inhabit throughout the city. What ratio of single-family dwellings to multiple dwellings is desired? Is it desired that the different types of dwellings be isolated from one another, or is it desired to "mix" them in some fashion?

It is probable that a legal method can be found to enable Santa Barbara officials to adopt and carry out any type of growth management plan they are likely to find desirable for the city. The legal discussion that follows, therefore, should be looked on as a guide to the discovery of the best methods, not as a series of obstacles in the path of the effort.

TEMPORARY ZONING: CONTINUATION OF
INTERIM ORDINANCE

It was originally predicted that eighteen months
would be required to complete the study which
was to culminate in the passage of a new zoning
ordinance. . . . In the instant matter the "temporary" ordinance has been in effect for more
than two years. However, as has been seen, the
mere passage of time alone is not the sole determining factor of the reasonableness or unreason-
ableness of the "stop gap" ordinance. We must
also look to the progress of the study being made,
its nearness to completion and the prospects for
passage in the new zoning ordinance, keeping in
mind at the same time that such a comprehensive
zoning plan requires considerable time for preparation and study. . . . It must be remembered that
zoning today is a more complex problem than it
was thirty years ago. What would require two
years then could very possibly require a longer
period of time today. Furthermore, this court
is impressed with the "good faith" attempt on
the part of the township and its planning consultant to expedite the new master plan, which
it is hoped will ultimately result in the passage
of a permanent zoning ordinance.

Campana v. Clark (N.J. Superior Ct., 1964)[1]

Extension of Half-Density Ordinance

If the city's planning and zoning efforts following receipt of
this work cannot be completed before the November 1974 expiration
date of the current Half-Density Ordinance,[2] extension of that ordinance or some equivalent measure should be considered. California
law authorizes a general law city to adopt an interim zoning ordinance
prohibiting any uses that may be in conflict with a contemplated zoning proposal that the legislative body of the city is considering or in-
tends to study within a reasonable time.[3] Such an ordinance may extend for a maximum of two years if notice is given pursuant to the
statute and other prescribed procedures are followed.

As a charter city Santa Barbara is not bound by this general
law city statute. The statute, however, does provide a useful pro-
cedural model for Santa Barbara to follow. Accordingly, if the City

Council wishes to extend the existing Half-Density Ordinance or some similar measure beyond 1974, it would be legally prudent for the council to hold a public hearing on the extension, after publishing notice of that hearing ten days before in the manner established by this court-approved general law city statute.[4] Since Santa Barbara is not subject to the general law city statute, the maximum duration of an interim rezoning ordinance there would be controlled by constitutional principles of due process and not limited by the arbitrary two-year rule.

The best reasoning found in a court case on due process in this connection is in the 1964 New Jersey case quoted from above, upholding an interim ordinance that had been in effect for 31 months. This had been enacted by the township of Clark, New Jersey, pending completion of a study on community needs intended to result in a new comprehensive zoning ordinance. The court examined the good faith of the city in extending the ordinance for such duration and (partially relying on a California case)[5] found the duration reasonable. In upholding the 31-month period the court further observed: "As might be expected, prior law on this question is inexact and sets no definitive guidelines. We can take judicial notice of the fact that it requires considerable time to prepare and put into effect a worthwhile and comprehensive zoning plan."

The California courts were among the first to uphold interim land-use restrictions.[6] In the case of regional commissions formed pursuant to legislation or initiative, restrictions for periods of up to three years have been upheld. These include the San Francisco Bay Conservation and Development Commission[7] and the California-Nevada Interstate Compact Commission[8] (relating to Lake Tahoe). The key factor in sustaining any interim restrictions is the findings as to the public health, safety, and welfare problems that would result from failure to enact the restrictions.

New Water-Service Moratorium and Rationing

Questions have recently been raised as to the adequacy of the city's water supply. If the City Council, after receipt of further information on the matter, concludes that the city has an emergency condition of water shortage within its service area, it may, under California law, adopt restrictions on the delivery and consumption of water for the purpose of conserving water supply.[9] These restrictions and regulations may include the denial of applications for new or additional water service connections,[10] and rationing of existing supplies.[11] These restrictions would be effective until the water-shortage emergency was resolved.

Other Interim Devices

Interim measures other than continuance of the Half-Density Ordinance or a moratorium on new water service could also be considered by the city under the emergency zoning authority discussed above. Such measures could include

1. Temporary rezoning of residential areas to densities even lower than those allowed by the Half-Density Ordinance;
2. Temporary rezoning of commercial and industrial property to residential or other uses. The presumed result of this rezoning would be reduction of the amount of land available for potentially growth-generating new employment opportunities.

Comment and Conclusions

In considering any of the interim measures discussed above, the following factors are pertinent:

1. What real effect will they have on reducing growth, pending completion of the final study?
2. What real need does the city have to reduce growth, pending completion of the study?
3. Has the Half-Density Ordinance actually reduced growth during the period of its application, or has it merely created a psychological climate that growth is being reduced when in fact it is not?
4. Does the city have the time and the resources to adopt an interim measure more comprehensive than the Half-Density Ordinance, considering the time and resource problems that will be created by working on any comprehensive permanent measure?

It is our opinion that Santa Barbara as a charter city may extend the Half-Density or similar ordinance for a total of at least two years from the original enactment of the Half-Density Ordinance and for a maximum of up to three years from that date. Such extension would require findings of fact by the City Council that this work and other data indicate sufficient problems to require the city to adopt a permanent growth management plan and to continue restrictions pending such adoption. The extension would also require steady, good faith progress by the city on adopting a permanent growth-management plan and associated ordinances.

The council should direct the agency responsible for preparation of any permanent plan to proceed with all due speed. The deadline for completion of the permanent plan should be established within the three-year period, and regular and continual review of the planning process should be made.

The information currently available indicates that the council should maintain continual scrutiny of the water situation but that there are not grounds for immediate adoption of a new water-service moratorium or rationing plan. This work indicates that a combination of existing water supplies plus that available through adopting the Phase I Conjunctive Use Plan described in the Toups Report could satisfy projected demand for three to four more years through 1979-80, if population growth occurs at the rate projected for attaining the Half-Density Zoning Probable PIP.

If, however, growth exceeds that rate, as it easily could if major water-consuming projects are approved, an emergency condition could arise, if alternative sources subsequent to Phase I Conjunctive Use did not become available in time. The water-supply section of this work should be carefully reviewed to understand fully the potential problems. This possibility provides a good basis for continuing the Half-Density or some other interim measure, pending adoption of a final growth-management plan.

If the city does reach the point where a water shortage emergency is found to exist, a system should be adopted, concentrating on rationing water to existing meters, based on the average consumption through those meters in recent years. Unlike Goleta-area property, most of the property in the city already has a water meter. Thus, denial of new service connections would not be so effective a means of cutting down water consumption as it is in an area containing large quantities of undeveloped land, such as Goleta.

This work indicates that the bulk of future population growth in the city would be made possible by replacement of single-family residences with multiple dwellings. Any water-shortage regulations, therefore, should be aimed at preventing the increase in water consumption that would follow from existing water meters supplying new multiple dwellings that would have replaced lower water-consuming single-family residences. Careful use of such a rationing plan, along with a moratorium on new service connections to undeveloped land, would be the most practical method to be followed by the city.

PREPARATION OF A GROWTH-MANAGEMENT PLAN

It is apparent that the plan is in short a constitution for all future development within the city. . . . Any zoning ordinance adopted in the future would surely be interpreted in part by its fidelity to the general plan as well as by the standards of due process.

O'Loan v. O'Rourke (Calif. Ct. of Appeals 1965)[12]

Reason for the Plan

Revision of the city general plan by adopting a comprehensive growth-management plan is vital as a step preceding adoption of any rezoning or other growth-restriction ordinances. This procedure not only represents a logical sequence of civic decision making but more importantly provides the soundest legal foundation for the ordinances that follow.

California law now requires a general law city to conform its zoning to its general plan.[13] Although not applicable to charter cities, this rule favoring comprehensive planning is a trend in California law that has been voiced on numerous occasions by California courts, including the 1965 case quoted from above.[14]

A growth-management plan and the factual findings supporting it would provide the public health, safety, and welfare reasons to satisfy judicial scrutiny of the exercise by the city of its police power in carrying out major rezoning.[15] The existence of such a plan would not make a zoning scheme impregnable to legal attack. It would, however, give such a scheme the best possible chance of being upheld in the courts.

Conclusions

If the city government wishes to make any major changes in the city land-use regulatory scheme following this work, it is our recommendation that it should do so pursuant to and following adoption of a comprehensive growth-management plan as outlined in this work.

REGIONAL CONSIDERATIONS

This case is a study in anti-planning. The refusal of a city to come to grips with the fact that it has joined a metropolitan complex and is no longer the sleepy small town that it once was. In a world in which nothing is as unchanging as change Petaluma wants to stay the same. . . .

In a large sense this case sets up the constitutional protections against a single small city's passing laws to keep people away, to maintain "small town character" at the expense of depriving people of mobility, their right to travel and of decent housing or perhaps any housing at all. . . .

> In a narrower sense this case [holds] . . .
> that the local police power may [not] be used to
> shift the burden of providing housing to other
> cities in a metropolitan region which have their
> own police power and their own problems. . . .
>
> A prospective resident turned away at Peta-
> luma does not disappear into the hinterland but
> presents himself in some other suburb of the
> same metroplex, perhaps in some town with as
> many problems or more than Petaluma. . . .
> By this means Petaluma legislates its problems
> into problems for Napa, Vallejo or Walnut Creek.
>
> Construction Industry Assn. of Sonoma
> County v. City of Petaluma (U.S. Dist.
> Ct., 1974)

Significance of Regional Issue

On April 26, 1974, the United States District Court for Northern District of California issued a permanent injunction prohibiting
the City of Petaluma, California, from enforcing its population
growth restriction plan.[16] This decision was based on a conclusion
that the city's plan interfered with the constitutional "freedom to
travel" held by every U.S. citizen. The court further found that
Petaluma was not faced with any water, sewer, or other health,
safety, or welfare problem qualifying as a "compelling State interest" sufficient to allow the city to interfere with this freedom.

In reaching this conclusion, the court made, among others,
findings of fact that the city had adopted building and density restrictions that would allow a maximum population of 55,000 by the year
1985, instead of the maximum population of 77,000 than an earlier
city study projected the city would achieve without the plan. The
figure of 77,000 represented Petaluma's share of the projected
growth for the San Francisco metropolitan region of which Petaluma
was found to be a part. The plan was rejected by the court on the
basis that Petaluma had no valid health, safety, or public welfare
reason for refusing to accept its share of the regional growth burden.

Whatever the ultimate fate of the Petaluma case,[17] it is clear
that for now legal prudence is added to common sense in support of
planning for the future of Santa Barbara in a manner giving consideration to regional factors.[18]

This work concludes that the City of Santa Barbara is now and
traditionally has been part of a natural planning and demographic region, encompassing what is generally referred to as the "South Coast"

portion of Santa Barbara County and, for certain planning purposes,
the Santa Ynez Valley portion of Santa Barbara County. The "South
Coast" portion of the county includes the territory and communities
bounded by the Ventura County border on the east, the community of
Gaviota on the west, the ridgeline of the coastal mountains to the
north, and the Pacific Ocean on the south. It is further the conclusion of the Task Force that for planning and demographic purposes,
Santa Barbara is not part of the Los Angeles metropolitan region. [19]

Regional Planning Methods

The city may approach regional planning in a variety of ways.
These include

1. Informal regional planning. The city in revising its general plan could simply study and incorporate information relating to
the surrounding region without making any official arrangements with
the County of Santa Barbara or adjacent communities. This work
provides some of the data on which such informal regional planning
could be based.

2. Informal planning agency conferences. The city could initiate and hold regular information meetings or conferences with
planning authorities of surrounding communities and the county
within the South Coast-Santa Ynez Valley region.

3. Joint powers authority. The city, adjacent cities in the
region, and the county could create a formal planning authority for
the region through the joint exercise of powers provisions of the
California Government Code. [20] Regional planning entities of this
type have been established elsewhere in California, including and
surrounding the cities of San Diego and Chico, respectively.

4. Effect of annexation. Annexation of the community of
Goleta would be partially equivalent to creation of a regional planning
authority. Such annexation, however, would still leave substantial
portions of the "South Coast" region outside the city's boundary. It
would thus not completely satisfy the regional planning "imperative"
that is an important trend in the law. [21]

5. Conclusions. The time made available through extension
of the interim zoning ordinance would not be sufficient to allow establishment of an effective regional planning agency. For purposes
of a growth-management plan, following this work, the city will be
limited to informal incorporation of regional considerations. This
work provides some of the data for these considerations.

For the future, the city should seriously consider initiating a
regional planning agency for the South Coast-Santa Ynez region along

with its efforts relating to annexation of the Goleta community. Such a regional planning agency could be of great value to the future of the region, considering the common nature of many problems, including air quality, water, waste disposal, and transportation. In this way the city could be at the forefront of a sensible trend in land-use-planning law instead of waiting until steps of that type are compelled by the courts or some other outside authority.

CONTRAST OF GROWTH ISSUES IN THE CITY OF SANTA BARBARA WITH ISSUES AND PLANS OF SELECTED OTHER CALIFORNIA COMMUNITIES

We can compare Santa Barbara with a number of other cities that have attempted growth management: Berkeley, Davis, Milpitas, Napa, Novato, San Diego, and Santa Rosa. Most of these cities share the common feature of a central "core" city surrounded by substantial quantities of open and potentially developable land. Each is thus faced with the common California problem of potential "leap-frog" or urban sprawl development manifested in the checkerboarding of tract houses with slowly deteriorating agricultural parcels.

The type of growth-management program developed by the City of Ramapo, New York (discussed below), requiring population growth to be time phased or sequenced with construction of necessary public capital improvements, is intended to alleviate problems faced by this type of community.

One of the studied communities, Berkeley, is a fully developed urban community with no significant quantity of open land. The growth patterns faced by Berkeley are not of the "leap-frog" or sprawl type, but rather are those associated with the conversion of old, single-family neighborhoods to multiple-dwelling neighborhoods.

The City of Santa Barbara as presently bounded is faced more with the type of urban growth patterns found in Berkeley than with the rural "leap-frog"-type problems. In the event the Goleta area is annexed, however, the city would be faced with both types of growth issues. Thus, Santa Barbara may be in a position to benefit from the experience of both types of communities.

RECOMMENDED PROCEDURES TO FOLLOW IN ESTABLISHING A SANTA BARBARA GROWTH-MANAGEMENT PLAN

Regional Status

The City Council should first investigate and make findings regarding the regional status of the City of Santa Barbara. As indicated elsewhere, it is the conclusion of this work that the City of Santa Barbara is part of a planning and demographic region consisting of the "South Coast" portion of the County of Santa Barbara.

Population-Growth Impacts

After making findings as to the city's regional status, the City Council should then make comprehensive findings as to the impact on the city of attaining certain levels of population growth. This work contains data on which such findings may be made as regards economic, environmental, esthetic, social, and other types of impacts on the city of achieving population levels potentially allowed by the existing city land-use regulatory schemes. These findings should be detailed and comprehensive, and they should clearly mark the points at which the impacts may seriously disrupt the quality of life in Santa Barbara.

This work indicates that attaining certain population levels would require major changes in the city's financial structure as well as in its physical structure. It is particularly apparent that major capital improvements in the form of water programs, sewer projects, and street widening would be required to allow the city to grow beyond certain population plateaus. These steps represent not only marginal expenditures to the city but also major changes in the character of the city that would have significant economic and social consequences.

The findings by the council regarding these items would represent the basis on which a "phased" or "sequenced" growth program would be based. They would also provide the public health, safety, and welfare factual basis of any "compelling State interest" that the city may wish to rely on in restricting further population growth. Without such findings as a foundation, any serious effort by the city either to restrict or to "phase" population growth would be vulnerable to legal attack.

Disasters

This work provides information to the city as to the variety of physical disasters that the city might face. Among these are earthquakes, floods, and tsunamis. The growth management plan should include findings as to the possible impact of such disasters as a foundation for rezonings or other land-use restrictions that would attempt to mitigate the impact of such disasters.

Projected Population

After making the above findings, the City Council should then make findings regarding the anticipated population range of the City of Santa Barbara at a selected point in the future. This could be the year 2000 used in this work, or some earlier year.

Our section on "Explaining Population Change" (Chapter 1) concludes that the city has not increased its population in the past eight years by more than 1.1 percent per year. That section contains additional data on which the City Council may attempt to project future growth trends. The section, however, stresses the point that population growth in Santa Barbara has been substantially unpredictable. This is because local growth has largely been based on major unforeseen individual events, such as expansion of the University of California and changes in the proportion of the city's population represented by elderly persons.

This work concludes there is no inevitable and "natural" population growth rate that can be projected for the city. The findings in this regard would allow public discussion to focus on the correct conclusion that future population growth of the city will depend upon responses by the city to local and regional problems and opportunities.

"Phasing" and "Sequencing" of Growth-Allowing Facilities

The council and city government staff should, using the results of this work, make findings regarding the cost and construction scheduling of capital improvements that will be required to attain the population range projected by the council. The needed capital improvements include those related to water supply, sewer capacity, street and transportation facilities, schools, and other public buildings. The street- and transportation-capacity findings should include references to the social and legal implications of air quality at various population levels.

Close attention should be paid to the neighborhood-growth projections provided by us at the various PIPs.[22] The city should require staff agency projections regarding the timing and cost of replacing street, water mains, and other capital facilities in neighborhoods in which future population growth is projected. The neighborhood growth projected in the various PIPs would have to be modified by any rezonings or other land-use-regulation modifications adopted by the city pursuant to the growth-management plan.

The type of "phased" or "sequenced" growth-management plan developed by the City of Ramapo, New York restricts residential development and population increase in a given area of a city until the planned civic capital improvements for that area are completed in the sequence preestablished by the local government.[23] Private developers wishing to build or increase density in that area prior to the date established for completion of the necessary roads, schools, water supplies, and the like to their property must pay for the civic capital costs of such "premature" development.

This type of "sequencing" would be most useful in the event that the community of Goleta with its areas of undeveloped land is annexed to the city. "Sequencing" of growth could be used to direct growth to areas immediately contiguous to currently developed areas and to prevent "leap-frogging" of development that would leave large islands of undeveloped property.

If annexation does not take place, sequencing could still be adapted to control the pace at which single-family dwelling neighborhoods are allowed to convert to the multiple-dwelling neighborhoods needed to accommodate significant population growth within the existing city boundaries. The sequencing concept could be applied on a neighborhood basis to prevent the "premature" overloading of streets, water mains, and other civic improvements in the various neighborhoods within the existing city boundaries.

Low-Income Housing

The final portion of the plan should include findings of fact and statements of policy regarding the city's efforts to provide low- and moderate-income housing for the projected population growth. This difficult problem is discussed in greater detail below.

ORDINANCES AND OTHER TOOLS TO CARRY OUT
THE GROWTH-MANAGEMENT PLAN

> . . . nor shall private property be taken for public use without just compensation.
>   Fifth Amendment United States Constitution
>   (the "Taking Clause")

Our strongest impression from this survey is that fear of the taking issue is stronger than the taking clause itself. It is an American fable or myth that a man can use his land any way he pleases regardless

of his neighbors. The myth survives, indeed
thrives, even though unsupported by the pattern
of court decisions. Thus, attempts to resolve
land use controversies must deal not only with
the law but with the myth as well.
       . . . Many courts have apparently treated
the idea of a regulatory taking more as a hypothetical possibility than a real one. The Supreme
Court of California, for example, appears unlikely to hold any regulation invalid under the taking
clause.

"The Taking Issue"[24]

A quiet place where yards are wide, people few
and motor vehicles restricted are legitimate
guidelines in a land use project addressed to family needs. This goal is a permissible one within
Berman v. Parker supra. The police power is not
confined to elimination of filth, stench and unhealthy
places. It is ample to lay out zones where family
values, youth values and the blessings of quiet
seclusion and clean air make the area a sanctuary
for people.

Village of Belle Terre
(United States Supreme Court 1974)[25]

Rezoning of Residential Property to Lower Density

The city government may utilize its police-power authority and
rezone portions of the residential property in the city to a lower potential density.

The California courts have historically supported rezoning decisions by local governments where the rezonings were based on circumstances changed from those that brought about the original zoning.[26] If these changed circumstances provide a rational basis for
changing the land-use patterns in the community so as to satisfy public health, safety, and welfare demands, the rezoning will be valid.

Where rezoning decreases the potential economic value of the
land, the same principles apply. The rezoning will be valid if the
private owners is left with some reasonable economic use of the property and so long as no public use of or access to the property is created by the zoning.[27]

Findings by the City Council that the city's anticipated population range would be substantially lower than that allowed by existing

zoning would be a basis for extensive changes in the existing zoning. Such findings would indicate that circumstances had changed from the time at which the current zoning patterns were established.

The section of this work dealing with "Explaining Population Change" concludes that population projections made a decade ago proved to be erroneously high. Acknowledgment of these errors, along with findings that future population growth is likely to remain low, would provide the factual basis for rezonings in the city that would bring about a lower population density.

Amendment of Multiple-Dwelling Density Ordinances

The neighborhood maps and PIPs developed by the Task Force show that the bulk of future population growth in the city would occur in areas currently zoned for multiple dwellings. Meaningful reduction of potential population growth would therefore require revision of zoning ordinances for those neighborhoods.

The simplest approach would be to amend the multiple-residence zoning ordinances to reduce the allowable density in the areas to which they apply. This is the approach followed in the existing Half-Density Interim Ordinance. That ordinance simply cuts in half the potential number of multiple dwelling units that may occupy the same quantity of land in the city that was zoned for multiple dwellings prior to its passage. It does not reduce the amount of land in the city available for multiple dwellings but instead reduces the potential quantity of those dwellings.

This approach, however, leads to a number of problems associated with having a portion of the city currently occupied by single-family housing slowly converting to multiple dwellings. These problems include

1. Property tax pressure on single-family dwellings due to increased assessments as potential apartment property;

2. Speculative purchases of single-family properties, forcing up the price of these properties;

3. The above factors combining to eliminate incentive for good maintenance and upkeep of existing single-family dwellings, creating a tendency toward deterioration in the neighborhoods;

4. Lack of concern for design controls that might more gently blend apartments with single-family residences, because of the anticipated elimination of all single-family residences;

5. Elimination of many esthetically or historically interesting single-family residences and of the neighborhood feeling they create.

Mixed Residential Zoning as a Possible Solution

One ambitious approach to solving the problems discussed above would be adoption of a zoning scheme encouraging an ultimately stabilized and well-designed mix of multiple and single-family dwellings within the same area. This "mixed" residential zoning would be based upon specific planning and rezoning of some or all of the multiple dwelling areas of the city to allow a total density within each area and upon each block within each area enabling the construction of sufficient multiple dwellings to satisfy projected population growth in the area but leaving room for a significant quantity of existing single-family residences.[28] The purpose of such a "mixed" residential zoning scheme would be to allow construction of apartments and multiple dwellings to accommodate both population growth and low- and moderate-income housing pressure without total elimination of single-family housing.

The ordinance would establish a method of transferring potential density from parcels on which the owners wish to retain single-family dwellings to those parcels on which owners wish to construct multiple dwellings. The density transfer would require city participation to insure enforcement and to provide restrictions on the single-family lot sufficient to allow the property-tax assessor to assess those parcels at single-family-residence values instead of at presumably higher multiple-residence values.

Design controls should be enacted and administered by the Architectural Board of Review that would blend the multiple dwelling units harmoniously with the existing and future single-family residences. This would be intended to eliminate many of the complaints that often arise from single-family-residence owners regarding the construction of adjacent multiple dwellings.

The success of such a scheme would depend upon the desire of purchasers to acquire some of the older homes for rehabilitation purposes, knowing that multiple dwellings would be constructed in the same neighborhood. The potential buyers, however, would also know that a sufficient quantity of single-family homes would remain on a permanent basis to eliminate the fear that they would be left with the last house in a neighborhood of apartments. In addition, they would be given assurance as to their property-tax status. By providing the potential single-family-residence purchasers with property-tax security, design harmony, and the knowledge of a stabilizing land-use scheme regarding other single-family residences, incentive would be created not only leading to purchase of the single-family residences but also to their enhancement and upkeep. Such efforts by the owners of the residences would benefit the community at large as well as the owners.

Presumably, reduction of a parcel from potential multiple dwelling to single-family residence status would reduce the assessed value of the land but would allow maintenance or increase of the assessed value of the structure. In this way the potential property-tax loss, if any, would be minimized.

The retention of single-family residences in neighborhoods zoned for multiple dwellings, if carried out with the type of stability proposed above, could have excellent social benefits. These include the maintenance of neighborhoods and community feelings now found in many of the older multiple-residence zoned areas of the city. It also could be a major force in preventing the "ghettoization" of the city into exclusive and expensive single-family residence areas contrasted with blocks of uninterrupted apartment houses.

Increased Minimum Lot Size: Open-Space Zoning and Substandard-Lot Problem

Potential population density could be held down in those portions of the city identified in the city open-space plan by significantly increasing the minimum lot size required for construction of residences. Increasing the minimum lot size from one to five or ten acres should be justified, however, if possible on the basis of geologic hazards, fire-protection problems, drainage and flood problems, and similar public health, safety, and welfare factors.

In adopting large minimum lot sizes, the city should specify in the zoning ordinance uses of the property allowed to the owners so as to provide as much economic value as possible, thereby minimizing any claims for compensation for "taking" of the land. Good examples of this approach are found in two recent cases from California and Wisconsin, placing very restrictive zoning on flood plain and wetlands property. [29] Along with restricting residential construction, the land-use authorities in each of those cases had also made positive efforts to develop a list of recreational, agricultural, and similar types of uses for the affected property.

Development-Right Acquisition

Outright purchase from owners of developable land of the owner's right to residential development of the property is one method of reducing population density and preserving open space. Appraisal should be made of the property with and without the residential or other development rights to be acquired. The difference represents the price of development-right acquisition.

Certain problems with this device limit its practical usefulness. Property having a valuable use remaining if the residential development rights were purchased quite possibly could be rezoned to the desired density without cost to the taxpayers and without representing a "taking" requiring payment of compensation.

On the other hand, if residential development rights represent substantially all the value of the property, as would be the case with much of the undeveloped open space within the city, outright acquisition of the entire fee would not cost much more and would be of greater benefit to the city.[30] Where an owner sold residential-development rights and was left with little or no remaining economic value, it is doubtful that the owner would be interested in paying property taxes and maintaining the property. In addition, the remaining tax value to the city would be minimal.

Therefore, while acquisition of residential development rights could be, in a given case, a valuable tool, it should always be considered very carefully along with rezoning as one alternative, and outright acquisition of the entire property as another. Considering it outside this context could lead to unrealistic results or unnecessary expenditure of tax funds.

Property-Tax Issues

The city should work with the County Tax Assessor's Office to make sure that assessment practices correspond as closely as possible to the land uses allowed on rezoned property. This is particularly important where property is rezoned in such a manner as to eliminate some of its previous potential economic value, such as reduction of potential density from multiple to single-family residence.

California law requires assessors to consider the effect on value of enforceable restrictions to which the use of land may be subjected, including zoning and contractual restrictions.[31] These restrictions may be ignored, however, if the assessor is convinced on the basis of past history and other evidence that the restrictions can easily be lifted. It is crucial, therefore, that any rezoning or density-transfer device, such as was discussed in the proposed "mixed" residential zoning above, be established with firm intent on the part of the city that it be and remain enforceable.

The County Assessor's Office should be consulted before the ordinances are enacted to determine that office's position as to the effect of the proposals on assessment practices.

Migration Opportunity Limitations

Employment-Related Migration
Opportunity Limitations

Since Santa Barbara is not a suburb or "bedroom" community
of the Los Angeles area, local population growth is heavily dependent
upon employment opportunities in the area. Employment opportunities, however, are not limited to those within the city boundaries;
they include those within the South Coast and Santa Ynez Valley region. Recognition of regional employment opportunities as a stimulus or deterrent to population growth within the city is an important
part of the regional thinking required for Santa Barbara planning.

The case law to date regarding the "right to travel," exclusionary zoning, and other constitutional limitations on a local community's power to control growth relates to schemes hindering in-migration
by restricting residential housing. By contrast, there seems to be no
authority mandating the creation by local communities of employment
expansion to attract migration to those communities. In this sense,
therefore, restrictions by local communities of labor-force growth
are among the legally safest approaches to population-growth restriction.

Any serious effort by the city to restrict, "phase," or otherwise have an impact upon future population growth has to take into
consideration population increase due to migration to the area brought
about by employment expansion. There are numerous tools a city can
use to accomplish this. None of these, however, would be completely
effective unless applied on a regional basis.

The available tools include careful scrutiny by the city any time
a city agency is involved in the decision-making process regarding
new employment expansion. Environmental impact reports prepared
by the city in relation to discretionary action that could increase employment there should include careful scrutiny of the in-migration
potential of the project.[32]

Where it is claimed that the project would not lead to additional
in-migration, careful analysis should be made to determine why the
given project would be exceptional to the general Task Force observation that virtually all job-producing projects are also growth inducing.

In the economic portion of this work the Task Force has concluded that the city's unemployment rate will tend to be unaffected by
increases in the size of the labor force or the resident population.
This is apparently caused by the replacement in the pool of unemployed persons newly hired by other persons newly arriving in the
city and joining the ranks of the local unemployed. Thus, arguments
that a proposed project would help solve local unemployment should

be examined carefully and not accepted on the basis of superficial
statements.

The quantity of land zoned in the city for light manufacturing
and industrial purposes should vary directly with increases or decreases in the potential population allowed by the city's residential
zoning plan. The city's power over the quantity of land zoned for
light manufacturing and industrial purposes is a critical tool regarding control of in-migration caused by labor force expansion. Ideally
the potential supply of employment opportunities in the city and the
region should relate directly to the potential housing supply.

If the city adopts any type of "phased" or "sequenced" growth-
management plan, one element of the plan should relate to labor-
force expansion. A permit system for major employment expansion
could be established to insure that in-migration caused by a project
would not increase at a rate in conflict with the balance of the city's
"phased" growth. This would be particularly useful as to previously
undeveloped land zoned for light manufacturing or industrial uses.

The new employment element of the growth-management plan
could act both as a brake where in-migration caused by new employment opportunities should threaten to put a strain on the city's housing supply and as a stimulus if the housing supply should reach any
type of surplus condition.

Monitoring of Migration-Inducing Housing

Another major element in population increase in Santa Barbara
is the in-migration of retired or otherwise nonemployed persons who
have some means of living not dependent upon regional employment
opportunities. A complete growth-management plan should include
an element and ordinances allowing the city to monitor major developments aimed at attracting in-migration of such persons to the area.
Such developments occur in many forms including "second-home" developments, retirement homes, nursing-care homes, and the like.
Particular scrutiny should be given to any proposed developments of
this type that plan to advertise or otherwise attract significant numbers of persons to the region from a national market.

A conditional-use-permit scheme tied to the residential growth-
management ordinances would be the most direct way to control in-
migration caused by such developments. As with the proposed em-
ployment-opportunity element, use could be made of the environmen-
tal-impact report system to determine the in-migration effect of
such proposed developments.

Subdivision and Subdivision-type Exactions

California subdivision laws authorize the city to require persons proposing to subdivide a parcel of five or more acres into five or more separate parcels of 20 acres in size or less each to exact land or fees in lieu thereof for park or recreational purposes as a condition to approval of a final subdivision map.[33] The amount and location of the land or the fee should bear a reasonable relationship to the use of the park or recreational facilities by the future inhabitants of the subdivided property.[34] The same law authorizes the city to require the subdivider to pay the fees needed to dedicate land for school purposes and to cover costs of constructing drainage facilities.[35] Rezonings, conditional-use permit approvals, the granting of variances and other discretionary acts by the city outside of the subdivision law may also be conditioned upon receiving negotiated exactions from the applicant.[36]

Exactions of the foregoing type must be reasonable and not confiscatory but may be obtained even if the exactions incidentally benefit members of the public other than those in the subdivision and even though the purpose may be to meet the needs of future as well as present population.[37] To be legally safe such exactions should have a demonstrable health, safety, and public-welfare basis (as with drainage and the provision of park facilities) and should be reasonable and primarily of benefit to the subject land.[38]

Another device for exacting revenue from increased building is the California court-approved practice of imposing a tax on the business of constructing dwellings measuring the tax with the number of bedrooms constructed.[39]

None of the above devices, except perhaps for the park dedication exaction, is primarily a growth-restriction tool. Instead, each is a tool allowing local government to make new growth pay a larger share of the civic marginal cost it creates. The city should carefully consider including some or all of these available devices as an element in any growth-management plan, particularly to help finance any "phasing" or "sequencing" of local growth.

Historical and Esthetic Zoning

The following quotation accurately summarizes the position of the courts regarding zonings and other land-use schemes enacted for esthetic reasons:

> . . . in Santa Barbara County scenic environ-
> ment is commercial. The trial court found that

> people come to the County because of its natural
> beauty and that the maintenance of billboards
> along the highway may reasonably be believed to
> have an adverse effect upon the economy.
>   (Calif. Court of Appeals 1967)[40]

Such schemes are legally safest where justified on economic grounds
and not simply on a local government's desire to foster beauty for
its own sake.

The city's growth-management plan should contain findings as
to the economic significance to the city of maintaining the natural and
man-made beauty of the area. Such findings would be supportive,
both of an overall growth-management scheme intended to maintain
that beauty and of more specific ordinances related to design controls
within the city. The frank acknowledgment in the decision above by
the California Court of Appeals of the significance to the regional
economy of esthetic features should be kept in mind by the city in developing both the growth-management plan and the associated ordinances.

Zoning to protect historic structures and areas has been upheld
by the courts upon economic and, in situations of significant historic
structures, on the basis of pure historic value alone. Examples of
these cases include those upholding special zoning of the French
Quarter in New Orleans and the birthplace of Abraham Lincoln in
Springfield, Illinois. [41]

Santa Barbara includes many historic sites, including the Mission and the Presidio. Less well known and lacking protection are
certain picturesque and historically significant portions of the city,
such as the West Downtown Area, El Cesario, and portions of the
Laguna area. The city should consider incorporation into the growth-
management plan of protective provisions for these and other areas.
Ordinances intended to protect the areas and their immediate sur-
roundings would best be based upon both their historic value and the
economic significance of the sites to the city as tourist-attracting
facilities.

Point or Scoring System for Proposed New Development

Numerous communities in California have adopted one or more
versions of the Ramapo phased-growth plan. Such plans typically include a scoring system for providing scrutiny of proposed new developments in the community. These scoring systems list the various
criteria considered important by the community regarding new developments, including accessibility to transportation, availability of

water supplies and sewer service, availability of schools, design features, provision of low- or moderate-income housing, and the like. Each proposed project of a given size and larger is typically judged by the Planning Commission or other reviewing agency on each of these criteria and is assigned a score on a numerical scale (for example one to ten) based on the evaluating agency's judgment as to how close the proposed development comes to meeting the maximum standard for each criteria. Typically, a proposed development is required to achieve both a minimum score on each criteria and a maximum total score to be eligible for approval.

Variations of this approach include the assigning of weights to the various criteria dependent upon their relative importance in the eyes of the community. For example, a given score of five on provision of low- or moderate-income housing may count one and one-half times as much in the final total as the same score on accessibility to transportation facilities.

Utilization of this device by the City Planning Commission and other agencies could be very useful in making discussions of proposed new developments more objective and more focused on the elements of such proposals desired by the city. The use of a scoring system or a matrix to grade proposed developments forces discussion of each planning commissioner's scoring of each criterion and would tend to eliminate much of the unfocused discussion allowed by the lack of such a system.

It is recommended that the city investigate the experience of the other California communities that have recently adopted such system, including Novato and Napa.

LOW- AND MODERATE-INCOME HOUSING

Two Problems

The city has two levels of concern regarding low- and moderate-income housing. One, the purely legal, is comparatively simple to deal with. The other, the social problem, is much more difficult.

The most common legal challenges related to low-income housing are those claiming that a zoning scheme is exclusionary of minorities[42] or that redevelopment and similar public projects do not adequately provide for relocation of persons whose homes are condemned for the projects.[43]

In our opinion the city need not be concerned with a challenge based on exclusionary zoning. The city can satisfy current legal standards on exclusionary zoning by allowing a reasonable portion of the city to remain zoned for construction of multiple residences.

Even under the Half-Density Zoning Ordinance, enough of the city remains zoned for multiple dwellings to prevent any challenge on this ground. So long as any rezoning plan did not substantially eliminate the opportunity to construct multiple dwellings in the city, this defense would remain.

Successful attacks against local zoning schemes on the grounds of minority exclusion have occurred in communities that either have attempted to zone out multiple dwellings entirely or in communities that have taken zoning or other steps actively to prevent construction of a proposed low- or moderate-income housing project. [44] So long as the city of Santa Barbara maintains multiple-dwelling zoning and continues an active public housing program of at least the same level it has in the past, it should have no problems regarding exclusionary zoning. [45]

While it is our opinion that Santa Barbara should have little difficulty in meeting the legal minimum standards regarding low- and moderate-income housing, the second and more serious concern arises as to what the city could do regarding positive programs to satisfy demand for low- and moderate-income housing beyond the bare minimum required by law. In this instance the social demands on the city may far exceed the minimum legal requirements.

Low-Income Housing Options

Federal Programs

The federal government has suspended much of its efforts regarding low- and moderate-income housing. Current reports indicate that the only program that will continue in effect is a form of rent supplement whereby low- or moderate-income persons may receive monetary subsidies to be used by them in addition to their own resources to rent existing dwellings. There will be no programs in the immediate future to finance the construction of low-income housing or to assist in the purchase of low-income housing by low-income persons. [46]

State or Authorized Programs

Public Housing Authority. The City Public Housing Authority[47] is authorized under State law to prepare, carry out, acquire, lease, and operate housing projects for low-income persons. [48] The authority has the power of eminent domain and the authority to issue bonds;[49] it is limited by law in the amount of rent it may charge tenants. [50] The limits are based upon the size of the tenant's family.

The Public Housing Authority is an administrative agency of the state government and thus is technically independent of the city. As a practical matter, however, the authority is substantially dependent upon city assistance for financing projects and is subject to all local zoning and land-use regulations.[51] It thus cannot function totally independent of the city but must work in harmony with it.

The Public Housing Authority is the one government entity established by state law that has as its primary objective the provision of low-income housing. It is also the only entity established by state law that has potentially full powers in carrying out this mandate. With all other low-income housing tools, however, the main problem with the Public Housing Authority is and will remain to be financing of its efforts.

Mass-Produced Housing. State law contains a provision authorizing the State Department of Housing and Community Development to approve mass-produced, factory-built housing.[52] If the manufacturer of such housing obtains this approval, compliance with local building codes, which often represent a significant cost factor, is unnecessary.[53] State law, however, leaves with local government the complete control over installation, zoning, landscaping, and esthetics of such housing.

Surplus Lands. State law requires cities to inventory surplus city land and authorizes the lease, sale, or grant of such land to the Public Housing Authority or other low-income-housing entity.[54] Making such land available to low-income-housing entities at a low cost or at no cost would be one of the most effective ways of reducing the cost of low-income housing.

Area Housing Council. State law authorizes the creation of area housing councils to create area or regional housing plans.[55] The Public Housing Authority could initiate or be part of the creation of such an area housing council for the South Coast area. This is a type of regional planning that could be incorporated into other regional planning efforts as described above.

Overhead expenses of an area housing council may be financed by a surcharge of one-twentieth of 1 percent added to building-permit fees issued within the area. The law contains a confusing provision, however, requiring reimbursement of this surcharge to the community generating it if that community adopts and begins carrying out housing plans pursuant to the area housing council's regional housing plan. It is unclear where the money would come from to make these refunds if it is already spent on expenses of the council. It appears that clarification of this law is needed before the area-housing-council device can be used effectively.

Referendum on Low-Rent Housing. The California constitution requires a majority vote of the people in a city before a city may itself
develop, construct, or acquire any low-rent housing projects.[56]
This requirement applies only to low-rent public housing projects
financed by long-term government bonds and constructed by a housing authority.[57] It does not apply to housing projects intended to be
sold (as opposed to rented) to low-income persons.

Low-rent housing projects can, however, be developed legally
by the city, without the referendum requirement. The city, for example, could lease existing private dwellings from private owners
and then sublet those dwellings to low-income tenants.[58] Projects
intended to be rented to moderate- and high-income persons as well
as to low-income persons similarly should not be subject to the referendum requirement. Additionally, the public financing of housing
to be sold as opposed to rented to low-income persons would be ex-
empt from the referendum requirement.

Financing Low-Income Housing Through Borrowing by the City. Efforts by the city to finance low-income housing by borrowing requires
consideration of the state constitutional provision limiting the incurring
of indebtedness by the city in any year to the total revenue and income
provided in taxes for that year. To exceed this limit requires a two-
thirds vote of the citizens.[59]

As indicated in the economic portion of this work, the city has
substantial unused borrowing capacity that could be utilized for low-
income housing purposes without obtaining two-thirds vote. The
two-thirds vote requirement can also be avoided by use of revenue
bonds, which require only a majority vote.[60] Another device suggested recently is the use of "moral obligation" bonds, which ex-
pressly are not made binding obligations of the issuing community.[61]

The city may utilize a private nonprofit corporation to construct
low-income housing on publicly owned land and then lease the housing
with an option to purchase at the end of the lease period. These devices have generally been approved by the courts as not requiring
two-thirds voter approval, even though in substance they are similar
to a long-term debt obligation.[62]

Entities set up pursuant to the Joint Exercise of Power Act may
also issue bonds without obtaining a two-thirds voter approval.[63]
Revenue bonds issued by such joint-power authorities are subject
only to the approval of the representatives of the government agencies comprising the authority.[64] A joint-powers authority operating
on a regional basis could utilize revenue bonds to help solve financial
problems of low-income housing on a regional basis as well as just
within the city. State law, however, provides that joint powers
authorities may construct only display buildings, public halls, and
"any other public buildings."[65] It is uncertain whether "public

buildings" includes low-income housing. Remedial legislation could
be obtained to clarify this issue.

Revenue-Sharing Funds. The federal Revenue-Sharing Act provides
that revenue-sharing funds may be spent by local governments on
"building code enforcement" activities. [66] There is no other reference in the act to use the revenue-sharing funds for public housing
or related purposes. This suggests that such funds could be used for
housing-rehabilitation purposes but not for original construction of
new low-income units.

Redevelopment Agency. A fundamental purpose of the California Redevelopment Law is the expansion of the supply of low- and moderate-
income housing. [67] The Redevelopment Agency has the authority to
acquire land, manage property it acquires, relocate people, and clear
land. It is specifically authorized to sell, lease, grant, or donate
land to a public housing authority or other public agency for public
housing projects. [68] The agency itself may not, however, construct
any buildings for residential or other uses, except for providing housing for persons displaced by the redevelopment project. [69]

The bulk of construction in a redevelopment project is new private construction. Apart from relocation housing, construction of
new low- and moderate-income housing faces the same problems of
financial risk to lenders and developers as in other parts of the community.

The redevelopment law, however, does offer the city a significant capacity for planning, land assembly, and land sale, lease, or
grant to assist private efforts in developing low- or moderate-income
housing.

The best opportunity for significant improvement of the low-
and moderate-income housing situation in the city of Santa Barbara
appears to be active cooperation between the Redevelopment Agency
with its ability to make land available and the Public Housing Authority with its ability to construct and operate low-income housing projects, both acting in conjunction with imaginative private finance
schemes. One such scheme is discussed at the conclusion of this
section.

Special Housing and Renewal Law. State law authorizes the creation
of a "renewal area agency" as an agency of the state government to
assist persons in deteriorating portions of a community to plan and
carry out rehabilitation and rebuilding of their area "to maintain its
neighborhood character. "[70] Such an agency is formed by a procedure
that begins with a petition signed by not less than 20 percent of the
persons residing within the boundaries of the proposed area. The

area covered by such an agency in cities or counties of less than 1 million population must be a minimum of three acres and a maximum of 30 acres (or 35 with Planning Commission approval).

The agency is managed by a 15-member board of directors, two-thirds of whom must be residents of the renewal area.[71] It has certain planning authority and even limited authority to suspend otherwise applicable local building codes to carry out projects.[72] The agency must submit its specific plans for rehabilitation and renewal of its area to the Planning Commission within nine months of its creation (with a six-month extension possible).[73] Upon receiving ultimate approval from the Planning Commission and the local legislative body, the renewal-area agency may issue tax-exempt bonds to finance its plan.

The intent of the law is to offer a government entity to residents of a particular area or neighborhood wishing to direct the destiny of their neighborhood. The local planning commission and city council, however, retain a great amount of authority over the agency.

Reports on this device indicate that no such agency has yet been created in the State of California. This seems to be due to the practical difficulties in establishing such an agency and a prospect of the complexities of administering it. Most residents of deteriorating neighborhoods lack both the technical expertise to work with the law or the money to retain technical advisors.

Mandatory Low-Income Housing Ordinance. The City of Los Angeles, the City of Berkeley, and other communities around the country have been experimenting with ordinances requiring developments containing a specified number of units (for example, five or more) to reserve a certain percentage of those units for occupancy by low- or moderate-income households. Typically, the ordinances require around 15 percent of the new units to be set aside for low-income tenants. This device conditions the issuance of building or occupancy permits upon the developers entering into a contract to set aside the specified percentage of his proposed units for low-income persons. Failure to agree to this results in denial of the building or occupancy permit.

Where such ordinances are enacted without compensation being paid to the private landowner for the low-income rental units, serious questions arise as to whether a "taking" has occurred as to the property. The Supreme Court of the State of Virginia has declared one such ordinance unconstitutional, on the grounds that it represents a taking of private property without the payment of compensation.[74]

The problem is that such an ordinance places the burden of providing low-income housing on one small group--developers and landlords--without offsetting compensation. If the provision of low-income housing is a valid public purpose, as it has been held to be by

the California courts,[75] the argument goes that the public at large
should bear the cost, instead of one small portion of the public.

One attempt to remedy this potential legal flaw is the requirement that government subsidies be available to compensate the land-
lord or developer for the difference between the market rent and the
low-income rent before compelling the developer to provide the low-
income units. Whether this resolves all the legal issues remains to
be determined.

Since substantial population growth in Santa Barbara will require an increase in multiple dwelling units there, the city may wish
carefully to consider adopting this type of ordinance. It is suggested
that, if the city considers this path, it should study the experience of
Los Angeles, Berkeley, and other communities around the country
that have adopted such an ordinance. Further judicial opinion can be
expected as to the validity of this approach to resolving the low-
income housing problem.

Private Financing Efforts. The best prospect for significant improvements in the city's low- and moderate-income housing situation
appears to be the development of a working relationship between the
Redevelopment Agency, the Public Housing Authority, and one or
more private groups. Such a combined effort would tie together the
Public Housing Authority's general authority to provide low-income
housing, the Redevelopment Agency's land acquisition and assembly
powers, and the financing sources of private groups pending increased
federal or state government financing support.

The Community Ownership Organizing Project (COOP) of Oakland, California, has devised a proposal for the City of Oakland,
calling for creation of a private cooperative low-income housing-
purchase program working with local governments. The program
calls for establishment of a private cooperative housing corporation
assisted financially by local and other government agencies enabling
low- and moderate-income persons to purchase housing at reasonable
prices through the use of various public financing schemes. The
sources of public finance for this type of program include accumulated
city reserve funds and city pension funds. Other suggestions include
the selling of bonds by the city for investment in the project, rental
of public land to the project at a low price, or the outright grant of
public lands to such projects. The Redevelopment Agency and the
Public Housing Authority, with their statutory powers, would be particularly valuable in this type of effort.

Conclusion. In conclusion, it must be stressed that the city of Santa
Barbara will not make any major steps regarding provision of low-
and moderate-income housing unless an aggressive and imaginative

program combining government assistance with efforts of private
groups and individuals is undertaken.

NOTES

1. 197 A.2d 711 (1964).
2. S.B. City Ord. no. 3591.
3. Cal. Govt. Code sec. 65858.
4. Metro. Realty v. County of El Dorado, 222 C.A.2d 508
(1963); Mang v. County of Santa Barbara, 182 C.A.2d 93 (1960).
See also the leading and well-reasoned early case on interim zoning,
Miller v. Bd. of Public Works, 195 C. 477 (1925), error dis. 273
U.S. 781 (1925).
5. Lima v. Woodruff, 107 C.A. 285 (1930).
6. Miller v. Bd. of Public Works, 195 C. 477 (1925), 273
U.S. 781 (1925).
7. People ex rel S.F. Bay etc. Comm. v. Town of Emery-
ville, 69 C.2d 533 (1968); Candlestick Properties, Inc. v. S.F.B.
C.D.C., 11 C.A.3d 557 (1970); Calif. Govt. Code sec. 66650 (pre-
1969), 66604.
8. People ex rel Younger v. County of El Dorado, 5 C.3d
480 (1971); Calif. Govt. Code sec. 66801.
9. Calif. Water Code sec. 353 (see generally secs. 350-58).
10. Calif. Water Code sec. 356; Butte County Water Users
Assn. v. Railroad Comm., 185 Cal. 218 (1921).
11. Calif. Water Code sec. 353.
12. 231 C.A.2d 774 (1965).
13. Cal. Govt. Code sec. 65860(a), 65803 (re inapplicability
to charter cities).
14. See cases cited in notes 7 and 8 supra.
15. O'Loan v. O'Rourke, 231 C.A.2d 774 (1965); Clemons v.
Los Angeles, 36 C.2d 95 (1950); Spindler Realty Corp. v. Monning,
243 C.A.2d 255 (1966); Topanga Canyon Assn. v. County of Los
Angeles, (Calif. Supreme Court, 5/17/74); Haar, "In Accordance
with a Comprehensive Plan," 68 Harv. L. Rev. 1154 (1955).
16. 375 F. Supp. 574 (D.C. Calif. 1974).
17. As of August 15, 1974, the injunction against the City of
Petaluma was under suspension by stay order issued by Justice Douglas, the United States Supreme Court Justice responsible for the
Ninth Circuit. This was based on a petition filed by the city government alleging water crisis grounds and relying substantially on the
Belle Terre decision (see note 23 infra). The case apparently will
be appealed and taken to the highest federal courts.

18. For additional literature and case law on the legal obligation of a community to consider the impact of its governmental action on surrounding communities, see Scott v. Indian Wells, 6 C.3d
541 (1972); "Phased Zoning," 26 Stan. L. Rev. 585, 606 (1974); "Regional Impact of Zoning," 114 U. Pa. L. Rev. 1251 (1966); Roselle
Park v. Union, 262 A.2d 762 (New Jersey 1970); "Metropolitaniza-
tion and Land Use Parochialism Toward a Judicial Attitude," 69
Mich. L. Rev. 655 (1971); "Regional Needs," 3 Conn. L. Rev. 244
(1970-71); Bozung v. LAFCO, 37 C.A.3d 842 (Cal. Sup. Ct. Hg.
granted 5/22/74 (1974) ("We do not perceive the significance attributed
by defendants to whether plaintiffs live within or without Camarillo
city boundaries. Effects of environmental abuse are not contained
by political lines."); c.f. Milliken v. Bradley, 42 U.S.L.W. 5249
(1974) (United States Supreme Court opinion in Detroit School Busing
Case re constitutional obligations of adjacent political entities vis-a-
vis one another in a different but analogous context).

19. See Volume 3, pp. 1-4.

20. Cal. Govt. Code sec. 6500 et seq.

21. See note 18, supra.

22. See Volume 2.

23. Golden v. Town of Ramapo, 334 N.Y.S.2d 138 (1972).
For commentary, some critical, on this leading case, see "note
Phased Zoning," 26 Stan. L. Rev. 585 (1974); Bosselman "Can the
Town of Ramapo Pass a Law to Bind the Rights of the Whole World?"
1 Fla. St. Univ. L. Rev. 234 (1973).

24. Bosselman, Callies and Banta, "The Taking Issue, an
Analysis of the Constitutional Limits of Land Use Control," Supt. of
Doc. U.S. Govt. Ptg. Office no. 4111-00017--written for the Presi-
dent's Council on Environmental Quality, 1973.

25. Village of Belle Terre v. Bruce Boraas et al., ___ U.S.
___, 94 S. Ct. 1536 (1974).

26. Robinson v. City of Los Angeles, 146 C.A.2d 810 (1956);
Johnston v. Claremont, 49 C.2d 826 (1958); c.f. Topanga Canyon
Assn. v. L.A. County, 11 C.3d 506 (1974) (findings required for
variance grant).

27. Goldblatt v. Hemstead, 369 U.S. 590 (1962); Hadacheck
v. Sebastain, 239 U.S. 394 (1915); Consolidated Rock v. Los Angeles,
57 C.2d 515 (1962); Turner v. Del Norte County, 24 C.A.3d 311
(1972).

28. Specific planning pursuant to Govt. Code sec. 65450.1 is
a little-used tool that appears to offer great planning flexibility to a
community. Use of this tool to "mix" multiple and single-family
residences would be an ambitious undertaking but probably the best
way to achieve the objective.

29. Turner v. Del Norte County, 24 C.A.3d 311 (1972); Just v. Marinette County, 201 N.W.2d 761 (1972).

30. Acquisition of development rights would not open the land to public use and access. It would leave the land as private property but without the potential for development. This may be fine for "scenic backdrop" or other land valuable for viewing purposes only, but it is of no value if public use of the land is desired. In many cases, acquiring the public-use right might not cost significantly more than merely purchasing the development rights.

31. Calif. Rev. & Tax Code sec. 402.1, 421-31.

32. This could be done as part of the required scrutiny of the growth-inducing impact of the project. Calif. Pub. Res. Code sec. 21151, 21110(g).

33. Calif. Bus. & Prof. Code sec. 11546.

34. Calif. Bus. & Prof. Code sec. 11546(e); Assoc. Home Builders etc. Inc. v. City of Walnut Creek, 4 C.3d 633 (1971). The court implied, however, that sec. 11546 could constitutionally be changed to allow dedication or fee usage in other parts of a community if adequate parks exist adjacent to the proposed subdivision, 4 C.3d 633 at 640 note 6 supra. See also Ayres v. Los Angeles, 34 C.2d 31 (1949); Southern Pac. Co. v. Los Angeles, 242 C.A.2d 38 (1960); Heyman & Gilhool, "The Constitutionality of . . . Subdivision Exactions," 73 Yale L. J. 1119 (1964); "Subdivision Exactions in California," 23 Hastings L. J. 403 (1972).

35. Calif. Bus. & Prof. Code secs. 11525.2, 11543.5.

36. Scrutton v. County of Sacramento, 275 C.A.2d 412 (1969).

37. Assoc. Homebuilders v. Walnut Creek, note 34 supra.

38. Scrutton, note 36 supra.

39. Assoc. Homebuilders v. Newark, 18 C.A.3d 107 (1971).

40. County of Santa Barbara v. Purcell, 251 C.A.2d 169 at 173 (1967).

41. New Orleans v. Levy, 64 S.2d 798 (1953); M & N Enterprises v. Springfield, 250 N.E.2d 289 (1969). See also the leading Supreme Court case of Berman v. Parker, 348 U.S. 26 (1954), Miami Beach v. Ocean & Inland Co., 3 S.2d 364 (1941) (Importance of esthetics to tourist industry); People v. Stover, 240 N.Y.S.2d 734, 191 N.E.2d 272 (1963).

42. The so-called "Pennsylvania Cases" are the main authorities in this area; see, e.g., Re Appeal of Girsh, 263 A2d 395 (1970); Appeal of Groff, 274 A2d 574 (1971); "Penn. Supreme Court and Exclusionary Suburban Zoning . . .," 16 Vill. L. Rev. 507 (1971). See also Ybarra v. Los Altos, 370 F.Supp. 742 (N.D. Cal. 1973).

43. See, e.g., Norwalk Core v. Norwalk Redev. Agency, 395 F.2d 920 (2d cir. 1968).

44. See, e.g., G. & D. Holland Construction Co. v. Marysville, 12 C.A.3d 989 (1970).

45. The obligations of a city toward both resident and nonresident indigents are well analyzed in Sager, "Tight Little Islands: Exclusionary Zoning, Equal Protection and the Indigent," 21 Stan. L. Rev. 767 (1969), and comment, "The Responsibility of Local Zoning Authorities to Non-Resident Indigents," 23 Stan. L. Rev. 724 (1971).

46. This was announced in January 1973 by the federal government. Speculation as to revision of this policy is beyond the scope of this document.

47. See generally Calif. Health & Safety Code secs. 34200-380.

48. Calif. Health & Safety Code sec. 34312.

49. Calif. Health & Safety Code secs. 34325, 34350, et seq.

50. Calif. Health & Safety Code sec. 34322.

51. Calif. Health & Safety Code sec. 34326.

52. Calif. Health & Safety Code sec. 19960-97--"The Factory-Built Housing Law."

53. Calif. Health & Safety Code sec. 19991.

54. Calif. Govt. Code secs. 50568-73.

55. Calif. Health & Safety Code sec. 37850 et seq.

56. Cal. Const. Art. XXXIV.

57. 51 Ops. Atty. Gen. 42 (1968); James v. Valtierra, 402, 402 U.S. 137 (1970).

58. 47 Ops. Atty. Gen. 17 (1966).

59. Calif. Const. Art. XIII sec. 40; Santa Barbara has a separate limit of 10 percent of the assessed value of property in the city--City Charter sec. 1209.

60. S.B. City Charter sec. 1210; Calif. Govt. Code sec. 54300 et seq. Charter cities may adapt this statutory authority to their own needs; see Santa Monica v. Grubb, 245 C.A.2d 718 (1966).

61. This device requires a pledge by the government to repay the bonds that creates a moral commitment but not a binding legal obligation.

62. County of Los Angeles v. Neswig, 231 C.A.2d 603 (1965); Dean v. Kuchel, 35 C.2d 444 (1950).

63. Calif. Govt. Code sec. 6500 et seq.

64. Calif. Govt. Code sec. 54386. For charter city issues, see City of Los Angeles v. Layton, 269 C.A.2d 567 (1969).

65. Calif. Govt. Code sec. 6546.

66. Pub. Law 92-512, sec. 103(a).

67. Calif. Health & Safety Code sec. 33071.

68. Calif. Health & Safety Code sec. 33442.

69. Calif. Health & Safety Code sec. 33440.

70. Calif. Health & Safety Code sec. 33701 et seq.

71. Calif. Health & Safety Code sec. 33709.

72. Calif. Health & Safety Code sec. 33713.

73. Calif. Health & Safety Code sec. 33717.

74. Bd. of Supervisors of Fairfax County v. De Groff Enterprises, 198 S.E. 2d 600 (1973).

75. Winkleman v. Tiburon, 32 C.A. 3d 834 (1973); Housing Authority of Los Angeles v. Dockweller, 14 C. 2d 437 (1939).

The Santa Barbara Planning Task Force first presented the findings of its studies on growth to the City Council at an evening meeting held September 17, 1974. The study was introduced by Dame Judith Anderson, a local resident for more than two decades, who read the poem about Santa Barbara by Galsworthy that appears in the section on esthetics in Chapter 4. Slide presentations accompanied the reading, which was followed by questions from the council members and the full-house audience. The Task Force subsequently took its slide presentation to about a dozen community meetings over the next several months, reaching an audience of several thousand. The distribution of the Task Force "Issues Booklet" (reproduced in the Appendix) in the local metropolitan daily provided access to the findings to thousands more. The study became the subject of classes held in local junior and senior high schools, the community college, and University of California campus.

In general, the study results were received favorably. Local planning associations and neighborhood associations praised it with enthusiasm, as did groups representing the poor; business groups—and particularly the real estate community—were either limited in their appreciation or actively hostile. Disagreement with the study tended to be vague and general; there was virtually no argument with either the evidence used in the study or with the concrete conclusions reached. Both radio and local newspapers gave the study extensive coverage; the one local television station ignored it. The weekly alternative newspaper praised it editorially; the daily paper took no position on its merit but did encourage citizens to turn out for the slide presentations.

A series of special meetings of the City Planning Commission were held in which the study findings were reviewed chapter by chapter. The Task Force staff was closely questioned on virtually all of its findings. Some of the commissioners took the time to confirm various findings with city staff members or to seek out original sources upon which evidence was based. The study held up.

After a series of legally required hearings, the City Council took up the matter of acting on the recommendations of the Planning Commission for General and Zoning Amendments for the city government, based on the findings of the Task Force. The Planning Commission recommended to the Council that "to protect the health, safety and general welfare of the residents of the City of Santa Barbara, the City should adopt amendments to its General Plan and Zoning

Ordinance which would provide for a probable approximate population
of 85,000." The justification for this action, which sharply reduced
the then-current Zoning Probable holding capacity of 120,000, was
explicitly based on water, sewer plant, and traffic capacities and
upon the fiscal costs of growth (complete references, including page
numbers of Task Force findings, were included in the Planning Commission Resolution).

The City Council, after hearing both praise and complaints regarding the 85,000 population limit, enacted it into law on April 22,
1975, through a major series of downzoning decisions. The vote was
four to three. The primary means used was to decrease maximum
apartment densities from 34 units per acre to 12 per acre. Realtors
and builders were especially critical of this action, citing deleterious
consequences upon the poor as a primary reason to avoid such downzoning. The debate was spirited but not acrimonious.

At this writing (1976) the council is considering various measures to set aside certain land parcels in the city for low-income
housing as a means of securing adequate acreage for such land-use
should the means come about in the future actually to construct low-
income housing. The council is also exploring new means, in conjunction with surrounding communities, to limit industrial expansion
in the area as another way to inhibit population migration. Although
citing budgetary constraints as its motivation, the council acted concretely in this direction by eliminating all community advertising in
its most recently adopted budget.

The group opposed to the City Council's action have subsequently formed a new organization, "Santa Barbara Tomorrow," and have
initiated legal action against the city government on the grounds that
the decision to enact the downzoning amendments without an environmental impact report was illegal. Additional technical complaints
were also raised. Attorneys for the city government contend that the
period provided to appeal this lack of an environmental impact report
had lapsed, and, since the complainants had not acted within this prescribed period, their argument was without merit. At the time of
this writing, the courts had not acted upon the case. Attorneys for
the city government are confident, however, that its actions were
legally sound.

Except for their periodic attendance at local community meetings as resource people, the members of the Task Force are no
longer formally linked together. Each has returned to his or her
respective duties and avocations.

Santa Barbara
HOW MANY PEOPLE SHOULD THERE BE ?

HELP YOUR CITY COUNCIL DECIDE

The following appeared as a supplement of the Santa Barbara News-Press on December 6, 1974.

WHAT IS OUR PURPOSE?

To Inform, To Involve.

What does population growth mean for Santa Barbara? What effect will additional numbers of people have upon the quality of life of this very special place? How will population growth affect:

* Jobs?
* Retail Business?
* Air Quality?
* Water Supplies?
* Taxes?
* Income?
* Traffic?
* Land Use?
* Parks?

In February of 1974, your City Council asked the Santa Barbara Planning Task Force, a group of local experts and citizen-volunteers, to conduct a unique study that would answer these questions so that an effective population policy could be set for the City. For years there have been many statements made about the effects of growth, but in the absence of detailed and authoritative study, there has been no way to discriminate myth from reality. The goal of the Planning Task Force was to utilize the tremendous research resources of the Santa Barbara area to lay the basis for the kind of sound planning that few cities ever achieve.

The Task Force studies are now complete; three volumes of evaluation, evidence and analysis have been presented to the City Council and the Planning Commission. But before decisions are made, decisions that may involve substantial rezoning of the City, the public must have an opportunity to know the study results and to make their opinions felt at City Hall. This brief booklet, a summary of the findings of the Santa Barbara Planning Task Force, is aimed at helping this process. Read it, think about it, and let City Hall know your views. The future of Santa Barbara is too important to be determined without your participation.

WHAT MAKES SANTA BARBARA GROW?

Primarily jobs.

Relatively few people are born in Santa Barbara; over the years the great bulk of the City's growth has come from migration. Why do people come to Santa Barbara? While the undeniable beauty of the area is clearly a major attraction, most people do not move from one city to another merely on the basis of aesthetics. Although some Santa Barbarans are here to retire, the vast majority of us are working people who would not be here if we could not find jobs in the local economy. In recent years, it has been the creation of new jobs resulting from the presence of the University and research and development industries that has been largely responsible for growth in the City and the South Coast region.

The graph below shows how growth in the City and surrounding area has paralleled increases in student enrollment at UCSB in recent years. The rapid expansion of University enrollment—from 3,500 students in 1960 to over 13,000 students in 1970—meant the creation of many new jobs. Whether these jobs were initially filled by unemployed Santa Barbarans or persons from out-of-town, the long-run effect was the same: as it became known that jobs were opening up, persons in other places came to Santa Barbara to join the local work force. Today population continues to grow, but at a slower rate, with expansion of research, manufacturing and the tourist industries.

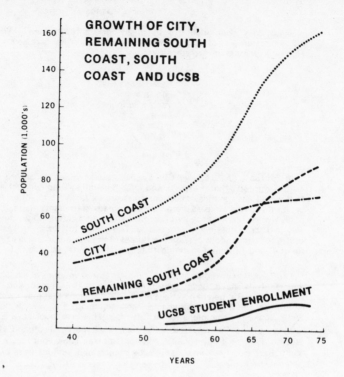

GROWTH OF CITY, REMAINING SOUTH COAST, SOUTH COAST AND UCSB

THE FUTURE OF GROWTH: WHO DECIDES?

That depends on you.

Attempts to predict growth on the basis of past trends have failed. For example, only ten years ago an effort was made by planners to estimate future population on the basis of past trends and foreseeable economic changes. Their efforts are summarized on the graph below. The predictions have proven to be substantially incorrect; the City currently has 7,000 people less than predicted; growth was overestimated by almost 100 percent. Such errors are unavoidable if we attempt to predict the future of Santa Barbara on the basis of current circumstance—because circumstances change. New industries may or may not come to Santa Barbara; existing ones may or may not expand. It is impossible to know in advance. If population grows it will be because decisions are made that will bring people here—decisions by corporations, University Regents, and public officials. The real problem is not to try to *predict* population, but instead to evaluate its effect and develop methods to achieve the population level that is desired.

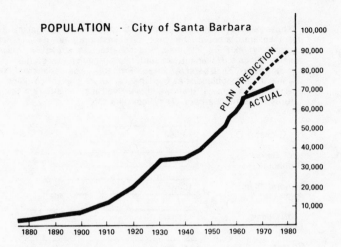

This graph, taken from the City's 1964 General Plan, demonstrates the difficulty of predicting population.

DOES SANTA BARBARA HAVE A GROWTH POLICY?

Yes, several.

The City's legal stance toward growth is contained in its Zoning Ordinance, which specifies the uses to which land can be legally put. Any proposed development—be it residential, commercial, or industrial—must legally conform to the Zoning Ordinance. Currently, the City's Ordinance permits housing for over 170,000 people—over two and one-third times the current population of about 73,000. Under the Ordinance, Santa Barbara can legally become a city of apartments, with densities (people per square mile) tripling in some neighborhoods. Furthermore, the Ordinance sets aside substantial amounts of land for future light industrial development—development which, if it were to occur, would generate more jobs and hence population growth through migration of persons searching for work.

Recently, the City Council temporarily amended its Zoning Ordinance, in an attempt to slow growth until long-range decisions could be made about the future of Santa Barbara. This Interim Half-Density Ordinance—originally adopted in May, 1973 and now scheduled to expire in May, 1975—cuts allowable densities in half in all those areas of the City zoned for apartments. Although the Half-Density Ordinance is sometimes regarded as a no-growth measure, it in fact permits substantial population growth—to about 117,000 people, two-thirds greater than the present level.

In addition to Zoning laws, the City also has a General Plan which is intended to serve as a guide to future development. Although the General Plan does not have the force of law (as does the Zoning Ordinance), it is taken into account by public officials when they made land use decisions. The General Plan, like the Zoning Ordinance, envisions substantial growth—to almost 140,000 people, or nearly twice the current population. If the Zoning Ordinance was brought into conformity with the General Plan, the ultimate legal development of the City would be reduced by about 18 percent.

These various population figures are based on ultimate legal maximums. They do not take into account the practical constraints on development caused by topography, existing lot lines, and construction already in place. When such considerations are taken into account, likely growth under each policy is lowered by a magnitude of 20-30 percent. These "Probable" populations were used along with the maximum populations as hypothetical future population points. Including the possibility of no growth at all, we thus arrived at seven different possible population futures for Santa Barbara. They look like this:

No Growth	73,000
Half Density Probable	94,000
General Plan Probable	103,000
Half Density Maximum	117,000
Zoning Probable	119,000
General Plan Maximum	140,000
Zoning Maximum	170,000

About each of these population levels, the study asked the same basic question: What would happen to the economic, environmental, and social qualities of life if the decisions were made to actually create city populations of this size? Some of the answers now follow.

PUBLIC OPINION: HOW MANY MORE PEOPLE DO RESIDENTS SAY THEY WANT?

Mostly, no more at all.

During the spring of 1974, Task Force sociologists carried out a telephone survey to determine the public's attitude toward growth. Santa Barbarans were asked a simple question: "Do you think there should be more people here, less people here, or about the same as now?" The citizens were chosen at random from the phone book, using standard statistical methods employed in surveys of this sort. We learned that any appreciable growth would be contrary to the expressed desires of a majority of citizens. And, in answer to a question about growth in their own neighborhoods, citizens were even more overwhelmingly opposed to growth. The table below summarizes the survey results, based on the responses of 192 people:

WHAT RESIDENTS THINK ABOUT GROWTH

	FOR CITY (%)	FOR NEIGHBORHOOD (%)
PREFER MORE PEOPLE	14.1	2.6
PREFER LESS PEOPLE	26.1	18.8
PREFER ABOUT SAME	56.7	78.1
OTHER	3.1	.5

WHAT WILL GROWTH MEAN FOR OUR LIFE STYLE?

Some changes would seem inevitable.

CRIME:

A Task Force study of 115 American cities found that crime rates are higher in larger cities than in smaller ones. This implies that higher population levels here will likely mean a larger number of crimes per resident. Visible effects of vandalism also increase as a larger number of people are concentrated in a fixed amount of space.

RACIAL SEGREGATION:

Residential segregation is higher in larger cities than in smaller ones. With more people in the City, Santa Barbara's minorities will tend to live in larger and more compacted geographical areas.

HOUSING:

At one time, the great majority of Santa Barbarans were homeowners. Now only a slight majority live in single family houses. If the city were to reach its maximum population under current zoning, the great majority of the city's people would live in apartments. Under a program that cuts back on apartments, such as that contained in the Interim Half-Density Ordinance, the majority of the people living in Santa Barbara would continue to live in single family houses.

HOUSING MIX

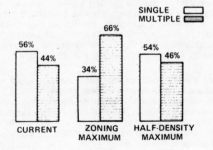

SINGLE ☐
MULTIPLE ▤

56% 44%	34% 66%	54% 46%
CURRENT	ZONING MAXIMUM	HALF-DENSITY MAXIMUM

COMMERCIAL SERVICES AND CULTURAL OPPORTUNITIES:

There is more to see and do in the big city than in the little city; there is a larger variety of stores, museums, and similar facilities in larger places. But Santa Barbara is an extraordinarily well-endowed small city. Among the 115 cities with which we compared Santa Barbara, only one (West Palm Beach, Florida) had a larger number of commercial services per resident. And the presence of the University combined with the traditional cultural sophistication, leisure, and wealth of its population, mean that Santa Barbara has an array of resources not often found in a city of its current size. If there were to be even more such people here, this variety would tend to increase.

THE QUIET LITTLE PLEASURES:

Additional population may mean that the secluded paseos, fragile street plantings, and the walkway benches will be subject to the press of more people. Large places tend to have crowding in their central public facilities. The tempo of life is increased; daily routines become more complicated as parking becomes more difficult, a place to sit harder to come by, and aimless pleasure a rarer experience.

Additional crowding of people, cars, and residences will mean that owning large pets, particularly horses, will become increasingly impractical. Public roads will be inappropriate for horse riding and complaints from neighbors will be more common. Dogs running loose will be larger in number and an ever-increasing nuisance.

On the other hand, more people may provide more social diversity, including ethnic communities in which the language, foods and other folkways of other cultures can be experienced. Another advantage of numbers is that anonymity is easier to come by; a certain kind of privacy only comes in large cities.

HOW MUCH MORE TRAFFIC CAN OUR STREETS HANDLE?

Not very much.

The Santa Barbara urban area has an unusual shape - a narrow corridor between the mountains and the ocean. These features make for dramatic views, but they also make for unusual predicaments for moving large numbers of cars. Our traffic problem is not primarily on the "up and down" streets running between ocean and mountains, but across the "length" of the City, between Goleta and Montecito. Particularly at the two ends of the City - the Goleta end in the area of San Marcos Pass, and the Montecito end, at Hot Springs Road - traffic will become critical with only modest amounts of additional growth. In the more central areas, traffic currently on the main streets will tend to divert to the less used side streets. This will have negative impacts on the environment of central area neighborhoods.

The result is that unless the carrying capacity of City streets is increased (by elimination of off-street parking, establishment of one-way streets, or adding additional lanes) most of the City's main routes will be overtaxed with only the low population growth that probably would result from the Half Density (a population of 94,000). Improving existing street capacities would provide for this additional growth but as City population moves much beyond 100,000 people, the majority of thoroughfares would again be congested beyond any reasonable standard of adequacy. And at this point, little could be done to carry the additional number of cars.

Once it was envisioned that Santa Barbara could solve its future traffic problems by making Foothill Road a four-lane highway, thus providing an alternative to 101. It was also once considered appropriate to even raise the possibility of a major highway through Hope Ranch. Today nobody takes such options seriously and the only alternative becomes to stabilize the number of autos at some point: either by limiting population or by somehow shifting a proportionate number of people to mass transit or bicycles.

WHAT WILL HAPPEN TO THE AIR WE BREATHE?

It will get better, but still not quite good enough.

The government has done two things to give us better air: it has created laws that restrict the *emissions* from cars and buildings, and it has mandated clean air quality *standards* which all parts of the country are required to meet. In some places, the current and scheduled emissions controls will mean that the clean air quality standards will automatically be met.

According to studies of the South Coast air basin carried out by the General Research Corporation, there would be a good chance that our air would be clean enough to meet government standards on the three major components of smog only if population growth were to cease in the area. But the government emissions controls will have the effect of making the air much cleaner even with high rates of population growth - it will just not be clean enough to meet government standards on one component, ozone. That could mean that with growth other measures may have to be taken to achieve really clean air: banning cars from the Downtown area, restricting gasoline sales, or some other means of diverting auto users to mass transit.

The table below shows the estimated number of hours per year that one particular pollutant, ozone, can be expected to exceed amounts permitted under federal standards, at various levels of city population by the year 2000. It shows clearly the significant air quality improvements expected under scheduled government emissions controls:

HOW GROWTH WILL AFFECT AIR QUALITY

	City Population	Number of Hours Per Year Exceeding Standard (Ozone)*
Current (1973)	73,000	314
No Growth (At Year 2000)	73,000	2-20
Half Density Probable (At Year 2000)	94,000	10-50
Zoning Probable (At Year 2000)	119,000	10-50

*According to the government regulations, the ozone standard cannot be exceeded more than one hour per year.

WHICH OF THE NATURAL HABITATS WILL REMAIN?

Very few.

If growth proceeds, land will become increasingly scarce and developers will be willing to pay even higher costs to build houses in remaining areas of open space. Some of Santa Barbara's hillside land is too steep to ever be developed, but the majority of such acreage is likely developable. Recent construction on Eucalyptus Hill is evidence of what could occur across the foothill backdrop of the City. Even low density development has the effect of eliminating the natural flora and fauna as new vegetation is introduced, as fencing is constructed, and a dogs and cats wander through previously undisturbed nesting and migratory grounds. A number of areas are additionally subject to increased dangers from fire and mud-slides.

With population growth, many species of animals are lost. In central city areas, increasing dog population results in the nuisance of dog wastes on city streets and lawns; more important, much of this waste ends up in the city's streams where it pollutes an aesthetic and biological resource, still used as a splashing ground (in some places with questionable health safety) by Santa Barbara neighborhood children.

Most of the natural habitats which once supported a complex array of wildlife have been destroyed by past development. The table below shows what was once here and what is now left. Each kind of habitat, taken for granted in the past, represents a unique support environment for the animal and vegetable species that remain in the area.

OPEN SPACE: WHAT REMAINS?

Type of Habitat	Original Acreage	Remaining Acreage	Percent Loss
Native Grassland or Foothill Open Oak Woodland	6,780 acres	676 acres	90%
Coast Live Oak Forest	750	215	71
Soft Chaparral	2,050	601	71
Hard Chaparral	350	179	49
Marsh	958	10	99
Riparian (Waterways)	156	77	51
Total	11,044	1,758	84%

PEOPLE AND BEAUTY: IS GROWTH UGLY OR LOVELY?

It depends on who you ask.

Questions of what is ugly or lovely are personal and subjective; beauty is in the eye of the beholder, not the object beheld. But we make the assumption that Santa Barbarans tend to have similar eyes and to cherish certain kinds of environmental qualities above others. They like open space and unimpaired views of the ocean and mountains. They prefer small scale to large, and appreciate the Spanish and Mexican motifs that lend to the area's architecture a bit of old world romance.

For those with such a vision, growth will tend to undermine the city's aesthetic resources. Additional construction in the periphery of the city will disturb views of the foothills and eliminate natural open space. The kind of Spanish architecture which distinguishes the older parts of the city is not being duplicated in the newer developments in the central area itself, and especially in other neighborhoods such as the Mesa and San Roque. There are also many fine irreplaceable Victorian houses, which, because they are in areas zoned for high density, will be lost with appreciable growth.

Other citizens view the new as evidence of dynamism and change; they have an appreciation for newer architectural styles and the visual variety they afford. Additional growth will mean more new construction, at least some portion of which may reflect handsome contemporary design.

As the city develops, the existing Spanish core will likely represent a smaller and smaller proportion of the existing building stock; it will increasingly represent an oasis, a special place, primarily for tourists and special occasions; it will not be the routine Santa Barbara of most people's daily lives.

WILL MORE PEOPLE MAKE US RICHER OR POORER?

It will generally make no difference.

In the Task Force study of 115 American cities it was found that wages in larger cities tend to be higher than in smaller ones, but that it also costs more to live in big cities than in small cities. The two opposite trends tend to cancel one another out: the net effect is that people's actual buying power seems unaffected by city size.

Population growth will bring more money to Santa Barbara and local merchants will have at least an opportunity to gain more business and higher profits. But along with population growth will come more competitors as well. In a free market economy, the number of competitors tends to grow in proportion to the profit-making opportunities. Only those businesses which have a monopoly on a local market or which make their money directly from growth (e.g. in land development, construction financing) will likely be assured of additional business with population growth. For most local merchants the consequence will be merely the addition of both more people and more competition. The size of the pie will grow, but not the size of each piece.

Size does have one important effect, however. With significant amounts of growth, Santa Barbara will attract additional regional shopping centers like La Cumbre Plaza. If located within the City limits, such centers bring additional sales tax revenues into the City coffers, but they tend not to increase the amount of private wealth in the community. Unlike more traditional forms of retailing, the proportion of shops in such centers which are locally-owned tends to be relatively low. Most of the profits go to chain stores headquartered elsewhere. So the amount of dollar volume in retail trade goes up with growth, but the amount of profits retained locally does not necessarily also increase.

WILL GROWTH SOLVE SANTA BARBARA'S UNEMPLOYMENT PROBLEM?

No.

Larger American cities have unemployment rates which are neither higher nor lower than smaller cities. But faster growing urban areas tend to have higher unemployment rates than slower growing ones.

Santa Barbara is not unique in having an unemployment problem: virtually all American cities have substantial numbers of workers without jobs and this has been so in most every year since World War II. Unemployment is primarily a result of the fact that, nation-wide, there are simply more people looking for work than there are jobs in the economy. The labor force is mobile and when jobs open up in a given locality, people from elsewhere migrate to the job-rich areas from the job-poor areas - and they often migrate in numbers even larger than the number of new jobs that are created. So a city that experiences new jobs gains not only more population, but also more people to join the ranks of the unemployed. The net result is that the local unemployment rate is unaffected over the long-term. Growth thus does not make jobs; it only distributes them to one city as opposed to another.

Santa Barbara's own history supports this idea that growth does little to solve the unemployment problem. During the 1960's this area experienced rapid population growth (the seventh most rapidly expanding population in the country), but at the end of the decade, the local unemployment rate was above the national average. The same was true for about half of the country's twenty-five fastest growing metropolitan areas; they had unemployment rates above the national average.

WHAT WOULD GROWTH DO TO OUR CITY PROPERTY TAXES?

They will go up.

Detailed study shows that new residents do not pay for themselves in additional revenues to the City. New industries do not pay enough in taxes to compensate for the additional services required by their facilities and by the employees they attract to the area. Even though the cost of certain city services, like fire protection, does not rise with growth, other city services, like police protection and the costs of park acquisition, tend to increase disproportionately under growth. The net result is that growth requires increasing amounts of revenue from each taxpayer.

Even without growth, the need to replace and improve existing City facilities will inevitably mean some increase in the tax rate, but this required increase will be much higher with additional population growth.

As an illustration of our findings, the present City property tax rate, by 1995, would increase by 10% if there were to be no growth at all; it would rise by 27% if there were very limited growth (as might occur if the current half-density ordinance were to become permanent). An extremely rapid rate of growth, one which would occur if the City actually developed fully under its zoning ordinance, would mean a city tax increase of 58% over the present cost to property owners.

The table below shows the percent increase in your city property tax rate at various population levels at the year 1995.

CITY PROPERTY TAXES GO UP WITH GROWTH

	City Population (Year 2000)	Increase in Taxes (Percentage)
No Growth	73,000	10%
Half Density Probable	94,000	27%
General Plan Probable	103,000	32%
Half Density Maximum	117,000	45%
Zoning Probable	119,000	45%
General Plan Maximum	140,000	52%
Zoning Maximum	170,000	58%

HOW MUCH WOULD NO-GROWTH COST THE CITY IN PROPERTY TAX REVENUE?

A little.

At present, city revenue from all vacant parcels in Santa Barbara amounts to $77,730, less than 0.7% of the city's annual General Fund budget. If a strict no-growth policy were instituted, most of this amount would be lost annually to city government.

A program of massive downzoning that would decrease the legal housing densities in apartment zones would similarly have only a minor effect on city revenues. Task Force studies show that owners of single family homes on land zoned for high density apartments are paying little more in land taxes than owners of nearby, similar types of property with low density (single-family) zoning. So it is doubtful that rezoning to lower densities will decrease to any significant extent current city revenues. The combined revenue loss from a policy which would have the extreme effect of removing all assessed value from the vacant land and eliminating all apartment zoning in the city would likely result in a total loss amounting to less than one percent of the city's current General Fund revenue.

WHAT WOULD GROWTH DO TO SCHOOL TAX, WATER AND SEWAGE COSTS?

Taken together, they will increase with growth.

But the pattern is different for each. *Water* is the most simple story: with higher levels of population, increasingly expensive alternative sources will be required to meet local needs. Over the next several decades, water costs would steadily rise and ultimately (at a population of 170,000) reach almost double the present per person costs.

Under current legislation for *school* financing, school taxes paid by city residents can be expected to decline—at any of the growth rates used in this study. It is the amount of the decline that will vary. Lower birth rates are going to mean lower attendence, less income and an increasing tendency for classrooms to be emptied over the next generation and for school buildings to be closed or less efficiently used. Partially for this reason, low population growth will lower total school costs while high rates of population growth will again require the building of new schools. This could, in turn, lead to higher school taxes than those which would occur under no growth or more limited growth.

Costs associated with treatment of *sewage* show a pattern similar to schools. With some population growth, the new wastewater treatment plant (about to be constructed) will be used to its full potential, thus resulting in a per person saving. But at high population levels, this capacity would be overtaxed, new construction would be necessary and costs per citizen would rise rather sharply.

Taken together, growth means that the costs of water, sewage treatment, and education will rise steeply, requiring that additional revenues be raised. These increases in revenue requirements will mean substantially higher utility rates for water and sewage even under moderate growth, while school taxes will decline somewhat regardless of growth. The table below illustrates how much additional revenue will have to be raised by 1995 at various population levels.

WATER, SEWAGE, AND SCHOOLS:
PER CENT INCREASE IN REVENUES REQUIRED WITH GROWTH , 1995

Population level		Water:	Sewage:	Schools:	Summary Rating *
No Growth	73,000	+ 22%	+ 80%	-25%	1
Half Density Probable	94,000	+ 47	+ 64	-27	2
General Plan Probable	103,000	+ 54	+ 63	-27	3
Half Density Maximum	117,000	+ 61	+ 59	-25	4
Zoning Probable	119,000	+ 63	+ 56	-25	5
General Plan Maximum	140,000	+ 79	+ 107·	-22	6
Zoning Maximum	170,000	+ 95	+ 123	-19	7

*(1 = Least Costs; 7 = Highest Costs)

HOW TO CONTROL POPULATION SIZE: WHAT ARE SOME METHODS?

*Residential Zoning

Most cities that have attempted growth control tend to use residential zoning as the key method. By limiting the number of housing units that can be built on various parcels of land, an effort is made to determine the number of people who will live in the city as a whole. Santa Barbara's Interim Half-Density Ordinance represents one example of such a strategy.

One problem raised by an across the board density cut such as the Santa Barbara ordinance is whether it leaves the right "mix" of multiple dwellings and single family dwelling units in a community. The Half-Density Ordinance left the same quantity of land zoned for multiple dwelling purposes while cutting in half the potential number of multiple dwelling units on that land. The citizens of Santa Barbara will still have to decide whether the ratio of land zoned for multiple dwellings to that zoned for single family dwellings is the one they desire.

While Santa Barbara has restricted potential growth through the Half-Density Ordinance, surrounding communities such as Goleta and Montecito have restricted residential growth as a result of water shortage problems. The coincidence of these events raises a major problem for the South Coast region. That is: If all South Coast cmmunities limit residential construction, where will the people live who come to Santa Barbara to work? This problem leads to a second growth control strategy, one which can influence population growth more directly.

*Industrial Planning

Task Force Report shows that Santa Barbara's population growth has largely been the result of expanding employment opportunities in education, research and development, manufacturing and tourism. This indicates that one way to limit population growth would be to limit the expansion of such industries.

Santa Barbara's population grows when industry creates more jobs which leads to migration of more people here. *The additional housing that is built for these people is in this sense not a cause of growth but a result of growth.*

If industrial expansion continues in the South Coast region while residential construction is limited, there will not be effective growth control. There will instead be a deterioration of housing conditions and steadily increasing housing costs under which the growing population will have to live.

The ideal solution is therefore planning for the entire South Coast region for the purpose of maintaining a balance between the quantity of available residences and available employment. The Task Force study indicates that the rate of unemployment is unrelated to population growth. This indicates that an effort to strike a balance between the restrictive residential condition in the South Coast region and employment opportunities in the region by limiting expansion of the latter would not result in a higher unemployment rate.

Industrial expansion can be limited in several ways. Land presently zoned for industrial use can be rezoned to non-industrial uses. The City could reduce its efforts of attracting even smokeless industry and new tourist facilities. Another possibility is for the City to require sponsors of new plant location and expansion to pay for all additional costs, including costs stimulated by the immigration of new employees.

Planning for the South Coast region to strike the balance between residential and employment opportunities could be carried out by a variety of formal or informal planning entities. Regional planning of this type has recently been encouraged by important court decisions including that of the Federal District Court in the much talked about "Petaluma case".

Finding the right combination of strategies to create a wise and balanced growth control program will be a major challenge for the people of the South Coast region.

GROWTH CONTROL: IS IT LEGAL?

- Yes—If it is done properly.

Virtually all United States cities now have zoning laws and these zoning laws are one form of growth control. They have been challenged in the Courts, and over the years they have been sustained many times. The question thus facing many cities today is not whether or not there should be growth control, but what the ultimate population should be. Should Santa Barbara's population be set at 170,000, the level permitted under current zoning? Or should it be at some point closer to the current city population of 73,000?

Any program of growth control must meet these requirements:
1. It must be shown to have some relationship to maintaining the health, safety and general welfare of the citizens. The Task Force Study sections dealing with water, sewage disposal, air quality, economic base and other growth-related issues provide a great deal of information pertinent to such health, safety and general welfare questions.
2. Any rezoning of private property must not only be based on sound health, safety and general welfare reasons but in addition must leave the owner with some reasonable economic use of the land. California courts have historically upheld rezoning even where the private owner's financial opportunities have been greatly restricted, if sufficient health, safety and general welfare reasons supported the rezoning.

The health, safety and general welfare data provided by the Task Force Study indicates that a growth control program aimed at a maximum population by the year 2000 of 100,000 or less could probably be devised and upheld by the courts. The details of such a program however would have to be carefully worked out.

A program of strict no-growth, by contrast, would probably be held invalid at this time since the City is not yet faced with any health, safety or general welfare problem adequate to justify a complete moratorium on growth. It is possible, however, that the City could be faced with a problem of this magnitude if, for example, the South Coast region water supply situation is not resolved within the next few years. Even now the law regarding the issue of growth control is being made, precedents are now being set. One way or the other, Santa Barbara might well lead in charting the direction of those precedents.

WHAT HAPPENS NEXT?

Again, that depends on you.

In the coming months, acting on the basis of recommendations from the Planning Commission, City staff, and interested citizens, the City Council will make decisions that affect everyone who lives here. The City has a choice. It can do nothing and continue to live under present zoning and traditional city outlooks on industrial growth. Or, it can set changes in motion: revision of zoning, changes in the General Plan, alternative approaches to industrial expansion.

Some residents are taking part in helping shape the choices. But most have been unheard from. Your opportunity to join the decision making process now begins, and will continue during the coming months.

Prepared for the City of Santa Barbara as the Summary
Issues Booklet for the Population Impact Study,

SANTA BARBARA: THE IMPACTS OF GROWTH

SANTA BARBARA
PLANNING TASK FORCE

Richard Appelbaum
Jennifer Bigelow
Henry Kramer
Harvey Molotch
Paul Relis

CITY COUNCIL

David T. Shiffman, Mayor
Gus Chavalas
Franklin Lowance
Leo Martinez
Alice Rypins
Lawrence D. Schatz
Nyle Utterback

PLANNING COMMISSION

Jeanne Graffy, Chairman
Warren Adler
Tomas A. Castelo
Sheila Lodge
Joanne Miller
Bruce O'Neal
Richard B.Taylor

COMMUNITY DEVELOPMENT DEPARTMENT
PLANNING DIVISION

Advisory Commission on Intergovernmental Relations (ACIR). 1968.
Urban and Rural America: Policies for Future Growth. Washington, D.C.: U.S. Government Printing Office.

Alsonso, William. 1973. "Urban Zero Population Growth."
Daedalus 102 (Fall): 191-206.

Appelbaum, Richard. 1975. "City Size and Urban Life: A Preliminary Inquiry into Some Consequences of Growth in American
Cities." Santa Barbara: University of California Department
of Sociology, unpublished.

_____ and Ross Follett. 1975. "Correlates of Growth in Middle-
Sized American Communities." Santa Barbara: University of
California Department of Sociology, unpublished.

Baum, Paul. 1971. "Issues in Optimal City Size." Los Angeles:
UCLA, Graduate School of Management.

Beck, Alan M. 1973. Ecology of Stray Dogs. New York: New York
Press.

Berry, Brian J. L., et al. 1974. Land Use, Urban Form and Environmental Quality. Final report, "Land Use Forms and the
Environment," Office of Research and Development, Environmental Protection Agency. Published as Research Paper No.
155, Department of Geography, University of California.

Betz, Michael. 1972. "The City as a System Generating Income
Inequality." Social Forces 51 (December): 192-98.

Bidwell Park Feasibility Study 1974. State of California Department
of Parks and Recreation.

Bikeway Master Plan. 1974. Santa Barbara Public Works Department.

Blalock, Hubert M., Jr. 1972. Social Statistics. New York:
McGraw-Hill.

Bolt, Beranek and Newman, Inc. 1970. "Chicago Urban Noise
    Study." Report No. 1411-1413. Downers Grove, Ill., November.

Bolton, H. E. 1927. Fray Juan Crespi Missionary Explorer of the
    Pacific Coast. Berkeley: University of California Press.

Brazer, Harvey E. 1959. "City Expenditures in the United States."
    Occasional Paper 66. New York: National Bureau of Economic
    Research.

Brown and Caldwell (consulting engineers). 1973. "Revenue Require-
    ments Study: Wastewater Utility." Santa Barbara: City of
    Santa Barbara, May.

_____. 1969. "Water Supply and Distribution Study." Santa Bar-
    bara: City of Santa Barbara.

Bruton, M. J. 1970. Introduction to Transportation Planning.
    London.

Buchalter, Howard, Anthony Nakazawa, and Frederick Schremp.
    1973. "Economic Effects in Santa Barbara County of an
    Amended County Zoning Ordinance and General Plan." Santa
    Barbara: unpublished manuscript.

Calhoun, John. 1963. "Population Density and Social Pathology."
    In The Urban Condition, edited by Leonard Duhl. Pp. 33-43.
    New York: Basic Books.

Caplovitz, David. 1963. The Poor Pay More. New York: Macmillan.

Chalupnik, J. D., ed. 1967. Transportation Noises: A Symposium
    on Acceptability Criteria. Seattle: University of Washington
    Press.

City of Newport Beach, Community Department. 1972. General
    Plan Program Cost Revenue System.

City of Santa Barbara. 1974a. Five-Year Capital Program: Fiscal
    Years 1974-75--1978-79.

_____. 1974b. Operating Budget, 1973/74.

_____. 1974c. Department of Public Works, Transportation Divi-
    sion, unpublished report of survey.

BIBLIOGRAPHY   321

_____. 1975. Operating Budget, 1974/75.

_____. 1973. Annual Report, 1972-73.

_____. 1972. Amendments to the General Plan, "Open Space Element."

_____. 1963-73. Police Department Annual Reports.

_____. 1963-64. General Plan.

County of Santa Barbara. 1974a. 1973-74 Secured Assessment Rolls.

_____. 1974b. Tax Rates and Assessed Valuations, 1973-74.

_____. 1974c. Comprehensive Transportation Action Plan.

_____. 1969. Master Plan of Library Services.

Daniel, Mann, Johnson and Mendenhall. 1969. "Santa Barbara Freeway Development Plan" (March 31).

Dickerson, D. O., et al. 1970. "Transportation Noise Pollution: Control and Abatement." Publ. No. N71-15557. Springfield, Va., National Technical Information Service.

Dodson, E. N., J. C. Eisenhut, and N. R. Yates. 1972. Forecasting Occupational Opportunities: Quantitative Procedures and a Case Study of Santa Barbara County. Santa Barbara: General Research Corporation.

Dodson, Edward, and Harry Fox. 1973. "Forecasting School Enrollment, Santa Barbara School District." Santa Barbara: General Research Corp. (December).

Duncan, Otis Dudley. 1951. "Optimum Size of Cities." In Readings in Urban Sociology, edited by Paul K. Hatt and Albert J. Reiss, Jr. Glencoe, Ill.: Free Press.

_____. 1949. Optimum Size of Cities. Chicago: University of Chicago Library.

_____, and Albert J. Reiss, Jr. 1956. Social Characteristics of Urban and Rural Communities, 1950. New York: Wiley.

Eisner, Simon. Undated. "Basis for Planning." Santa Barbara County Planning Department.

_____ and associates. 1971. "Recommended Amendments to the General Plan." City of Santa Barbara.

_____ and associates. 1964. Santa Barbara County General Plan. Pasadena.

Engineering-Science, Inc. 1971. "Regional Wastewater Management and Water Reclamation for Santa Barbara, summary report.

Federal Water Pollution Control Administration. 1970. Industrial Waste Guide on Logging Practices. Portland, Oregon: USDI FWPCA.

Field, Ronald. 1972. "Urban Rat Control." Pest Control 40, no. 4: 20-30.

Flaim, P. O. 1968. "Jobless Trends in Twenty Large Metropolitan Areas." Monthly Labor Review 91, no. 5: 16-28.

Frank, Ronald E. 1966. "Use of Transformations." Journal of Marketing Research 3 (August): 247-53.

Fuchs, Victor R. 1967. "Differentials in Hourly Earnings by Region and City Size, 1959," Occasional Paper 101. New York: National Bureau of Economic Research.

Gebhard, David, Robert Montgomery, Robert Winter, John Woodbridge, and Sally Woodbridge. 1973. A Guide to Architecture in San Francisco and Northern California. Santa Barbara: Peregrine Smith.

Gebhard, David, and Harriette von Breton. 1968. Architecture in California, 1868-1968. Santa Barbara: University of California.

Geotechnical Consultants, Inc. 1974. Wastewater Treatment Plant. Santa Barbara: City of Santa Barbara.

Gold, David. 1969. "Statistical Tests and Substantive Significance." The American Socialism 4 (February): 42-46.

_____ and John Sonquist. 1973. "Recreational Beach Use Survey,"
report to the University of California Sea Grant Program.
Santa Barbara: unpublished.

Gruen & Gruen and associates. 1974. Redevelopment Study for the
City of Santa Barbara. Santa Barbara: unpublished interim
report to the city.

_____. 1972. The Impacts of Growth. Berkeley: The California
Better Housing Foundation, Inc.

Hadden, Jeffrey K., and Edgar F. Borgatta. 1965. American Cities:
Their Social Characteristics. Chicago: Rand McNally.

Hanna, Frank A. 1959. State Income Differentials, 1919-1955.
Durham, N.C.: Duke University Press.

Harper, Edwin H. 1974. "Recalculation of the 1973-74 Revenue
Limit." California State Department of Education, Memorandum (July 11).

Hawley, Amos H. 1951. "Metropolitan Population and Municipal
Government Expenditures in Central Cities." The Journal of
Social Issues 71, nos. 1-2: 100-08

Henningson, Durham, and Richardson. 1974. "Preliminary Draft,
Las Positas Inn Environmental Impact Report." Santa Barbara,
Calif.

Hoch, Irving. 1972a. "Income and City Size." Urban Studies 9
(October): 194-328.

_____. 1972b. "Urban Scale and Environmental Quality." In Popu-
lation, Resources, and the Environment, edited by Ronald G.
Ridker. Washington, D.C.: U.S. Government Printing Office.

International City Management Association. 1972. The Municipal
Year Book, 1972. Washington, D.C.: The Association.

International City Managers' Association. 1961. The Municipal Year
Book, 1961. Washington, D.C.: The Association.

Isla Vista Planning Commission. 1971. Isla Vista Transportation
Study. Isla Vista, Calif.: The Commission.

Jacobs, Jane. 1961. The Death and Life of Great American Cities. New York: Random House.

Johnson, D. Gale. 1951. "Some Effects of Region, Community Size, Color and Occupation on Family and Individual Incomes." In Studies in Income and Wealth, vol. 15. New York: National Bureau of Economic Research.

Kasarda, John D. 1972. "The Impact of Suburban Population Growth on Central City Service Functions." American Journal of Sociology 77 (May): 1111-24.

Keisker, Albert, and associates. 1973. "Environmental Assessment Draft, Hyatt Regency Hotel Development." Santa Barbara, Calif.: Keisker Associates.

_____. 1970. Economic Base Analysis, Santa Barbara, California. Pasadena, Calif.: Keisker Associates.

Kelley, Robert. 1972. Presentation to the Environmental Quality Advisory Board, City of Santa Barbara, Regarding Proposal of U.S. Army Corps of Engineers for Channelization and Diversion of Mission Creek.

Klein, G. E., et al. 1971. "Methods of Evaluation of the Effects of Transportation Systems on Community Values," Publ. No. PB199-954. Springfield, Va.: Technical Information Service.

Levy, Shephan, and Robert K. Arnold. 1972a. "An Evaluation of Four Growth Alternatives in the City of Milpitas, 1972-1977," report of the Institute of Regional and Urban Studies, Palo Alto, for the Planning Department, City of Milpitas, Calif.

_____. 1972b. "An Evaluation of Four Growth Alternatives in the City of Milpitas, 1972-1977," technical memorandum report. Palo Alto, Calif.: Institute of Regional and Urban Studies.

Livingston and Blayney. 1971. Open Space vs. Development: Final Report to the City of Palo Alto. Palo Alto.

Lomax, K. S. 1943. "The Relationship Between Expenditures per Head and Size of Population of County Boroughs in England and Wales." Journal of the Royal Statistical Society 151, no. 1: 51-59.

Los Angeles County, Environmental Resource Committee. 1972.
Habitat Types in Los Angeles County. Los Angeles: The
Committee.

Los Angeles Times. 1974. "L.A. and State in Conflict over Reading of Smog Instruments," July 27.

Lynch, Kevin. 1960. The Image of the City. Cambridge, Mass.:
MIT Press and Harvard University Press.

Margolis, Julius. 1957. "Municipal Fiscal Structure in a Metropolitan Region." The Journal of Political Economy (June): 225-36.

Martinez, J. R., R. A. Nordsieck, and M. A. Hirschberg. 1973.
"User's Guide to Diffusion/Kinetics (DIFKIN) Code," Publ. No.
CR-2-273/1. General Research Corporation.

Menchen, William. 1974. "Santa Barbara County Transportation
Study," private communication. April.

Menzie, Archibald. 1924. "California Journal of the Vancouver Ex-
pedition." California Historical Society Quarterly 2, no. 4:
265-340.

Mercer, Lloyd J., and W. Douglas Morgan. 1973. "Estimation of
Commercial Industrial and Governmental Water Use for Local
Area. Water Resources Bulletin, forthcoming.

Molotch, Harvey. 1976. "The City as a Growth Machine." American Journal of Sociology, forthcoming.

_____. 1972. Managed Integration: Dilemmas of Doing Good in the
City. Berkeley: University of California Press.

Moore and Taber. 1974. Seismic Safety Element, preliminary.
County of Santa Barbara: County Comprehensive Plan and Implementation Program.

Morgan, James N., Ismail A. Sirageldin, and Nancy Beerwaldt.
1966. Productive Americans, Monograph 43. Ann Arbor:
University of Michigan Institute for Social Research, Survey
Research Center.

Muir, K. S., U.S. Geological Survey Water-Supply. "Ground-Water Reconnaissance of the Santa Barbara-Montecito Area, Santa Barbara County, California," Paper 1859-A.

Munz, P. A. 1968. A California Flora. Berkeley: University of California Press.

Nordsieck, R. A. 1975. "Air Pollutant Emissions Factors Estimates for California Motor Vehicles: 1967-2000." Los Angeles: California Department of Transportation, January.

Ogburn, William F. 1937. Social Characteristics of Cities. Chicago: International Managers' Association.

_____, and Otis Dudley Duncan. 1964. "City Size as a Sociological Variable." In Contributions to Urban Sociology, edited by Ernest W. Burgess and Donald J. Bogue. Chicago: University of Chicago Press.

Oliver, Henry M. 1946. "Income, Region, Community Size, and Color." Quarterly Journal of Economics (August): 588-99.

Olsen, Phil G. 1972. "Seismic Micronization in the City of Santa Barbara." Reprinted in Proceedings: International Conference on Micronization for Safer Construction, Research, and Application 1: 395-408.

Pereira Associates. 1970. "Master Plan for the Santa Barbara Municipal Airport." Los Angeles, April.

Phillips, Hugh S. 1942. "Municipal Efficiency and Town Size." Journal of the Town Planning Institute (May/June): 139-48.

Pignataro, Louis J. 1973. Traffic Engineering. Englewood Cliffs, N.J.: Prentice-Hall.

Puskarov, Boris. 1969. The Atlantic Urban Seaboard: Development Issues and Strategies. New York: Regional Plan Association.

Richardson, Harry W. 1973. The Economics of Urban Size. Lexington, Mass.: Lexington Books.

Rosenberg, Morris. 1968. The Logic of Survey Analysis. New York: Basic Books.

Rossi, Peter. 1965. Why Families Move. New York: Macmillan.

Sadler, R. R. 1970. Buffer Strips--A Possible Application of Decision Theory, technical note. Eugene, Ore.: USDI Bureau of
Land Management.

Sage, Cynthia. 1972. Environmental Hazards as a Basis for Land-
Use Planning in a Rural Portion of the Santa Barbara Coastal
Area. Santa Barbara: unpublished manuscript.

Samuelson, Paul A. 1942. "The Business Cycle and Urban Development." In The Problems of the Cities and Towns, edited by
Guy Greer. Cambridge, Mass.: Harvard University Press.

Santa Barbara County-Cities Area Planning Council. 1974. Comprehensive Transportation Action Plan for the Santa Barbara
County Area (revised version).

Santa Barbara Coast Survey Map, 1852. Santa Barbara: University
of Cartography Archives.

Santa Barbara School District. 1973. Annual Budget, 1973-74.

_____. 1969. "Master Planning for the Future," August.

Schmandt, Henry J., and Ross Stephens. 1963. "Local Government
Expenditures Patterns in the United States." Land Economics
39 (November): 397-406.

Schmitt, Robert C. 1966. "Density, Health, and Social Disorganization." Journal of the American Institute of Planners (January): 38-40.

Schnore, Leo F. 1963. "Some Correlates of Urban Size: A Replication." American Journal of Sociology 50 (September): 185-93.

_____, and D. W. Varley. 1955. "Some Concomitants of Metropoli-
tan Size." American Sociological Review 20: 408-14.

Scott, Stanley, and Edward L. Feder. 1957. Factors Associated
with Variations in Municipal Expenditure Levels. Berkeley:
University of California, Bureau of Public Administration.

Shapiro, Harvey. 1963. "Economics of Scale and Local Governmental Finance." Land Economics 39 (May): 175-86.

Shefer, Daniel. 1970. "Comparable Living Costs and Urban Size."
    Journal of the American Institute of Planners 36 (November):
    417-21.

Sierra Club of San Diego. 1973. "Economy, Ecology, and Rapid
    Population Growth." San Diego, Calif., mimeographed.

Silverman, Sybil. Undated. "Impact of Irvine Industrial East,
    Jurisdictional Economic Analysis," mimeographed.

Sorensen, Annemette, Karl E. Taeuber, and Leslie J. Hollingsworth,
    Jr. 1974. "Indexes of Racial Residential Segregation for 109
    Cities in the U.S., 1940 to 1970," Studies in Racial Segregation,
    No. 1. Madison, Wisc.: University of Wisconsin.

Stuart, Darwin B., and Robert B. Leska. 1971. "Who Pays for
    What: Cost Revenue Analysis of Suburban Land Use Alterna-
    tives." Washington, D.C.: Urban Land Institute, March.

South Central Coast Regional Commission. 1974. Coastal Land En-
    vironment 1974. California Coastal Zone Conservation Com-
    mission: San Francisco.

South Coast Transportation Study (SCOTS). 1969. 1990 Progress
    Report Analysis and Forecast. Santa Barbara: SCOTS.

_____. 1967. SCOTS Base Year Report, vol. 1. Santa Barbara:
    SCOTS.

State of California. 1973a. Annual Report of Financial Transactions
    Concerning Cities, 1972-73.

_____. 1973b. Annual Report of Financial Transactions Concerning
    School Districts, 1972-73.

_____, Department of Education. 1974. "Recalculation of the 1973-
    74 Revenue Limit," memorandum from Edwin H. Harper,
    July 11.

Taeuber, Karl E., and Ama F. Taeuber. 1965. Negroes in Cities.
    Chicago: Aldine.

Toups (consulting engineers). 1974. Water Resources Management
    Study. Santa Barbara: Toups Associates, February.

United States Army Corps of Engineers, Los Angeles District. 1973.
    "Flood Insurance, 1973," preliminary study.

United States, Department of Commerce, Bureau of the Census.
    1973a. 1970 Census of Population. Vol. 1, "Number of Inhabi-
    tants and General Social and Economic Characteristics." Wash-
    ington, D.C.: U.S. Government Printing Office.

_____. 1973b. County and City Data Book, 1972, statistical abstract
    supplement. Washington, D.C.: U.S. Government Printing
    Office.

_____. 1972. 1970 Census of Housing. Vol. 1, "Detailed Housing
    Characteristics." Washington, D.C.: U.S. Government Print-
    ing Office.

_____. 1971. City Employment in 1970. Washington, D.C.: Bureau
    of the Census.

_____. 1970. City Government Finances in 1969-1970. Washington,
    D.C.: U.S. Government Printing Office.

_____. 1963a. 1960 Census of Housing. Vol. 1, "General Housing
    Characteristics." Washington, D.C.: U.S. Government Print-
    ing Office.

_____. 1963b. Census of the Population: 1960. Vol. 1, "Number
    of Inhabitants and General Social and Economic Characteristics."
    Washington, D.C.: U.S. Government Printing Office.

_____. 1962. County and City Data Book, 1962. Washington, D.C.:
    U.S. Government Printing Office.

_____. 1961a. Compendium of City Government Finances in 1960.
    Washington, D.C.: U.S. Government Printing Office.

_____. 1961b. City Employment in 1960. Washington, D.C.:
    Bureau of the Census.

United States, Department of Health, Education and Welfare, Public
    Health Service. 1973. Vital Statistics of the United States,
    1969. Vol. 2, "Mortality," Part B. Washington, D.C.: U.S.
    Government Printing Office.

_____. 1963. Vital Statistics of the United States, 1960. Vol. 2, "Mortality," Part B. Washington, D.C.: U.S. Government Printing Office.

United States, Department of Justice, Federal Bureau of Investigation. 1971. Uniform Crime Reports for the United States, 1970. Washington, D.C.: U.S. Government Printing Office.

_____. 1961. Uniform Crime Reports for the United States, 1960. Washington, D.C.: U.S. Government Printing Office.

United States, Department of Labor, Bureau of Labor Statistics. 1973. Handbook of Labor Statistics 1973. Washington, D.C.: U.S. Government Printing Office.

Urban Land Institute. 1972. The Dollars and Cents of Shopping Centers. Washington, D.C.: The Institute.

Weschler, Henry. 1961. "Community Growth, Depressive Disorders, and Suicide." American Journal of Sociology 67 (July): 9-16.

Wirth, Louis. 1938. "Urbanism as a Way of Life." American Journal of Sociology 44 (July): 1-24.

RICHARD P. APPELBAUM is Assistant Professor, Department of Sociology, University of California at Santa Barbara. Before joining the Santa Barbara Planning Task Force, he was Technical Advisor to Isla Vista Community Council Incorporation Studies and Principal Investigator at the Institute for Juvenile Research. He is author of Theories of Social Change and has published journal articles both in the United States and in Peru, where he served as an urban planning advisor and researcher. Dr. Appelbaum holds a Ph.D. in sociology from the University of Chicago.

JENNIFER BIGELOW is Research Assistant, specializing in housing and urban renewal, at the Community Action Commission of Santa Barbara County. She earned a B.A. and California Secondary and Elementary Teaching Credentials, both from the University of California at Santa Barbara.

HENRY P. KRAMER is President of the Pattern Analysis Corporation. He was formerly with General Electric at the Center for Advanced Studies in Santa Barbara, was President of Kramer Research Inc., and was Vice-President at the Data Recognition Corporation. Dr. Kramer earned his Ph.D. in mathematics at the University of California, Berkeley.

HARVEY L. MOLOTCH is Associate Professor, Department of Sociology, University of California at Santa Barbara. His forthcoming book is entitled The Political Economy of Place: A Reconstruction of Urban Sociology. He has published articles on a wide variety of current social issues in numerous sociological journals. Dr. Molotch holds a Ph.D. in sociology from the University of Chicago.

PAUL M. RELIS is Director of the Community Environmental Council, Inc. He is author of Today's Action, Tomorrow's Profit: An Alternative Approach to Community Development, and coauthor of A Plan for East Beach. He holds a B.A. from the University of California, Santa Barbara.

URBAN GROWTH MANAGEMENT THROUGH
DEVELOPMENT TIMING
David J. Brower, David W. Owens,
Ronald Rosenberg, Ira Botvinick,
and Michael Mandel

URBAN NONGROWTH: Planning for People
Earl Finkler, William J. Toner,
and Frank J. Popper

SYSTEMATIC URBAN PLANNING
Darwin G. Stuart

NONGROWTH PLANNING STRATEGIES: The
Developing Power of Towns, Cities, and Regions
Earl Finkler and David L. Peterson

THE POLITICAL REALITIES OF URBAN PLANNING
Don T. Allensworth